Pueblo Chico

PUEBLO CHICO

LAND AND LIVES IN GALISTEO SINCE 1814

LUCY R. LIPPARD

Pueblo Chico, Infierno Grande

MUSEUM OF NEW MEXICO PRESS
SANTA FE

Director: Anna Gallegos
Editorial director: Lisa Pacheco
Art director and production director: David Skolkin
Designer: Ann Lowe
Composition: Set in Adobe Caslon Pro and Trajan
Manufactured in Korea
10 9 8 7 6 5 4 3 2 1

Library of Congress Control Number: 2019958032

ISBN: 978-0-89013-649-2 (hardcover)

Museum of New Mexico Press
PO Box 2087
Santa Fe, New Mexico 87504
mnmpress.org

Frontispiece: Lucy R. Lippard, *Cross on old church mound, The Hill*, ca. 2010.

Edward Ranney, *The Author Interviewing Simona Baros García*, 1999.

In Memory of Simona Baros García and all the Galisteo elders who are at the heart of this book and generously shared their memories with a newcomer before passing on, among them: Serapio Anaya, Onésimo and Mela Montoya, Rudy Sena, Remedios and Luis Chávez, Tacho Sandoval, Clarita and Manuel Anaya, Sarapio Montoya, Andrés and Josefina Anaya, Richard Griscom, Joe Cooper, Linda McKee, and Priscilla Hoback. Que descansen todos en paz.

And thanks to everyone in Galisteo who advised and encouraged me, including those who inadvertently passed on bits of information, gossip, and stories over the years. And to those who happily are still among us: Stella Maestas, Michael J. Anaya, María Ortiz y Pino, Yolanda Ortiz y Pino, Antonio Chávez, Mary Alice Anaya, Clyde and Mary Peña, Modesta Presley, Terry Vasquez, Henry Anaya, Romona Scholder, Dianna Gwyn, Phillip and Judy Tuwaletstiwa, Charlie Holloway, Rod Hall, Patrick Mehaffy, Harmony Hammond, Denise Lynch, Johnny Pack, Wayne King, and Jean and Steve Moya. And from beyond the village: Estevan Rael-Gálvez, Jan Willem Jansens, Steve Post, and Mike Marshall.

CONTENTS

ACKNOWLEDGMENTS

I OWE A GREAT DEAL to the late Joe M. Anaya, who told me, "If you want to know about Galisteo history, you have to talk to Simona García." My thanks to Joe D. Anaya, whose impressive memory greatly illuminates these pages, and to the late José Ortiz y Pino III, who whetted my curiosity at the beginning. Anna Cárdenas helped research and graciously criticized the manuscript in the name of her many Galisteo ancestors. Sabra Moore was a godsend with her knowledge of photo research and permissions. Thanks to the late Mela and Onésimo Montoya for access to the crucial Cadial book.[1] The late Bill Baxter, friend and colleague, opened his research on some thousand pages of newspaper references to local names over a century. John Benjamin shared his own extensive knowledge and research materials. I am deeply grateful to David Snow, who read and commented on the manuscript; to Sylvia Rodríguez for her brilliant writing and for lively conversations about village life; and to Antonio Chávez, who has lived it. I learned a lot from Kay Matthews and her writings in *La Jicarita News* about *norteño* village issues. Malcolm Ebright advised me on land grants in the early stages of this book but cannot be blamed for the chaos I've made of them. Enrique R. Lamadrid has been patient with my questions about La Tañita.

Photographer friends Ed Ranney, Joan Myers, and Caroline Hinkley have generously donated their time to fill in some crucial gaps, while Richard Shuff and Nicolas Trofimuk made available their vast archives of Galisteo photographs. Ed Epping kindly scanned the images for me, and Angie Beauchamp answered frantic cries for help with computer crises. Mira Burack helped with research. Librarians and archivists at the State Library, Hannah Ablebeck and Daniel Kosharek at the Palace of the Governors Photo Archives, and Cindy Abel Morris at the University of New Mexico made the never-ending research go more smoothly, not to mention all the families who responded to my pleas for images.

Anna Gallegos, Lisa Pacheco, and David Skolkin at the Museum of New Mexico Press patiently and expertly shepherded this third New Mexico book of mine toward publication, and copy editor Beth Hadas was also invaluable.

Last but not least, thanks to my partner, Jim Faris, whose cantankerous questioning and love of his native New Mexico spurred me on, and to Chino and Yazzie, whose runs in the bosque always lift my spirits.

NOTE ON SPANISH ACCENTS

Most Galisteans today generally do not use traditional Spanish accents in their names. I intended to ask my editors to omit them, bowing to colloquial use, until I was warned about "linguistic imperialism" by Sylvia Rodríguez. She led me to linguist María Dolores Gonzales, who informed me that

> the suppression of Spanish (lack of literacy classes or punishment for speaking) contributed to the loss of the traditional New Mexican variation, which has been spoken for 410 years. My work continues to focus on the preservation of my mother tongue. This includes informing and/or educating the public [about] the importance of using accents in all publications as well as honoring family names. Most New Mexicans are open to their use upon learning their value. By not using them we corrupt the Spanish language.[1]

Joan Myers, *Aerial View of Downtown Galisteo*, 2007.

INTRODUCTION
OTHER PEOPLE'S MEMORIES

Interpretation is critical, for history is a contest of stories.
—ESTEVAN RAEL-GÁLVEZ, "Testifying to the Silence of Servitude"[1]

I WRITE THIS looking out my workroom window in November at a post-Thanksgiving twilight. The familiarly ragged band of the Ortiz Mountains (featured in ads for the TV-show *Longmire*) is a sharp black silhouette against a vast sky bleeding upward from yellow to turquoise to blue to a dark blue gray. Venus is brilliant and alone in the southwest. How many former inhabitants of the Galisteo Basin have stopped in the pre-winter chill to contemplate this view before continuing tasks or comforts or trials in war and in peace? It is a cultural landscape that has become familiar to me, simultaneously enriched with the stories I have been told by those long time residents who value memories and veiled by those I have not been told. From its inception, this book has been about the vortex of land and lives, about the ways the land reveals its coexistence with people, the ways people have changed it, and the ways the land has in turn changed the people who lived here long enough to become part of it.

Joan Myers, *The Ortiz Mountains from the Author's Home*, 2018.

As of this writing, I have lived in Galisteo for only twenty-seven years. So this history is based largely on other people's memories—those of the descendants of the original settlers in the early 1800s, most of them mestizos, heirs of the Spanish colonizers and the indigenous colonized who courageously settled this isolated valley despite official neglect and threats of Indian raids. The memories of those who came later, Hispano and Anglo, also echo through this book. I hoped to track the vortices of land and lives with relative specificity. But too many lives have already receded into the land. Few remain to tell the stories, and the accounts themselves are often too detailed, too contradictory, and go too far back to be clearly recalled even within oral traditions. The land itself has the longest memory, harboring traces of towns, trails, agriculture, and other land use that go back thousands of years. Like traditional New Mexico adobe homes, cultural landscapes are settled, lost, resettled, and expanded when need requires, the old and new merging into each other until specific history is blurred by real life. Nevertheless, history is how we got here, and the more we know about it the better.

Landscape studies or cultural/historical geography encompass a vortex of social, esthetic, and scientific disciplines. I have to pay parenthetical homage to the peripatetic scholar and brilliant essayist/geographer John Brinckerhoff (J. B.) Jackson, who lived just northwest of the Galisteo Basin. He defined the cultural landscape as "a concrete, three-dimensional, shared reality" rather than just a detached view beyond where we huddle in our own homes.[2] He was criticized for being too involved in "the multifarious details," which can indeed be seductive, as this book all too clearly demonstrates. But the details build up and finally illuminate aspects of local place that remain stubbornly hidden from the generalizers who normally control representation.

I was consumed with curiosity when I moved to Galisteo, and I soon became inextricably inundated by historical detail. I wanted to know everything about the place. George Henderson warned: geographers turn "their attention to fine-grained, ethnographic approaches developed in anthropology and sociology in order to ferret out the hidden details of resisted, negotiated landscape."[3] Remember, my partner keeps reminding me, you don't have to know *everything*. Despite his admonitions, I managed to create a morass of information; I've often despaired of a book ever emerging from such chaos. Beneath the rubble of my research—cartons and drawers and files full of "anything about Galisteo"—lie multiple truths that have emerged from collective memories.

Historical facts are notoriously elusive. Putting this place in words has been for me part of the slow process of belonging, a commitment to intimacy that will never be fully consummated. The history of the Galisteo Basin is in flux, and I won't pretend to have the last words. The more you know about a place like this, the less (you realize) you actually know. My task has been to balance often contradictory sources, without being able to decisively select the one that is "correct." Any text attempting to take in multiple viewpoints must be a collage, a patchwork of images. How do you overlay different world views and conflicting oral histories without obliterating everything? And without subjecting them to a dominant cultural overview, which amounts to forcible assimilation? The context doesn't exist for a nice, seamless narrative, so this book may not always resemble a conventional history. Each family story is different, many conflict with others. My own memories are equally suspect.

Lucy R. Lippard, *View of the Galisteo Basin with Cerro Pelón*, ca. 2009.

Lucy R. Lippard, *Village Home*, 2017.

Years ago, a local man told me, "I wouldn't pay a dollar for a book on New Mexico by some New York writer or even *published* in New York." I don't think he knew at the time what I did or where I was from (New York), but he went on to warn me about my own investigations into local culture: "Nobody will tell you the real stories, and if they did, you couldn't print them." In many cases, Will Mares turned out to be right. So why forge ahead? Curiosity and self-indulgence on one hand, and on the other, a sense of obsessive responsibility to a place I love, a need to tell at least some of its story, no matter how fragmented and inconclusive. I have been encouraged in this project by Galisteans who are angered by the lack of local Hispano history taught in the schools. They hope this book will remind educators of their responsibilities to people and place.

And then there are the historical documents themselves, purported to be more trustworthy than individuals' memories. New Mexico historian Marc Simmons has wisely observed, "The value of every historical document depends on its accuracy and completeness of observation. Unhappily, faithful testimony is not the rule, since human beings are prone to falsify their statements, either deliberately or unconsciously. When to this impediment is added the fact that for any past event or period only a limited quantity of evidence is ever available, it will be seen how difficult it is for the historian to speak with confidence. The good scholar takes these limitations into account."[4]

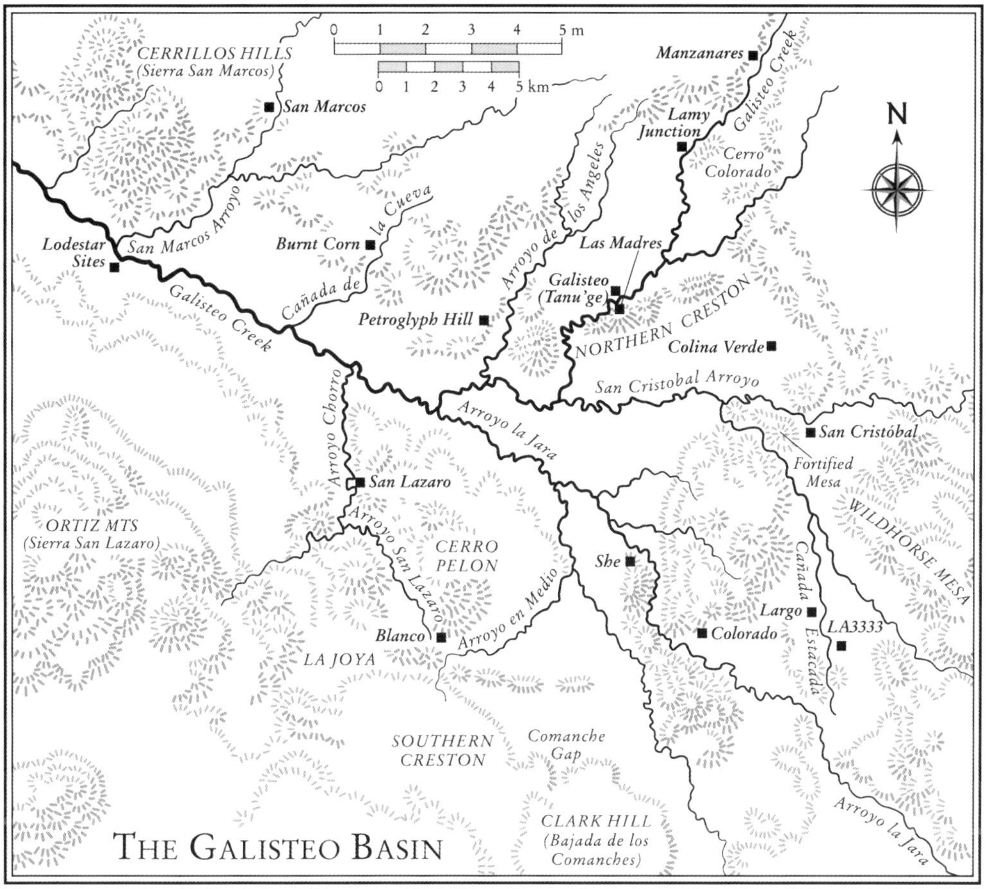

Deborah Reade, *The Galisteo Basin*, showing Galisteo Basin Pueblos (Lippard, *Down Country*, 33).

My research over almost two decades has been fragmentary and spasmodic, as other projects and making a living took precedence. I began with the plan of a single volume covering the entire history of the Galisteo Basin. This proved too big a bite. In 2010 I published *Down Country: The Tano of the Galisteo Basin, 1250–1782*, primarily concerned with the lives of the Pueblo peoples who first built their impressive pueblos here—the Tano or Southern Tewa and the Keres—and their interactions with the Spanish explorers and colonists who first wandered through the basin in 1541. Embarking on this second book, I decided to hone in on Galisteo village, founded after the departure of most of the Pueblo people in the late eighteenth century, and on its environs—the eastern part of the basin, where farming/ranching continued as the primary livelihood. At the same time, I cannot ignore the fact that our local stories are interwoven with those of other, newer local villages: the railroad town of Lamy, five miles to the east; Cerrillos, on the western side of the Galisteo Basin, where mining was the primary industry; and the later company mining town of Madrid, to the south in the Ortiz Mountains, now a tiny, funky, tourist attraction and an old hippie hangout. The western basin was the turf of the late lamented historian Bill Baxter. I refer readers to his books for stories of "the other side."

There are few models for an in-depth history of such a small village. *Pueblos chicos* like Galisteo are usually mentioned in the contexts of major historical events, urban centers, or larger landscapes. In order to understand this place, I have to shake off my own native geography, outwardly defined by my upbringing in New York, Maine, Louisiana, Virginia, and Connecticut. As I write about Galisteo, I'm looking for the full fabric, a place in a landscape woven of natural, historic, and current events, or history up to the moment. At the same time, I am all too aware that I have not even begun to solve the eternal land grant questions that lie beneath the surface. The village's past is integrally tied to its "continuous present" (as

Denise Lynch, *Southern Creston*, 2007. Traces of an old road and El Central Railroad bed are barely visible through Comanche Gap.

Gertrude Stein put it). Whatever the first impression of these vast spaces, this is in no sense a "timeless" landscape. It is a landscape of many times that—once the history is known—can be experienced almost simultaneously, which is the point of this book.

And now for a rapid road trip to and through the tiny village of Galisteo. I want the reader to be able to visualize entering the Galisteo Basin before being inundated with its intricate histories.

Galisteo lies on the eastern side of the Galisteo Basin in north central New Mexico, on the border between the Rio Abajo and the Rio Arriba, between the Rio Grande and the Sangre de Cristo mountains. It is embraced by two volcanic dikes, or crestons, that cut east-west across the eastern basin, both densely adorned with petroglyphs, or ancient rock art. The crocodilian form of the largest landmark, Cerro Pelón (Bald Hill) runs north/south, anchoring the valley. To the west, the pyramidal Lone Mountain is silhouetted in front of the Ortiz

Edward Ranney, *Río Galisteo and the Galisteo Pueblo from Las Madres*, 1999.

Mountains, which are echoed to the south by the San Pedros and the monolithic Sandías. The basin is best described as a circa 730-square-mile watershed, defined by the Río Galisteo, an often intermittent stream that descends from Thompson Peak in the Sangre de Cristos and enters the basin proper above the town of Lamy. This "river"—usually an ankle-deep creek or wash—is fed by the more robust Arroyo San Cristóbal, becoming a major tributary to the Rio Grande, a force to be reckoned with when in flood.

Lucy R. Lippard, *Northern Creston and Rock Art*, 1999.

To descend into the Galisteo Basin from the plains of the south or the encroaching suburbanization of the north is to enter an intimidatingly arid place that has meant something different for every new cultural group settling here, depending on climate, belief systems, larger economic-political frameworks . . . and weather, always the fickle weather, now subsumed by climate change. It is a rare moment when this *entrada*, from any direction, is not amplified by a stunning play of light on landforms—long, wooded mesas and red, pink, and yellow outcrops to the east, with higher blue mountains to the west. The Tano people, who arrived in the late thirteenth century, called their pueblo Tanuge, the Down Country Place, Near the Sun. The basin is a luminescent place, or a series of constantly shifting luminescent spaces.

Although this harshly beautiful landscape can be admired by tourists dashing through, it is ultimately defined by its inexhaustible secrets. On foot, you may come across prehistoric water diversions and check dams, the remains of corrals and lambing pens, tin cans from

Caroline Hinkley, *Coming Down Clark Hill into the Galisteo Basin from the South*, 2018. During road construction.

cowboy camps, failed nineteenth-century irrigation scams, or a brand-new road and the green metal boxes that signal new housesites. On row upon row of sandstone cliffs, volcanic dikes, and mesas is the rock art, some a thousand years old, some with bullet holes and graffiti near pot-hunted archaeological sites and landscapes defiled by sprawl or extraction industries.

Arrival from the south is the most dramatic introduction. The two-lane highway, NM 41, gives way to open space and an illusion of timelessness as the road descends abruptly from the broad plains of the Estancia Valley into a more intimate and varied space where the light seems to take on an extra dimension. My breath is always taken away by this descent into

home. But it has changed a good deal since I first saw it thirty-five years ago. For all the fleeting sense of unspoiled natural beauty that marks the basin's southern entrance, one has only to look left and right to be jolted by future reality. On one side "the biggest house in New Mexico" is poised on a ridge high above the highway, where once the Teyas, Apaches, and Comanches poured down to raid the Galisteo pueblos. On the other side of the highway, just before the descent, ugly gates announce an unsuccessful subdivision.

Joan Myers, *Entering Galisteo from the South*, 2018.

But ignore, for the moment, these harbingers of the future. Instead surrender to the stunning views of hilly open ranchland on both sides of the road. On our left the ragged humps of the southern creston create dramatic shadows and Cerro Pelón looms over them, its languid form echoed by the much smaller Loma Montosa. On Chapatalito, a small, perfectly pyramidal hill below the slope, there are more petroglyphs and sheepherders' signatures. Occasional herds of pronghorns graze contentedly alongside Angus cattle, even in drought years, since tax-break ranchers can usually afford to bring hay to their beasts. Thanks to their ranches, there are almost nine miles of open space ahead of us.

A few more miles north on NM 41, the church spire of the village of Galisteo appears and disappears as the curving road rises and falls. My little tin-roofed house and solar tracker appear, then disappear with the next curve. Then the road aims straight for it. We pass the Galisteo Rodeo Grounds, a huddle of corrals, arena, trailers, and old cars that for over forty

Nicolas Trofimuk, *Entering Galisteo from the East in 1987*.

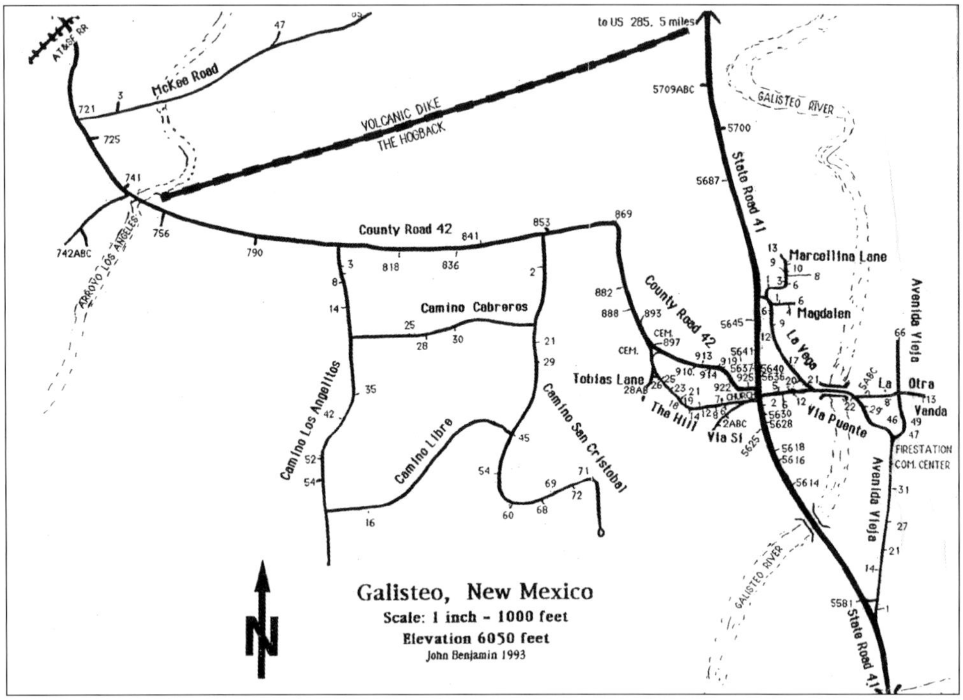

John Benjamin, *Village Map*, 1993. Printed annually in the Galisteo Volunteer Fire and Rescue Phone Directory. Benjamin made this to scale, using a topo map, when he created the first village directory as a Christmas gift to the community, including names of all roads and rural addresses to facilitate emergency responses.

years awakened annually in late July. We cross a cement bridge twenty feet above the San Cristóbal Arroyo, then cross the Galisteo Creek on another bridge, and we are in the village. Slow down. Don't blink. Welcome to Galisteo (population circa 260, altitude 6,056 feet).

The village was once a major crossroads, but the eastern wing, County Road 33A, has been subsumed by the locked gates of San Cristóbal Ranch. Entering the village from the west, on County Road 42, recently renamed Camino los Abuelos, we drive around a sharp curve, pass between the old and the new cemeteries and a modern residence with giant wings. Below lies "downtown Galisteo," the center of town life, marked by the roof of the 1884 village church, Nuestra Señora de los Remedios, with its distinctive two-way

Joan Myers, *Entering Galisteo from the West*, 2018.

Joan Myers, *Entering Galisteo from the North*, 2018.

cross, reflecting the crossroads. Here is the bank of locked mailboxes that replaced a long line of old ones decorated by a kids' art project. If we turned back and drove around eight miles to the west, we would arrive at NM 14 (aka the Turquoise Trail, after the pre-European and historic turquoise mining district).

Once in the village, the visitor has the choice of a few short dirt roads: tree-lined Via La Puente, across the highway from CR 42, leads east across the Rio Galisteo on an old wooden bridge to La Otra Vanda, the "other side" of the village, making an abrupt right turn to meet Avenida Vieja, once the main road, which now dead-ends at a private home to the north and meets NM 41 to the south. Back toward the center are three dirt roads called Magdalena, La Vega, and Marcellina Lane. Behind the church a road winds up "The Hill," where the original settlement began. Some old homes survive, drastically altered, and the remains of others recall the village's busier days. Short drives called Via Si and Tobias Lane branch off The Hill, which leads to the mound that was the original church and the old cemetery, paired by the "new" one across the road.

Leaving Galisteo, NM 41 continues north roughly following the river, between two handsomely tended "haciendas," past two shiny "silos" and a swooping white modern structure (both artists' studios), past a sliver of the San Cristóbal Ranch, through the *puerto* of the northern creston, and we're back in ranchland, most of it now subdivided. We pass the former Nizhoni School for Global Consciousness, the equestrian center Goose Downs, the new subdivision officially misspelled Hacienda Tranquilas, the Chi Center, the invisible ruins of ancient Tanuge, and a foreclosed subdivision called Saddleback Ranch. NM 41 ends at US 285, the four-lane route south to WIPP (the Waste Isolation Pilot Plant nuclear depository in Carlsbad), and indirectly north to Santa Fe. To the right the hamlet of Lamy huddles against the rising wooded mesas, guarded by the stepped Cerro Colorado (quarried for the construction of the cathedral in Santa Fe) and another invisible pueblo ruin, and onto the state capital, the Villa of Holy Faith, or Santa Fe, some twenty miles away, where Cerro Pelón is visible from high points, its distinctive form hovering on the horizon as I go about my urban errands, reminding me of the little-known land and lives surrounding it.

Edward Ranney, *Shrine at Las Madres, above Tanuge/Galisteo Pueblo*, 1999.

ONE

A Village Rises on The Hill (1799–1840)

In 1706, the surviving Tano/Tewa population was forced back into the deserted Galisteo Basin and a crumbling Tanuge (the Down Country Place, or Galisteo Pueblo) to provide a buffer for the Spanish between Santa Fe and raiding tribes. By 1782, the pueblo had dwindled to some fifty people. Having suffered starvation, smallpox, and raids by nomadic Indians, those who hadn't already migrated to other pueblos finally fled down the Rio Galisteo to the Keres pueblo of Santo Domingo (now Kewa), forgoing permission from their Spanish rulers. From the moment the last of the Tanuge people trudged down the riverbed, the story is allabout land—land use, land grants, land grabs, land losses, division and subdivision, development and preservation, and the declining health of land coveted by and affecting everyone. If water is life (el agua es la vida), land is luck, and always has been for the residents of the Galisteo Basin. Because land without access to water is perceived as worthless, the two are inextricably entwined in the social lives of those living here.

It is not known how many, if any, Spanish settlers (other than part-time clergy and the soldiers necessary for their occasional defense) shared the Tanos' eighteenth-century exile in the Galisteo Basin. The Comanche Peace Treaty came in 1786, just too late to save Tanuge. It held for more or less forty years and was crucial for the Spanish colony of Nuevo Mexico. "It might be but little exaggeration," notes one historian, "to conclude that had there been no Comanche peace in New Mexico, there might have been no New Mexico."[1] Once the merciless Comanche raiders were calmed, if not entirely neutralized, the good grazing land of the Galisteo Basin should have attracted settlers.

This does not, however, seem to have been the case. Any reference to Galisteo on sixteenth through early-nineteenth-century maps and documents is to Galisteo Pueblo rather than to the future Hispano village a mile and a half to the south. Village and pueblo never coexisted as living settlements. In the 1790 Spanish census Galisteo is not mentioned at all, and there is no Galisteo on a 1795 map, suggesting that although the Tanos had departed, no one else had yet legitimately settled in the area, despite a garrison in the vicinity of the present-day village. (In fact, in the mid-eighteenth century, the beleaguered Tanos isolated at the Galisteo Pueblo might have welcomed Hispano neighbors to help defend against raiding tribes, just as Pueblo allies often rescued Hispano settlers before the 1680 Revolt.) In the Salinas Basin to the south, Apache, Navajo, and Plains tribes continued to raid, holding off settlement there until around 1800. Similar conditions afflicted the eastern Galisteo Basin.

Edward Ranney, *San Cristóbal Pueblo*, 1999.

There was never a formal Galisteo Pueblo grant of land by the Spanish crown that survived the departure of the Tanos. This is curious because in the seventeenth century, before the Pueblo Revolt of 1680, missionized pueblos were the only extant "towns" in the Galisteo Basin.[2] In the eighteenth century, Galisteo and Pecos were the only surviving pueblos in the area. Yet the long unoccupied San Cristóbal Pueblo was the sole Galisteo pueblo included in the Cruzate grants, purportedly drawn up in 1689 during the Spanish exile in El Paso after the Pueblo Revolt, by governor-in-exile Domingo Jironza Petriz de Cruzate with Zia leader (and accused turncoat) Bartolomé de Ojeda. These documents are now determined to be mysteriously credible forgeries, or possibly nineteenth-century copies of authentic documents.[3] Four square leagues—to be measured from a central church or a cross—had been decreed as reserved for each pueblo, but the Cruzate grants were submitted to the US surveyor general in the 1850s and became law when they were confirmed by the US Congress.

Although these four-league pueblo grants were not recognized in 1782, the deserted villages should have been held in trust for the Tanos when they were forced out by adversity.[4] It makes sense that the pre-European pueblos in the basin that were already unoccupied when the Spanish arrived in the 1500s (Largo, She, Colorado, and Blanco) were considered up for grabs once colonization began in earnest (though to this day, descendants of their original occupants continue to visit the sites for ceremonial purposes). But it is more puzzling that after the 1693–96 Reconquest, no rights to the previously missionized and colonized pueblos of San Lázaro, San Marcos, San Cristóbal, and Galisteo were retained by their Pueblo owners through the Spanish, Mexican, or US governments.[5] No Pueblo people seem to have made legal claims to any of the ancestral Galisteo Basin pueblos, and if they did, it was ignored. They were not yet threatened by Hispano encroachment in the eighteenth century, unlike many other New Mexico pueblos, because there was little if any settlement in the basin, thanks to raiding tribes.[6] After the Tanos departed, of course, there was no longer an official

Protector of Indians to support their claims.[7] It is also possible that Galisteo Pueblo's last population was so mixed, comprising a few surviving Tanos along with Tewas from Tesuque and other pueblos, that those who saw the basin as their homeland were in the minority. Or perhaps the widely dispersed and decimated Tanos felt powerless because they were so few, or because they had departed without official sanction, or they faced punishment for leaving without permission. All four of the pueblos in the Galisteo Basin that were occupied historically soon became private property, as are most of the pre-Spanish ruins.

The eighteenth century redefined the economic and spatial world of both Pueblos and Hispanos.[8] The Spanish had learned something (if not enough) from the Pueblo rebellion. While to the north of Santa Fe, Spanish and Mexican land grants (*mercedes*) overlapping Indian lands were already contentious issues, settlers to the south did not spread very far from the historic pueblos until the beginning of the nineteenth century. By the late 1700s, despite continuing threats from nomadic tribes, both *ricos* and *pobres* were undoubtedly eyeing or actually staking out land in the Galisteo Basin, especially along the rare waterways. There were rumors of settlers near Tanuge by 1794, but the western side of the basin was settled first, perhaps because of easier access to Santa Fe and proximity to the Camino Real and the mines. As early as July 26, 1754, Governor Tomás Vélez Capuchin granted the westernmost historic pueblo, the long unoccupied San Marcos, to Antonio Urban Montaño, whose 1772 will refers to the land once occupied by San Marcos Pueblo and describes an arroyo called "lo de Vasques" (Juan de Oñate and many other early settlers were Basques). Mount Chalchuihuitl (Nahuatl for "turquoise") is mentioned. One boundary was "the road leading to the Pueblo of Galisteo," which may have roughly followed the route of present-day County Road 42. Another boundary was "Sabinos Altos de Chuacaco" (the Tall Cedars of Chaquaco).[9]

The empty Galisteo Pueblo lands may have been unofficially utilized by the turn of the century. The possibility of the Tanos returning was apparently never considered, but no formal recognition of land ownership around the old "Pueblo de los Tanos" came until more than a decade after their departure. In 1799 a petition was made by Juan Cruz Aragón ("an aging and infirm soldier") with other unnamed citizens for a grazing grant at the Ojito de

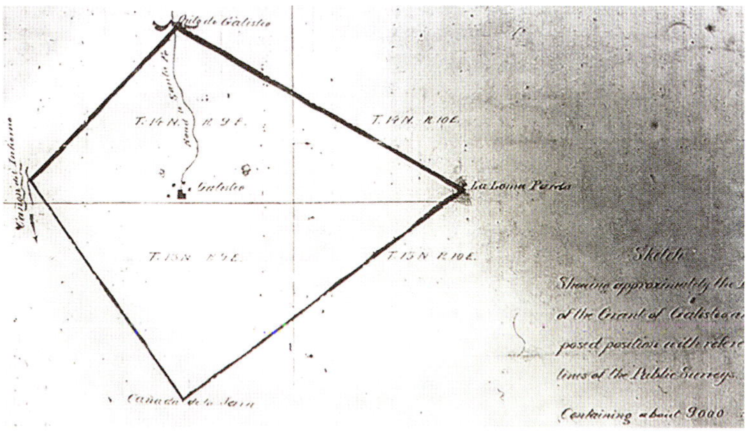

Ojito de Galisteo/Galisteo Grant Sketch, undated (after 1848). (Private Land Claims case #164, Spanish Archives of New Mexico [SANM] I 49:862.) "Showing approximately the Boundaries of the Grant of Galisteo and its supposed position with reference to the lines of the Public Surveys. Containing about 9,000 acres." The "Road to Santa Fe" from Galisteo village leads directly to the Ojito.

Edward Ranney, *Ojito de Galisteo*, 1999.

Galisteo—a reliable spring along the wagon road from Galisteo to Santa Fe, today a few stone foundations, a former stock tank, and a small wetland on Thornton Ranch/Commonweal Conservancy. Although known as the Ojito de Galisteo grant, its boundaries as drawn in a later, inaccurately geometric sketch do not include the spring, and it has been conflated (or confused) with the original Galisteo grant.

It is unclear if Aragón or anyone else took possession of, occupied, or utilized this grant, which seems to have been subsumed or revived by a Royal Edict of January 1813. By then, Aragón's name had disappeared. In fact, even the existence of the Aragón grant has been questioned. Like so many other valid Spanish/Mexican grants, it was eventually deemed a forgery by the US courts, which does not mean that it was not legitimate. A connection between the 1799 Aragón grant request and the powerful Pino family is possible, since almost a century later, in 1893, Nicolás Pino made a half-hearted claim for the grant on the grounds (not further explained) that he was an heir of, or related to, Aragón.[10] A rough rectangular sketch (unrelated to the diamond-shaped plat of Ojito/first Galisteo grant) marks the following boundaries: on the north, by the high ridge (La Ceja Alta) of Reconocida; on the east, by the slopes of the high hills (los caidos de los lomas) west of Galisteo and continuing to Las Cuchillas Pedrogosas at the northeast corner of the San Cristóbal del Monte plain; on the south, by the slopes of the Galisteo River; and on the west, by La Cañada Colorada and Cerrito Huerfano (possibly Lone Butte or Lone Mountain).[11] The "Galisteo" mentioned was, of course, the unoccupied pueblo, and the accompanying document states that the confirmation rituals took place at the Ojito de Galisteo.[12]

Indicative of the continuing dangers in outlying regions, the Aragón grant stipulated that the claimant have bow and arrows or a firearm "for defense because of the open nature of the place." After four years, firearms would be mandatory. An 1807 edict required all those traveling abroad to be armed. Mule trains were required to have three lances and one musket. The poor had to have at least a slingshot when in the countryside. Settlers and Indians alike used bows and arrows.[13] Well into the nineteenth century, life in the Galisteo Basin, and travel anywhere in New Mexico, was hazardous. All journeys, trading with nomadic tribes, or attending frontier-town tradefairs, required a permit, which didn't keep footloose wanderers off the roads. Anyone traveling aimlessly was considered a "vagabond" and a danger to society. This included laborers looking for work and criminals disguised as Apaches so that the tribe would be blamed for their crimes.

That the rigorous scholarship devoted to larger communal grants by scholars like G. Emlen Hall, Victor Westphall, and Malcolm Ebright has never been applied to the small grants in the Galisteo Basin reflects the complications of the local land grant morass, although J. J. Bowden tackled the details in her 1969 MA thesis.[14] Documentation of the labyrinthine trajectory of San Cristóbal Pueblo is a partial exception to this void. One reason for the scarcity of attention is probably the comparably smaller scale of the other local grants. There may have been too few grantees to garner the attention given to those elsewhere who were gobbling up thousands of acres.

Seventeenth-century Spanish grants were awarded primarily to individuals, for major service and/or as class privilege, but over the next two centuries, grants of house and farm plots and common lands to groups and communities became more common, as they were vital to the colony's survival in the *tierra adentro*, in dangerous areas that trespassed on tribal homelands. The Crown needed settlers to push the tribes out of their traditional territories. Colonists were encouraged to consider the land "their mother"; "as sons" (and patriots) they would "love, honor, and defend her."[15] After the Reconquest, mercedes replaced the exploitative encomiendas as the best way for settlers to acquire property. Native peoples struggling to keep their own lands were pitted against landless Hispanos willing to risk their lives to become property owners. Mercedes served something of the same purpose in the Spanish and Mexican periods as homesteading would for the United States in the late nineteenth century, the major difference being the Spanish *ejido* tradition of shared or common lands. Many settlements were periodically abandoned because of Indian attacks, and if the government had not bestowed permission for withdrawal, the lands reverted to the Crown. Though Mexico's vast and richly appointed haciendas were not found in New Mexico, the hierarchy was clearly delineated. Poor people received less land. The lower classes could not expect the bounty due the upper classes. Galisteo grantees sometimes held plots as small as 30–50 varas wide.[16] As one friar put it, where land is concerned, "It is not suitable that everyone should be an equal."[17]

By 1805, northern New Mexico was dotted with loosely grouped, small ranches, or poblaciones.[18] Plazas, or villages, the smaller *placitas*, and the still smaller *lugares* and *sitios* began as communities of extended families and were often named after the founding family (Los Chávez, Los Lunas). These hamlets offered scant protection against raiding Indians, but the tough, contrary New Mexicans could not, even after the 1680 disaster, be persuaded to group together in larger towns, as recommended/required by the Spanish Crown. Although Indian raids made the eastern Galisteo Basin a *tierra de riesgo* (risky, or dangerous place), land speculation and colonization began, first spasmodically, then in earnest, by the early 1800s. There were sheepherders, camps, and corrals in San Cristóbal Canyon. Unidentified, undated stone stock pens and foundations exist within the ruins of several of the basin's pueblos, including Galisteo/Tanuge.[19]

To obtain a grant during the Spanish period, the applicant wrote a petition to the governor describing the desired parcel, stating that it was not occupied, and explaining how it would be used. Among the requirements for a community grant was the digging of acequias (irrigation ditches), a protected plaza, and a church. The local *alcalde mayor* was ordered to investigate, and the request was announced in public so that protests could be lodged. Neighbors, Indian or Spanish, were to be notified. Then a document was drawn up, including a sketchy map of the claim and a statement signed by two witnesses giving the distance between the grant and neighboring communities. Each grantee received a private homesite (*solar*) on which to build a house on the mandatory town plaza, as well as a *suerte*, a strip of agricultural land with access to water, that could be irrigated in one day. The strips were usually 100–150 varas wide. The grander grants were measured in leagues. As the most desirable farmlands were handed out, new groups applied for more peripheral areas. If the governor was satisfied that the title was clear, official transfer was granted, followed by a traditional ceremony of possession, when the alcalde, accompanied by twelve witnesses and neighbors, went to the boundary markers. There the grantees tore up grass and threw rocks, in a ritual derived from medieval Spain, while the crowd shouted "Long Live the King." In order to receive final title, the applicants had to live and work there for four years. Eventually, virtually every *vecino* (neighbor) held title to some grant land. Well into the twentieth century, writes Frances Swadesh, the first question asked when Nuevo Méxicanos met was, "Que es tu merced?" (Which is your grant?)[20]

Sometime before 1807, Diego Antonio Baca was given a grant in Cañoncito, overlooking the eastern Galisteo Basin on the road from Santa Fe to Pecos, in exchange for a house and lot used for barracks by government troops stationed in the presidio in Santa Fe. His southern border was the road leading to Galisteo to its junction with the Soldiers' Bridle Path, and on the west by that path and Cerro Colorado. Carlos de Herrera bought the Cañoncito grant land from Baca around 1817, stocking it with sheep under a *partido* contract with a group of Penitentes (La Cofradía de Nuestro Padre Jesús Nazareno Hermanos) called La Nuestra Señora de la Luz, later the name of Lamy's church. Five hundred of these sheep were stolen by a band of Comanches (despite the treaty) on their way to a fair in Albuquerque, and Herrera gave the land back to the Penitente Brotherhood. The godson of Diego Antonio Baca was Domingo Fernández, a Santa Fe prosecuting attorney, who was appointed custodian and tithe collector of the property for the Church (although the Church was supposedly not permitted to own land in New Spain). He was to play a major role in Galisteo's land grant history, as was the Pino family, arriving in Galisteo roughly around the same time.

The Pinos, originally from Albenga, Savona, Italy, via Mexico City, arrived in New Mexico in the eighteenth century and became "among the most influential residents of the Territory."[21] They first emerged as major landowners in Tomé and Belen. Don Pedro Bautista Pino, the most illustrious family member, was born circa 1752 in Tomé. His wealthy father, Mateo José Pino (born 1720 in Mexico City) and grandfather Juan Bautista Pino (birth date unknown, from Albenga) were merchants trading up and down the Camino Real. His mother was Teresa Sánchez, a New Mexico native from the vicinity of Isleta Pueblo and Rancho de

1795 Garrison Barracks at the Ortiz y Davis Hacienda, 1980. (Courtesy of Yolanda and María Ortiz y Pino.)

San Clemente. Don Pedro ranched in the Belen area and was alcalde of Tomé, then moved to Santa Fe in 1801 (or "sometime after 1780").[22] His main claim to fame is that on August 11, 1810, after "drawing lots with two men of the Ortiz family," he was selected by Governor Manriques and an assembly of his peers to be the New Mexico delegate to a *cortes*, or congress, of the disheveled Spanish Empire in Cadiz in 1812. Fray Angélico Chávez writes: "What is of main significance for New Mexico in this period is that Mother Spain finally remembered her long lost tribe after more than two hundred years, and that one tribal son sailed back across the ocean sea to plead in his people's behalf."[23] Pino claimed to be "the first native of the province who [came] to Spain," boasting that "the patriotic people [of New Mexico] contributed $9,000 to the cause of the King of Spain."[24] Though only fifty-eight, he was referred to by his colleagues in the cortes as the "Abraham of New Mexico." His report, (Exposición sucinta y sencilla de la provincia del Nuevo México) (A Brief and Succinct Exposition of the Province of New Mexico), is considered the best information on life in New Mexico in the last years of Spanish rule.[25] "Is there any other province six hundred leagues from the seat of administration of justice?" he asked rhetorically, lobbying hard for his forgotten province in its "doleful condition." Among his recommendations: "1) the establishment of a bishopric in Santa Fe; 2) the establishment of a seminary college of higher learning and of public schools for the instruction of the youth; 3) uniformity in military service, the additions of the five presidios mentioned and payment of salaries to all settlers who may been listed . . . as is done in Durango, Sonora, Texas and other adjoining provinces; 4) the establishment of a civil and criminal *audiencia* in Chihuahua."[26] These were adopted but never implemented, inspiring the locally popular rhyme "Don Pedro Pino fue; Don Pedro Pino vino" (Don Pedro went [to Spain], Don Pedro came back). And that was that.[27]

Don Pedro's third wife, whom he married in 1816, was Ana Maria Baca.[28] They had two never mentioned daughters (Encarnación and María Guadalupe de la Trinidad) and four sons—Nicolás, Miguel, Germán, and José Facundo—all of whom figure in the history of

Galisteo, along with cousin Ambrosio and half-brother Juan Esteban.[29] In the late 1700s the name Pino was associated with grazing lands in the Galisteo Basin. By the early 1800s, Don Pedro "was the wealthiest man in Santa Fe, being the owner of vast flocks of sheep and goats that were pastured along the Galisteo River."[30] "We just came and took what we wanted. That's how people did it in those days. The Pinos held land all over," a descendant told me.[31] One undocumented source holds that in the late 1700s the Pino ranch house was the only house in the Galisteo valley.[32] Its location is unknown, but it was probably in the western valley.[33] Like many of the nineteenth-century ricos, he would have resided in the city and visited his outlying holdings when necessary. Don Pedro Pino lived in Santa Fe until his death on April 19, 1829. He is said to be buried there, but the church records for that year are lost.

The only documented activity on the present site of Galisteo village in the eighteenth century was the construction, between 1792 and 1795, of a "square compound and a house for soldiers," ordered built "7 leagues South Southeast of Santa Fe." This *destacamento* (garrison, or outpost; the presidio was in Santa Fe) was the first recorded post-Revolt Spanish building beyond the pueblo and in the vicinity of the eventual village. It was built to protect the government's horse and sheep herds. In earlier days, as many as thirty soldiers were assigned to guard military stock grazing in the Galisteo Basin. Yet by the beginning of the nineteenth century, the basin had already been overgrazed and was parched by drought. Government sheep herds (to feed the hundred or so soldiers at the presidio) and the remudas (each soldier was assigned three horses and a pack mule) had to be rotated, often to Pecos. In the winter, when there were no campaigns against the Indians, eight to ten soldiers camped in the Galisteo Basin with their own livestock. An August 30, 1800, report on Indian depredations and reprisals mentioned the destacamento at Galisteo,[34] while a report dated June 15, 1808, from Governor Alberto Maynez to the alcaldes, lists a detachment of three soldiers at Galisteo.[35] The presence of a garrison would also have attracted settlers to the eastern Galisteo Basin.

The garrison's location is still in question.[36] It would have seemed more practical to build this little structure amid the ruins of the recently abandoned Galisteo Pueblo rather than a mile and a half downstream in the middle of nowhere, in indefensible lowlands next to the river. Archaeologist Adolph Bandelier was told in the 1880s that there "were formerly two detachments of troops, one at the old pueblo of Galisteo and the other at San Cristóbal, both against the Comanche."[37] However, testimony in an 1871 trial suggests that it was built at the village site. John Benjamin, current owner of what could well be the 1790s barracks, part of the former Ortiz y Davis "hacienda" in Galisteo, is convinced that this is the site. Students of University of New Mexico architectural historian Bainbridge Bunting came to the same conclusion.[38] Benjamin speculates that the Spanish government hauled the stones to build their garrison "from the abandoned Pueblo two miles to the north." The Galisteo Pueblo was constructed primarily of adobe; the rocks might have come from foundations, from the mission church, or from the small Las Madres site on the bluff above, though there were much closer sources of uncut sandstone. Perhaps the siting depended on the health of the grasses and the fact that the Rio Galisteo runs above ground in the village site and is intermittent farther north. Traces of earlier stone structures detected in the corners of the approximately square Ortiz y Davis hacienda compound may have been defensive torreones, though probably from a later date, as Indian depredations continued in the area into the 1860s.

The date of the founding of "the Mexican village of Galisteo" ranges in the literature from 1808 to 1846. In the early twentieth century, ethnographer J. P. Harrington was unable to learn "how old this settlement is."[39] Bandelier was told by Ramón Cháves in Galisteo that the first settlers arrived around 1810.[40] According to historical archaeologist David Snow, "not until the second decade of the nineteenth century is there evidence for serious reoccupation of the vicinity of former Galisteo and its environs."[41] He suggests that the village of Galisteo was settled 1814–16, but "not permanently until c. 1822," as Indian raids were still taking their toll.[42] According to archeologist Steve Post, who has studied many of New Mexico's early villages, this was typical: "Settlers would come out (or send their grown children out), build some shelter, begin to settle, and then someone would be killed by Indians and they would go back to town."[43] The Comanches finally began to drift away from the Galisteo Basin around 1822, which would have encouraged settlers.

Despite the garrison and probably some illegal settlers, Galisteo appears to have been officially founded in 1814–16 when Hispano families petitioned to take over Tano lands. Donaciano Vigil testified on December 2, 1871, "I know the place mentioned and have known it all my life. . . . It is situated eight leagues south of this city and in the county of Santa Fe. . . . When the United States took possession of the country, the town of Galisteo existed the same as it does today."[44] His father (Juan Cristóbal Vigil) "occupied a portion of the land under one of the grantees," and Vigil himself lived there as a child from 1819 to 1820, "while part of my father's family."[45]

The grant Vigil referred to was petitioned to Governor Alberto Maynez (Maynes) in February 1814. It read in part: "We, Felipe Sandoval, José Luis Lovato, Julián Lucero, Matías Sandoval, and Pedro Sandoval, for themselves and *in the name of other associates* [my italics], citizens of this village [totaling nineteen individuals] having large families to support, we are desirous of some pieces of land sufficient for the maintenance of our large families the place, Galisteo, being the old field of the Indians called the Tanos, and the same Indians having become extinct, there remaining but few, who are scattering among the other pueblos of this province, they having no intention of living at their old homes, we therefore pray" that 9,000 acres be donated to the petitioners by the Crown. Some or many of those named may already have been in the area, waiting to be legitimized.

By February 14, 1814, when the petition was signed and granted by Governor Maynez, the name Galisteo was already well enough known to be logically inherited by the new Spanish village. Grantees were "to understand that the pastures and waters [should] be free to the inhabitants of this village and its ranches for pasturing and herding their horses and cattle thereon." The petition was certified by Trinidad Barceló (of Taos, brother of the famous Doña Tules), with no date or place. The diamond-shaped plat displayed in later trials, "showing approximately the Boundaries of the Grant of Galisteo and its supposed positions with reference to the lines of the Public Surveys containing about 9,000 acres," would seem to be the actual Ojito de Galisteo grant since the Ojito is its northern boundary. "Approximate" though the plat is, the place names are all familiar to the area around both the pueblo and the village.

The boundaries were, north, the Galisteo Spring; west, the Arroyo del Infierno (later renamed Arroyo de los Angeles by Archbishop Lamy); east, Loma Parda (Gray, or Dark, Hill, defined elsewhere as "tablelands" two or three miles east of Galisteo); and south, Cañada de la Jara, although the diamond shape does not exactly fit these landmarks.[46]

The government probably hoped that the Spanish village would help protect Santa Fe, a function previously served by the old pueblo and the garrisons, which were not replaced in 1814. The settlers thus inherited the precarious role of buffer between Santa Fe and the raiding tribes, as they noted in their petition: "And said place will in part be a protection for this village and ranches, owing to the great risk from the enemy who passes to and fro with his spoils, after having committed many murders"; in order to respond to recent depredations, "a strong detachment of Pueblo Indians and citizens was kept stationed there; and by granting to us the said place as a grant the said detachment would then be unnecessary."[47]

The 1814 grant seems relatively straightforward. But in 1816, almost the same list of petitioners made a second request, suggesting that something was amiss with the initial plea. The year 1815, just when the villagers would have been trying to settle in, was known as "the year without summer," due to a global chill caused by the eruption of the Indonesian volcano Tambora, ten times bigger than that of the better known Krakatoa. Crops were diminished, and it may be that the settlers were unable to meet their obligations under these conditions. In 1816, however, the petitioners were successful, though it is unclear exactly what acreage they requested or received. Decades later, in the American courts, this approval was to work against the existence of the apparently much larger 1814 grant. Someone unfamiliar with New Mexico land grants erroneously claimed that there was no reason to believe the same piece of land would be awarded twice. Nevertheless, in 1816, nineteen families were "ordered to build their houses adjacent to one another around a central plaza" and to build a community dam at "a spring nearby" for irrigation. But locals were soon trading and selling. The 1821 census shows that of the original nineteen grantees of 1816, only seven of those listed, or their households, remained in the village five years after the original grant was made.[48]

The conclusive documents, however, were not forthcoming until April 7, 1822, when Governor Facundo Melgares confirmed the 1814/16 grant. By that time, New Mexico no longer belonged to Spain but was annexed to the Republic of Mexico. On April 8, the ayuntamiento (government) ordered Santa Fe Alcalde Pedro Armendaris to give each of nineteen grantees an *hijuela*.[49] On April 29, Armendaris came to Galisteo to formalize possession with fourteen of the original grantees, heirs of two deceased grantees, and three new settlers. Grass and rocks were thrown, and each individual was awarded strips of land measuring 100 by 1,000 varas. Larger tracts, 150 varas wide, were given to Rafael Luján and Felipe Sandoval (in 1815 he was the official Protector of Indians).[50] The boundaries were those of the diamond-shaped plat. In subsequent years the Mexican government granted requests to some thirty-eight other individuals along the creek.[51]

The Galisteo grant's trajectory is often oversimplified, and I am duly recomplicating it here, from a local vantage point. For years of research, I labored under the illusion that there were several relatively distinct grants: the 1799 Aragón grant, the 1814/16/22 Galisteo grant,

Edward Ranney, *The Hill from the Galisteo Grant to the South*, 2018.

the 1843 Tacubaya and 1846 Cadial grants on the east side of the river (not to mention the overlapping San Cristóbal, Baca y Terrus, and Mesitas Blancas grants). Yet, given the massive documentary confusion that has to be sorted out legally or historically, they were all sometimes labeled the Galisteo grant, and they all overlapped at various times. Estimated acreage for the Galisteo grant has varied from 9,000 to 21,740 to 24,000 acres. The founding village grant is sometimes called the Townsite or Town of Galisteo grant.[52] As described in the 1822 version, it embraced not only the former Galisteo Pueblo lands but also the entire townsite of the nascent village of Galisteo and parts of the later San Cristóbal grant. However, it was never surveyed, beginning a long and conflicted history that has taken its toll on scholarship. New Mexico land records are a mess, offering fragmentary documents from three nations over more than four centuries, their interpretation and misinterpretation (innocent and intentional) fueling ongoing disputes over speculation and stolen lands as each successive culture appropriated property from its predecessors when it took power.

Whatever its legal base, or lack thereof, a community rose above the Rio Galisteo. The settlers built their homes on La Loma, still officially named "The Hill," overlooking their fields and the Rio Galisteo. The site was a good choice, with water in two directions, as the Galisteo Creek makes an *arco*, or almost ninety-degree turn at the site, embracing the village on both east and south, and the Arroyo Atascoso (now the San Cristóbal Arroyo) branched off to the east. The defensive height, along with surrounding hills, commanded a broad, though not totally unobstructed, view of the surroundings. "The townsite" is mentioned here and there. Homes were often built of stone found at the old pueblo ruins and/or outcroppings to the west.[53] Along with a wall, an acequia, a church, and houses close together around a central plaza, the settlers were expected to build an irrigation dam at Galisteo Spring—probably not the Ojito but something nearby, perhaps around the northern creston east of the *puertocito* (to the east of the *puerto* where the current road runs). Presumably the grant was still 9,000 acres,

Joan Myers, *Up The Hill*, 2018. Benny Anaya ruin at the right.

as in the 1814 version. The farming village was to focus "the immensity of unsettled lands" and "to relieve the almost annual shortage of crops of this Capital."[54]

The new village was located where several ancient trails met, leading north to the Galisteo Pueblo and Santa Fe, south to the Salinas, and east/west to Pecos and San Marcos/ Santo Domingo. In an 1871 trial, seventy-four-year-old Agustín Durán testified that Galisteo had been "continuously occupied as a town since 1814." The people living there in 1821 were Felipe Sandoval, Luis Lovato, Julián Lucero, José Antonio Sandoval, "alias Bachicha," and others Durán could not recall.[55] Librado Valencia added that the settlers built their houses on a hill and a church in the middle so as to be protected from the Indians. Anastacio Sandoval observed that "they were afraid of the Navajos, the Apaches, Mescaleros, afraid of the Comanches, afraid of the Cayguas [Kiowas] . . . and the Apaches that lived close to Picuris [Jicarillas]. Galisteo at that time was nothing but a desert. Further I have had knowledge enough [that] when a man died a natural death there were ten to twelve that were killed by the Indians that had to be buried."[56]

Speaking during a court case in the early twentieth century, Anastacio Sandoval reiterated that "the first settlers who went to Galisteo went there on the 14th year of the last century" and petitioned for agricultural land. Each settler got 100 varas and "decided to build their houses on top of a hill." They stayed in the "little town they had settled" because there was good drinking water and "the Indians at that time were threatening to fight against the settlers and that was the reason they stayed all together at the time, and that is the reason the town [of Galisteo] stands there today."[57]

Under the Spanish and Mexican ejido systems, the bulk of a grant was common land, shared and deeply depended upon by poorer settlers who were unable to enlarge their holdings. In northern New Mexico, the common village settlement pattern was "one of multiplying, not enlarging," with each new group spread out along the narrow valleys into new plazas, or placitas, some of which eventually became villages.[58] In the Santa Fe Parish Census of 1821, el Partido de Galisteo was the "outlying district," probably the entire Galisteo Basin, not just the village, implying that villagers, or others, had already spread out. A later copy (in English) of this census shows 125 people (a large number of them children) in twenty-five households.[59]

I have not found any record of the names of Galisteo's alcaldes mayores in the early to mid-nineteenth century, but they would have had some impact on the town. In the early Mexican period, the alcalde ruled locally, though in 1828 the power to award land grants reverted to the governor. The alcalde registered cattle brands in a *libro de registro*, went after crooks, extortion, and other illicit activities, completed census reports, regulated public travel, and publicly proclaimed official edicts and royal decrees, calling attention with a drum, reading the decree out loud in the plaza, then posting it in public places. Pueblo people, who had seen life improve somewhat after the Reconquest, began to suffer abuses again under this new wave of bureaucracy. The clergy, too, complained about the local authorities. "Strict honesty [was] in short supply."[60]

Lucy R. Lippard, *Stone Lines Marking Fields on the Former Galisteo Grant*, ca. 1998.

In the Galisteo Basin, where the river wound between rolling grazing lands, no other towns arose until the railroad arrived in 1880. In the early 1800s, the nearest settlements were Cañada de los Alamos, Pecos, and La Ciénega. It would have taken a day's ride to travel the eight leagues over rough country to Santa Fe, and more in a carreta (ox-drawn wooden cart) or on foot. Few human marks on the landscape would have been visible in any direction, aside from occasional grazing livestock. The arrival of visitors—friends or foes—would have been an event. In the early nineteenth century, a husband accused by his wife of maltreatment with words, including a threat of death, was banished to Galisteo until he could prove his good intentions.[61]

At its inception, the village of Galisteo probably consisted of a few low adobe and stone buildings and brush (jacal) corrals perched on La Loma.[62] The suertes lay below on the plain along the creek to the south, irrigated from a newly dug *tanque* and an acequia that ran through the area's low hills and at field level. No defensive walls remain on The Hill itself, although there are traces of ruins and piles of rocks, most of which have long since been reused for other purposes in later, safer years.[63] Stone lines marking old fields are still visible west of the property now known as El Tanque Viejo.

Perhaps within the first five or ten years of the village's life, a small adobe church was built, providing a center and small plaza on top of the hill. The Archdiocese of Santa Fe holds no records of the church's construction, although an anonymous handwritten note card in a file there says it was erected in 1824.[64] Tony Anaya, lifelong Galisteño and self-taught painter

J. R. Riddle, *Old Galisteo Church*, 1884. (Palace of the Governors Photo Archives, NMHM/DCA neg. no. 76052.)

Lucy R. Lippard, *Old Cemetery*, ca. 2000.

of New Mexican churches, told Marion Steele in the 1980s that the old church "closely resembled the church at Picuris built in the same era." An elder told me that babies were buried beside the old church, where the campo santo was traditionally located. The "old" cemetery, therefore, is probably not the oldest. It is popularly believed that the oldest grave markers in the original cemetery on the western crest of La Loma date to the early 1800s, although none survive today. The earliest (legible) stone standing today marks the 1879 death of José Montoya, age sixty-six. (Wooden crosses disintegrated, were taken for firewood, or were eventually stolen for sale in antique shops.)

Place names have been crucial to land rights cases. The complex claims made around Galisteo were often dependent upon the lay of the land and residents' knowledge of impermanent landmarks. Identifying these places is a difficult task, since their names have often proved to be as ephemeral as the boundary markers—the vanished cottonwoods, chicken coops, boulders, and mounds of stone, even *mojoneras*, or small mounds of earth. For instance, Loma Parda, the gray or dark hill that formed the eastern boundary of the early Galisteo grant, could apply to almost any ridge or mountain, but it was certainly well known to early settlers. One now unknown boundary is actually called Reconocida, or "Familiar."

In September 1821, the Republic of Mexico declared its independence from Spain, a fact that was duly celebrated when the news finally reached Santa Fe in 1822. This change of nationality, which lasted only twenty-five years, did not immediately mean much to New Mexicans, who were for the most part uninvolved in Mexico's war for independence. Having received little enough attention from Spain, they may have been resigned to the same neglect from their new rulers. However, "the Mexican Revolution was a strongly anti-clerical mestizo uprising,"

William Baxter, *Ruin of Mission Chapel at San Cristóbal Pueblo*, 1990s. (Courtesy of Ardeth Baxter.)

according to Roxanne Dunbar-Ortiz, "which put an end to relentless missionary pressures upon unwilling Indians and softened Indian-Spanish relations ingeneral."[65]

The Mexican government was anxious to increase the population of the province in order to ward off Indian raiders and covetous European nations, and this regime brought more settlers to the Galisteo Basin. Although the population was growing in this period, the giant San Cristóbal grant was the only land officially awarded in the eastern Galisteo Basin between 1814/22 and 1840. San Cristóbal has woven histories as a Tano pueblo, a Spanish/Mexican land grant, and finally an Anglo ranch. But since the early 1800s it has been entangled with the history of the adjacent Galisteo village. By the time Galisteo was formally founded, Domingo Fernández, described by G. Emlen Hall as "a skillful, manipulative, educated and corrupt native Santa Fean"[66] and elsewhere as "never harried, reclusive, religious,"[67] had set his sights on the long uninhabited San Cristóbal Pueblo lands. After an initial attempt in 1816 (perhaps not coincidentally the year the Galisteo grant was reconfirmed), Fernández petitioned Governor Melgares on April 26, 1822, the same month the Galisteo grant was formalized. This transaction also included lands that would have belonged to the remaining Tanos. Presenting his request virtually as a religious crusade, Fernández described "the site commonly called El Pueblo de San Cristóbal where, in truth, the ruins of the pueblo [could] be seen and the walls of a sacred temple in a dilapidated condition and almost entirely razed to the ground." (This was the seventeenth-century mission chapel.) Church repair was his "principal object" as "the temple" was "a lodging for brutes [livestock], unoccupied, uncultivated, without any hopes of its first owners ever occupying it." Perhaps protesting too much, he declared, "Divine Majesty [has] moved my spirit for so great a purpose [to repair the chapel] and . . . it may not possibly be thought that I solicit said land through avarice."[68]

The San Cristóbal grant bordered and incorporated parts of the 1814/16 Galisteo grant, not to mention later ones that would seriously curtail common usage of the land on the east side of the Rio Galisteo, so its acquisition at the very same moment as the Galisteo grant is somewhat suspect. A vast domain much coveted by Hispanos and Anglos alike, it has stayed more or less intact as the Eaton grant or San Cristóbal Ranch, despite a chaotic history of often fragmentary ownership. Exhaustively documented and contested, constantly in and out of the courts as a major pawn in Galisteo Basin land speculation through the twentieth century, it has been and is still a bone of contention within the village of Galisteo. (See chapter 6.)

The San Cristóbal boundaries were, on the east, "where the can[y]on in the direction of the Baca spring [Ojo de la Vaca] commence[s] to disappear"; on the west, the "Puertosito" designating the boundary of Galisteo; on the north, "the descent of the Pueblito"; and on the south, "the ascent called Las Comanche" (actually known as the "descent," La Bajada de los Comanches, east of what today is known as Comanche Gap in the southern creston, near Clark Hill). On June 13, acknowledging that water was "very scarce in this place," Santa Fe Alcalde Armendaris inquired how much water was at San Cristóbal and who the petitioners were so that he could grant necessary land to raise wheat to support families. Twelve springs and eight ponds were reported—the Lagunita (the now dry "Galisteo Lake") was full of water. "Tes [*sic*] Canoncites, below the Cueva" are mentioned, and Fernández states that Don Luis Lovato, resident of Galisteo, examined the site with him "to count water from the spring called El Cavallo."[69] On July 8, "Lucero," José Miguel Baca, and Rafael Sarracino went to the site and found El Cavallo consisted of two, not twelve springs.[70] The Tanos were still a remembered presence; the document mentions that "natives in those times had their fields in the Cañon of la Casita, where the ruins can be seen of the houses in which they watched their fields."

In 1824, Fernández got his grant, but it was neither forwarded nor documented. The government claimed the papers couldn't be found. In 1827, he was still petitioning. The governor wanted more information on access to water. On June 25, 1827, Fernández reported that he had gone to San Cristóbal with two Indians ("Francisco the white-eyed" and Ramón of Pojoaque), who told him there was abundant water under the land: "[But] it is covered up, also . . . the ornaments and sacred vessels are buried, which [one of them] promised to show me and discover."[71] These Indians may have been descendants of San Cristóbal Tanos who remained in the north after the Reconquest or among those who lived at Galisteo Pueblo until the late 1700s. In any case, Fernández reported back that due to the "immense amount of public land existing in this province," each settler should get a decent portion, or they would not choose to settle there. There was to be no objection to "this noble neighborhood" (the people of Galisteo village) obtaining "wood, watering animals and even horses, much more in time of war," and he hoped for their assistance in Indian raids. Despite the lack of water, the Santa Fe Asemblea declared, "If the petitioners labor with as much perseverance as it is seen [the Tanos] did, they will be rewarded for their labor if they are aided by God our Father, with water from heaven to fill their tank, as in truth from the existing springs they will reap very little benefit."[72] In other words, "pray for rain."

On August 21, 1827, a new governor, Manuel Armijo, finally awarded Fernandez half of the 81,032.67 acres he requested. The other half was to be shared with thirty other settlers (many of whom are names familiar in the various Galisteo grants); the Mexican government was following a Spanish edict of 1813 requiring that half the land be used for agriculture and the rest be communal, where "the public" could "pasture their animals in the vicinity thereof."[73]

The land acquisition ritual took place on August 21, the very day of the grant. The constitutional justice "having taken the said Fernández by the hand, he entered upon and walked over the said land, he pulled up weeds, scattered handfuls of earth, broke off branches from the trees and uttered loud exclamations of joy and pleasure . . . 'Long Life to our actual president Don Guadalupe Victoria, long life to the Mexican nation'" and performed other ceremonies and acts of possession.[74] Boundaries were pointed out, "the said Fernández receiving lands between the Mesita de las Lagunitas and Oho [*sic*] de Baca" and the remaining agricultural lands on the plain and in the Cañon de la Cueva going in 100-vara parcels to each of a long list of names.[75]

There was land left for the formation of a new town. A hundred varas were designated for "gardens." Settlers promised to work on the church, ditch, and tank. They were permitted to keep a hundred head of "small stock" (goats and ewes), should erect houses at the plaza and "make their gardens in common . . . thereby preventing dissentions and lawsuits." They owned the land and could donate or sell it as they wished. And "they should live ever grateful to Domingo Fernández, who owning and being the oldest settler and proprietor of the tract of San Cristóbal, is entitled to the same, and that they are confined to the surplus portions thereof, for so he has agreed."[76] The document was signed by owners and Antonio Sena, "there being no notary public in this department."

Fernández never did repair the "sacred temple," the walls of which remain standing to this day, having been slightly restored at some unknown point. On September 24, 1829, he went to a new governor, José Antonio Chávez, complaining that none of the other grantees had shown up to clean springs and build ponds as agreed. It was decreed that if the settlers didn't work, "industrious individuals [would] be substituted in their place."[77] Things got done through communal work. There were no fences; sheep and goats on common pastureland were branded. There is no record of Fernández himself ever building a house on San Cristóbal,

Prairie Schooners under Convoy—A Santa Fe Caravan of the Third Decade. Based on the illustration *March of the Caravan* in Gregg, *Commerce of the Prairies*, 1844. As reproduced in William G. Ritch, *Illustrated New Mexico* (5th ed.), 1885. (Palace of the Governors Photo Archives, NMHM/DCA neg. no. 087450.)

Ben Wittick, *Panning for Gold, New Mexico*, ca. 1880–90. Probably taken in the Cerrillos area. (Palace of the Governors Photo Archives, NMHM/DCA, neg. no. 102147.)

but later witnesses testified that other grantees did build, open springs, and begin to farm. "Ruins of stone walls, which may have been sheep corrals, are scattered over the grant, remains of stone dwellings can also be seen," writes one of the current owners of the ranch.[78]

In November 1821, Don Pedro Ignacio de Gallego, captain of the Militia Urbana, with 445 men, including settlers and Pueblos, "123 armed with guns and the rest with bows and arrows," was pursuing some Comanches who had raided the village of San Miguel. They left Abiquiú and went over Glorieta Mesa via Galisteo, taking ten hours to travel the "path" along the Galisteo Creek. At the Puertocito de le [*sic*] Piedra Lumbre, they encountered six Americans, among them Samuel Becknell, traveling from Independence, Missouri, with several wagons of commercial goods. They sent him to see the governor at Santa Fe and tracked him backwards to see how he had entered the territory.[79] But the Spanish policy of banning foreigners was about to become irrelevant. The Mexican government welcomed trade. The Missourian arrived at a serendipitous moment, sold out, made a fortune, and soon returned. Thus began the Santa Fe Trail. As it neared its goal, the trail was braided into alternative routes, one of which was the old track from Cañoncito to Ojo de la Vaca (aka Cow Spring) to Galisteo, and the village became a tax-collecting pause on the trail. With trade barriers lifted and New Mexico open to new influences, the Santa Fe Trail set in motion the most drastic social changes since the early Spanish entradas.

Given the absence of regular troops in New Mexico, the province was given an allowance to maintain forces for internal defense: "All males native of the province between the ages of sixteen and sixty were prima facie members of the militia."[80] Officers were the younger sons of large landowners. In another economic milestone, gold was discovered in the 1820s by José de Jesús García and Rafael Alejo in the Oso Mountains on the southwestern border of the Galisteo Basin. (The Ortiz range was first called the San Lázaros, then the Osos, and then the Oros—after an ancient pueblo, bears, and gold.) The boomtown that sprang up around the strike was known variously as Oso, New Placer, Old Placer, Oro, and Real de Dolores del Oro. Dolores became the hub of the New Mexico gold rush, which preceded the better-known California event.

José Francisco (Juan Nepomuceno) Ortiz, purported ancestor of today's Galisteo Ortiz y Pinos, became involved in the Real de Dolores around 1832 as a military commander and superintendent of the Dolores mining district.[81] He purchased his first interest in a lode mine in the now Ortiz Mountains in 1832, and in 1833, with merchant Ignacio Cano, he bought from García and Alejo an "undeveloped gold vein" that became the Santa Rosalia Mine. In December of that year, Ortiz and Cano acquired the extensive mine grant connected to that property. As a mine, the Santa Rosalia was not very successful and operated only intermittently, but by 1836, through various machinations, its less than three acres had expanded to 69,458 acres, stretching into the Galisteo Basin, solely owned by José Francisco Ortiz.[82] This enormous chunk of land (and water and mineral rights acquired with it) was worth a fortune. It became known as the Ortiz Mine Grant. Another major player, Luis Lobato, settled in and owned land around Galisteo. (Lobatos are listed on all the early grants.) The story of the Dolores mines and widespread chicanery is a fascinating one, told with great gusto by William Baxter in his two books on gold in the Ortiz Mountains.

In the 1830s, relations with the Apaches worsened, though local harassment was more common than large-scale attacks. Josiah Gregg, plying the Santa Fe Trail, complained that the Apaches stole thousands of sheep, boasting that they could have taken all of them: "But . . . they prefer leaving a few behind for breeding purposes, in order that their Mexican shepherd may raise them new supplies."[83] By the mid 1800s, the vecino population of New Mexico had also been enriched by the innumerable captives (Comanches, Apaches, Utes, Navajos, and Kiowas, among others) raised as servants or *criados/as* in Spanish families. When grown and on their own, those detribalized and hispanicized Indians from "pagan" tribes were called *genizaros* (a word derived from *janissaries*, a mercenary army in Turkey also made up of child captives). In the nineteenth century, there were genizaros in every community, some of which (Tomé, Abiquiú) were founded specifically for them.[84] There is a growing scholarship focusing on the genizaro heritage, but Galisteo is never mentioned, although the presence of Native servants (probably slaves) from "Apache country" or "Navajo country" is documented in the censuses.

After 1821, as Mexico tried to encourage Spanish settlement and discourage American expansionism, grants became larger, and quite a few were even awarded to foreigners.[85] According to Roxanne Dunbar-Ortiz, 1821–48 marked "the conquest of the merchants," turning the province away from Chihuahua and central Mexico and bringing a new set of values to New Mexico. The province gained, but "it was the elite who benefitted, while the villagers and Pueblos . . . were increasingly impoverished by the introduction of exchange values and money."[86] Donald Meinig describes New Mexico as "suddenly changed from the northern-most province of New Spain to the southwestern province of a new transcontinental nation . . . from a terminus to a pathway; from having only tenuous longitudinal ties with the outer world to a position astride several latitudinal strands within a national network"; from "a forlorn gateway to imaginary cities of gold on the barren plains" to "a well trampled corridor to some very real cities of gold on the Pacific shore—for California became the new Cibola and New Mexico and Arizona were again caught up in the quest."[87] One of the stops along the way was Galisteo.

TWO

Land Is Luck, Water Is Life (1840–1870)

De la tierra fui formado (Of the earth I was formed).
La tierra me da de comer (The earth gives me food).
La tierra me ha sostenido (The earth has sustained me).
Y al fin yo tierra he de ser (And in the end I shall be earth).
—From a Penitente alabado[1]

In the early 1840s, the demand for land intensified, sparking a dizzying train of sales and resales, inheritances, divisions, and exchanges in Galisteo. "As population increased around New Mexico pueblos in the latter part of the Mexican period, New Mexico governors and local officials . . . were more often concerned with protecting their own interests through the making of new land grants to Hispanos as a US invasion began to seem certain."[2] Indian threats persisted, but Galisteo villagers expanded their fields beyond the early protected site on and below The Hill onto the rich flatland to the east, across the Rio Galisteo. (The western bank, just below their homes, was apparently still owned by the government.) In the region immediately surrounding the village, six land grants overlapped—a recipe for chaos.

Just west of the village lay the Baca y Terrus grant (aka San Francisco de Arroyo de Galisteo or Cañada de San Francisco grant), awarded on June 28, 1840, to José Francisco Baca y Terrus.[3] He had applied for the grant in 1839, under the condition that Agustín Durán (who owned the adjacent ranch to the west on the Santo Domingo de Maragua grant) be permitted to use its water for irrigation.[4] The boundaries "approximately" were the "Arroyo del Infierno" in the northeast, "lands of Agustín Durán" in the west, "Hills of the Matadero" in the north, and Alto de la Jara ("Hills of the Arroyo de la Jara") in the south. The Galisteo Creek runs east/west right through the middle of the Baca y Terrus grant.[5] When it came before the American Court of Private Land Claims on May 16, 1871, Antonio Cháves y Alire of Galisteo, "about 49 years old," described the north and south boundaries as "the Ceja" (Summit) and "another ceja."[6] Cháves had been present when the claimants were placed in possession by Fernández (officiating as alcalde) and had assisted "by carrying the measuring cord." Witness Esteban Sena of Galisteo, sixty-two, who had also assisted, stated that the claimants had worked that land ever since. Witness Agustín Durán of Santa Fe, seventy-nine, a member of the Departmental Assembly in 1840, declared that Fernández was alcalde (presumably of Santa Fe) in 1840 and all the other signatures were genuine. Witness David J. Miller, a translator from the Office of the Surveyor General, stated that the grant document was in the archives. Everything seemed to be going smoothly.

Then Durán, stating that the acting governor of New Mexico in 1840 was Juan Andrés Archuleta, said some of the documents had been "mislaid" or lost after "diligent search." The

Lucy R. Lippard, *View across the Cadial toward Loma Parda from the Boundary of the San Cristóbal Ranch*, 2018.

original was genuine and complete except for the act of possession, the latter portion of which was missing from the archives, so there was no clear documentation of the identity of the grantees excepting Baca y Terrus and the last applicant, one Benavides. On November 25, 1871, the Surveyor General signed off on the grant's validity but decreed that the parties would have to arrange it among themselves or through the courts. Ominously, it was observed that confirmation of this grant would "sever [land] from public domain." The Baca y Terrus case was apparently reopened on November 20, 1877, before Justice Agapito Sena of Galisteo. Twenty years later, in 1897, US justice had its way with a letter rejecting the "Cañada de San Francisco Grant."[7]

Grants such as the one awarded in June 1840 to "Juan Ortiz of the Río del Oro" (Juan "Grande" Ortiz of Dolores), who registered for "300 varas of land for cultivation" at the ford (*badito*) of the Galisteo Creek, were part of larger donations, "whose general boundaries are already set forth in the original title to said grant."[8] Ortiz's application either was never decided was rejected when he reapplied in 1848.[9] Nevertheless, on a 1900 map, "Juan Ortiz's" is shown north of the northern creston, just west of today's NM 41. Years later, Donaciano Angel said his land was, like Juan Ortiz's, "fronting on the place commonly known as the Cañada de Puertocito."[10]

Southeast of the village was a small "donation" called El Tacubaya, named by a Mexican woman after a still extant Mexico City neighborhood known for an 1859 massacre of liberals by conservatives. The word is Nahuatl for "the place where water is gathered." Granted on February 3, 1843, to twelve or thirteen Galisteo residents, it was of indeterminate acreage, lying near Gavilán Hill, south of the San Cristóbal Arroyo. This is the first mention of Gabilón (Gavilán, Gavilanes) or Hawk Hill, a crucial and elusive landmark; the name is not familiar to contemporary villagers and I have yet to find it on old maps.[11] Prominent Galisteño Librada Valencia farmed on Tacubaya, where Agapito Sena had a house. My contemporary Onésimo Montoya said his father had a house there when he was a child. Up to four houses on the Cadial and Tacubaya are mentioned in various sources.

The Mesita(s) Blanca(s) grant (also known as Meritas Blancas—probably an Anglo misspelling), awarded on February 15, 1843, only days after Tacubaya, consisted of small allotments ("more or less" 200 varas each, plus 100 varas each for a plaza and a public garden) on land south of the San Cristóbal/Atascoso Arroyo.[12] The eight "new petitioners" for 18,000 acres were "Luis Griego, Francisco Provençal, Juan Silva, José Silva, Florencio la Garza, Vicente Roibal, Benito Varela and Marcelino Ortiz,[13] citizens of this city [Santa Fe] and residing in Galisteo. . . . Having large families and having no land of our own to cultivate . . . we ask that there be granted to us the place known as the Mesita Blanca, having the drains of San Cristóbal on the north, on the West the hill called Gabilón Hill, and on the south the elevation called La Jara."[14] No eastern boundary is cited, but there is a reference to "the Western boundary of the tract of Domingo Fernández," an irrigated rancho on San Cristóbal. (It has been suggested that the grant, awarded on February 15, 1843, was made under pressure from Fernández.)

Significantly, the Mesitas Blancas allotments were said to be "within the Galisteo Grant," which implies that the original 9,000-acre Galisteo grant was still acknowledged

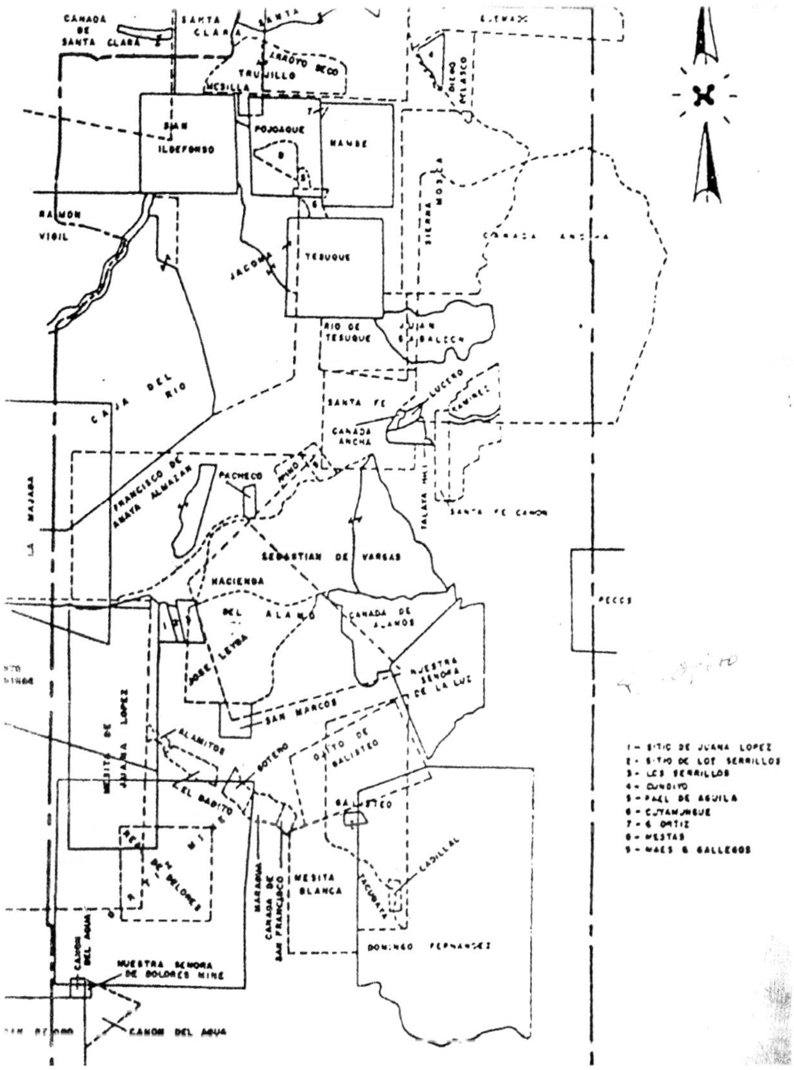

Map of Galisteo Area Land Grants (Bowden, "Private Land Claims in the Southwest," vol. 2, 269).

and that it probably overlapped with both the 1846 Cadial grant (see below), which crossed the San Cristóbal Arroyo to the La Jara, and the earlier San Cristóbal grant south of the Arroyo Atascoso. To further complicate matters, Mesitas Blancas included a section called La Santisima Trinidad, later granted to thirteen applicants. Nevertheless, the land was officially declared to be public domain, vacant, unencumbered by other claims, and uncultivated, "occupied only as pasture." The settlers were to enclose their properties; if they didn't, they lost the right to claim damages by others' animals—the long-standing protocol known as "fence out." The document was signed in 1843 by Domingo Fernández as secretary and by Antonio Sena. With no objection from anyone, they performed the traditional ceremony to "enter peacefully into possession." They "walked over the tract and plucked off grass, cast stones, plucked off boughs, and shouted aloud, 'Long Live the Mexican Nation!'"

And finally there is the never-forgotten San José de Cadial (or Cadillal, cocklebur pasture) grant east of the village, awarded in 1846, just before the American invasion. Known locally as the Cadial, its relation to the Galisteo and San Cristóbal grants is ambiguous, presenting a classically convoluted case that is close to unintelligible in its complexity. Area lands were parceled out at various times in the early 1840s. In 1846, twenty-nine people applied. The ayuntamiento investigator decided that there was enough land for more, dividing it into small lots for sixty-two people.[15]

Outside the Spanish and Mexican archives themselves—which, given their disarray, were easily disregarded and later sometimes literally discarded by the impatient Americans—the best general sources of land history remain the surviving original grant papers and the transcripts of court cases and property abstracts of the large ranches in the area around the turn of the twentieth century. A village family owns a treasured printed transcript of the 1909–17 Cadial trials (with extensive references to the 1871 lawsuits), which I quote as the "Cadial book" throughout this volume.[16] Confusing as it is, given the near impossibility of untangling the geographical evidence, this 597-page volume is a rich source of information about Galisteo's land claims, land use, and genealogies and the political relations among the Santa Fe Ring, Hispano ricos, and working Galisteans in the early twentieth century. The Cadial's boundaries and ownership were examined in detailed and often conflicting testimonies that frustrate determination of the actual lay of the land and are yet invaluable in determining the way it was perceived by those who lived upon it. And, of course, much in these accounts must be taken with a few grains of salt, given the inevitable inaccuracy of translations and the instability of memory itself.

I have found no credible maps of the Cadial. Descriptions vary widely from 1,000 to 7,500 acres, with different boundaries, depending on the source and probably the date. Its boundaries roughly followed some of the original Galisteo grant's outlines, extending from the Puertocito or the northern creston's middle hump (*de en medio*) south to a hill near La Jara Arroyo (Alto de la Jara) south of the Galisteo Lake (La Lagunita).[17] The northern boundary—marked by "a volcanic stone, set half in the ground and marked 'SCNW Beg. Cor.,'" according to the 1880 Atkinson survey—was around two miles long, "a portion of it cut off on the west

Caroline Hinkley, *Nicolás Pino Outbuilding Ruin (and New Home)*, 2018. The ruins of a small home and sheep corrals are all that remain of the Nicolás Pino/Pedro Ortiz y Pino hacienda on Avenida Vieja. Beside it is the Morin/Diggs and Epping home, designed by Beverley Spears and built in the 1990s.

Old Fort on Loma Tejana, n.d. (Courtesy of Yolanda and María Ortiz y Pino.)

side."[18] The grant extended east a mile (or two, or in some accounts three miles) into the San Cristóbal ranchlands. The western boundary is blurred but lay somewhere near the Galisteo River. J. J. Bowden's map inaccurately draws Tacubaya far larger than the Cadial, which formed its western boundary. Sixty-two versus twelve grantees should make it clear that the Cadial is much larger, as all contemporary villagers confirm.

In the later trials, Juan Ortiz described the Cadial de San José as "almost a square," noting that there were some markers: "But as we already know all the lands so well, we don't care very much about the marks of the land."[19] Nicolás Pino owned seventeen strips on the Cadial, which may have included his home on the east bank of the river. Anastacio Sandoval testified that the Cadial lay 600 to 800 yards from the last structure on the east, "the house of Don Nicolás Pino."[20] At one point during the various trials, Attorney Catron claimed that the entire Cadial was subsumed by San Cristóbal, whose western boundary ran across the creek through the center of the village, in the yards of Antonio Ortiz (present-day Kerstetter) and Sylvester Davis's hacienda (present-day Gwyn and Benjamin). Anastacio Sandovald is agreed: it was at least 100 yards "from the wall of the yard of Sylvester Davis to the arroyo."[21] He was referring here to the west bank of the Rio Galisteo; the use of "the arroyo" for both the San Cristóbal and Galisteo creeks adds another level of confusion to these statements.[22]

Librado Valencia, who later sold his two suertes on the Cadial, testified that there were no houses on the Cadial (except for the "wooden house of the herder") due to lack of good water. (The town of Galisteo was located where "there [was] good water.")[23] Anastacio Sandoval testified that he believed there was only one house within the grant, belonging to Ascensión Chávez.[24] During the late-nineteenth and early-twentieth-century Cadial trials, Juan Ortiz said his father (Juan "Grande") had a lot of land on the Cadial, though his father had never lived there, and he saw the hijuela of Joaquín Chávez first "from the hands of [his] mother in '65 before… [coming] over [to Galisteo] for the first time."[25] Only those with hijuelas issued by

Kenneth Chapman, *Raising the American Flag over the Palace of Governors August 18th, 1846*, painting, 1909. In a 1932 letter about this image, Chapman noted that many of his illustrations for Ralph Emerson Twitchell's *History of the Military Occupation of the Territory of New Mexico from 1846–1851* were "drawn from imagination": "The portal of the Palace of the Governors . . . is particularly unfortunate, as I had then made no study of New Mexico architecture on which such a restoration should have been based." (Palace of the Governors Photo Archives, NMHM/DCA neg. no. 006725.)

Governor Albino Chacón were entitled to use the land; Librado Valencia's father had one. In a later trial it was claimed that Chacón had no authority after August 18, 1846, when the United States took over. Most of the precious hijuelas were created after that date.[26]

There were several big landowners in Galisteo in the 1840s. An 1844 news item announced that "the prominent Chávez family from Galisteo donated the bulls" to a bullfight in the Santa Fe Plaza.[27] "In 1846 Galisteo family names identified with the prestige and wealth" of large herds were Leyba, Pino, Sandoval, Chávez, and Anaya.[28] While the Pinos may have owned or appropriated grazing land in the Galisteo Basin since 1800 or earlier, the first of the family to actually settle in Galisteo was Nicolás de Jesús Pino.[29] Known as a great gambler and once described as the best-looking man in New Mexico, he apparently established a home on family lands in Galisteo around the time of his marriage in 1842 to Juana Rascón (1821–93), who was born in Chihuahua, a niece of the Mexican vicar general. It may have begun as a *pied à terre* for inspecting family lands. Most ricos owned several ranches and had homes in Santa Fe, as well as in the outlying villages. An 1846 destacamento housed in the home of Nicolás Pino is noted in several documents as "east of Galisteo" and as the house farthest east in Galisteo, as well as "the first grand house in Galisteo," east of the river, 200 yards south of the bridge. The small adobe ruin of servants' quarters still stands on Avenida Vieja, and traces of the large foundations of the Pino hacienda itself remain next door, as well as a rectangular concrete reservoir. When a new home was built there in the late 1990s, large numbers of sheep bones were unearthed.

"Indian problems" from nomadic and raiding tribes persisted. On September 8, 1844, a force of Utes, camped in a vacant lot at the corner of Shelby and Water Streets in Santa Fe, almost killed Governor Martínez and engaged Mexican soldiers in a bloody battle on the plaza.[30] Elderly Galisteans recalled stories told in their families about raiding Indians.

Galisteño Tacho Sandoval recalled his grandmother Francisita Chávez y Sandoval telling stories of Indians stealing food; she would open the door and throw lard at them. Carmelita Chávez Anaya told of a woman making sopaipillas in the fireplace when she realized that Indians on the roof were stealing them with a long, pointed stick. She then burned hot chile in the fireplace and drove the pilferers away with a choking smoke.[31] A family who lived in Cañon Blanco, to the southeast, handed down this more benign experience from their great-great-grandmother Ciria Pineda Perea (b. 1854):

> On one occasion, when the menfolk had gone out on the eastern prairies to hunt buffalo, a band of Navajo Indians came to the house. Ciria, her mother and the other girls barred the door and waited, terrified that they would be attacked and killed. Nothing happened. When they looked outside again, they noticed that the Indians were half starved. Again they closed the door and waited. The ladies had been cooking sopaipillas. They heard the Indians climbing onto the roof and noticed that they had dropped a wire down a vent in the roof, attempting to fish the bread off the table. The ladies hooked some bread to the wire and the Navajos pulled it up. After being supplied with a few sopaipillas, the Indians left.[32]

But not all the intruders were indigenous. In 1841 and 1843 soldiers from the Republic of Texas (declared in 1836 and annexed by the United States in 1845) unsuccessfully invaded New Mexico, hoping to corner some of the Santa Fe Trail's profits. They were intercepted at Pecos, and some of the prisoners evidently passed down the Galisteo Creek to Santo Domingo.[33] The small hill northwest of the new church was known as La Loma Tejana because from there the Galisteños watched the Texans retreat. According to José Ortiz y Pino III, the Eugenio Velásquez house on that hill (current home of Judith Masin) was the high point overlooking the river, where attackers hid in the arroyo: "There was a big building there called the Fortress, square and fortified. There were other fortresses, one on the east side of the river, near Luis Chávez's, one on The Hill."[34]

Then came the changing of the guard that was to transform New Mexico, though deep cultural roots were not so easily disturbed. In August 1846, the United States, in the person of General Stephen W. Kearny, Commander of the Army of the West, marched in from Missouri to take New Mexico, at the time including Arizona and parts of Utah and Colorado. Having prepared for battle by building barricades in Apache Canyon, New Mexican governor Manuel Armijo suddenly declined to engage with Kearny's troops at Cañoncito, on the mesas east of Galisteo. Discharging those who refused to accompany him on his ignominious retreat, he fled to Chihuahua, to the disgust of many of his countrymen, although others approved of his avoiding the bloodbath that would have ensued in battle with the far stronger US Army. The New Mexicans lacked military training and were armed mostly with bows and arrows and lances.[35] Among those who were raring to fight the invading Americans were the Pino brothers and José Francisco J. N. Ortiz (whose signature is on the report on Armijo sent to Mexico City). On his way south, Armijo passed through Galisteo, abandoning two brass six-pounders and a brass mountain howitzer said to have been taken from the Texans, plus three unserviceable gun carriages.[36]

"Here we are in Santa Fe—AND NEW MEXICO IS OURS!" crowed one of Kearny's men, Richard Smith Elliott, as here called the bloodless conqueston August 18, 1846. He was among those sent south to "Galasted," or "Galasteo," immediately after the invasion, and his memoir provides us with a blurry snapshot of the village: "To give an idea what the people of New Mexico were like when fresh conquered, and as seen at Galisteo, where I was sent the morning after the capture of Santa Fe, with all the horses and half the arrangers to graze the animals . . . on the lush grass . . . found 200 inhabitants, living in small, flat roofed, adobe houses which were whitewashed inside. The town is on a knoll, affording an excellent view in all directions."[37]

Elliott does not mention any major buildings below La Loma, which suggests that he saw only the remains of the destacamento and that the "hacienda" was not yet constructed. The people, Elliot tobserved, were raising corn and wheat; they used Pueblo earthenware and had looms and spinning wheels under sheds. The little church on La Loma "was 20 x 30 feet, whitewashed inside . . . walls were partly of stone, topped by adobe. The door opened opposite the pulpit. There was a gallery over the door." Elliott also remarked on "the arrival of Señor Pino, the owner of the village," or alcalde, described as an old man. It has often been stated that this was Nicolás; if so, he must have been endowed with great gravitas, since he was then only twenty-seven years old. Anastacio Sandoval was alcalde in 1841 and possibly still in 1846.[38] A few years later, a forty-niner passing through Galisteo met "a very intelligent old Spanish Gentleman who could speak indifferent English, and who proved to be the Alcalde of the Town. He did not hesitate to condemn our Government for its injustice in robbing Mexico of its Territories without just cause or compensation."[39] This is presumably the same unnamed alcalde (possibly still Anastacio Sandoval) who was removed around 1850 by Governor J. S. Calhoun "because of his political views." This "caused a storm, and an open protest to the people of New Mexico by many prominent figures of the day was circulated among the people. The circular read: 'An alcalde of the town of Galisteo, in the county of Santa Fe, was removed against the known wishes of the citizens resident in that place, as expressed both by a public meeting and petition from the people, desiring that he be retained.'"[40]

Kearny established aprovisional government in Santa Fe and stationed a tax collector in Galisteo, charging two dollars for wagons and carriages coming through on the Santa Fe Trail. Then he departed to conquer California, leaving the Missouri Volunteers in charge. On August 23, under command of Lt. Col. Ruff, "a heavy detail was made from the different companies to conduct the horses and other animals belonging to the command into the neighborhood of Galisteo, 27 miles southeasterly from the capital . . . forage being scarce [closer to Santa Fe]." Ruff 's encampment changed constantly as pasturage demanded. The stock revived "So fine and nutritious is the grass in the hill-country of New Mexico." A week later, another group under Captain Sumner marched on foot to Galisteo.[41] When Colonel Alexander Doniphan's expedition set out for the west on September 2, he, too, stopped at the "grazing encampment near Galesteo," at the Pueblo of the Tanos: "We were badly supplied with water and grass after a tiresome day's march of some 25 miles" from Santa Fe.

Nicolás Pino and Juan Ortiz, n.d. (Courtesy of La Herencia Foundation.)

The next day they "pursued our way down the Galesteo—the Sierra Nevada to the right and high ridges on the left—sandy barren country—Flint and Sandstone."[43] Henry Smith Turner, camping with Kearny's troops on "Galiesteo" creek on September 2, 1846, described "but little grass—pass over a barren country—a few ranches or farms—but no vegetation except along the margins of streams." They camped "on the Galisteo Creek at Del Gardo," where some stock was left, "about fifteen miles from the gold mines in the Galisteo [Ortiz] mountains, commonly known" as El Placer (Dolores), after which they continued west.[43]

George F. Ruxton (a twenty-four-year-old racist and misanthropic British travel writer/spy) had not a good word to say for anyone or anything he encountered in New Mexico. Coming north from Albuquerque, he observed disdainfully:

> The families of Armijo, Cháves, Perea and Ortiz are *par excellence* the *ricos* of New Mexico—indeed, all the wealth of the province is concentrated in their hands; and a more grasping set of people, and more hard-hearted oppressors of the poor, it would be difficult to find in any other part of Mexico, where the rights or condition of the lower classes are no more considered, than in civilized countries is the welfare of dogs and pigs.
>
> In his rabbit burrow, and with his tortillas and his chile, his *ponche* [ersatz tobacco] and cigar of *hoja* [corn husk], the New Mexican is content; and with an occasional traveler to pilfer, or the excitement of a stray Texan or two to massacre now and then, is tolerably happy, his only care being that the river rise high enough to fill his acequia, or irrigating ditch, that sufficient maize may grow to furnish him with tortillas for the winter, and shucks for his half-starved horse or mule, which the Navajos have left, out of charity, after killing half his sons and daughters and bearing into captivity the wife of his bosom.[44]

On the way to Santa Fe, Indians (supposedly "Mansos," defined as Pueblos or "half civilized Indians" from San Felipe Pueblo) stampeded the mulada. The next day Ruxton camped on the "Galisteo, a small stream coming from the mountains" in "wild broken country, covered with pine and cedar," where they noticed "a curious ridge" running east to west, "broken here and there by abrupt chasms, which exhibit[ed] its formation in alternate strata of shale and old red sandstone," with "indications of coal."[45] When Ruxton reached Santa Fe, he found "a wretched collection of mud-houses" comparable "to nothing but a dilapidated brick kiln or a prairie dog town." The Americans who had just arrived were "the dirtiest, rowdiest crew [he had] ever seen collected together."

The arrival of the US government in New Mexico was tolerated but hardly popular. In December 1846, three Pino brothers, several Ortizes, and others, led by Tomás Ortiz, concocted a plot to overthrow the American regime. It was to take place the night of December 19 but was later postponed to Christmas Eve. Donaciano Vigil (already an official in the American government) was told about the plot, supposedly by the indomitable Doña Tules (Gertrudis Barceló, ca. 1800–1852), proprietor of a thriving Santa Fe gambling business and a player in the Dolores mining boom in the 1830s. She was reputedly Nicolás Pino's mistress, though she was some twenty years older; he was said to have joked that he lost more money gambling than anyone else because he was sleeping with her. An alternative version has it that the source of the leak about the plot was another of Doña Tules's lovers, a Mexican general in Santa Fe.

Some of the conspirators escaped arrest. Tomás Ortiz, disguised as a servant girl, fled to the home of his mistress, La Peregrina, for provisions, then proceeded to Galisteo, presumably to Nicolás Pino's home. There he was met by pack mules loaded with provisions for his trip to Chihuahua via Manzano and Abo. (He returned to become a leading territorial citizen.) Others were arrested, including Nicolás Pino as he sat in front of a Santa Fe hotel in 1847.[46] A decade after the fact, Don Clemente Ortiz recalled, "I was serving as a volunteer at the government post at Galisteo in 1856 and 1857, at the home of Don Nicolás Pino, [and was told] that the written plan for the conspiracy was taken by Don Miguel E. Pino and hidden at the house of his [and Nicolás's] mother, Doña Ana Maria Baca, who was the widow of Don Pedro Bautista Pino. It was hidden in the ceiling. It was never found."[47]

Once released from prison in Santa Fe, after what must have been a very short sentence, Nicolás Pino took the oath of allegiance to the United States, proving his loyalty in 1847 when, along with his friend and fellow former conspirator Don Manuel Cháves, he helped defeat the revolt by his compatriots and members of the Taos Pueblo who had killed the American governor Charles Bent. This persistent Taos- and Mora-based Rio Arriba revolt posed a real threat to the new regime, attracting thousands of Mexicans and Indians and causing hundreds of deaths. In contrast, the Pinos' and Ortizes' short-lived Rio Abajo conspiracy has been characterized as merely the work of "disgruntled *ricos*."[48] Nicolás Pino settled in Galisteo (and on his other properties), became an upright United States citizen, and did very well indeed in the next fifty years, holding various offices. Like most ricos, he invested diversely in land speculation and mining, sometimes partnering with various Ortizes and with members of the Santa Fe Ring.[49]

In the Treaty of Guadalupe Hidalgo, ratified by the United States Congress March 10, 1848, Mexico ceded two-fifths of her territory, in exchange for $15 million. New boundaries were set and Nuevo Mexicanos adjusted to their latest change of nationality. Articles VIII and IX of the treaty guaranteed all the rights of US citizenship to the former Mexicans and promised, "Property of every kind . . . shall be inviolably respected" with "free enjoyment at their livery and property." However, the deletion of Article X (which allowed additional time for claimants to confirm unexecuted grants) had long-term consequences for New Mexicans. (On July 26, 1848, a supplemental document, the Protocol of Querétaro, affirmed that the United States government, in suppressing Article X, "did not intend to annul the grants of lands made by Mexico.") The treaty was ratified on July 30, and despite the promise to respect the cultural and property rights of the former Mexicans, it dismissed ejidos, or common lands, all over New Mexico, depriving many people of their livelihoods.

By the late 1840s there were probably "70,000 Hispanos in NM and no more than 10,000—perhaps as few as 6,000—Pueblo Indians."[50] Guadalupe Hidalgo granted Mexicans the legal status of being "white," which did not deter racism. No US anti miscegenation laws were passed against Mexicans, though marriage was prohibited at the time between "Mongolians" and whites. Native Americans and Asians were denied citizenship. Americans with one-sixteenth Indian blood were still "white," but one drop of African blood made anyone "black."

This tumultuous period was further complicated locally by hordes of travelers through New Mexico heading for the California goldfields. Their wagon trains often stopped in Galisteo. Within the state, where the gold rush of the 1820s and '30s in the Ortiz Mountains had preceded the California boom, rumors of gold continued to flourish, if not to pan out. Among those passing through was the self-described "Quaker Forty-Niner," Charles Edward Pancoast, who wrote up his adventures on the way to the California goldfields. He and his "Boys" were traveling by wagon train from Santa Fe "through the Desert Plains of Ojo de la Vaca until [they] arrived within a mile of the old Spanish Town of Galisteo, where [they] found Pine woods and a large Plain of grass. Many acres, planted with Corn and other Vegetables, and irrigated by waters from a branch of the Pecos [the Galisteo Creek, not a Pecos branch], surrounded this little Adobe Village. On account of the starved condition of our Stock, we permitted them to run at large all night, and in consequence came near getting in trouble with the Law, as our Cattle got into these irrigated fields and destroyed some of the corn."[51]

They paid for the damage and remained for several days to recuperate. "The next morning a large party of us went up to Galisteo to have a good time and were received very cordially by the inhabitants." The forty-niners visited the jail and a tavern where only one drink was available, "a vile mixture of Turpentine, Muscat and Whiskey that they called Agua di Ente [Aguardiente]." Pancoast overindulged in this vile mixture and staggered back to camp on a plank across the creek, coming upon an ox that had been "gnawed and hamstrung by wolves." The next afternoon the Americans went to a fandango in the village. The women were in church, emerging around four o'clock. They "trailed over to the Ball Room, and in a short time the Dance commenced. Their dancing figures were very unique and interesting, some of the sets accompanied by a beautiful chant." He commented on "a number of pretentious young Hidalgos . . . gaudily dressed in feathered caps, woven shawls called Serapos, and an abundance of lace and Navajo Silver, with Pistols, Stilettos and Bowie Knives in their belts, which Weapons they removed and placed on a ledge." Later a fight broke out, with the locals "flying for their weapons; the Ladies screaming and running out of the doors." A cheating American gambler was wounded. The next day there was "a Foot Race with the Mexicans," but an American blacksmith beat their "splendid looking muscular Fellow" and won some livestock. That evening a soldier arrived to report the massacre of a wagon train by Comanches (later thought to be Apaches), and the forty-niners "left Galisteo regretfully," crossing the basin for fifteen miles through flat farming country where people were plowing with a stick drawn by oxen, "just as in the days of Abraham."

New Mexico was declared a US Territory in 1850. The second half of the nineteenth-century was for Hispanos "a period of great demographic and geographic gains but of irrevocable political and cultural losses," writes Meinig.[52] The real break with the deep affinity between people and land came with the rugged individualism of the Americans in 1846, when the clash between indigenous connectedness with all types of life and Western anthropocentric views came to a head, changing forever many New Mexican lives. In addition, the Catholic Church's complicity in colonization did not help its constituents or the Pueblo peoples. God was exhorted or evoked in civil documents about land and water that were as foreign to Natives as the imported European tenets of individual landownership.

There were dispersed pockets of settlers along the Rio Galisteo and in scattered *ranchitos* throughout the basin, some owned by Galisteo residents. The 1850 census is hard to decipher as it is organized by county and towns are not identified. What might be Galisteo (given the names of some residents) was surveyed by one Charles Blumner in October of that year. The population was young. Most were listed as "farmer," although Jesús Anaya, age twenty, was a "musician" and several men were identified as "golddigger," which meant that they were panning for gold in the Ortiz mountains when farm work was out of season. The familiar names are Anaya, Montoya, Benavides, Silva, Lucero, Baros, and lots of Chávezes. Nicolás Pino does not appear. He may have been counted in Santa Fe, where he owned a home, and he may have been in Mexico at that time with his Mexican-born wife, Juana Rascón, since his daughters Concepción and Margarita were both born there.[53] The Dolores Ortizes appear in a different section: Juan (Grande) Ortiz, age thirty-four, Paula, age twenty-three, Antonio José, age seven, and Cayetano, age three.[55]

In 1854 the Office of Surveyor General was created to recommend actions on land grant claims to Congress, "placing tremendous power in the hands of one official."[55] The legal intricacies and injuries that accompanied the American conquest of New Mexico continued to destroy the villagers' land-owning dreams. "Some residents of Galisteo took advantage of the nearby public domain and filed homestead claims where they then grazed their livestock."[56] Those who could afford it sometimes preferred to buy land rather than get it "free" with so many strings attached. The hard-won suertes surrounding Galisteo were immediately challenged, but the *herederos* (heirs) were often ignorant of their rights, did not speak English or comprehend the legalese, and were easily bilked. All land not granted by courts became federal domain and by the time these claims were decided, much of that land had been homesteaded out for timber, farms, and grazing. Americans had lost the old tradition of the "commons," which historically held sway in England and New England. While occupancy and use had traditionally determined ownership, written title was paramount in American law. As one native New Mexican has explained, the rationale for this process was probably due to "the Anglo mindset of legal order. Common ownership was a well-established tenet of Spanish and Mexican law. But Washington probably saw it as too imprecise, too messy. . . . The Anglo mind needed land to be divided up into precise townships and ranges and sections and quarters, neatly fenced off by barbed wire, and deeded in identifiable parcels, recorded on a piece of paper. Private property was sacred; common property was confusion."[57]

As the Hispano population continued to struggle with new ways, the Americans were busy assessing their new possessions. The federal Donation Act of 1854 granted 160 acres to every white male citizen over twenty-one living in New Mexico Territory and even to those who simply declared an intention to become citizens and had resided in the territory before January 1, 1853. At the end of that year William Pelham, the first surveyor general, arrived in New Mexico to survey only "truly arable land"—no easy task.[58] One hopeful sign in this era was the fact that the "Little Ice Age," which had lasted some four hundred years began to wind down in the 1840s and came to an end around 1850, which would have provided a longer planting period and improved the area's farming potential. However, it soon became clear that 160 acres was not enough to support a family in arid New Mexico. In 1862 the Homestead Act replaced the Donation Act. Former grantees could homestead small parts of their former common lands. But even these fragments soon fell to speculators. Instead of fulfilling the American dream, the law, according to Victor Westphall, "was not suitable for any except limited portions of New Mexico and it was greatly abused," becoming "another way of acquiring large amounts of grazing land."[59] Vast tracts were acquired by unscrupulous speculators, Anglo and Hispano. Only 58 percent of the original homestead entries were patented. Unsurveyed land could be squatted upon and preempted. One person could legitimately acquire 1,120 acres, live on 160 acres for five years, or pay cash and move onto another preemptive claim for six months, and so forth. Family members could acquire separate claims. If homesteaders did not stay long enough to prove up, the government took the land back, but if they did hold on, big ranchers could buy them out, despite initial bitterness about the settlers' role in closing the free range. Ranchers profited from temporary use of land; a calf worth five dollars could be raised on grass in the public domain and sold for forty or fifty dollars with no tax paid. Foreign cattle ranch investors were often cheated; the same cattle could be counted over and over.

Once the US territorial Office of Surveyor General was established, surveying on the ground took almost forty years to complete. Land claims were to have been settled by 1858, but some years Indian raiders were so dangerous that survey parties never ventured out. Up to 1860 the Surveyor General's office confirmed sixty-four valid grants, but "later in that decade it stopped confirming grants altogether. Only one grant was confirmed between 1870 and 1890," leaving a hundred claims pending.[60]

Colonel Ethan W. Eaton, Founder of Socorro Vigilantes; Mrs. Marcelina Chávez Eaton, ca. 1900. (Palace of the Governors Photo Archives, NMHM/DCA neg. nos. 122150 and 122151.)

Deborah Reade, *Map of the Eaton (San Cristóbal) Grant* (Mednick, *San Cristóbal*, 167).

In March 1850 Col. George McCall was sent to New Mexico by the secretary of war to convey information on the newly acquired territory and encourage statehood among its citizens (ironically, since statehood would be denied them for another sixty-two years). He found "no beauty of scenery, absolutely nothing but sand hills and snow-covered mountains."[61] On the other hand, William Anderson Thornton, Chief of Ordinance for the Department of New Mexico, wrote in his diary for May 26, 1856:

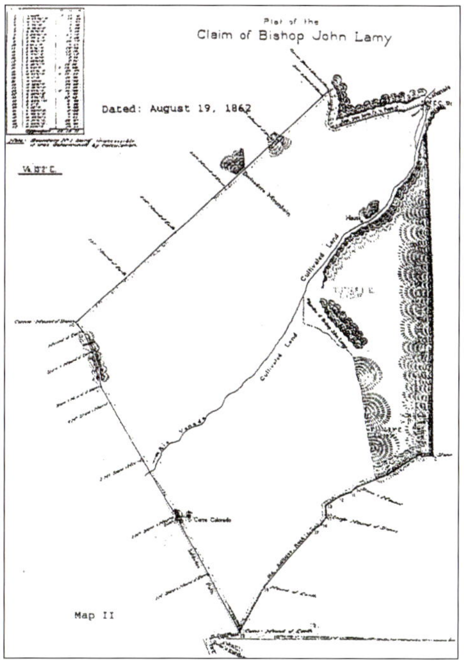

Plat of the Claim of Bishop John Lamy (aka Nuestra Señora de *la Luz Grant)*, August 19, 1862, showing the Soldier's Path leading toward Galisteo from Cerro Colorado (*lower left*). The boundaries were described: "On the north, by the road leading from Santa Fe to Pecos, the lands of Loreiyo Marquez, deceased, and El Cerro del Divisidera; on the east, by the Canoncito de los Apaches, including the water of said Canon; on the south, by the road leading from Galisteo to its junction with the soldiers' bridle path; and on the west, by the soldiers' bridle path and the Cerro Colorado, including said Cerro" (Records of the SGNM, no. 10).

At 7 am came abruptly on the Valley of Galisteo, affording the grandest landscape view I have ever seen. . . . We came abruptly to the termination of this table land [where they had traveled for days] and our road descended rapidly into a valley of a thousand or more feet [deep]. . . . Around us on every side arose towering mountains, some of which are covered with snow almost the year round, while thousands of others poked their heads of every shape high in the air. The scene burst so unexpectedly on us that we all shouted with surprise and halted to take a long look. The deep furrow cut on the face of nature by the long chisel of time

Jesse Nusbaum, *Old Spanish Convent Near Lamy, New Mexico*, ca. 1910. (Copyright Fred Harvey, Palace of the Governors Photo Archives, NMHM/DCA neg. no. 040298.)

Lucy R. Lippard, *Convent Ruin*, ca. 2016.

> showed many a deep gorge, many a bold bluff of rocks, many a pile of earth partly shaded by the deep green of pine and cedar trees. Nature had labored hard but her work as a whole was perfect. We passed down into the valley and trotted along through Galisteo and other Mexican towns.[62]

Col. McCall also found in New Mexico an inefficient army, helpless against the Indians who were stealing their horses, and no effective forts beyond Santa Fe. Fear of Navajo and Apache raids had cost the livestock industry its grazing lands, and export of sheep to Chihuahua was almost nonexistent. Like so many scattered settlements, Galisteo was vulnerable. In 1849 it was raided by the Navajo, perceived as the major offenders, with a long history of mutual raiding between the tribe and Nuevo Mexicanos.[63]

The first and foremost of the *gabachos* (gringos) who turns up in the censuses and land titles around Galisteo is New Yorker Ethan (Eathan) W. Eaton (1827–1913), who arrived in New Mexico in 1849 to prospect for gold. On January 20, 1851, Domingo Fernández sold his part of the San Cristóbal grant ("one undivided 26th part," larger than all the others) to Eaton and Alexander Reynolds for $500.[64] Eaton soon bought out Reynolds for $262. He married Marcelina Chávez (1830–1920), daughter of Ramón Chávez. They built an impressive stone home on Rancho San Cristóbal, opened a store in Galisteo, and had nine children.[65] In 1854 Eaton petitioned the surveyor general for confirmation, but he received only "a triangular area 'from the Mesita of the Lagunitas upwards as far as the spring of La Vaca,'" which was Fernández's parcel. Eaton, who thought he had bought the entire grant, began a long battle for a resurvey. In 1854, he prohibited Galisteo sheepherders from grazing on the Cañada de la Casita, a tributary of the San Cristóbal Arroyo, but both Tacubaya and the Cadial were recognized."[66] These of course were the last Mexican grants, where the villagers were accustomed to farm, cut firewood, and graze and water their stock.

Kenneth Chapman, *Chávez/Peña/Durán House in Galisteo*, 1926. (Palace of the Governors Photo Archives, NMHM/DCA neg. no. 009318. Courtesy of the Durán/Peña/Chávez families.)

In 1855 Eaton petitioned the surveyor general, "stating that all of the original grantees except Fernández had forfeited their rights" by failing to meet the Mexican government's conditions and claiming their lands as Fernández's assignees.[67] In 1856 it was ruled that if grantees on the rest of San Cristóbal didn't cultivate the land, they would lose it.[69] In 1857 Surveyor General William Pelham recommended confirmation, but Congress took no action until June 21, 1860, when Eaton's claims were finally confirmed. The subsequent survey, however, showed only 27,854.056 acres, and Eaton immediately protested. It was not patented until December 1880.

On the heels of the Americans, another powerful foreigner, from France, arrived in Santa Fe in 1851. Bishop and soon-to-be Archbishop Jean-Baptiste Lamy (1814–88) put more priests in the field, diminishing New Mexico's isolation, but he disliked the local culture, architecture, and clergy and tried to get rid of the Penitentes, the lay group that had sustained the Catholic faith in the days when priests were few and far between. In 1856 Bishop Lamy secured a quit claim deed for the Church from Francisco Herrera, acquiring 16,546 acres from the Cañoncito/Diego Antonio Baca grant on the eastern border of the Galisteo Basin. In 1857 it was investigated and in 1860 approved by Congress and became known as the Bishop Lamy grant. In the meantime, a convent was built on the land, perhaps intended for the Sisters of Loretto, whom Lamy brought to the state in 1852. Little or no information about it survives, though its picturesque adobe ruins remain on private land and postcards of the ruins were sold to tourists.[69]

Perhaps in the hope that the Americans would offer rural areas better protection from Indian raids, there was an influx of Hispano/Mexican population into the Galisteo Basin, and building surged during the Territorial period after 1846. By the 1850s, it became relatively safe to build houses and livestock pens on the flat, well-watered land along the Rio Galisteo. Several substantial homes—long, low, flat-roofed, and linear in plan—were built from the 1840s to the 1860s.[70] From November 1851 to January 1852, the First Dragoons, "Companies F and I of the US Cavalry under the command of Colonel Summer were briefly stationed at the Fort in Galisteo," before they were moved to Fort Howe in Colorado because the Indian problem was more severe there.[71] This "fort" may have been the late eighteenth-century, government-owned barracks on the creek's west bank or at Nicolás Pino's house, where a destacamento was once noted. In any case, its demise was unlucky for Galisteo. On January 13, 1855, nine Mescalero Apache rustlers stole some hundred head of cattle from the Eaton Ranch. They "killed one man, stripped one dozen women, and ran off seventy mules." Some Indians were killed and four were wounded. Word was sent to Fort Marcy in Santa Fe, and Lieutenant Sturgis of the First Dragoons was sent in pursuit, along with some unnamed militiamen from Galisteo. On the third day out, they found the offending Indians 160 miles from Galisteo. Three soldiers were wounded and one died as a result of this chase. Eaton himself was wounded "in the thigh by an arrowhead two and a half inches long."[72] Probably as a result of this raid and to protect surveyors working in the area, an escort of "mounted rifles" was stationed in Galisteo village between 1855 and 1859.[73]

In a casually racist letter dated November 4, 1860, John Kingsbury reported:

> The Navajoes are becoming very bold and have nearly got possession of the whole Territory. The fact is they go just where they please, killing and robbing all the while. We have had much excitement here with them this week. They first killed a herder near Rock Corral [above Lamy], cry of Indians soon filled the town, several Americans who started out that way on their regular business were turned back by the reports of Mexicans. There was no mounted troops here. The Col. finally sent out all he had here which was only a small detachment here in charge of Gov't property [probably those stationed in Galisteo], about 15 strong and they went out against the foe in two wagons. Of course they saw no Indians, reports continuing to come in, and the dead bodies of three herders. [Miguel] Pino of Delgado & Sandoval, also having arrived, created much excitement. Finally Simon Delgado applied to the Governor for arms, and got up a party of mounted Mexicans about 45 strong, and started out. Found the Indians concentrated near Galisteo, a large number some say 40 others as high as 60. Any rate the Indians were strong and bold enough to stand in the open plain and did fight from Eleven A.M. until 3P.M. Jesus Baca, Miguel Pino and other good fighting men were of the party. They lost three men killed on the ground and 5 wounded, two of which have died since. They all report having killed 13 Indians and wounding many more. The Mexicans also lost about half their horses, two or 3 shot but the balance run off by the Indians. My boy Talisforo went and was in the fight. From him I learn that only about half the men went into the fight (Mexicans I mean) the others were about 2 miles behind, staid there looking on and left the foremost party to fight it out alone. They were in too tight place to

Cibolero (Buffalo Hunter), painting on wooden panel from a house in Santa Cruz de la Cañada, redrawn by Jerry L. Livingston after E. Boyd, *Popular Arts.* (Palace of the Governors Photo Archives, NMHM/DCA neg. no. 101496.)

U.S. Soldiers Guard Navajo Camp at Fort Sumner, Bosque Redondo, After the Long Walk, 1864–68. (Palace of the Governors Photo Archives, NMHM/DCA neg. no. 028534.)

> run and had to stand and fight it out. From him I infer that the Mexicans were whipped and that both Mexicans and Indians were glad to quit.[74]

Despite US promises to rid the territory of the Navajo "scourge," the tribe was raiding in full force during the early 1860s, when the Civil War distracted US troops. New Mexicans took advantage of the situation to step up slave raiding, exacerbating warfare with Navajo desperate to regain their stolen children.[75] The territorial government passed laws in 1856 and 1859 designed to limit the number of free blacks entering New Mexico, and given the small African American population, mostly fugitive slaves escaping from Texas, most slaves in the Southwest were Native indentured servants and Mexican peons. In 1862 the US Congress outlawed slavery, and in 1865 the Thirteenth Amendment abolished involuntary servitude.[76] Many Rio Arriba families had captive Native "servants" (that is, slaves). Women, often Navajo, valued for their weaving, were integrated into the population by marriage, as were some Pueblo people. Joe Martínez tells that his great-great-grandfather Ramos Valencia was a sheepherder at the age of six or eight when Comanches took him and he wound up in Jémez, near the Valle Grande. Years later, when he was around twenty-one, someone from the pueblo showed him the way home to Galisteo, and his father hid him for a year. Later he returned to Jémez to see Native family.[77]

By the late 1860s, Comanches rarely came west of the Pecos, but in October of each year, until 1879, when the Comanches held their last full-scale buffalo hunt, leather-clad New Mexicans and Pueblos set out for the eastern plains to hunt the disappearing buffalo with long lances and bows and arrows. As many as two hundred men traveled in caravans of oxcarts and pack mules, accompanied by almost one hundred women and children to help with the dirty work of butchering and processing. The meat was hauled back to camp and dried into jerky; buffalo tongues were preserved in brine.[78] Texans saw it as "bloody criminal commerce and a conniving with savages which could only deepen their hatred and contempt for the Hispano New Mexican. To the latter it was a continuance of fragile but long-standing trade relations with neighboring Indians—a relationship essential to peace on their own frontier—and a measure of their view of Texas as a foreign country full of potential enemies."[79]

Comanchero trade was dangerous but profitable work, since in addition to a winter's supply of dried meat, the hides, tallow, brined tongues, and marrow bones could be sold. With its relative proximity to the Plains, Galisteo may have been one of the departure points for these caravans. WPA interviews yielded a corrido about the accidental death of Manuel Maes, with an enigmatic reference to "Lauriano Peak," which could be seen from his "humble *jacal* in far away Galisteo." The composer, Cecilio Roybal, asks that prayers be said for the cibolero, who fell on his own lance when his horses tumbled while chasing a galloping buffalo herd. He was "left in a lonely grave near the Colorado River."[80]

"For the nomadic Indians [the fifty years between 1820 and 1870] was a disastrous time, ending in their defeat and capture, the loss of most of their lands and much of their freedom."[81] The Pueblos, their reluctant adaptation to Spanish customs already over a century old, were less drastically affected, though their losses were significant and well remembered. In 1864, after Kit Carson's scorched-earth campaign throughout Navajoland, Gen. James Carleton put into effect a notoriously ill-conceived project—to relocate 12,000 Navajos (as well as a small band of Mescalero Apaches) to Fort Sumner at the Bosque Redondo on the Pecos River in eastern New Mexico and force them to become sedentary farmers. Nine thousand Navajos took the "Long Walk," or forced march, from their beloved homeland in 1864, remaining at Bosque Redondo in terrible straits on unproductive farmland until the project's failure was finally acknowledged. The survivors were sent home in 1868 to a shrunken but familiar reservation within sight of their four sacred mountains. There were braided routes to and from Fort Sumner, one of which ran through Tijeras Canyon, Galisteo, and San José to Tecolote, then south along the Pecos River to Bosque Redondo. A return route also ran near or through Galisteo.

When Capt. R. B. Marcy conducted a survey seeking the best wagon road from Fort Smith in Arkansas to Santa Fe, he recommended the route from Anton Chico through Galisteo, "used by Spaniards and Mexicans for many years as a grazing for the horses of the Santa Fe garrison owing to the fine grass lands in the locality."[82] This may have been a section of the military supply route south of the Santa Fe Trail that crossed the Galisteo Basin en route to Albuquerque. As population grew, and despite Indian raids on every front, there was regular stagecoach service to Santa Fe. In the mid-1850s, there was a stage stop at Rock Corral Station, on the west side of Apache Ridge, where fresh horses and water from a natural well were available.[83] Two sites have been suggested as Galisteo's stage stops, one on today's Avenida Vieja and the other where today's CR 42 crosses the Arroyo de Los Angeles. Topographical engineers Lts. J. W. Albert and W. G. Peck mapped the region, under the command of a Captain Pope, who resided in Galisteo from October 1, 1858, to May 31, 1859.[84] They were charged with drilling artesian wells at strategic sites; one near Galisteo village struck water at twenty feet. The project was finally discarded as too costly; the water quality in most of the basin was no better then than it is today.

Salt was an important local commodity. From the seventeenth century on, caravans of carts had gathered for the *cosecha de sal* (salt harvest) at Galisteo Pueblo—and later at the village—for three-day marches to the salt lakes (Las Salinas) in the Estancia Valley, accompanied by soldiers for protection against Indians. Marc Simmons describes nineteenth-century expeditions: "Leaving Galisteo, often after a wild fandango the night before, the throng of salt gatherers was in a festive mood. The men knew that weeks of hard work lay ahead, but they were accustomed to that." Once they reached the largest lake, Laguna del Perro, they raked pure salt from its shallows and shores, stashing it in ox carts lined with dried hides. Salt sold for a dollar a bushel and was necessary not only for human nutrition but for the stock: "ranchers with large flocks needed huge quantities." In 1854 a territorial law decreed that salt in the lakes was free, but that did not keep people from trying to sell the lakes, which, according to an unnamed Galisteña, "was equivalent to a New York visitor buying the Brooklyn Bridge."[85]

During the Civil War, Galisteo became a crossroads for both Union and Confederate troops, the latter hoping to make New Mexico a slave state like neighboring Texas. The Confederates—mostly Texans based in San Antonio, despised by New Mexicans for their previous failed attempts to annex the territory—entered New Mexico during the winter of 1861. In December, the Battle of Valverde, south of Socorro, was won by the drunken Confederate Gen. Henry H. Sibley, related by marriage and old school ties to Edward R. S. Canby, leader of the Union troops. New Mexico militiamen, led by Galisteans Brig. Gen. Nicolás Pino and his brother Col. Miguel Pino (a hero of the Battle of Valverde), were ordered out of nearby Fort Craig in March 1862 to follow the victorious Confederate troops as they marched north to take Albuquerque and Santa Fe, occupying northern New Mexico from February to April 1862. (Union captain Enos evacuated Albuquerque when he learned that the Confederates were approaching.) Among the number of Galisteños in the militia was José Dolores Montoya, an

A. B. Peticolas, *The Church at Galisteo, 25 March 1862.* (Courtesy of the Arizona Historical Society.)

ancestor of today's Montoyas and Anayas, and Pedro Peña, who enlisted as a private under Captain Gaspar Ortiz in Santa Fe on December 5, 1861, and was discharged on February 28, 1862, before the Battle of Glorieta Pass.

Lt. Col. William Scurry and the 4th Regiment of Texans camped briefly in Galisteo, then conquered an undefended Santa Fe on March 13. The initials *CS* (Confederate States) are carved in the north porch door in what became the Ortizy Davis hacienda below The Hill, and there is some evidence that the soldiers cooked on the roof.[86] Among the Confederate soldiers who camped at Galisteo for one night on March 25, 1862, was A. B. Peticolas, who described the voyage down from the Real de Dolores gold mines in the Ortiz Mountains: "Four miles down a long slope and out of the piney country, we have reached the valley [Galisteo Basin] and traveled a good distance over a first-rate road and camped twelve miles from the gold mines at Galisteo. This is a small town situated on a small creek of the same name. We are not on one of the main roads from [Fort] Craig to [Fort] Union and considerably fatigued with our march. We were not sorry to know that we had at last reached a point where we could rest a little."

On the way, the troop "captured a large flock of sheep . . . and pressed them into service, as we are just now rather short of meat." In his journals, Peticolas created the first known image of Galisteo, a pen-and-ink sketch of the church and flanking buildings, giving some notion of what the early defensive plaza on The Hill looked like.[87] The victorious Confederates hoped to go on to capture Fort Union and the desperately needed supplies there, but this was not tobe.

In the meantime, the territorial government fled from Santa Fe to Fort Union, where they were joined by Union reinforcements from Colorado, sent to dislodge the Texans from Galisteo, although they had already departed. The Confederate troops were on their way to the three-day Battle of Glorieta Pass, which began on March 26. There was no fighting on March 27, but the next day both sides took the field in a major skirmish at Pigeon's Ranch. The Confederates appeared to be winning, but the same day, a battalion of "Pikes Peakers"—Colorado Volunteers of the Union Army led by Col. John M. Chivington (displaying the cruel efficiency that was later to mark his leadership at the unforgivable Sand Creek Massacre) and a local captain named Cháves—serendipitously came upon the eighty Confederate supply wagons hidden near the Galisteo Creek at Apache Canyon. They destroyed the supplies, killing twenty-seven soldiers and all their horses, which led to a Confederate retreat. Thus the South's hopes to make New Mexico a refuge for slavery were dashed. After the victory at Glorieta, the Colorado volunteers pursued the retreating Texans to Galisteo, but they escaped.[88]

In 1863, a stagecoach traveler from Albuquerque to Santa Fe reported eating "a first-rate breakfast" at the rancho of Don Nicolás Pino near La Ciénega, where the Pinos had extensive holdings. An interesting footnote to Galisteo's Civil War is an undated letter in code, found in the State Archives, and attributed to Pino. It reports the movement of Confederate forces to an unknown recipient, presumably Union leadership: "Sir, rumors are that the Confederates are organizing a force that will march through New Mexico. This will need confirmation. If

Photographer unknown, *The Ortiz y Davis Hacienda*, ca. 1890. (Courtesy of John Benjamin and Dianna Gwyn.)

such news exists and gets to this remote area of mine, you shall be informed."[89] Don Nicolás was later commended officially for having "rendered valuable services to the Union during the Civil War."[90]

Years later, Josefa Ortiz y Davis told vivid (though apparently fabricated) tales to her granddaughter Victoria Sánchez about the Ortiz y Davis hacienda during the Civil War. As recounted by Sánchez, "An entire platoon was quartered for many months in my grandmother's corrals and courtyards, turning her house into a mini-fortress. I spent many hours listening to her stories about Yankee soldiers chasing Confederate rebels on hit-and-run missions. Grandmother and her two maids cooked and cared for the Yankee soldiers."[91] Josefa was only nine years old in 1862 and still living with her family in Dolores. Her father, Juan Grande Ortiz, owned land in Galisteo, and it is possible that by then he had acquired the site of the Galisteo hacienda from the government. But her older brother Juan Ortiz later testified that in 1863 (at age twelve, a year after the Civil War battle), he went to the village of Galisteo for the first time to help his father gather corn fodder. They stayed a few nights and returned to Dolores: "where we lived."[92]

The origins of the expansive Ortiz y Davis compound below the settlement on The Hill—the largest and most storied home in the village, once bordering the Rio Galisteo and surrounded by orchards and farmed fields—are unclear. Former owner John Benjamin contends that the earliest structure was a seventeenth-century trading post.[93] If the separate eastern building was the site of the 1792/95 destacamento, the rest of the current hacienda (as it is still called) may have been built at the same time or in the late 1840s, when Doniphan established another military post there. In the 1850s, it was a government commissary. (Piles of forage are visible in a photograph from the 1880s.) At some point it was enlarged and transformed into a home, perhaps in the mid-1860s, when the Ortizes and soon Sylvester Davis moved in.[94] According to John Benjamin, "they did not have a title until a homestead act patent for the 164 acres of 'vacant land' [in 1891]. For unknown reasons, the hacienda was never described as being here in legal papers, even in the 1890s. It was still called 'vacant land' when I bought it in 1987. From day one I have known that the history and even the existence of this place were purposefully hidden and obscured."[95] If the property was the site of the destacamento, it seems logical that it belonged to the Spanish, then Mexican, then US government, at least until after the Civil War, as suggested by Kingsbury's account of soldiers guarding "government property." This would also explain why the settlers on The Hill requested grant land on the east side of the creek rather than on the more convenient west side. But it still does not explain how Juan Grande Ortiz acquired this choice piece of land.

Most Ortiz y Pino family trees and histories assume an unbroken line between today's Ortiz y Pinos and the prestigious line of Nicolás Ortiz Niño de Ladrón de Guevara. However, the 1848 will of his descendant José Francisco (Juan Nepomuceno) Ortiz[96] and his wife, Malaquita Montoya, states that they had "no living heirs."[97] In some genealogies, Juan or Juano "Grande" (born ca. 1816 or 1818) is presumed to be their son, though family members have said

Juan Ortiz's Mercantile (Palace of the Governors Photo Archives, NMHM/DCA neg. no. 9715). The building dates to the late 1860s and this photo is dated ca. 1905, although given the store's poor condition, it seems likely to be later, perhaps in the 1920s, when Ortiz had already handed the business over to his son, Don José Ortiz y Pino, who had his own store on Calle Grande.

Sylvester Davis and Josefa Ortiz y Davis with George Davis, Their First Child, 1869. (Courtesy of La Herencia Archive.)

he was "from Chihuahua," and his lack of several names suggests a more plebeian ancestry than the elaborately denominated Ortizes. He might have been an adopted relative, an illegitimate child from within the family, or even a captive Indian servant, a genizaro.[98] Family sources say that he ran wagon trains into Chihuahua and was also a trader and merchant; he may also have been a Comanchero, trading with Plains Natives for cattle.

Whether he was a bastard, a former servant, or an estranged son, Juan "Grande" Ortiz was prosperous. By the 1860 census he was age forty-two and illiterate, a "farmer and *placero*" (gold digger), living in Dolores with his wife and children. He owned land in Galisteo and real estate worth $1,400, with a personal net worth of $12,500. Although unacknowledged in the will of his purported parents, he owned mines in the Placer de San Francisco (now Golden) and elsewhere, and he married well, wedding María Paula Ortiz from the same large and generally wealthy extended family on June 7, 1843.[99] They had at least five surviving children: Antonio José (b. ca. 1842), Juan (b. 1851), Josefa (b. 1853), and Susano (b. ca. 1856).[100] Cayetano, (b. ca. 1847), was listed as both male and female in different censuses and described as an "idiot" or "dumb." He was still living with his sister Josefa in 1900.[101]

Within six weeks of Juan "Grande" Ortiz's death and burial in Dolores, in 1865, his widow moved her family to the hacienda below the original fortified village in Galisteo. (According to one of his granddaughters, the patriarch believed "there were too many American hoodlums in Santa Fe."[102]) His son Juan Ortiz, who was fourteen when they moved to Galisteo, eventually built his own home and mercantile on La Vega. He married Nicolás Pino's daughter Concepción in 1873, and their children were José, Pedro, and Manuela. Concepción died in 1894 and Juan later married her sister Margarita; Trinidad, another

Nicolas Brown, *The Palace of the Governors, Santa Fe*, 1868. (Palace of the Governors Photo Archives, NMHM/DCA neg. no. 045819.)

sister, the widow of cousin Ambrocio Pino, was also in the household.[103] According to his great-grandson, Juan Ortiz was a trader like his father, "hauling freight from Durango, Mexico, making the long hauls from St. Louis and Kansas City to Santa Fe and Galisteo." He owned one hundred wagons and five hundred oxen, and told stories "about the storms, the Indians and the Outlaws. . . . Juan Ortiz was not large in stature, but a giant in courage."[104]

At the age of fourteen or fifteen, Juan's younger sister Josefa married Sylvester Davis. The couple met in Dolores, but the courtship and marriage took place in Galisteo.[105] According to her granddaughter, Victoria Davis de Sánchez, Josefita Ortiz, "a dynamic young girl of Spanish and Native American ancestry,"[106] met Sylvester when she was still a child, but "the tall adventurer fell in love and asked for Josefita's hand in marriage when she was only thirteen years old."[107] Family lore has it that Josefa Ortiz had vowed not to marry a Spanish man because of their imagined mistreatment of local hero Pedro Bautista Pino, to whom her maternal family was related. Another account says she refused to marry Spanish boys because they had no ambition and cared only about horses.[108]

The marriage record shows that "José Silvestre Davis" and Josefa Ortiz were married on May 5, 1868, in *la capilla de Galisteo* (the first church on The Hill). Davis, born in Concord, New Hampshire, in September 1834, was a bachelor, legitimate son of John Davis and Elizabeth Douglas Davis.[109] Josefa was "the legitimate daughter of Juan Ortiz, deceased, and Paula Ortiz." Their sponsors were her older brother Antonio Ortiz and his wife, María de

Jesús Durán. Victoria Sánchez wrote, "On their wedding day my grandfather brought his bride several jars of gold nuggets from his Dolores mine. Some of these she later had made into jewelry."[110]

Josefa and Sylvester's first surviving child, George Davis, was born May 22, 1869, when Josefa was sixteen. In the ensuing years they had three more sons and two daughters: Joseph, Frank, John, Carlota Leyba, and Pablita Davis Ortiz y Pino, who married her first cousin, her uncle Juan's son, who became Don José, the "last *patrón*" of Galisteo. The Davis children grew up in the hacienda, which remained the family base. When George married, he homesteaded a ranch in Moriarty, a new town thirty miles to the south.[111] As adults, his children used the simple name of their Anglo father, while their cousin José Ortiz adopted the more prestigious maternal name, becoming Ortiz y Pino.[112]

Sylvester Davis's descendants tell differing versions of his life story, describing him as a "blue blood Bostonian" and as Scots Irish: "Captain Davis . . . left his native Concord, New Hampshire in his twenties to look for gold. Having crossed the Mississippi in 1859," he headed for Pike's Peak and the goldfields of Colorado, passed through Denver, went over Ratón Pass and landed briefly in Mora in mid-September. He proceeded to Las Vegas, New Mexico, noting in his brief diary that "the valleys are generally covered with Sheep, goats, cows & oxen, mules, Ponies etc."[113] In "Sapio" (Sapello) he noted, "Men & women are Returning on mules and Jack asses from the fandango which they have bin to during the night at Las Vagas [*sic*]." They came to "Antoncheco" (Anton Chico) and enjoyed the fruit of the "Nut Pine" (piñon), which grew in abundance. On October 4 they arrived in "Canion Seat" (Cañoncito), where he got a job at the sawmill.[114] That winter he was in Santa Fe and then worked on a grist mill in Bernalillo for the wealthy Perea family before starting out again in search of gold in the Sandias and in Dolores, where he met the Ortiz family. A man named Manuel Stevenson, half African American and half Cherokee, possibly a former slave, who enlisted in the Union Army in 1865, came to New Mexico with Sylvester Davis, though little is known of his background. He worked in the Dolores mines and in 1879 married Julianita Ortiz, an Indian servant.[115]

After the Civil War, US surveying teams laid a grid of townships over the public lands—the common lands that villagers had depended upon.[116] Government appropriations, Indian attacks, and relative poverty not withstanding, Galisteo had thrived since the American takeover, when it was a small but growing village on a branch of the Santa Fe Trail, with a population of perhaps two to three hundred people, most of whom lived on The Hill. By the 1860s, the village had spread down to the river and boasted around seven hundred residents.

THREE

La lucha es tu herencia (1870–1900)

The victors write the history, but the vanquished write the songs.
—Irish ballad singer Frank Harte[1]

New Mexicans have long memories. "La lucha es tu herencia" (Struggle is your legacy) remains a battle cry.[2] Well into the twentieth century, the small landowners of Galisteo fought fiercely in the American courts for their miniscule allotments and thousands of acres of common land, but none of their cases achieved a final title. In 1869, the well-named territorial governor William Pile "sold a large number of the colonial and Mexican archives as waste paper."[3] A later governor kept all the archives in an outhouse, where many rotted beyond use. The surviving documents show endless comings and goings of Native, Hispano, and Anglo people whose hopes and dreams were often dashed on the arid legal landscape. To this day, ambitious politicians promise to seek justice for land grant heirs, though the depth of centuries-old passions embedded in New Mexico lands remains difficult for Congress and outsiders to comprehend.[4]

The social and legal contexts in which Galisteo's legacy of struggle took place are revealing. Under US law, six steps were required to prove ownership, and if any documents related to a Spanish or Mexican grant were missing from the archives, otherwise valid claims were tossed out. Long-standing grants incompletely documented before a governor left office at the end of his term were also declared invalid.[5] Claimants had to sue the US Court of Private Land Claims, which would honor only those grants supported by documents from the

Santa Fe Ring, cartoon from *Thirty Four* (Las Cruces), Oct. 27, 1880.

incomplete Mexican Archives in Santa Fe. To add insult to injury, claimants were required to pay for the survey. [6] Few poor families could shoulder the financial burden. Even if they could afford a lawyer, the supporting documents for many claims could not be found. Lawyers sometimes claimed as much as a third of the disputed land as payment for representing grantees in court. When cases were strongly contested, they were sent to the US Congress, the equivalent of exporting the law to another country that understood very little about New Mexico's history or economy.

Spanish/Mexican land grant boundary markers were natural and ephemeral, not up to American standards. For instance, in discussions of the Baca y Terrus grant, one boundary on Agustín Duran's land was described by the point where "a cottonwood tree formerly stood." The tree, "having great age," was destroyed "by persons camping here years ago. . . . This point is where it stood." Witness Antonio Cháves y Alire of Galisteo also cited the cottonwood tree and a "mound of stone."[7] Local claims were marred by disagreements about which boulder, lone tree, cross, stone, or landmark, which obsolete place name, which lost or nonexistent documents, not to mention dates available only through oral history that were summarily dismissed by Anglo judges.

The young Americans who entered New Mexico after the Civil War coveted the Spanish/Mexican land grants that accounted for most of the arable lands. Whereas initially the sale of land grants was illegal, by the end of the century they could be partitioned by sale of the whole, with the profits divided among unwilling grantees who often did not want to sell. San Cristóbal is cited as an example of this process.[8] Many properties were eventually transferred to the "public domain," to be homesteaded or to become national forests or other federal public lands. Once in the public domain, the old common lands could be leased at low prices to savvy Anglos and ricos. Grant heirs left with nothing but home lots and small fields were "forced to file homestead claims on land their families had farmed for generations."[9] Speculators were in hog heaven.

Some influential Hispanos (including Galisteños Nicolás Pino and later Don José Ortiz y Pino) also seem to have profited from disinheriting their fellow grantees. Extensive and expensive legal wrangling in the US courts often resulted in lands being "alienated" from their proprietors. In 1885 it was estimated that 40 percent of five-year homesteads in New Mexico were fraudulent. Victor Westphall considered this a conservative figure, since in 1883 alone, 67.5 percent were fraudulent: "This traffic in land grants worked to the detriment of the Territory."[10] Surveyor General Henry M. Atkinson, who supervised most of the New Mexico surveys from 1876, turned a blind eye to irregular practices. Despite all the property available, there was a national distrust of New Mexico land titles and a feeling that most of this land was unusable (part of a "low culture" of snakes, Mexicans, and Indians), so legal sloppiness didn't matter.[11] New Mexico's only Washington voice before statehood was one nonvoting delegate to Congress. Low settlement joined racism in retarding statehood. Moreover, the pay was inadequate for good survey work. One has to agree with James Elkus when he writes, "The fact of the matter is that the United States really didn't want anyone to own land in New Mexico, and the way they treated the problem showed it."[12]

At the core of these machinations was the Santa Fe Ring, a consortium of mostly Anglo lawyers and politicians, led by Thomas Benton Catron and Stephen Benton Elkins, who arrived in the mid 1860s and dominated the territory between 1872 and 1884, though their power was not truly dismantled until statehood in 1912. John Greiner has been credited with inventing the Ring's political strategy for dubious land acquisitions—"to buy semi worthless or cheap land grants and to control the survey of their boundaries and assemble the political forces needed to get the grant approved by Congress"—a method that became "a staple industry of New Mexico for the next century."[13] T. B. Catron was at one time the largest landowner in the United States. As Violle Heffernan observed, "Only a portion of T. B.'s immense landholdings were acquired by direct purchase. Much of it came into his possession because he followed the then prevalent practice of taking claims for the original Spanish and Mexican land grants to court to have them confirmed."[14] Westphall calls Catron "the greatest single force in the land grant saga," citing his dealings with the San Cristóbal grant as an example of the methods used "to consolidate the individual interests of various grant claimants into a merchantable title to the entire property."[15] T. Rush Spencer, surveyor general in 1869, was the first of three surveyors general to align with dominant Republican politicians for mutual gain. He was in the land grant business with Catron, Elkins, William Pile, John S. Watts, John Pratt, and Miguel Otero, as well as Stephen W. Dorsey and Max Frost.

While Catron has come to epitomize the Ring's excesses, journalist Charles Lummis, also a Republican, contended, "Steve Elkins is the boss thief of the lot . . . universally detested and feared throughout all New Mexico."[16] With Catron, Dorsey, and Springer (who is occasionally referred to as "anti–Santa Fe Ring"), Elkins, "after massaging the [Maxwell] grant to eighteen times larger than originally determined . . . tried to have his survey paid for out of public funds!"[17] The Ring was described by New Mexico governor Miguel A. Otero II as "one of the most corrupt, unscrupulous, and daring organizations ever connected with [New Mexico's] history. Nothing was too rotten for the well-known Santa Fe ring to undertake."[18] Yet in 1897, former governor Lew Wallace wrote: "That governor Oterro [*sic*] has submitted himself to the domination of Mr. Catron does not surprise me. One of the curious incidences pertaining to Mr. Catron is his astonishing influence over New Mexicans. I cannot recall one instance in which he did not absolutely submerge and control all persons who came in contact with him speaking the Spanish tongue."[19] This scenario was played out in Galisteo as well as in other communities.

On December 5, 1881, Elias Brevoort, a receiver in the Land Office in Santa Fe, wrote to Commissioner N. C. McFarland: "I have quite recently become impressed with the belief that there has been for some months past a system of frauds perpetrated in making entries of lands," and he proceeded to list the principal suspects.[20] In 1884, Clarence Pullen became surveyor general and tried to clean up some of the errors. Then in 1885, when the Santa Fe Ring's influence had somewhat declined, George Julian took over.[21] Known as "Old Malaria" by the Santa Fe Ring,[22] he was considered by some to be "unimpeachably honest"[23] and a partisan for actual settlers, which explains his lack of popularity with the power structure. In 1887, he published "Land Stealing in New Mexico" in the *North American Review,* attacking

"Traffickers in land grants . . . politicians for revenue only." "Forged and fraudulent grants," he wrote, "covering very large tracts, were declared valid . . . and the Surveyor General's office very often became a mere bureau in the service of these claimants. . . . Millions of acres of the public domain were thus appropriated to the uses of private greed."[24] But Julian's honesty was selective. The settlers he championed were usually Anglos and ricos, not the beleaguered Hispanos. Within two years he was removed and replaced by E. F. Hobart (1889–93), another "reformer," and the commissioner general of the US Land Office suspended all surveys because they were faulty.[25] Frank Springer, who arrived in Cimarron, New Mexico, in 1873, once said of land grants: "The territory would be far better off if there had never been any."[26]

Ethan Eaton, owner of parts of the San Cristóbal Ranch since 1851, was listed in the 1870 census as a "farmer," worth $4,000 plus $1,000 of personal property. For the most part, he allowed Galisteo villagers to continue to graze, farm, and gather wood on the Cadial, as guaranteed by the Treaty of Guadalupe Hidalgo. But that did not protect them from hovering predators. Eaton was a natural ally of the Santa Fe Ring.[27] T. B. Catron's machinations as a Ring leader, and his acquisition of large parts of the grant, played a major role in San Cristóbal's tumultuous history. In 1869, Catron began covertly to acquire interests from Domingo Fernández's "companions" in the grant, under the name of Nicolás Pino. He played both sides by acting as attorney for grant litigants, cozying up to the Galisteo villagers around election times, then bilking them when it suited his agenda. They complained publicly that Anglos only spoke to them around election time.

In the 1870 Census of the Galisteo Precinct (not just the village), there were 497 people in 106 houses, averaging 4.7 people per household.[28] There had been, since the last counts, twelve births and four deaths. There were 48 farm laborers, 38 laborers, 15 farmers, 4 servants, one alcalde, one miller, one washer woman, a tailor named Nazel Klein, one musician, one teamster and, curiously, only one housewife. Livestock were oxen and a few milk cows; only Antonio [José] Ortiz had more than twenty cattle.[29]

Irrigated parcels on both sides of the river accounted for 384 acres, where mostly corn, wheat, and some pinto beans were grown, but Nicolás Pino grew apples, peaches, and grapes in his orchard east of the creek. In 1870, he is listed as a wealthy farmer in Galisteo, with real estate worth $1,500 and other assets of $1,500. In 1872 he owned seventeen strips in the Cadial and a large piece of land at Stinking Springs (Ojo Hedionda), southeast of the village.[30] Pino also owned a flour mill in Galisteo, located "by the bridge." It was "a five horsepower, water powered, rimstone machine." In one ten-month period, he milled 47 barrels of flour, 2,400 pounds of short logs, 3,600 pounds of bran, and 6,500 pounds of corn.[31] Nicolás's brothers Miguel and Facundo Pino also settled in Galisteo and/or were landowners in the Galisteo Basin, as was their cousin Ambrocio Pino, who in 1870, at the age of thirty-two, was even richer than Nicolás, with a combined income of $1,500 and $2,500.[32] In 1876, Don Ambrocio "staked two flocks of sheep and a herd of cattle in a bet against Santiago Baca of Pecos on a rooster pull" and won.[33] An 1878 corrido by Estevan Encinas tells the story of Don Ambrocio staking his entire fortune, wagering that his team from Galisteo could win. "And, lo, it did."

Doña Josefa Ortiz y Davis, then in her seventies and sightless, proudly recollected to reporter Mary Coan that it was her late husband's horse, Chiquito, that saved the day, being ridden to victory by one Marcelino Baros, who was also famed as the best village fiddler.[34] Another version of this story is that Galisteo had suffered a drought all summer, and its horses were weak, so Pino borrowed a fast steed from someone in Albuquerque.

Despite the odds stacked heavily against them, Galisteo land grant heirs did not give up easily. On July 20, 1871, a group of herederos took the bull by the horns and sought confirmation of the larger, overlapping, original 1814/22 Galisteo grant "situated in the abandoned Indian pueblo of Galisteo . . . said to contain about 9,000 acres." Among others, Sandovals, Anayas, Chávezes, and Nicolás Pino and their heirs testified that they had been in "quiet and peaceable possession" of the 9,000 acres of land since 1814, though there was no survey. Their lawyer was Samuel B. Elkins, brother of Stephen Elkins, who, like T. B. Catron, played both sides of these land cases, boding no good for the claimants.

The nature of the grant—individual or communal—was a point of contention. Witness José Antonio Anaya, "who had resided at Galisteo for twenty-odd years prior to 1840," testified he never knew of a formal town grant, and Anastacio Sandoval agreed, citing his grandfather, a principal petitioner in 1815 [1814], whose title came from the alcalde. Joaquin Chávez, resident in Galisteo since 1822, also knew of no community grant but "was aware that the land had been divided out to 18 or 19 individual tracts of 100 x 1000 varas in size on the Galisteo River, under the verbal authority of Governor Maynez in the year 1815 or 1816 and afterwards in 1822 given possession to said individuals."[35] These tiny suertes, eventually the only lands confirmed by the United States, would have been a fraction of the entire grant. The rest was presumably common land.

Another bothersome point was raised by Eaton's lawyers: why, if the 1814/22 Galisteo grant was valid, did some of the same people already living in the area apply in 1816 for a much smaller tract that overlapped with that original Galisteo grant? Donaciano Vigil, now an influential figure in the US government, whose memories were taken as gospel, contended: "There being no standard history of the country, the yet more reliable data . . . [of the old, incomplete archives] must determine the question." The original grant was not produced: "From these documents [it] is rationally deducible that there was no general or community grant to the town of Galisteo" and there was "no written grant or title for the lands at Galisteo" except those to individuals who held the five surviving acts of possession dated April 19, 1822: José Antonio Alarid, María Nieves Mirabal, Matias Sandoval, Rafael Sena, and Felipe Sandoval.[36]

In the end, the case balanced on one point: whether or not Governor Maynez, who had awarded the grant, was actually governor in 1814/16.[37] The irregularities of New Mexico governors' terms were ignored, thanks to the fact that "no register or book of records of the acts of the provincial governments of about the period of Governor Maynez incumbency" could be found, and the surveyor general was depending on (what was left of) the "old archives preserved in his office." However, "it appears that Maynes did make, in the year 1814, a verbal grant to a number of individuals at Galisteo for a grant there, and that in the year 1822 the alcalde by direction of the ayuntamiento of April 8 of that year placed certain individual parties in formal possession of those lands which he states they had been occupying and cultivating during the previous six years, some of them, it appears, being the identical individuals named as grantees in the claim of 1814."[38]

Nevertheless, it was decided by the courts that José Manrique (1808–15), not Alberto Maynez (1815–17), was governor in 1814. So the trial ended badly for the heirs of Galisteo. On December 2, 1871, the claimants were forced to relinquish all right and title to "that portion of the said Galisteo Town Grant which conflict[ed] with or [lay] within the limits of the grant confirmed to E. W. Eaton [San Cristóbal]."[39] The confirmation of the 1814/16 grant by Governor Melgares in 1822 was disregarded, and nothing seems to have been decided about all the land contained in that original grant that did *not* conflict with the San Cristóbal grant.[40]

When the case was lost, Galisteo men apparently made some kind of private settlement with Eaton that allowed them some use of the land they had claimed, which now lay officially on the San Cristóbal grant.[41] So at least part of the Cadial/Tacubaya remained in some sense an ejido, or common grazing/agricultural land. This quasi-resolution of the eastern tract was not, however, the end of litigation on the Galisteo grant, since in its original form it also included land west, south, and north of the village.

In February 1878, the iron horse that would transform the landscape as much as flesh-and-blood equines had done three centuries earlier came roaring into New Mexico. The Atchison, Topeka & Santa Fe (AT&SF) Railroad won the race with the Denver and Rio Grande (D&RG) to get over the Ratón Pass, becoming the main line between New Mexico Territory and "the States"—its eastern terminus at Atchison, Kansas, on the Missouri River. In February 1880, the tracks reached the foot of Apache Canyon at Galisteo Junction (renamed Lamy Junction in January 1881), where pusher engines were stationed to assist trains over Glorieta Pass. A different company, the New Mexico & Southern Pacific Railroad, continued

Ben Wittick, *Atchison, Topeka & Santa Fe Engine #137 ("Baby"), at Glorieta Summit*, October 1880. (Palace of the Governors Photo Archives, NMHM/DCA neg. no. 015870.)

Joan Myers, *Cerro Colorado*, ca. 2013. The track is still visible where stones were slid down from the top. At the foot of the hill is a gravel quarry on the south bank of the Río Galisteo.

westward through Cerrillos, reaching Albuquerque by April.[42] Thanks to its altitude, the capital, eighteen uphill miles away, had been bypassed by the main line—an indignity as well as a major economic blow. The Church sold Archbishop Lamy's land grant to the railroad, and Lamy was instrumental in raising money for a branch spur to Santa Fe. His zeal for the spur line may be partially explained by the fact that it made possible the transportation of stone from Cerro Colorado for his new cathedral, then under construction in Santa Fe. The Cerro, adjacent to the burgeoning town of Lamy, was quarried into a stepped form resembling a cloud terrace that would have been meaningful to the Pueblos who had built a shrine on the eastern side of the hill centuries before. The shrine was left undisturbed, although the six-hundred-year-old Pueblo ruins at Manzanares and at Lamy Junction underwent their share of damage when the Rio Galisteo was displaced from its natural bed to accommodate the railroad, causing disastrous floods.

The arrival of the railroad was rivaled in 1880 by the extraordinary sighting of a monstrous air machine, or "Asian balloon," that dropped a "magnificent flower" and a message in "Japanese" on "fine silk-like paper" in Galisteo Junction/Lamy—forerunner of UFOs that have been spotted in the area to this day.[43] The same year, there was a major train wreck near the raw new railroad town, which boasted boarding houses, bars, gambling establishments, and probably a brothel, and a new hotel opened in April 1881.[44] Lamy became a hangout for gangsters and outlaws. A newspaper reported the arrest of gamblers headquartered in Lamy who had "made themselves obnoxious to the public." Deputy Sheriff Tony Nels "went down on the train yesterday to take the wanted in out of the wet."[45] A May 1, 1881, newspaper article headed "The Trouble at Lamy" noted the arrest of one "Winter Monkey Jack."[46]

Librado Valencia of Galisteo had a saloon and store in Lamy, but Browne and Manzanares was the largest mercantile establishment, and it was robbed by the "Ike Stockton clique" from Farmington and southern Colorado; one of the culprits was hanged in Socorro. "Good brick [was] made in Lamy Junction" in 1881; in 1883, "rocks from Lamy or Manzanares" (a hamlet just east of Lamy) were sold for $5 per 100 pounds.[47] Despite its reputation, Lamy acquired a post office in 1884. As late as May 7, 1890, a report in the *Daily New Mexican* headlined "Desperadoes at Lamy" named two men who "terrorized the town," holding up two trains and "a number of Prominent Citizens."[48] Lamy's population in the wake of the railroad briefly soared to 2,000, leveling off at about 200 by 1890 when it settled down as a small Hispano village. One factor in its decline was the switch from coal to diesel, eliminating the need for the roundhouse.

Along with overgrazing, the deforestation of the highlands, aggravated in the 1880s when the railroad arrived and began to cut timber for ties, was a major cause of flooding and erosion. The railways also cut across streams, changing their natural courses. Soon plans were being hatched to reroute the tracks. On October 30, 1884, the *New Mexican* reported: "Several leading citizens of Galisteo . . . bring in the good news that the officers of the AT&SF at Topeka headquarters are considering the advisability of running the main line of the road direct through Galisteo. . . . The intention now, it is understood, is to straighten the line and run it over the line originally surveyed. This would seem to be a wise move. Galisteo is a flourishing settlement of one thousand inhabitants. . . . The annual wool clip (twice a year) of the Galisteo region is estimated at not less than 300,000 pounds a year, and with any accommodations at all for shipping cattle, the railroad company could here also do a large business. But the railroad never came through Galisteo proper. A Señor [Agapito?] Sena, who owned land near today's CR 42, refused to have it run through his ranch, forcing a change of plans. The tracks were laid a few miles to the west.

Galisteo, for decades the only town in the basin, was now joined by Lamy to the east and Cerrillos, a mining boomtown, to the west. The railroad brought workers and immigrants from all over the world, including Jewish and Lebanese merchants and several Chinese.[49] The 1880 census noted two new Anglo residents—John Adams and his wife, born in Ohio and Kansas, never mentioned again—as well as David Filleton ("black") married to Maria ("Indian"), both born in New Mexico. One Frank Gornes was a "huckster" born in Portugal. Curiously, medical conditions were documented, including a sixty-three year old "mother" with "disease of the brain" and a child with "inflammation of the brain." A number of children appeared to have serious disabilities.

Cerrillos, once a candidate for state capital, boasted a hotel, an opera house, and many cantinas.[50] It beat out Lamy as a hotbed of murder and intrigue. In 1893 the newspaper referred to a "half breed" named Friday who was involved with a "notorious woman" called Bronco Mary (María Sisneros).[51] The robberies, ambushes, and shootings were covered by two newspapers: the *Cerrillos Rustler* in 1888 and the *Galisteo Valley Democrat* in 1893.[52] Several photographers were already at work in Cerrillos. George C. Bennett made photos and stereo cards of mining districts in spring 1880. He worked for W. Henry Brown's Studio in Santa Fe. The anthropologist Adolph Bandelier refused to work with Bennett because he "call[ed] every Spaniard a dog and every Indian a brute."[53] Nicolas Brown was also in the area and in 1906, Aaron B. Craycraft went "again" to San Cristóbal, where he photographed the Pueblo ruins, and then went west to the petrified forest in a covered wagon.[54]

While these newcomers thirsted and thrived in the 1880s, old Galisteo remained an isolated farming town, although it was not free of the late-nineteenth-century propensity for violence. (Marc Simmons reports that "things were so bad that some dance hall keepers installed signs that read: 'Please don't shoot the musicians. They're doing the best they can.'"[55]) Constable Frank (Francisco) Chávez from Galisteo brought in Aban Lucero, who was charged with the murder of sheepherder Teodoro Romero, through evidence of footprints in the snow. In 1892 Chávez himself, who had resigned as sheriff of Santa Fe County under suspicion of corruption, died in an ambush.[56] In 1893 Juan Gonzales shot and killed Severiano Peña, a clerk in a village store.[57] A year later, another murder was reported: "The town of Galisteo has been having quite a lively time, according to reports, A day or two ago Felipe Trujillo was assaulted with stones by a young man named Eulogio Ortega. . . . [He was] placed under a $300 bond. Yesterday Atanasio Padilla was also assaulted seriously though not fatally hurt . . . a mixture of whiskey and politics seems to have been at the bottom of both troubles."[58]

A decade later, similar reports were still hitting the papers. Dario Mora and Pedro López were badly cut in a drunken fight in Galisteo; Mora ended up at a doctor's office in Cerrillos with his arm half cut off. The newspaper reported that "there was trouble" near Galisteo: "Perhaps too much of the stuff they drink in Kentucky had a hand in getting up the bad blood which made things look ugly for a little while."[59]

In the early 1890s, the Las Vegas area was plagued by the notorious outlaw Vicente Silva and his gang, known as the Society of Bandits. One of their victims was an unnamed Galisteo man who kept his cattle near Ojo de la Vaca. The story goes that one day when he went to check on his herd, he found the Silva gang killing cows. They murdered him and

"1850s" Photograph of Donaciano Angel House and the Old Church. The date of this photograph, from an undated newspaper article, ca. 1970s, is probably later, at least the 1880s. The caption reads, in part: "LOOK INTO THE PAST. . . . Galisteo shortly after New Mexico became a territory of the United States more than 100 years ago. Valentino Anaya . . . who was born and raised in the village, said the old photo was sent to him by another former Galisteo resident from Arizona. He said [it] was taken by a visitor to the village in the early 1850s . . . the old Galisteo church, demolished some 40 years ago, is in the background. Except for the old Angel home in right foreground and the adobe residence adjoining the church, all other buildings have long since vanished."

J. R. Riddle, *Galisteo Church and Plaza*, 1884. (Palace of the Governors Photo Archives, NMHM/DCA neg. no. 76054.)

threw his body on a fire. His little dog was shot at but escaped, running home with one of his owner's boots to alert the village, leading them to the scene of the crime.[60] There were some Silvas living in Galisteo, but nothing indicates they were involved. During this period, Lamy was invaded by Apaches, Comanches, Kiowas, and Navajos traveling to and from Taos, Picuris, and Pecos fairs. Never a dull moment.

Galisteo's old adobe capilla on The Hill was still in use in 1880, though in poor condition. In 1882–84 it was replaced by a brand-new church across from the Ortiz y Davis home on "El Camino Real" (as villages' main roads were called, although the famous Royal Road lay to the west). The church was built under the auspices of Archbishop Lamy on land donated by the Ortiz y Davis family. Lamy is said to have been a frequent visitor to the Ortizes and the Pinos and the source of their heirloom fruit trees. The new church, with its pitched roof, was perceived as "French," due to Lamy's influence.[61] A photograph taken soon after its completion shows the building standing alone in the midst of a vast empty plaza backed by many houses on and around The Hill; no trees are visible anywhere. The stained-glass window of Santa Lucia, stone buttresses, low spiked wall, double facing cross, and handicap ramp were all added over the next centuries.

J. R. Riddle, *View of Galisteo from the West (The Hill)*, ca. 1884. (Palace of the Governors Photo Archives, NMHM/DCA neg. no. 76053.)

In the 1880s, Adolph Bandelier was told by a Father Mailluchet, "There is a Saint here [in Galisteo] from [Pueblo] San Cristóbal, and an old painting from 1648."[62] A painting of the Virgin holding the Christ Child purportedly had hung over the altar of Galisteo churches for centuries, but Doña Josefa Ortiz y Davis kept it in her home for many years, citing the old church's bad condition; the painting and its frame were deteriorating. She said the canvas had once been "much longer" and the earlier frame was "very beautiful."[63] Archbishop Lamy took the painting to Santa Fe, and for some reason it was cut down to its present size. Bandelier was also shown several paintings on "buffalohide" (buckskin, or *gamuza*), one of which was a "San Cristóbal of that pueblo, a horrid picture, and a better-executed painting of Nuestra Señora de Begonia, 1608." The latter is one of two hide paintings still in the current church. The former is a crucifixion.[64]

Aside from the Civil War Peticolas sketch, there are no known images of the Spanish-speaking village of Galisteo before the 1880s, when J. R. Riddle's photographs, taken around 1884, show a flourishing town. The Ortiz and Pino orchards lay along both sides of the Rio Galisteo, bordered by mostly unfenced grazing lands. The east side of The Hill was built up with corrals and houses. Across the roughly defined, dirt plaza in front of the new church stands the Ortiz y Davis hacienda and some small adobes. Beyond the fields and orchards lining the river, the village was windy, sunbaked, and treeless except for an occasional cottonwood in the sparse bosque. Precious water could not be wasted. Door-side cisterns on The Hill were filled by rain or water from the river, hauled by local men in wagons, a system that continued until the early 1960s. Into the next century, the early settlement on The Hill and the community below continued to expand with new and larger homes.

Galisteo House with Well or Cistern, ca. 1926. (Palace of the Governors Photo Archives, NMHM/DCA neg. no. 21083.)

The new church and plaza created a village center that lasted until 1936, when NM 41 was rerouted to barge right through it. José Ortiz y Pino III visualized the old days when "the houses in the center all had benches out front. Girls would walk across the bridge to La Otra Vanda. The plaza was a promenade, a park, a place to see people."[65] As architectural historian Chris Wilson writes, plazas "capture social interaction from intimate to public in one frame. . . . Plaza, church, and congregation became the three-part module for the creation of a community." He and his coauthors point out that one of the culprits for the neglect and abandonment of many New Mexico plazas was the automobile. Another is the "American predilection for privacy, mobility, and sprawl."[66] Short of an unlikely bypass of downtown Galisteo (an idea that is periodically raised, and razed), the village will never be able to revive its plaza, but plans to commemorate it continue. Religious processions on various saints' days often took place around the church, a tradition that barely survives today.

Meanwhile, the histories of the western and eastern Galisteo Basin were diverging. There are amazingly few crossovers of names and references between Galisteo and Cerrillos, where land uses differed. While the two sides of the basin share grasslands and forested borders, the mineral-rich west, with its exotic rock formations, engendered far more "modern" commerce, while the east remained traditionally pastoral. Galisteños farmed to sustain their families, raising sheep, cattle, horses, corn, pinto beans, wheat, and probably a few other crops, as well as hay, on the Cadial. Although some villagers worked as hardscrabble miners in the winters, and wealthier ones, like Luis Lobato, invested in the mines to the west, most remained attached to the land. The Galisteo Mining District (named not for the village, but for the river downstream) was formed in 1879, when "over a thousand Colorado miners"

William Baxter, *Gold Mine Scar on the Ortiz Mountains*, 1990s. Almost two centuries later, this huge scar was the end result of the 1820s gold rush in the Ortiz Mountains. It has since been largely restored by the Santa Fe Botanical Gardens. (Courtesy of Ardeth Baxter.)

descended upon the Cerrillos Hills, setting off the 1879–84 Cerrillos mining boom.[67] San Marcos Pueblo west of Galisteo had been the source of much pre-European turquoise trade, but the gem was not valued by colonial powers. In 1889 turquoise was no more valuable than hard coal. By 1893 it was worth more than gold, spurred by the American Turquoise Co., agent for the Tiffany jewelry company. That year 63 percent of all turquoise produced in the United States was mined in the Cerrillos Hills, much from the largest source at Turquoise Hill, renamed the Tiffany Mine. By 1912 the turquoise market had crashed and the "sky stone" was valueless again, only to be resurrected in the 1930s with the burgeoning popularity of Navajo and Pueblo jewelry.

The Timber Culture Act enacted in 1873 and the Timber Culture and Stone Act of 1878 were intended to "transform bleak plains of the west by having land-hungry men cultivate trees in exchange for a farm. This was a visionary dream and no more," since people took the land and planted no trees.[68] When it became obvious that the Homestead Act's 160 acres was not enough to support a family in arid lands, the US Congress passed the Desert Lands Act in 1877. Now 640 acres could be acquired, but that was still too small for stock range and too large for a small farmer to irrigate. It required no residence and became yet another abused source of free land. A rancher or speculator had only to secure title to the water supply to control land for miles around. In the 1860s and 1870s there was "an almost complete encirclement of the Hispano domain of New Mexico" by Anglo cattlemen. One settler could apply for a whole township and not even settle it. Most land around the settlements was already private property. False proofs abounded, and constant boundary disputes ensued.[69]

Since around 1850, the western cattle industry had been extremely profitable. Millions of pounds of beef were shipped out as far as Europe. In the 1870s, as population increased, the biggest change in the landscape was the ever-growing herds of sheep (and goats) whose sharp little hooves and strong teeth devastated the fragile grasslands and sparse water sources. Livestock in New Mexico increased from 300,000 head in 1870 to over 2 million in 1890. But the benefits from industrialization of farming and livestock brought by the Americans toward the end of the nineteenth century rarely trickled down to small farmers like those in Galisteo unless they were working for large landowners. In 1884, Demetrio Leyba, described as a "well-known citizen of Galisteo," was in Santa Fe trying to sell wool, found no buyers, and had to go to Las Vegas to sell.

Until the 1880s, livestock ran free throughout the Galisteo Basin, identified by brands and earmarks. In keeping with the western "fence out" tradition, Galisteo farmers in the Cadial were ordered to enclose their farmlands to keep San Cristóbal cattle out. Fences also protected the acequias from damage by free-range stock. In the 1870s, much of the Southwest was gullied by floods. By 1885, cattle had trampled the banks of the Rio Galisteo, causing erosion and silting up the streams that were the villagers' sole water supply. In the late 1880s, severe winters and blizzards in the Northern Plains caused huge cattle losses. The rapid decline of the cattle industry in New Mexico was also due to droughts, overstocking, and low prices.[70]

Galisteo's irrigation ditch system must have suffered, but some farmers apparently did not. In 1884, Nicolás Pino painted a rosy picture of a "prosperous" Galisteo for a local reporter: "Grass is abundant and cattle of all kinds are rolling fat. Lambing season closed most satisfactorily. The wool clips are all that could be expected. Several thousand head of cattle and sheep are fattening on adjacent ranges. Nine thousand pounds of wool were shipped from Galisteo this week."[71] In his journals of September 1889, Bandelier noted that a bad drought had resulted in failed crops in Anton Chico and Pecos: "Galisteo alone has fair crops. It rained there more, although only three good rains in the summer, and they have been able to irrigate in the Arroyo of San Cristóbal."[72]

Fences—their types and locations—tell a story. Widespread fencing over western ranchland is a relatively recent phenomenon.[73] Fencing the frontier meant domestication of both the wilderness and the "wild" people it contained. Before the American invasion, fences were unnecessary because sheep were guarded by herders, usually small boys facing Indian rustlers and wild animals in the course of a dangerous day's work. A number of these children were kidnapped or killed. Well into the twentieth century, boys were taken out of school in the spring to spend long lonely months in distant pastures. As open range diminished, cattle ranchers began to fence in their pastures, interrupting the routes of some of the great cattle drives. Individual ownership began to overwhelm communal uses and open range. In 1885–88, New Mexico was one of the top three states for land fenced, although laws alternated for and against. Around 1895, open-range ranching diminished, and in 1899, the New Mexico Territorial Assembly passed an act to prevent overgrazing due to fencing and overstocking.[74]

Back in the day, the barriers were made of thorny Osage orange or even elk antlers; adobe walls were topped with prickly pear, forerunner of razor wire. Photographs of Galisteo

Gorras Blancas, A Re-enactment, 1975. Taken by an anonymous photographer from the *Las Vegas Optic* during the Mora Fiestas, 1975. (Courtesy of Claudio Chacón.)

from the 1880s show corrals made of adobe or masonry walls or the still common "coyote fences"—tall, slim, cedar or aspen posts tied together and grounded sporadically by a thicker cedar post. Stone walls were loose or mortared, reserved for valuable crops such as orchards and vineyards, to discourage local plundering and wildlife. San Cristóbal was fenced, then unfenced, then fenced again. Juan Ortiz testified that he helped fence the Cadial in 1885. The first wire fences were flimsy and dangerous for livestock, but barbed wire, perfected and patented in 1874 by J. F. Glidden—was far more effective, heralding major changes to the land: "As Light as air, Stronger than whisky, Cheaper than Dust," claimed an advertisement in the 1870s.[75]

There is a certain finality to fenced land, even if the boundaries marked are inaccurate (as they often are) or even illegal. A fence was a claim, defining private property and manifest destiny. It represented spatial power, somewhat subtler than invasion but with similar results. Like any power struggle, it sparked violence. The Anglo appropriation of common lands and the depletion of the traditional land grants by speculators did not go unchallenged. Las Gorras Blancas (the White Caps, or Hoods) was an Hispano guerrilla group formed in 1889 to protest land issues in the area. Based in Las Vegas, then New Mexico's largest city, it was led by brothers Juan José, Pablo, and Nicanor Herrera. Anselmo Arellano calls them "probably the most secretive and close-knit association of men ever to exist in the Territory of New Mexico."[76] Native Hispanos composed close to 80 percent of the state's population, and the movement spread to other communities, including Galisteo, joining ranks with the national populist labor party, the Knights of Labor (Caballeros de Labor). Their norteño movement was called La Mano Negro (the Black Hand). Standing up for the poor and the workers, Las Gorras Blancas destroyed bridges and railway tracks, demanding fair prices for lumber and ties. When Governor Bradford Prince investigated, he found many prominent citizens were sympathetic to their activities. Apparently modeled on the White Caps of Illinois, in action they eerily resembled the Ku Klux Klan. With white hoods hiding their identities, they tore down fences restricting access to communal grazing and water and destroyed barns and other property belonging to those profiting from land grant grabs. They were taken seriously enough that Charlie Siringo, a Pinkerton detective from Denver, was hired to infiltrate the group. In 1890 Adolph Bandelier noted in his journals, "It seems that [the White Caps] committed some damages in Galisteo, cutting wire fences." In 1891 he cites an article in the *New Mexican* about "a brutal attack on Pablo Ortiz in Galisteo several nights before. Pablo, son of Rafael Ortiz y Pineda, a prominent Republican, had been attacked by six masked men, who had beaten him and left him for dead," departing to find Librado Valencia, another prominent Republican of the community.[77] The attackers were believed to have been Gorras Blancas.

An anonymous poem, "Desorden de Dia, Desorden de la Noche [Confusion by Day, Confusion by Night] From Galisteo, N.M. Agosto 1891," printed in *El Nuevo Mexicano*, was written by someone skeptical of the Gorras Blancas. It read in part: "De noche causando ruinas [By night causing ruin]/ Y de día a lo señor . . . [And by day acting like gentlemen . . .]/ ¡Caballeros de Labor! [Knights of Labor!]/ Paseandose en las cantinas . . . [Strolling through the saloons]/ Y contra el gobernador [And against the government]/ Y codiciando oficinas [And coveting offices]/ Ahora, si que estamos peor [Now we're worse off]."[78] In 1891 the group claimed 1,500 members "and growing," but by the end of that year they were subsiding, and the United States had appointed the Court of Private Land Claims for former Mexican territories. A newspaper article remarked, "The reign of terror that has existed in the southern part of Santa Fe County has ended." No one was ever convicted of the Gorras Blancas' alleged crimes.

Although many Anglos invested in properties in the Galisteo Basin from the mid-nineteenth century on, only Sylvester Davis put down deep roots in the village itself. He spoke fluent Spanish, and his wife, Josefa Ortiz, was related to powerful families and fully integrated into local culture. In some of his ventures Davis partnered with his in-laws, the increasingly prosperous Ortiz (then Ortiz y Pino) family. Juan Ortiz II and Antonio José Ortiz were among Galisteo's wealthier citizens. Davis had several vocations. He had built and worked at mills, and once settled in Galisteo, he opened a saloon and a store and became the postmaster in 1879.[79] He held the government contract for a foraging station and commissary until the 1890s,[80] visible as piles of hay behind the hacienda within the walled compound in the Riddle photograph of the village around 1884.[81] Concha Ortiz y Pino de Kleven recalled that "although the Davis family was relatively well-off financially, it was not 'terribly rich.'"[82] However, in June 1891, the *Rustler* mentioned "the commodious mansion and fine ranch of Captain Sylvester Davis," who belonged to the Republican Club of Galisteo. In the 1870 census, Josefa's

Pedro Ortiz y Pino, Pablita Davis, and Manuela Ortiz y Pino, ca. 1880s. (Courtesy of La Herencia Archive.)

mother, Paula (Pablita) Ortiz, was the richest person in Galisteo and knew how to read and write (though in an earlier census she was listed as illiterate).[83] She died in 1881, according to some documents, or in 1880, as inscribed on her gravestone. Concha Ortiz y Pino describes Josefa's "beloved brother Juan" Ortiz, "who ran a small store and let her maintain a generous charge account there. . . . The family had many cattle, but after the rustlers were through stealing, there wasn't that much left. Yet there was always food for all."[84]

According to one villager, Davis had a reputation for grabbing any land that was not nailed down, which would not have been insignificant, since little was fully titled. (One of his descendants disputes this account: "We owned everything already.") Many villagers had and have no official deeds; if they were lucky, they possessed an hijuela. Victoria Davis Sánchez writes: "Initially, Sylvester Davis acquired the Cadial land grant and raised sheep." Davis did own land in the Cadial (though certainly not the whole grant) and participated in some of the early twentieth-century lawsuits. In 1891, he patented 164 acres on "a strip located between the Galisteo Creek and the townsite on the hill" that included his hacienda. "Although parcels within the Davis patent have changed ownership over the past century," writes historian David Kammer, "many of the contributing properties within the historic district lie within the patent area or just to the east of it and can be traced to members of the extended Ortiz and Davis y Ortiz families."[85] The Davises "allowed many villagers to build homes on the land but they never gave them deeds for the land."[86] Mineral rights remained the property of the US government.

Marion Steele (with a little help from José Ortiz y Pino III) imagined rooms in the busy hacienda where smiths, wheelwrights, harness makers and others worked, rooms where sick animals were treated, and rooms where ammunition was stored, as well as "hornos blackened from baking. It was the long, north portal where women worked at their ceaseless jobs."[87] Helping Josefa in the house were "an Ortiz cousin named Ambrosia," her thirteen-year-old granddaughter Angélica Leyba, and "a Santo Domingo woman named Felipa [Lucero]."[88] "Grandma loved the Indians," recalled Concha Ortiz y Pino. "She was one of the few people who did," perhaps because of her own alleged Native blood.[89]

In 1894, Juan Ortiz's wife, Concepción Pino, died at the age of forty-two; she is commemorated by a tall, elegant tombstone in the old campo santo. Their eldest son, José Ortiz y Pino, born in 1874, married his cousin, Sylvester and Josefa Davis's daughter Pablita, and built his family compound across from her family's hacienda on what was then Calle Grande (now Via La Puente), where they produced nine children. Nicolas Pino, who sported a voluminous white beard in his illustrious old age, died of Parkinson's disease in Galisteo in 1896 at age 77. He and his wife, Juana, who died in 1893, are said by the family to be buried in unmarked graves beneath the oratorio in Galisteo's "old cemetery."[90]

Meanwhile, the San Cristóbal grant story rumbled on. In 1873, Eaton once again requested a resurvey of the San Cristóbal grant and once again he was denied.[91] In 1874, he and his wife sold a large part of the grant (one-third to one-half) to Saron and Hattie Laughlin of San Francisco for forty-five cents an acre.[92] Eaton mortgaged his remaining portion several times, once to Seligman Bros. of Santa Fe. In 1875, he tried again to have his land resurveyed.

Lucy R. Lippard, *Tombstone of Concepción Pino in Old Galisteo Cemetery* (at right). On the gravestone: En Memoria de Concepción Pino y Ortiz que fallecio el 17 de Nov. A.D. 1894 a la edad de 42 años 3 meses 16 días . . . nació en Chihuahua esposa de Juan Ortiz la hija de Nicolas Pino y Juanita Rascon de Pino.

By 1876, he had sold an undivided half of the grant (except those interests in that half which had already been purchased by Laughlin) to T. B. Catron, who also owned the four to five thousand sheep involved in a partido contract ending September 15, 1877. Eaton was to raise them and split all profits with Catron, a common sharecropping contract among *patrones* and other landowners, usually peons. A mortgage of half the grant (a quitclaim deed) went to Charles Gildersleeve, Eaton's son-in-law, a prominent Santa Fe Democrat and not incidentally an occasional business partner of T. B. Catron. Nicolás Pino was still involved as well; his and Catron's agreement with Eaton stated that they owned half the grant, although all the interests of the original claimants had not yet been acquired. In 1878, Eaton sold his share of San Cristóbal to Gildersleeve for $1,000.[93]

At first, the resurvey looked encouraging for the land grant heirs. The US secretary of the interior decided Eaton was entitled to part of the grant, but so were the descendants of the original grantees, who had only been threatened with loss of their lands but had not forfeited their claims. However, the "triangular" survey of the "rectangular" grant on which this decision was based was "obviously erroneous," and a new survey was ordered.[94] The Shaw survey of 1879 showed San Cristóbal's full 81,032.67 acres belonging to Eaton and moved the boundary four miles to the west, cutting heavily into Galisteo's pastures and timberlands. Villagers learned of this expansion only through posted notices in English, which many could not read, and they protested: "We would be reduced to great misery and calamity and as though we were imprisoned and oppressed with only our little tracts of land, without the consolation of having liberty where to feed our animals . . . which every poor man may have for the support of his poor family."[95]

On July 14, 1879, James Williamson, commissioner of the US General Land Office, decreed that the Shaw survey was accurate but that the grantees had not lost their land; it only remained to determine the boundaries, which he cavalierly left "to the interested parties to identify and adjust their respective claims within the grant by mutual agreement and by partition or other appropriate proceedings in the proper judicial tribunals."[96] In 1880, the San Cristóbal grant was owned by a passel of people, including Saron Laughlin, who had one-third, Gildersleeve, who held "a large portion," a group of twenty-three to forty Hispano settlers with unspecified shares, and the Catron/Pino interests. However, on December 8, 1880, President Rutherford B. Hayes assigned the entire grant to Eaton (who had already sold half his share) and to "the remaining original grantees [twenty-three Galisteo landowners] who had not forfeited their rights to the land by a non-compliance with the conditions of the grant . . . their heirs and assigns forever." This sounds favorable for the Galisteans, but Bowden says Williamson dismissed their claims on the grounds that they failed to show title or interest.[97] At the same time, according to Christina Mednick's summary of the San Cristóbal land grants, the grantees still owned "perhaps 1,000 acres" mostly near Galisteo (the Cadial/Tacubaya portion), along with Catron and Nicolás Pino, who had picked up a sizeable number of tracts. From 1880 to 1888 Catron, continued to buy small plots on the San Cristóbal grant from original grantees and heirs.[98]

Frank Mendoza (Mendonca), a Portugese immigrant, lived at the ranch as "agent," representing the owners at San Cristóbal from 1895 to 1905, after which he moved to Galisteo. During one of the Cadial trials, he said he was ordered to "run the sheep off," as well as trespassers; he took care of the grant but not the Cadial, because he "didn't want to fight the people of Galisteo . . . Laughlin told me it would be all right." In 1883, Mendoza was permitted by "old man [Nicolás] Pino" to stake horses on the Cadial when there was no crop.[99] Others also testified that Eaton, who was generally known for beneficence along these lines, perhaps because he was married to a local woman and was a compadre of Juan Ortiz, never obstructed their use of the Cadial. Although this statement was repeated by virtually every witness in the multiple trials, the history of "interference" with village agriculture on the Cadial does seem to go back to Eaton. Anastacio Sandoval testified that before 1884, Eaton got an injunction to keep Galisteans from cutting hay on San Cristóbal. Cadial strip owners Luciano Chávez and Fernando Peña opposed it and were prosecuted. Then Eaton came to Galisteo and in 1855–56 asked the Cadial owners for "portions of grass that was good to cut" and *they* gave *him* permission to cut in the Cadial. Sandoval, who was raised in Galisteo, living "down on the plains," testified later that Eaton gave *them* permission to cut hay there and he got a third of the crop.[100]

In October 1883, Juan Sandoval had paid $200 to have a survey made of a large area including the Galisteo Spring (Ojito), in preparation for the legal action nine years later concerning the original Galisteo grant, though he is not named. He may have died in the interim, as Jesús Gil Sandoval seems to have taken his place. While that grant had been virtually determined null and void in 1871, the part that overlapped the Cadial was resurrected in 1892 before the Court of Private Land Claims. Parallel to and intertwined with the San Cristóbal case, this one involved the common-lands Cadial/Tacubaya grants overlapping San Cristóbal, and also the original Galisteo grant. On August 19, lawyer James Brady filed a protest on behalf of Galisteños Ramón B. Chávez, Nicolás Pino, Antonio J. Ortiz, Juan Ortiz, Sylvester Davis, Luciano Chávez, and around thirty others, to reconfirm the Cadial and Tacubaya grants against the San Cristóbal resurvey, suing the United States for compensation for lost pasture and timberlands.[101] The resurvey had aided the Galisteans by upholding their rights, although simultaneously abetting Catron's plans to buy up those rights.[102]

Invoking the Treaty of Guadalupe Hidalgo, the claimants declared that San Cristóbal's resurvey "[would] result in damage not only to our lands, but also to a large number of the houses in our town, all against our rights. . . ." These landowners, disclaiming links with the 1871 Galisteo grant document that had been declared fraudulent, separated the Cadial from the Galisteo grant, producing legal proof of Mexican grants in 1822 (which of course *was* the Galisteo grant), 1843, and 1846, with evidence that their families had continuously occupied the area. (The lengthy list of names suggests that everyone in town, old claimants and newcomers, had signed on.[103]) There is a reference to an 1846 lot sold in 1856 "as a part of the public lands within the Grant of Galisteo, lying in the Cañada de San Cristóbal," implying that the Cadial was still considered part of the original Galisteo grant.[104] Among the witnesses was Robert B. Willison, who had surveyed the Cadial for fencing around 1885. He referred to a conversation in which Nicolás Pino said that no part of the Cadial was enclosed in the 1860s, when everybody ranged and grazed livestock over the "entire grant without any disturbance whatsoever," whether or not they claimed land there. Clearly the open land was usually used by mutual consent; it was only disputed when outside interests became paramount.

José Manuel Sandoval was among thirty or forty grantees who "agreed among themselves in regard to the boundaries; on the east they showed some old stone monuments" recognized by Tomás Roybal as the east boundary of the Cadial. The north and south lines were "mere arbitrary lines." The lands surrounding the house of Nicolás Pino ("his place of residence, I never knew of his claiming that under any written title"[105]) were cited, as well as his interests in the Cadial, where he cultivated lands, also in Tacubaya and San Cristóbal.

The court rejected the grantees' claims in 1894. They appealed, and this case was noted in a 1915 reprisal by more or less the same defendants. Kammer says the grantees were claiming 21,740 acres including the "townsite on the hill where the grantees had built their houses above the cultivated fields."[106] This is a new, expanded acreage figure. To further complicate matters, the original 9,000-acre Galisteo grant was referred to in 1892 as 24,000 acres, although the boundaries remained the same. The 1814/16 version of the Galisteo grant preceded and should have subsumed all the other grants, but its fate at the hands of the US courts (based on the inconclusive dates of the Maynez administration) eventually doomed the Cadial and Tacubaya grants. It also eternally complicated the San Cristóbal grant and by extension the remains of the overlapping Galisteo grant, forever muddying the waters of land titles in and around the village.

In 1895, a land tax was imposed, accelerating the loss of individually owned property on the grant lands. In testimony on the Cadial from August 10, 1895 (read into the 1909

Lucy R. Lippard, *Arroyo Atascoso/ San Cristóbal from Highway 41 Bridge*, 2018.

proceedings), Sylvester Davis, who lived in Galisteo and "kept a small store there," said he had "heard" that the land was donated to the people of Galisteo but no one ever occupied it. Nicolás Pino noted that he had begun to buy lands in Galisteo "since he removed there."[107]

Most of the Cadial on the east boundary of the village was good only for "temporal" or "dry" farming, mostly haying, although flood irrigation was used wherever possible when the San Cristóbal Arroyo, which ran through the center of the Cadial, was running.[108] The Sierrita del Jaspé—the highest land in the Cadial, on the south side, above the marshes (Las Lagunitas)—was used for grazing but not for haying. Three or four animals per allotment were allowed to graze on the whole Cadial after haying and after individuals' crops had been harvested. Grass was cut in La Vega (probably not the meadow on the west side of the creek after which the present-day road is named).[109] Everybody who claimed interest in the San Cristóbal grant ran stock on it when it was unfenced.

At one of the Cadial trials, José Antonio Anaya testified that the San Cristóbal Arroyo was dammed at both the east and west so that the floodwaters could be spread over a large tract of land. The arroyo water was used for animals and irrigation but was too alkaline for domestic use. The farmers came to Galisteo for drinking water. In the northwest corner of the grant, at the Cañada de Puertocito, which was "at a height," there was always "a great deal" of water, according to Anastacio Sandoval. Juan Ortiz and José Antonio Anaya were able to irrigate these northern lands even after the San Cristóbal Arroyo dams were destroyed.[110]

Transcripts of the twentieth-century Cadial trials provide fascinating, if often contradictory, recountings of socio-political interactions in the village. In 1890, when he was running for office, Catron was meeting with Galisteños and promising, under pressure, to respect the traditional ownership of the Cadial.[111] Librada Valencia testified that after Catron "got into politics," he often came to Galisteo "to have meetings with [them]. . . . During politics when he was there he was friendly with the people." Anastacio Sandoval testified that he saw the notices about the San Cristóbal resurvey in 1890, signed by Laughlin, Catron (whom Sandoval considered a "personal and political friend"), and Gildersleeve, posted on the north corner of Nicolás Pino's house at Galisteo. But the notices were in English and he couldn't read them. He was told that they prohibited people from cutting wood and grazing animals. That was why Sandoval went alone in October 1890 to Catron and told him he would lose the Eighth Precinct because of the San Cristóbal resurvey: "[The new line] goes right by the wall fence of the house of Don Nicolás Pino and the donation of the Cadial is cast 500–600 yards East of the San Cristobal line." Sandoval told Catron that the Cadial inside the San Cristóbal line was "the land that [was] part of the town and the inhabitants of the town," consisting of sixty-two sites "from the high hills of the Cañada del Norte to the foot of the hill of La Jara on the South there, maybe 2 1/2 miles more or less."

Catron told Sandoval to return the next morning and instructed him "to go to Galisteo and hold the meeting and . . . tell them in my own name that if I happen to have a right to that grant [San Cristóbal], I will respect their homes and their residences." Sandoval replied, "The donation of the Cadial is inside of the west line of the San Cristóbal Grant and that is the land that the town of Galisteo wants to have because that is the land that is a part of that town." Sandoval met with villagers and afterwards met Catron at Sylvester Davis's house, telling him, "Mr. Catron, they are satisfied. The ill feeling has stopped already and it is now as before, only among Democrats." Catron was a Republican at the time.[112]

In April 1890 Gildersleeve sold his portion of San Cristóbal for $1,000 to Laughlin, who became the majority owner of the grant. On April 24, 1890, the *Santa Fe Daily New Mexican* reported that Saron Laughlin ("a California Capitalist") "[would] fence the grant and stock it with several thousand head of graded breeding cattle, and that he [would] also seed large tracts of irrigable land to alfalfa. Mr. R. R. Elder [was] superintendent of the ranch." In June, the first large herd of cattle arrived. Catron and Pino then sued Laughlin on behalf of the grant heirs (i.e., themselves) for full title of all the farming lands they had been purchasing, itemizing ownership from Fernández's twenty-six original co-grantees to their ever-multiplying heirs, then to Catron and Pino. Laughlin claimed that the original grantees had abandoned their allotments, so it all reverted to Fernández to Eaton to him. A seven-year court battle ensued, ending in favor of Laughlin. On September 2, 1897, Catron and Nicolás Pino "entered into a supplemental agreement with Eathan W. Eaton whereby Catron and Pino were acknowledged to own a one-half interest in the grant" except for Laughlin's part. Eaton owned the other half, though not all the original claimants had yet been bought out. Catron, having acquired Pino's portion, appealed in his own name. "From this point on," writes Victor Westphall, "the arrangements became unbelievably complicated in a manner typical of Catron's financial affairs."[113]

The territorial population in 1890 was 153,076, excluding Indians, who were not citizens. In 1891, it was 158,000, and only 22 of 212 land grant claims had been patented. Eight were rejected outright, and almost 35 million acres were still in dispute. The territory thrived on wheeling and dealing. But ranchers were encountering growing competition from farmers. In 1893 the national economy collapsed, leading to a five-year depression. Prices for wool and meat dropped. Still, 1899 was reportedly the peak year in New Mexico for sheep, totaling some 5 million. By then only nine people in Galisteo owned sheep, with flocks ranging from 20 to 1,500. All listed losses to wild animals and exposure.[114] On March 3, 1899, the *New Mexican* reported that Antonio Gómez lost 300 sheep to wild animals and thieves, while Ambrocio Pino lost 350. Grizzlies were still being shot in the Ortiz Mountains. In November 1893, "a party of Nimrods went up to Galisteo" to hunt ducks on La Laguna, now a dry pan, rarely filled with water (although in the 1970s some young residents once tried hilariously to windsurf on it). A number of well-to-do Hispano families ran sheep at the turn of the twentieth century on considerable tracts of land to the west of Galisteo, among them Antonio and José Antonio Anaya, José de la Cruz Chávez, the Sandovals, and the Senas. Throughout this era the wealthier citizens of the village would go up to Santa Fe, registering at the Bon Ton Hotel and the Palace Hotel.[115] The newspaper recorded their visits. In 1894 Demetrio Leyba, who often stayed at the Bon Ton, was described as "Galisteo's handsomest citizen."[116]

Searching the legal records of property transfers over the past century and a half reveals a grotesquely complicated and often misrepresented history of land use from the various surveyors general and later from the federal Court of Private Land Claims (CPLC), founded in 1891, inspired by Hispano outrage at the broken promises of the Treaty of Guadalupe Hidalgo to protect the land rights of formerly Mexican citizens. By the time the CPLC adjourned in 1904, Congress had only approved around 155 grants, a little over two million acres in thirteen years.[117] In 1897, the controversial Sandoval case decreed that Spanish/Mexican common lands had never been legal, that the Mexican nation rather than the local grantees held title to all common lands granted before 1848. Over fifty-two million acres became federal lands, many of which were then opened up to homesteaders, who were required to build a one-room house and improve their properties.[118] This was a devastating loss to those small farmers and ranchers whose livelihoods depended on grazing, woodcutting, water, and resource gathering on the larger shared lands to augment the limited production from small farm tracts. At some point around the 1890s there was a small and short-lived community called Colorado on the Rio Galisteo between Galisteo and Lamy.

But they had competition from newcomers. "The country is settling up considerably," a newspaper reported. "A half dozen families from Fort Worth, Texas located near Galisteo this month, and others are en route. They appear to be thrifty people with good range stock. The citizens are glad to welcome them." The article goes on to mention Ambrosio Pino's herd of one hundred brood mares foaling well: "Losses by loco weed were none, whereas in the last five years, many died." One A. Kirschner had 75–100 horses on the Galisteo range, and two unnamed Portuguese brothers had started a chicken ranch. Even the fruit crop was "bountiful," doubling the ordinary yield. Galisteo was noted as "a delightful overnight stop" in the "Sunshine State," as New Mexico was dubbed by Governor Bradford Prince.[119]

Map of Reduced Galisteo Grant, 1898. "Santa Fe County, New Mexico. ALLOTMENTS. Surveyed by George H. Pradt, U. S. D. S., Sept 17, 1898 . . . Galisteo Grant 260.79 acres."

Yet all was not rosy. In the late 1880s, an outbreak of diphtheria (*litéria*)—the "child killer" caused by polluted water—ravaged the village.[120] Simona Baros García's mother lost

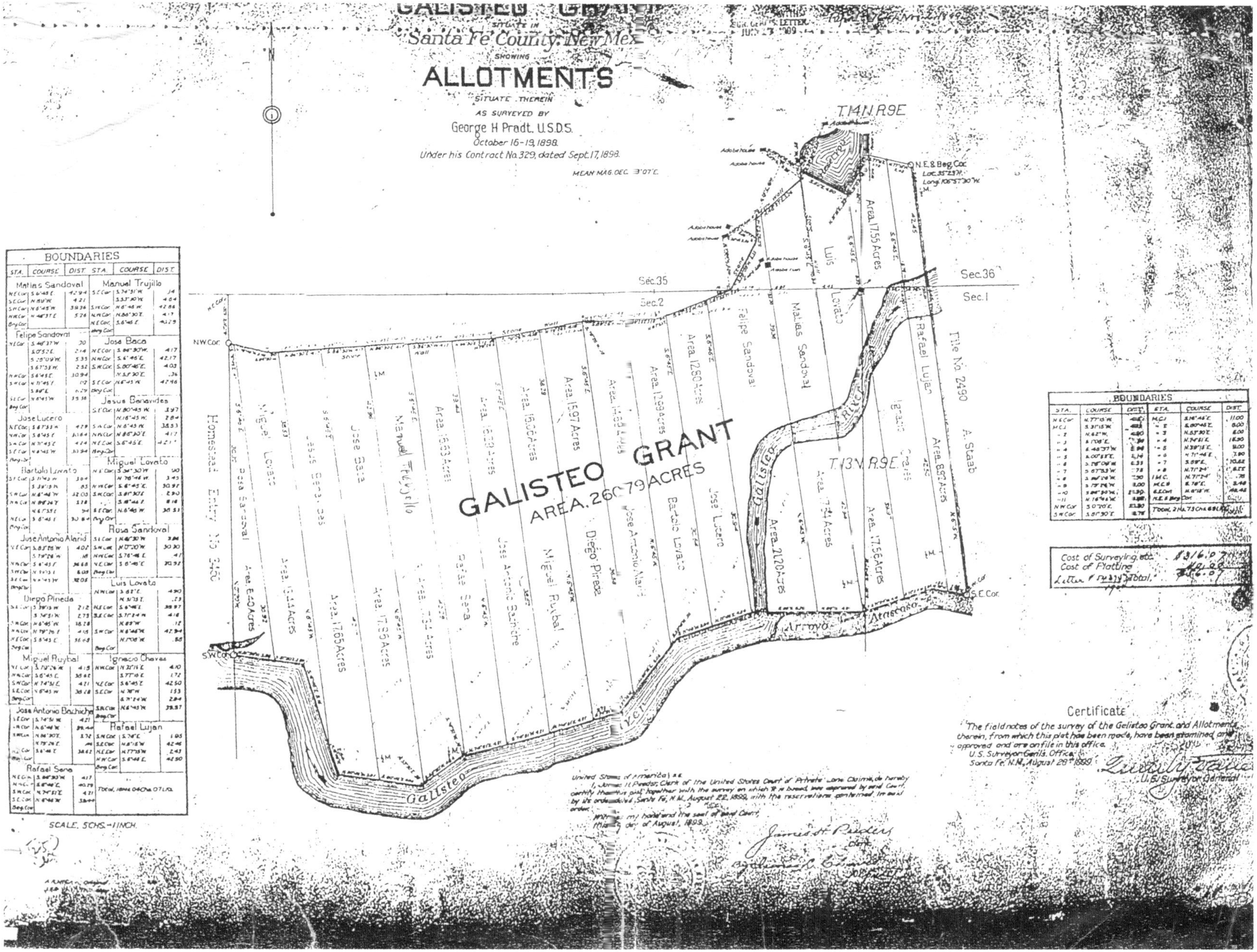

GALISTEO GRANT
SITUATE IN
Santa Fe County, New Mex
SHOWING
ALLOTMENTS
SITUATE THEREIN
AS SURVEYED BY
George H Pradt, U.S.D.S.
October 16-19, 1898.
Under his Contract No. 329, dated Sept. 17, 1898.
MEAN MAG. DEC. 13°07'E.
GALISTEO GRANT
AREA. 260.79 ACRES
T.14 N. R.9 E.
T.13 N. R.9 E.
Sec.35
Sec.36
Sec.2
Sec.1
NW Cor.
SW Cor.
S.E. Cor.
N.E. & Beg. Cor.
Homestead Entry No 3460
File No 2490 A. Staab
Galisteo River
Arroyo Atascoso
BOUNDARIES
Matias Sandoval
Manuel Trujillo
Felipe Sandoval
Jose Baca
Jesus Benavides
Jose Lucero
Bartolo Lovato
Miguel Lovato
Rosa Sandoval
Jose Antonio Alarid
Luis Lovato
Diego Pineda
Miguel Ruybal
Ignacio Chaves
Jose Antonio Bachiche
Rafael Lujan
Rafael Sena
SCALE. 5 CHS. = 1 INCH.
Cost of Surveying, etc.
Cost of Platting
Certificate
The fieldnotes of the survey of the Galisteo Grant and Allotments therein, from which this plat has been made, have been examined and approved and are on file in this office.
U.S. Surveyor Genl's. Office
Santa Fe, N.M., August 28th 1899.
U.S. Surveyor General

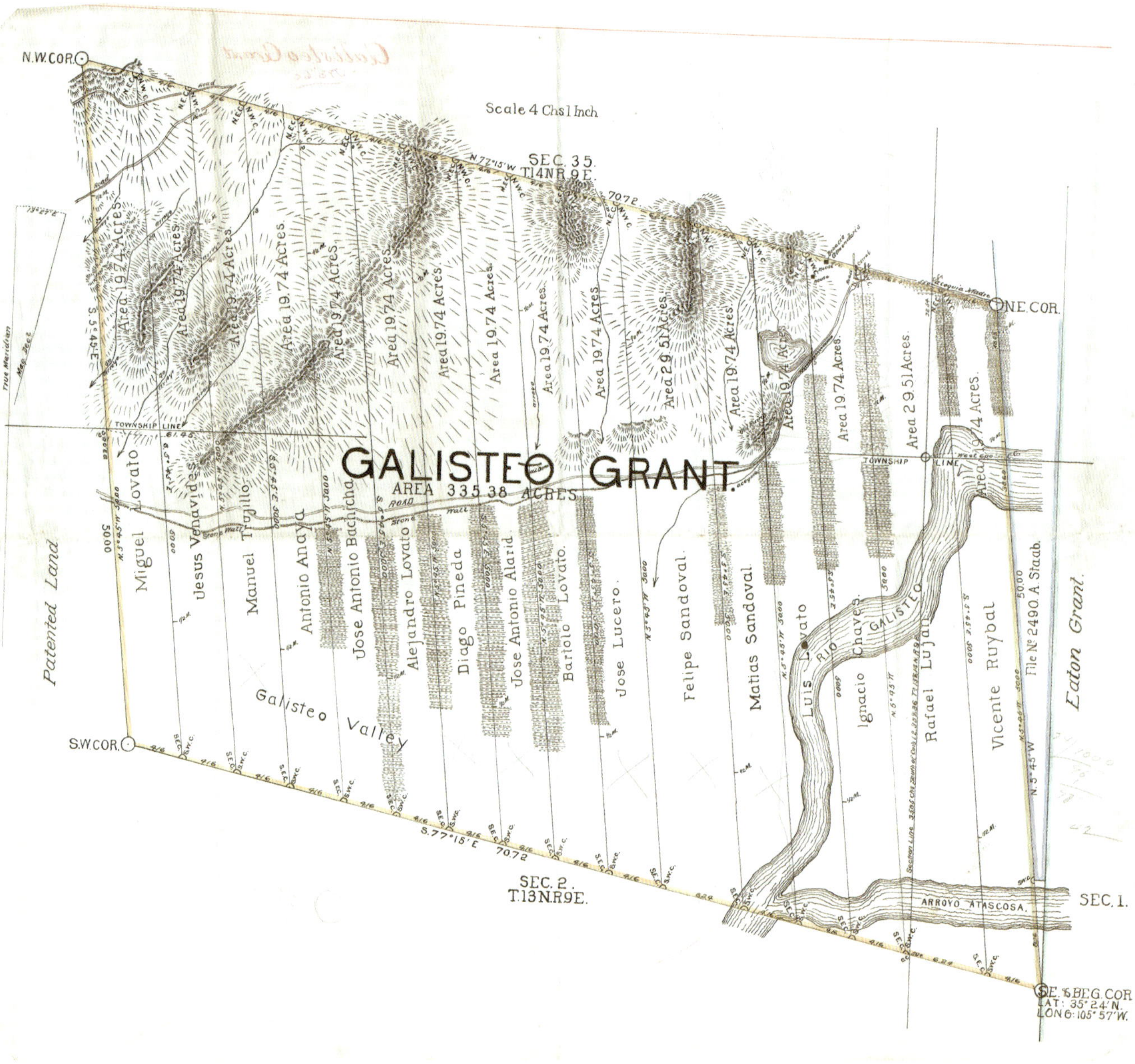

Alternative Galisteo Grant Map, 1898. (Courtesy of the University of New Mexico Thomas B. Catron Collection, Center for Southwest Research, mss29BC301#31.)

her entire first family and started over again. On May 15, 1891, the *Cerrillos Rustler* reported its sympathy on the death of Sylvester Davis's "bright little five-year-old daughter, which occurred at the Galisteo home." Then on May 29, it reported that the Davises had lost "Isabel, the bright four-year-old girl," apparently the second daughter lost in ten days.

On August 28, 1899, the almost century-old tale of the "Galisteo Grant" was concluded to no one's satisfaction. With a stroke of the pen it was whittled down to 260.79 acres and confirmed by the CPLC. More or less evenly divided into seventeen long rectangular suertes lying between the Rio Galisteo and La Loma, each with frontage on the river, this tiny fraction of the 1814/22 grants was all that remained of the thousands of acres originally decreed, and of the perhaps nonexistent Galisteo "Town Grant."[121]

Lucy R. Lippard, *Stone Lines on the Former Galisteo Grant*, ca. 1999.

As though all of this were not confusing enough, the 1898–99 grant is variously described on contemporary maps and documents as 300, 317, 335, 420, or 425 acres (perhaps reflecting the difficulty of translating varas into acres), and there are two almost identical maps that differ ever so slightly in names and acreages.[122] On both of them, each grantee was designated with his or her long-lot field "irrigated by gravity-based ditch," despite the fact that the original settlers were deceased and their suertes had already been broken up, combined, sold and resold, and consolidated for the most part into a single parcel known as the Rancho de Galisteo—or the Miguel E. Pino Galisteo Ranch, the Loya Ranch, or the Sena Ranch, which may be more or less the same property despite varying acreages.[123] This ranch (or these ranchos), sometimes described as synonymous with the vestigial Galisteo grant, also as "part of the Galisteo Grant" of 24,000 acres, was located in the "western part of the village of Galisteo along the North bank of the Galisteo Creek," including "water rights and tank or tanks, ditches, houses and buildings thereunto." Much of this diminished grant is currently incorporated into the Cerro Pelón Ranch.[124]

The Rancho de Galisteo/Loya Ranch on the Galisteo grant, confirmed in 1899 "for about 300" acres, was the subject of a 1901 lawsuit, which offers yet another example of how confusing these conflicts could be. Eloisa Luna de Bergere sued Luciano Chávez and other heirs of José de la Cruz Chávez for trespassing on the former Galisteo grant.[125] When the case was heard in 1902, it was incumbent upon Chávez to show that the land he claimed to own had not been previously conveyed to anyone else. Testimony seemed to prove that it had.[126] By this time, Don José Ortiz y Pino apparently owned the entire parcel. It was still designated "an unconfirmed Mexican grant," which, as someone noted during the proceedings, "does not make a 'perfect' grant" (one that can be affirmed with no conflict, loss of papers, etc.)—quite an understatement.[127]

Meanwhile, corn, wheat, beans, chile, tobacco, cabbages, and alfalfa were grown on the disputed properties. At one point, three quarters of the land was cultivated; the rest was vega (grazing land) or *chical* (underbrush). A fence kept stock out of the crops. It was testified that the south and east sections were very poor, but where the land was ditched, it was fertile. Court records offer interesting glimpses into the ever-pressing problems of irrigation. "We worked a sort of dam in the arroyo so as to have water for the lands," testified Juan Ortiz. (This may be the "reservoir" at the northernmost tip of the grant map.) Apolonio Chávez told

Galisteo Houses, ca. 1920s. Palace of the Governors Photo Archives (NMHM/DCA):

Cristóbal Peña/Francisco Montaño/Basilio Anaya House, neg. no. 36454. Anaya bought it in 1919;

Angel or Sandoval House, neg. no. 026178;

Remy and Luis Chávez House, neg. no. 021096;

Sena/Griscom House? neg. no. 009315;

Larrañaga House with Adobe Wall, neg. no. 009313;

Sage H. Goodwin, *Romona Scholder Residence, Galisteo, New Mexico*, 1920–30?, neg. no. 119396. Former Epifanio and Remedios Mora House.

how tenants were given a tract in return for their work in the arroyo. Each year in March a dam of brush, stone, and dirt was built or restored "so as to raise the water above the arroyo to carry it to the tanks to irrigate the ranch."[128] Downcutting was already a problem in the early 1900s. At some point, landowner Jerry D. Romberg built a house next to an old tank and then put up a wire fence. He made a new ditch from the reservoir to a new "big, long tank . . . for the purpose of getting water away from some houses" and planted alfalfa.[129] The earlier tanque had been "filled up and could not gather any water at all." Water was brought "through the town to irrigate the ranch" (the Plaza de Galisteo ditch).

The population of Galisteo in the 1890s remained around seven hundred. A number of houses were built in the village during that decade, among them, on Avenida Vieja, the Pantaleón Montoya home and the Cayetano Chávez home (recently reclaimed by descendants), both apparently built on some incarnation of the Cadial. After more than fifty years of American rule, much had changed for Galisteans, though culturally much also remained the same. While eastern visitors were still struck by the "biblical antiquity" of farming methods and living conditions, the influx of railroad-imported consumer items greatly affected many aspects of village life, not always for the better. Beautiful old hand-carved wooden saints were replaced by saccharine plaster counterparts, hand weaving was replaced by factory goods, Pueblo pottery, by metal pots and manufactured goods from the east. In some areas, tin roofs replaced traditional flat ones topped by layers of turf . . . and so it went.

Don José Ortiz y Pino among His Sheep, ca. 1920s–30s. (Courtesy of Yolanda and María Ortiz y Pino.)

Cooks for Sheep Herd[er]s Ortiz Ranch, 1900. Frank Sandoval on right; possibly Climaco Sandoval on left. (Courtesy of the Anaya and Montoya families.)

FOUR

From Prosperity to Desperation to Renewal (1900–1945)

When the fields are lost, only the love of the land is left.
—Irish saying

The 1900 Galisteo District census listed farmers and stock raisers, as well as a clerk, a teacher, a blacksmith, a boot repairer, servants, laundresses, and 142 day laborers, an increase since 1870, suggesting that fewer villagers were operating their own farms for profit and more were working for larger landowners. The ricos bought out small homesteaders blocking their ways, and by 1910 many had abandoned their dryland farms after crop failures. Local farmers were also still losing their ancestral lands to legal tricks or tax deficits. Even when the cattle and sheep industries boomed,"land grant alienation" continued apace, leading to a parallel social alienation within formerly cohesive communities. Today's cultural stress, poverty, resentment, addiction, and grief in New Mexico are attributed to the deracination of traditional farmers and ranchers. Yet in many cases, the Cadial among them, common lands continued to be used by the community long after paper claims had made it invalid.

Over the next two decades, Don José Ortiz y Pino, the well-connected "last patrón," saw his fortunes rise exponentially as he set about consolidating inherited properties to become a sheep baron. He acquired thousands of acres of homestead and grant lands in the basin, and his holdings extended south to today's Clines Corners, as well as "miles to the east," in an area then called Agua Verde, where he ran both sheep and cattle.[1] Thus one of largest grazing empires in New Mexico was headquartered in Galisteo. His compound, along with his father's mercantile and his in-laws' hacienda, constituted a village power center. An active member of the Republican Party, a state legislator and member of the State Highway Commission, Don José became a figure to be reckoned with in New Mexico politics, as well as a feared and often reviled patrón. The Ortiz y Pino ranching empire exacerbated levels of class inequality that had flourished for centuries. Galisteo became a company town, in which workers' wages were balanced against their debts.

Sheep remained Galisteo's cash crop. Herded by man, boy, and dogs, they were more desirable at the time than cattle since they "could go 2–3 days without water, grazed on marginal land, and they stayed together."[2] But thousands of acres were necessary for financial success. The partido system worked in the landlords' favor. The patrón would loan some 2,000 sheep to a shepherd who was to return them in the same condition after five years. The owner got a 20 percent return in wool and additional sheep as interest. The shepherd had to be lucky

T. Harmon Parkhurst, *New Mexico Central Railway, Southbound Coal Train in the Vicinity of Arroyo de la Jara, South of Kennedy, near Galisteo*, 1919–20. (Palace of the Governors Photo Archives, NMHM/DCA neg. no. 166098.)

to pay his debt and make a profit. He could keep half the lambs born in the five-year period, developing his own flock if weather, predators, Indians, and other obstacles did not interfere. "Every animal that was lost to wolves, lightning, rattlesnake bite, or other mishap was charged to the poor herder who had to make it good from his paltry wage."[3] On December 7, 1907, the *New Mexican* reported, "The sheep raisers of the territory have enjoyed good and prosperous times during the past few years. . . . Therefore, this season they could afford to sell their lambs and ewes to the feeders on time and wait for payment of the purchase prices." The end of the free range for livestock came around 1911, when barbed wire triumphed, although young boys were still herders for two or three months in the summer, a lonely life for a child.

In 1902 more local jobs became available when another railroad entered the Galisteo Basin. Cutting south from Buckman, northwest of Santa Fe, the New Mexico Central (aka Santa Fe Central and known locally as El Central) ran between today's NM 14 and Eldorado, meeting the AT&SF at Kennedy Station a mile or so west of Galisteo. Don José was of course involved. Francis J. Torrance and William H. Andrews completed the main construction in 1903, opening the Estancia Basin to homesteading. El Central transported passengers and freight over 115 miles between Santa Fe and the now extinct town of Torrance, southwest of Vaughn, stopping at stations Kennedy, Clark, and Stanley (all named after railway employees). Beans were the southern area's prime crop, and Moriarty boasted of being "the Pinto Bean Capital of the World."

For a brief period Kennedy was a raucous little town, a hub in its own right. In its hayday, it included coal houses, an agent's cottage, a twelve-room concrete bunkhouse with pump and cistern, and livestock chutes. Farther down the AT&SF track, there were privately owned stores, bars, a railroad car bordello, a hotel, and houses. In 1902 the newspaper reported that the Leybas, who owned a cantina in Galisteo, had opened another in Kennedy, joining two already licensed there. On October 14, 1907, "two carloads of outfits" from the east arrived

Lucy R. Lippard, *Ruins at Former Kennedy Station*, 2018.

on El Central—some of the homesteaders pouring into the Estancia Valley. But in 1910 the railway went into receivership and in 1915 began to reduce service. After 1925, its unprofitable routes were abandoned and dismantled. In 1926, it was sold to the AT&SF, which abandoned all track in the northern Estancia Basin, although it ran to Stanley until 1938. Only a few stone ruins remain.[4] Among the Galisteo men who worked at Kennedy were Manuel Anaya and Luis Chávez. They often walked back and forth from the village and at times slept over in boxcars. Many Galisteans, including Sylvester Davis, left their marks on the interior walls of the walk-through culverts under the tracks, where graffiti continues to accumulate.[5]

Jesse Nusbaum, *El Ortiz Hotel at Lamy Train Depot*, 1912. (Palace of the Governors Photo Archives, NMHM/DCA neg. no. 61669.)

Richard Shuff, *La Lanera*, 2001. Don José's wool warehouse, now an artist's home. Information from José Ortiz y Pino III about those who signed the rafters in the building: "Feliberto N. Anaya, clever, a good worker, his family was from Cerrillos; Isabel Adams, 'held in esteem' by Don José. . . . He was half Indian and an all-around handyman; Clemente Martínez; Juan Martínez built the lanera and lived in Galisteo; Glennes Parker, a homesteader in Moriarty who drove a truck to bring wood to Kennedy around 1940; Juan Montoya; Romolo Leyba; Betty and Tony García, 1947, Tony liked his booze and women; Pite (Pepito) lived and worked in Galisteo, was very short, about 4 ft. tall, had a hunchback and one arm . . . he could beat anyone arm wrestling; Mateo; Felipe Chávez; Jack Salter. . . a well driller from Stanley/Moriarty who had sheep" (*El Puente*, Summer 2001).

Development continued locally. On October 10, 1908, El Ortiz, an elegant new $90,000 Harvey House, opened across the tracks from the Lamy Depot. (Rumor has it that its initial name was Los Pinos, but in English that sounded too close to male anatomy.) It closed its doors in April 1940 and was dismantled a few years later. Around 1907 or 1912, Don José built a *lanera* (wool warehouse) in the center of Galisteo, on the recommendation of Robert Seligmann, a wool buyer from Boston who wanted to have his product shipped by rail. Don José's carpenters, Galisteans Juan and Clemente Martínez, were told to construct a large building "from stone, with good ventilation and wooden floors . . . east of the stable, close to the alameda on the river front." Ortiz y Pino brokered wool from his own sheep and those of neighbors and others around the state, getting better prices by pooling the product and selling large quantities. Each family had a stall-like area in the lanera, where their wool was stored. (Some of the men painted their names or brands on the trusses and window sills of the shed; rival José Antonio Anaya did not participate.) The wool was shipped out of Kennedy, where Don José's men built the depot.[6]

Miners and oil and gas prospectors also invested in the Galisteo Basin during this period. A few got rich; most failed. In 1904 a delusional Fayette Jones published an outrageous boast: "The whole channel of the Galisteo River is one vast sluice box, the gold collecting in the depressions and seams of the rocks that form the river bed. The same thing will apply to the Rio Grande . . . a vast storehouse of gold."[7] However, mining continued in the western basin and some Galisteans panned for gold in their off hours. Mine owners in the early twentieth century brought in Mexican workers as scabs, widening the breach between "Spanish" New Mexicans and their southern cousins.[8]

In 1912, New Mexico became a state, next to last to enter the lower forty-eight, finally overcoming the racism that had prevented this from happening for so many years. Perhaps more significant for the Galisteo Basin, in July 1912, eminent archaeologist Nels Nelson (a Danish immigrant farm boy who had been studying in California) and his brand-new wife, Ethelyn (who had been secretary to the Berkeley anthropologist Alfred Kroeber), were sent by the American Museum of National History to explore the basin's archaeological resources. Research into the Ancestral Pueblo past has played a consistent role in the Galisteo Basin since Adolph Bandelier began poking around in the late 1800s, often staying in Galisteo as he pursued his local jaunts. The eight major pueblo ruins of a thousand rooms or more (most of them adobe, now subsided into grassy cholla-covered mounds), stunning rock art panels, and hundreds of minor sites were beginning to command scholarly attention.

The Nelsons arrived at "the desolate little railroad station" at Kennedy, "whose newly appointed agent seemed scarcely aware of the existence of" nearby Galisteo. They walked three miles:

> [Then] we came suddenly to the edge of a rise of ground and looked over on what appeared as an oasis in the desert. A little white church stood in the midst of a group of adobe houses, while apple orchards and great cottonwoods shaded the whole. Just beyond, the new bridge spanned the stream that winds its way through the town. We . . . were soon resting in a room in the cool depths of the rambling adobe structure where Señora Davis, mother-in-law of the only English-speaking resident of the place, the merchant [Don José Ortiz y Pino], puts up chance wayfarers. From this vantage point we began to explore the surrounding country for ruins, being ably assisted by a Mexican driver whose name [was] Anaya.[9]

The Nelsons soon exchanged Josefa's hospitality for several months of camping, mostly at the ruins of San Cristóbal Pueblo, where they began to put the Galisteo Basin's archaeology on the national map. In the fall of 1912, they worked their way around to Pueblo Blanco, south of Cerro Pelón, via Pueblos Largo, Colorado, and She.[10] They excavated only 47 of its 2,000 or so rooms while simultaneously working at the even larger historic ruins of Pueblo San Lázaro a few miles to the west. Winter was approaching, and Nelson was to spend only four days at the end of the tour at the Galisteo Pueblo and its adjoining Las Madres site. After two years of excavations, the ruins slept peacefully for decades, though occasionally plundered by pothunters and often visited by amateur archaeologists and sightseers who pilfered surface sherds and lithics. A number of archaeologists have worked in the basin since then, making surveys when land is for sale or easements are permitted, but the major legacies were left by Bandelier, Nelson, and their successor, Bertha Dutton, who worked at Las Madres and Pueblo Largo.[11]

In her 1912 notes, Ethelyn Nelson mentions the "Mexican" workmen, who did most of the excavating, one of whom they called "Old 'Socrates' . . . because of his great knowledge of everything on earth or in the heavens above. No question could be put to him that he was not prepared to answer, and he had a name and a use for every plant that grew in the vicinity. . . . He had stories of buried treasure, supposed to be well guarded by the Indians."[12] Years later, in the course of WPA interviews, this treasure story resurfaced when Higinio Tórrez, a man from Córdova (then Quemado), told researcher Lorin Brown about a wagon trip returning from the salt lakes south of Galisteo "during the war" (World War I): "I usually camped at San Cristóbal near that old Indian village. . . . I noticed when I was making camp a group of men near the old church. They went by my camp as I was getting supper and I noticed they were covered with dust. Soon my little grandson Remigio came back from picketing the horses where they could graze. 'What could those men be doing digging near the old church, grandpa?' *Quien sabe, hijo.* How many were there?' 'There were four and a fat Americano was watching them.'"[13]

Sam Hudelson, *Nels Nelson's Excavation of the San Cristóbal Pueblo Ruins*, 1912. (Palace of the Governors Photo Archives, NMHM/DCA neg. no. 046539.)

Tórrez and his grandson met the men and were told not to snoop. They wondered "what they could be digging for, maybe one of those springs which the Indians stopped up when they left, or maybe digging up graves. Why couldn't they leave the poor dead Indians in peace?" Then the Americano offers them two days work digging, as "the rest of the *tontos* [were] afraid of being bewitched." Tórrez accepts and they start

> With my compañero, a man from Galisteo, I can't remember his name. . . . Toward evening of the second day we struck some poles laid crosswise in the earth. Now the fat man was all excited. He almost fell in the hole trying to tell us how to dig. Following his instructions we dug around the cedar poles and lifting them up carefully uncovered a sort of pit walled and floored with the same kind of cedar poles. In it were several articles wrapped in buckskin and tied with thongs. As I was lifting the largest of these out, and it was very heavy, the buckskin wrappings came loose and it fell back in the hole leaving the buckskin in my hands. I stooped to pick it up, and you will not believe me but it was a golden image of San Cristóbal about so large [around 18–20 inches].[14]

The Americano got angry, paid them, and told them to leave. Tórrez didn't get to see the other objects but could feel them through the buckskin: "Oh, some felt like big cups and plates, others just like heavy bars. There were not many, and none weighed as much as the gold image, if it was gold. On the way past my camp I asked my compañero from Galisteo who the American was. He called him El Panqueque, something like those little tortillas I ate in a restaurant once."[15] Presumably, "Pancake" is Pankey, then owner of San Cristóbal. The "gold" appeared to be ecclesiastical objects buried at the time of the Pueblo Revolt in 1680.

Galisteo's population in 1913 was 800, with around 110 households in the village. Sylvester Davis died that year, and Josefa Ortiz y Davis was running a boarding house in their hacienda. She had borne twelve "live" children, of whom six were still living, according to the 1900 census. (None of the women listed on the same census page had much better luck with their children; Josefa's daughter Pablita had some twenty-three pregnancies, and only seven offspring lived to adulthood.) "My grandmother Josefa was a fascinating paradox," wrote Victoria Sánchez. "Although she married an eastern Anglo, she refused to learn English. She became the legal authority in Galisteo, yet her schooling was limited to having been tutored."[16] As a younger woman, according to her great-grandson José Ortiz y Pino III, she "could ride, rope, saddle and work with the horses, sometimes better than most men."[17]

Granddaughters Victoria and Concha remembered Josefa as a midwife, a *curandera* (healer), and an apprentice doctor, "the heart and brains of the community . . . the complete boss of Galisteo. . . . She remembered all the important dates, who people were, when they were baptized, and by whom. . . . Grandmother was the one the community turned to in times of need. . . . She buried the dead, fed and often housed the homeless, and kept the keys to the church, seeing that it was properly maintained. . . . People valued her sense of judgment. She always ruled through gentleness."[18] Simona Baros García, like other poorer villagers who were around Concha's age, contradicted this benign familial view: "People were afraid of her." She and other villagers recalled Josefa hitting and "being mean to" Bluebell Jackson, Josefa's "adopted daughter" (servant).[19]

Bluebell's is an extraordinary story. The 1910 census notes a seven-year-old *mulata* living under guardianship with the Ortiz clan.[20] Dr. Friend Palmer, an AT&SF physician based in Cerrillos, found a baby and a small child left at the railroad tracks at Kennedy, reportedly

Alice and Bluebell (standing); *Frank Ortiz y Davis, Concha Ortiz y Pino, and Cousin Reynalda Ortiz y Pino* (in wagon), ca. 1913. (Courtesy of La Herencia Archive.)

Galisteo School, ca. 1917. Among those pictured (not in order), according to a handwritten list on the back of the original: Lupe Baros, Delfino Anaya, Juanito Anaya, teacher José Villanueva, Rosario Chávez, Simona Baros, Annie Peña, Lugarda Leyba, Catalina Chávez, Lola Chávez, Bluebell Jackson, Juan Mendoza (Mendonca), Lucas Anaya, Frank Sandoval, Alex Valencia, Camilo Chávez, and Antonio Chávez. (Photo and identifications courtesy of Simona Baros García, who recalled that the photo was taken by the county nurse when she came to the school to give shots.)

by an African American prostitute known there. He brought them to the Davis/Ortiz y Pino families. Josefa took in Bluebell (aka Brauglia), said to be "half white," and her daughter Pablita took Bluebell's assumed half-sister Alice (born 1905, called Alma in another account), said to be "all black." Their surname was Jackson. In the 1920 census Josefa was listed as a sixty-six-year-old widow who could not read or write, while Bluebell was a thirteen-year-old servant who could. (She was listed first as white and then it was scribbled over, presumably to read "black.") Concha Ortiz y Pino, who lived with Josefa when she was in Galisteo, considered Bluebell her "sister."[21]

Bluebell appears in a 1917 Galisteo school picture, but Alice does not. Simona García recalled that Alice ran away after an altercation with a member of the Ortiz y Pino or Davis family. On March 23, 1917, the *New Mexican* noted that a Deputy Sheriff took Alice Jackson, "aged 12, colored," to Springer, where she was sentenced to serve a year in the reform school; on arrival he was informed they did not take girls. Alice is never mentioned again in Galisteo stories.[22] Bluebell remained in Galisteo, marrying Ramón Hurtado from Estancia, who was working in the village. They had two children, Frank and Clara. Villagers remember Bluebell fondly. She "came to be a Spanish lady with us," said Simona García. Her little house on La Vega is now a picturesque ruin.

In 1907 the oldest school in Galisteo—behind the church on The Hill, although no trace remains—was said to be flourishing, but it was replaced in 1914 when the Ortiz y Pino family donated land on La Vega and met the building cost of $1,400 without state aid. Paulita Peña Chávez (1905–2000) recalled: "In our community there was a large public school where elementary through high school classes were taught. In those days very little English was spoken. . . . We were not allowed to speak Spanish, only English. My favorite teachers were Elena Dominguez and Magdalena Dominguez." (The latter was described by Simona García

Entrance of the Galisteo School on La Vega, 1926. (Palace of the Governors Photo Archives, NMHM/DCA neg. no. 001014.)

as "a little fat lady who belonged to Cerrillos Road in Santa Fe" and rented a room in Galisteo from the Baros family.) The schoolteacher in the circa 1917 picture was José Villanueva.[23] Nicolás López of Aqua Fria recalled his school years, which probably resembled Galisteans' experiences: "The teacher was very good at punishing and our text book was the Catechism and our arithmetic problems were worked on the surface of the schoolhouse door with charcoal."[24]

A curious document that lies under the radar of all the familiar local land struggles is a federal land patent dated May 21, 1908, and recorded on December 8, 1909.[25] Raising more questions than it answers, it states, "Full payment has been made by Candelario Martinez, Probate Judge of Santa Fe County, New Mexico, for the southeast quarter of the southwest quarter, the southwest quarter of the southeast quarter and the Lot one of Section Thirty five in the Township fourteen north and the Lots one and two of Section two in Township thirteen, north of Range Nine East of the New Mexico Meridian Containing two hundred eight and ninety-eight hundredths acres."[26] This land was granted by the United States to "Candelario Martinez in trust for the general use and benefit of the occupants of the townsite of Galisteo, in said County, according to their respective interests and to his successors in trust as aforesaid. And there is received from the lands hereby granted, a right of way thereon for ditches or canals constructed by the authority of the United States." Thus the core of the original settlement "remains in trust to this day with individual parcels only having been removed from the trust through quiet deed claims."[27]

Who was Candelario Martínez and why did he establish this trust for Galisteans?[28] How did he profit from this transaction? Why was this 209-acre tract forgotten? Is it still valid? "Public land that had never been deeded could be acquired by patent, which established the rights of ownership just like an invention patent establishes ownership to a design," I was told by former Galisteo resident Patrick Mehaffy. The question is, did Candelario Martínez "acquire the patent as an individual or as an official representing Santa Fe County?" Mehaffy put this question to a Santa Fe County attorney, who "thought that a case could be made for the latter. If that could be done, then the County of Santa Fe holds title to the remaining land in this patent. It also bears the responsibility of protecting and defending the land."[29] No one has ever pursued this puzzling situation or opened the can of worms that would ensue, given successive private ownerships of the land in question.

Meanwhile, the machinations surrounding the San Cristóbal grant continued. Although he did not testify in person, T. B. Catron was a major presence behind all the Cadial trials. In 1903 the courts decided the San Cristóbal grant for Catron on his appeal of the case won by Laughlin in 1897, decreeing that the original twenty-six grantees never surrendered their legal rights, even if they had left the land, and those rights were somehow to be parceled out. After Laughlin and Catron had become partners, the early 1903 decision was bowled over by another that year, declaring that forty-six claimants were too many for the available water and that the grant must be subjected to public auction, announced in the *New Mexican* on January 25, 1904. On January 30, Catron was, not surprisingly, the highest bidder, acquiring 18/26ths for $5,200. Then, as previously agreed, in 1906 he conveyed San Cristóbal's eastern 40,000 acres to Laughlin (who already owned 4/26ths). "Thus Catron, who invested only $468

José Abel Anaya and Family, ca. 1900. José Abel Anaya (5/13/1859–1/21/1940) lived on what is now Marcellina Lane. In the back row are the sisters Remedios Anaya (who married a Mora), Ursula Anaya (who married a Portugese man named Díaz), and Martina Anaya (who married the schoolteacher José Villanueva), their parents, Simona Baros Anaya and José Abel Anaya, and brother Desiderio Anaya. In the front row the children are Basilio Anaya, Remeditos Anaya (who married a Flores from Pecos), and baby Antonio Anaya. (Another child, Faustín, was born after this picture was taken.) Anaya, the patriarch of this substantial family, was a prominent citizen and the owner of many sheep. (Photo and identifications courtesy of Simona Baros García in *El Puente*, June 2000; additional information from Anthony Burns, José Abel's great-great-grandson.)

in the small farms he'd bought over the years, and not much more in the actual purchase price (much of the $5,200 cost was returned to him since he held a major percentage of the grant), ended by making a profit of about fifty times his original investment."[30]

Witnesses testified to the ongoing manipulation of Galisteo villagers. When the Cadial grantees discovered that Catron was trying to sell the San Cristóbal grant, they came again to Anastacio Sandoval, who said he hadn't seen his friend Catron since 1890. On January 17, 1904, a paper was signed by the Cadial landowners appointing a committee to confer with Catron. The next night, January 18, a "commission meeting" took place, attended by Catron, Sandoval, Juan Ortiz, Don Apolonio [Chávez], Don [José] Abel [Anaya], and "those now dead": Sylvester Davis, José León Madril, and Antonio José Ortiz.[31] Both Spanish and English were spoken at the meeting. Catron said he would survey at his own expense and if he died, his son would also keep the promise. (In 1915, that same son was representing the ranch owner.) Madril said, "Mr. Catron, we don't want this promise to be like the promise that you sent us with Don Anastacio Sandoval some time ago" (1890), to which he replied, "Of course not." At this point in the meeting, Marcelino Ortiz (then county assessor, who had lived in Galisteo and was invited to the meeting) piped up and asked him to put his promise in writing. Catron got angry and said, "I haven't got no business with you." Ortiz recounted, "[Catron] didn't want to talk to me, he wanted to discuss the matter with the other fellows." Ortiz retorted, "Of course you don't want to do business with me, you can't make an agreement of that kind with me without putting it in writing. You might make it with them . . . he got more angry then." José Abel Anaya recalled that Ortiz spoke English and the others didn't understand the exchange. They all agreed that Catron said, "I don't want to fight with the Galisteo people." According to Juan Ortiz, Catron told the Galisteños that even if the Cadial was inside the Eaton grant,"he would see that [their] lands were going to be protected by anyone purchasing the grant."[32] (At some point during these events, absurdity triumphed. The original 26ths were broken up into infinitesimal parts; for instance, "two of the six children of said Juan Mares making 2-6 part of 1-4 of 1-26 part of entire grant.")

Don José Ortiz y Pino testified that he was present in October or November 1906 when Catron went to his father's house in Galisteo, wanting to know what Juan Ortiz could do for him in the election. (Catron was now running as a Democrat.) Juan said "What can I do, Mr. Catron, when the people are so awfully sore at you?" Catron wanted to buy his Cadial strips and Ortiz refused: "I need that land to cut grass and also to graze my animals." Catron claimed that Luciano Chávez and others had already agreed to sell; Ortiz would not budge. So Catron drew a map with the San Cristóbal Arroyo going through the Cadial and said he would not give anyone titles south of the arroyo but on the north he would give titles. Ortiz said, "That is not right. You have agreed to give us our deed for all the lands enclosing the fence of the Cadial and you must do it." So Catron said he would, but he wasn't sure whose name he would make the titles to "so that this one [would] be able to give title to every one of the others." Then Catron promised, "But I will see how I can do it."[33] However, the 1907 quitclaim was made out not to the settlers, already in place for almost a century, but to Catron and his wife, Julia.

T. Harmon Parkhurst, *Front of B. F. Pankey Ranch House (San Cristóbal Ranch)*, ca. 1915. The ranch never exceeded 81,033 acres. (Palace of the Governors Photo Archives, NMHM/DCA neg. no. 012725.)

In the early 1900s, Laughlin, then major owner of the San Cristóbal grant, had grandiose plans.[34] He proposed to subdivide into 4,867 tracts to be sold at $6 per acre. There was to be a townsite with hotel, school, and reservoirs, but he found no buyers. In August 1907 he mortgaged the grant to T. B. Catron, and the same month they sold out for $141,000. The entire 81,032 acres of the San Cristóbal grant went to Benjamin F. Pankey, "a Capitalist of Topeka," who was to become a Republican state senator, lieutenant governor, and state land commissioner in New Mexico.[35] Like the Singleton family, current owners of San Cristóbal, he was once the largest landowner in New Mexico. By 1908, Pankey was in cahoots with Catron.

Though their claims had been rejected in 1894, a number of Galisteans were listed as taxpayers on the Cadial from 1904 to 1911, and four houses were said to exist there. Part of the 1907 agreement was that Pankey would cede 250 acres in and around the village most of it

Caroline Hinkley, *Ruin Behind Cháves/Peña/Durán Compound*, 2018.

Edward Ranney, *Ruin on The Hill*, 1999.

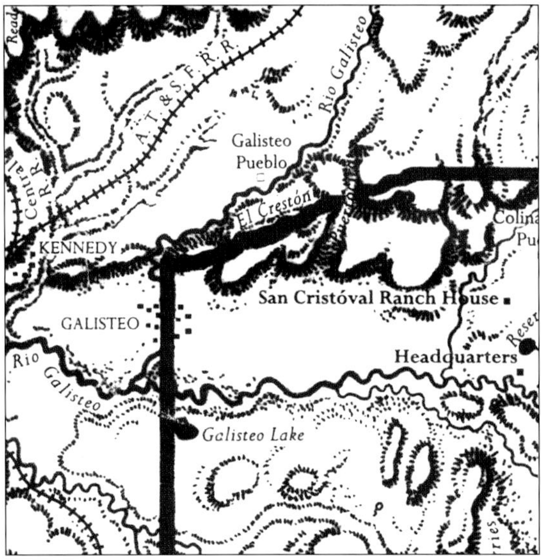

Detail of Deborah Reade's *Map of the Eaton Grant Showing Overlap with the Village of Galisteo*, the infamous "250-acre exception."

already settled, to Catron. This "250-acre exception" from the San Cristóbal grant surrendered rights to the ranch's northwestern quarter, mostly on the east side of the village, but extending across the river in places. It was outside the barbed wire fencing that enclosed the rest of the Eaton grant, and it was to be used for the people of the village of Galisteo. However, when the villagers continued to use the Cadial for subsistence farming and grazing and continued to fight for their property rights, Pankey began to crack down on them.[36] At one point he was said to have destroyed Antonio Anaya's crops in the Cadial and planted oats instead.[37]

Fencing was still a major issue. When Pankey bought San Cristóbal, he was told that the fenced area (the Cadial) had been abandoned. He did not "pay much attention" to people

T. Harmon Parkhurst, *On Guard, Cattle on "el Chico" on the B. F. Pankey Ranch*, ca. 1915–20. (Palace of the Governors Photo Archives, NMHM/DCA neg. no. 005350.)

cutting hay there and made no inquiry about other claims to the land, though to protect himself, he did get a $3,500 bond from Laughlin (which he soon sold for $5,000). His cattle grazed everywhere, including the Cadial, since the fence was broken and there was nothing to keep them out.[38] In 1908, Galisteans were accused of fencing the Cadial and "cultivating the soil of said tract without permission, consent, or approval." However, in 1909 witness after witness took the stand to affirm that the fence had been built in 1885 in response to an April 1884 law; it could be seen from the village.[39] They may have *repaired* it in 1908, as it was constantly being destroyed by Pankey's stock (and admittedly by stock inside the fence as well).[40] "We were repairing the fence years ago," testified Juan José Silva, "when Mr. Pankey came over and asked us why we were repairing what belonged to him. It wasn't his. We had built that fence . . . to prevent stock of Pankey's coming in."[41] It was a three-strand, post-and-wire fence, four to five feet high, parts of which had fallen down. José Antonio Anaya testified that he was one of three fence commissioners who repaired it every year before crops were planted. "We made up a collection to buy wire, then appointed the people accordingly to fix up the fence."[42] Donaciano Angel cited an old agreement that each owner could put four animals inside the fence after the crops had been harvested.[43] But "freshets in the creek come down and wash [the fence] away," and animals broke through.

In April 1909, Pankey filed suit against eleven villagers[44] for quiet title to some 7,500 acres: "a certain piece, parcel and tract of land commonly known as the Cadillal or Cadial Tract," originally bounded on the east by "Tecubaya," on the west by La Joya, on the south by the foothills near the La Jara Arroyo (Alto de la Jara), and on the north by the hills of the Cañada de en Medio, the middle hump of the northern creston, or hogback.[45] His lawyer was C. C. Catron, son of T. B. The Galisteños were defended by Frank Clancy, another Catron colleague,[46] who contended that the US patent to San Cristóbal did not include the Cadial and other tracts and that the Cadial was entirely outside the bounding lines of the Eaton [San Cristóbal] grant.[47] Each defendant was "owner of one or more pieces of land in the Cadial, having had titles since 1846," from "Old Mexico" ("before the US got us," as Anastacio Sandoval put it). (Clancy argued, "[Because] each chain of title is different, each is entitled to a separate trial by jury before he can be lawfully dispossessed," but this did not happen.)[48] The defense also insisted that the 1871 case, in which the original Galisteo grant had been rejected, was "entirely disconnected" from this case, since it dealt with the 1814 grant rather than the 1846 Cadial grant and the same applied to the 1892 Luciano Chávez petition to confirm the original Galisteo Grant. Many of the defendants were said to be "insolvent" and unable to pay damages, although several ricos were among them and the lawyer appears to have been paid by Don José Ortiz y Pino.[49] After opening statements were made (with complaints of "frivolous" and "irrelevant" scattered through the proceedings),[50] nothing happened until 1914, and the bulk of the trial took place in July 1915. Sixty-four hijuelas and deeds of sale were presented as evidence by the defense. Apolonio Chávez testified that he and his father raised corn there, and some milk cows for the use of the town of Galisteo were pastured at the Cadial: "In times gone by we were never interfered, but in 1909 then we were interfered by Mr. Pankey."[51]

At the end of the trials covered in the transcript, "Findings of Fact" were presented to District Judge Edmund C. Abbott: the Cadial was bounded on the east by Tacubaya, west by La Joya, north by "the hills of the Cañada de en Medio and South by the Alto de la Jara." The "Conclusions of Law" (stating all the positions again) were presented, and on December 20, 1916, the "Final Decree" stated (despite evidence to the contrary) that there were no residential houses in the Cadial, all the hijuelas were void, and there was no proof of ownership. Pankey received a complete title, but the Galisteo landowners' appeal to the Supreme Court was granted and on June 3, 1917, Apolonio Chávez, José Ortiz y Pino, and his brother-in-law José N. Gonzales signed a document saying they would pay the costs of the appeal for all the appellants.[52]

In 1921, it was their turn to win. Then T. B. Catron stepped in again, doing "all in his power to extinguish or cause to be extinguished as soon as practicable either by purchase or legal proceedings or otherwise [!] all of said adverse claims."[53] Although he died that year, he had made some kind of a deal with the landowners while still claiming a "small parcel" of San Cristóbal, as well as interests in six other grants, all "heavily encumbered." In 1922 the matter was set aside "for want of prosecution." According to José Ortiz y Pino III, the Catrons were responsible for the final settlement: "The Rio Galisteo became an official dividing line, with everything east of the river belonging to San Cristóbal and everything west belonging to Galisteo."[54] This actually applied only to the northernmost section of the grant, where an east/west fence still brings the border across the river today, rather than in the disputed part of the village proper.

Pankey lost his fortune after a three-year drought in the 1920s. In January 1924 he leased the mineral rights to over 13,000 acres of San Cristóbal to Walter E. Wood of Lamy, who drilled for gas and oil but found none. Other portions of the grant were leased to cattle ranchers and fuel prospectors, but in April 1926 Pankey surrendered the San Cristóbal grant to Missouri State Life and its president, M. E. Singleton.[55] In December 1926, Samuel and Minnie Fullerton and their friend Wayman Dobson bought the San Cristóbal grant and kept it for twenty-two years, passing it on to other owners until the Singleton family acquired it. In the mid 2000s, like a ghostly signal from the past, a sign reading "Pankey Co." appeared on a disputed lot in the eastern village (the "OK Corral" described in chapter 6), deepening the mystery of this endless case.

Lucy R. Lippard, *"Old Wooden Well" (or pigpen?) in Galisteo Creekbed*, ca. 1998.

In the high desert, any hint of moisture brings a strange acrid smell, like the spirit of dust. Water, its presence and absence, is local in every sense. Agua es vida, water is life, is a saying long associated with the Southwest, where moisture's shortage has always rendered it sacred. (Since Standing Rock, when Native Water Protectors united in 2015–16 to oppose potentially leaking fuel pipelines beneath their water supply, "agua es vida" has become a familiar slogan nationwide.) For centuries, preconquest Pueblo farmers depended on water from the sky for dryland farming and water in the streams and springs for drinking and "pot watering" of crops. Only shallow wells or reservoirs were dug. The early Spanish hand-dug wells went deeper. Galisteo's community well on Quartermill Farm, once Ortiz y Pino property, is fifty feet deep. Today drilling down as far as two thousand feet is not uncommon.

The Rio Galisteo (aka Galisteo Creek) has been the main artery of its valley's heart and history, sustaining lives with an increasingly less generous runoff from the Sangre de Cristo

Joan Myers, *Rio Galisteo Bosque*, 2018.

Mountains and a contribution from the San Cristóbal Arroyo. After its right-angle turn to the west at the village's southern border, the creek empties through a dam constructed to stop excess silt from entering the Rio Grande above Santo Domingo Pueblo. The Galisteo is one of the six major tributaries to the 725 miles of the "Great River." (This name is increasingly incongruous; in 2018, large stretches were totally dry.) Ecologist Jan Willem Jansens, who has worked in the Rio Galisteo watershed for many years, reads the landscape features around the village and upstream to conclude that the Galisteo Creek was once a narrow, gently meandering stream through grasslands at the level of the older houses bordering the creek. He believes that between 1880 and 1892 one of several cataclysmic floods hammered the creek, drastically changing its course and shape. The narrowing of the creek bed and floodplain was caused by the railroad's realignment of the river upstream between Glorieta and Lamy in 1879–80. Concrete dams and levees in and along the floodplain led to more stream erosion on the opposite dirt banks, exacerbated by overgrazing and deforestation on the mesas.[56] There was also the 1886 flood that damaged old Santo Domingo Pueblo where the Rio Galisteo meets the Rio Grande, and it is possible that weather changes resulting from the eruption of Krakatoa, halfway around the world, had some effect as well.

Over time, says Jansens, floods widened the creek's trench and created the current hundred-yard-wide arroyo floor, which was almost entirely barren, full of sand and clay with patches of grass. Historically, there were no big trees in the Rio Galisteo bosque except for an occasional clump of willows and a grove of big old cottonwoods between the current Hammond and Griscom properties. Around 1912, non-native Russian olives and salt cedars (tamarisks) were introduced across the West to stabilize stream beds—a really bad idea, as it turned out, because they stole water from the cottonwoods and poisoned the soil. (See chapter 6.)

Charles A. and Anne Morrow Lindbergh, *Aerial Photograph of Galisteo from the West*, 1929. Note the church in the center, the treeless creek bed, the irrigated fields on the reduced Galisteo Grant and maybe Tanque Viejo. (Palace of the Governors Photo Archives, NMHM/DCA neg. no. 130327.)

John Watson-Jones, *The "Tornadic Event" Coming at Galisteo over Highway 41*, October 2017.

Steel Truss Bridge across the Rio Galisteo, before 1923. (Courtesy of the Concha Ortiz y Pino de Kleven Photograph Collection, Center for Southwest Research, University Libraries, University of New Mexico, neg. no. v000-457-0110B.)

In any case, floods (*venidas*) were common. Around 1910, Galisteño Antonio Mendoza and his son were drowned in the Atascoso/San Cristóbal. El Puente, the old bridge over the Rio Galisteo leading to La Otra Vanda, was often washed out and eventually replaced. One bridge was destroyed before Carmelita Anaya's wedding in 1905. The "new" bridge seen by the Nelsons in 1912 may have been a handsome steel truss structure shown in an undated photograph. The current steel-beam and wooden construction of what is now known as the "old" bridge, or El Puente, has undergone various incarnations since 1927 when the previous bridge fell to the elements.

Property along the creek southwest of the village was homesteaded in 1917 by a Dr. Dooley, who had a dairy farm, raised alfalfa, and ran a feed store in Santa Fe.[57] The Galisteo Basin is now primarily residential land, ranchland, and wasteland. It is hard to picture acres of bright green alfalfa within my viewshed or to imagine the deeper past, when land-based lives depended on the acequias and the Galisteo Creek supported many small farms. However, even in its intermittent/ephemeral weakness, thanks to a number of little springs, the creek flows shallow year round, sometimes underground, except through the village proper, where there has almost always been (in historical memory) a trickle or a flow aboveground, no matter how drastic the droughts. That is, until the record hot July of 2016, when patches of the riverbed along the bosque were just drying mud, for the first time in local memory but not the last. We are not immune to climate chaos.

John Wesley Powell, in his famous *Report on the Lands of the Arid Regions of the United States* of 1878, made an impassioned and prescient plea for bioregional boundaries to replace political ones in the arid West, which unfortunately went unheeded. In this dry land (Galisteo's average annual rainfall is around twelve to fifteen inches), little rain reaches the aquifer before it evaporates or is gulped up by plant roots. Braided and meandering drainages are healthier than the arroyos that run only in the rainy season, often too fast to trap water in the ground, riddling the land into gullies. Arroyos can replenish groundwater, but they also send overloads of unfertile sand- and gravel-laden sediment downstream. As they deepen with erosion, narrowing the channel, increasing velocity, and lowering the water table, irrigation becomes more difficult. This is what happened in Galisteo, which lost its last irrigation ditches around 1926 to human-caused erosion.

In small farming villages like Galisteo, water or lack thereof is deeply embedded in the social fabric. Under Spanish and Mexican laws, land and water were inseparable. Water sharing was based on "equity and need," common rather than individual property rights. Belief and practice once coincided. Sylvia Rodríguez's important book, *Acequia,* is subtitled *Water Sharing, Sanctity, and Place*, acknowledging the spiritual component of communally built and maintained irrigation ditches in New Mexico. In a later paper, she expanded on "the enacted but unspoken moral economy of the ditch." Acequias, from the Arabic *assaqiyah* for "hand-dug, gravity-flow, small-scale, farmer-managed irrigation systems," were the first mandate for any community land grant.[58] They were laboriously and collaboratively constructed for miles. As one *acequiero* put it, "land without water is dirt."[59]

New Mexico water allocations are based on seniority and a "use-it-or-lose-it" or "beneficial use" rule. Thus the Pueblos can claim senior rights, and acequia *parciantes* should be next in line, though this is constantly challenged by internecine squabbles and Anglo latercomers or corporate interests.[60] The 1907 New Mexico Water Code attempted to determine "the amount, priority in time, and location or point of diversion of every drop of water in the state."[61] There is wet water and paper water, surface water and groundwater, with different legal protocols for each. Under US law, water rights were not shared, but adjudicated according to seniority, or "prior appropriation"—"first in time, first in right"—and they became a transferrable commodity. Water rights come with land but can also be sold away to distant places, leaving a damp property officially dry. As northern New Mexico became more crowded, the ditch systems and their accompanying socio-dynamics became more complicated. Adjudication became the focus. The nineteenth-century maxims hold all too true: "Whiskey is for drinking, water is for fighting," and "Water runs uphill toward money." Amid perennial droughts, management of a watershed is a subtle and demanding task. Several settlements might depend upon the same stream for sustenance, although Galisteo was alone in the eastern basin until the advent of the railroad. Despite the contentious history, there are still about a thousand working acequias in the early twenty-first century in cities and villages across New Mexico, especially in the north.

The Galisteo community once had at least three acequias. The earliest settlement on The Hill must have had its irrigation source below the first suertes in the Rio Galisteo as it turns west. (An 1839 petition for land for José Manuel Angel and others at "El Arco de Galisteo" may refer to that bend.) At some point it seems to have been replaced by La Plaza de Galisteo Acequia, running from the north along the "Camino Real" (predecessor to NM

41). Its source was apparently a spring and a pool where water was trapped by rock around the puertocito in the creston, mentioned as the Ojo de la Creston. (There are remains of a large dam at the present-day Chi Center, and there is a now mostly dry pond at the Nizhoni property that is another candidate for the acequia's source.[62]) It ran through village backyards on La Vega east of present NM 41, then across the old plaza to La Sala, behind the church, in front of the current Sandoval homes to El Chical, then around the two low hills below La Loma to a tanque below to the west that fed the fields of the truncated Galisteo grant.[63] There were two tanques. The original was farther west than the one now called Tanque Viejo, below The Hill, perhaps the one mentioned in documents as constructed circa 1874-78, which was once called Tanque Segundo or Tanque del Día. Today, almost imperceptibly, the acequia's path greens first in the spring or after rains.[64]

A second acequia, dating presumably from the 1840s, fed the Cadial from the south, with its source in the Arroyo Atascoso/San Cristóbal. Its downcutting seems to have occurred before 1892, when the Cadial farmers "no longer repaired their irrigation dams because the stream had cut too deep to feed the acequias."[65] In the Cadial trial of 1909–17, Apolonio Chávez testified that you could see the ruins of the dams on the San Cristóbal,[66] which were no longer repaired ("because the arroyo is very deep now") and because they did not have the materials to build the dams.[67] Juan José Silva was mayordomo for the last dammed ditch, "until Mr. Pankey prevented [their] bringing the brush and rock" from "La Mesita de San Cristóbal," three to four miles from the Cadial, the only viable source of materials.[68] Evidence was noted of an old dam that was "broken out." José Antonio Anaya said that when the summer rains broke the dam, "it was very urgent, you know, to fix both those places."[69] A third, entirely private ditch ran parallel to the east side of the creek on Ortiz land, where the banks are now some twenty feet high in places. "The Ortizes had water because they had money," says one villager.

The major source for Galisteo's ditch erosion history, Charles K. Cooperrider's 1937 book, notes "a period of land degeneration" in the Galisteo Basin between 1896 and 1913. He identifies six acequias and the acreages they affected in the Galisteo watershed, conceding that these were "very early" ditches, before 1850, and the irrigated acreage figures may have been much larger than what he documents. Those ditches in the village area are "private" (300 acres); this was probably the Ortiz y Pinos'); Colorado Plaza (100 acres); San Cristóbal (100 acres); Galisteo Plaza (400 acres); and "Ortiz" ("00" acres, unexplained, though probably also "private").[70] Remarking on the great change since Pancoast's glowing description of Galisteo agriculture, he states that in 1931,"the stream channel both above and below Galisteo Plaza was a vertical-walled earth canyon from 15 to 25 feet deep and from 50 to 200 feet wide."[71] The ecological impact was severe: acequias once extended "the riparian habitat and transformed watershed ecology throughout the region."[72] Environmental historian William deBuys guesses that "the end of irrigation in Galisteo occurred in stages, ditch by ditch. . . . Memory no doubt varies depending on which ditch one used."[73]

The end came when all of Galisteo's acequias were "destroyed beyond repair" by the great flood of August 1926. Roaring down from the mountains, it almost obliterated the village of Lamy. Downriver, the "acequia and small reservoir feeding the fields of the Galisteo

Sharon Stewart, *Walking the Ditch in Cerrito, New Mexico*, 2003.

Lucy R. Lippard, *Ladder Stranded by Downcutting of the Galisteo Creek,* ca. 1998.

Lucy R. Lippard, *Defunct Water Works East of the Creek,* ca. 2008

Grant, which had broken and been repaired periodically over the years, ceased to operate."[74] The channel of the Galisteo Creek was so deeply eroded as to destroy all the ditch headings. The acequias were left stranded above. No land irrigation was practiced after 1928. In later decades attempts were made to pump river water up to the fields. The remains of old water-works can still be seen in the bosque and above. By the late 1920s, a forty-foot dam was built on present-day Cerro Pelón Ranch, for the unsuccessful Galisteo River Project, now in ruins.[75]

The loss of acequias was tantamount to a loss of both community and culture, destroying Galisteo's farming potential and undermining traditional society. Moreover, it coincided with the early onset of the Depression in New Mexico. I'm still amazed at how little has come down in the oral histories about the ditches. Most of the elders I've been able to interview over the past two decades were born in the 1920s and 1930s, so their memories do not include working acequias. Joe D. Anaya, born in 1925, remembers the presence of a clearly defined ditch through central Galisteo, but it was already disconnected from its source, running only when it rained. There are few historical references to the mayordomos, *comisionarios,* or parciantes of this or any other Galisteo ditch, which ceased to exist around 1935, probably when NM 41 rolled through the plaza. Nevertheless, the tradition of cooperative self-governance, which was rooted in acequia culture, continues in unincorporated villages like Galisteo, where volunteers run the town.

I have found no direct evidence of ongoing relationships during the nineteenth century with the Tanos who had inhabited the deserted Tanuge Pueblo or of anyone descended from those who remained in the area, although Galisteños were known colloquially into the 1930s as "Tanos." Adolph Bandelier noted in his journals of the 1880s that Ambrocio Pino lived "at Galisteo, where there [were] about seven Tano Indians left."[76] In 1940, in Placitas, Lou Sage Batchen collected a story for the WPA that she titled "El Indio Viejo," about an old man named Martínez from Galisteo who was a *resador*, or prayer man, and known as "the old Indian." Around 1865, he taught local children what appeared to be Indian dances and collected money; when the townspeople got tired of handouts, he lost his pupils and left town.[77] Joe D. Anaya recalls Tanos living at Cochiti who were related to Galisteo families. Another Keres pueblo, Santo Domingo/Kewa, that was a refuge for fleeing Tanos in 1782, provided Galisteo labor and sometimes friendships into the late twentieth century.[78]

"Tañita de Galisteo"—a milagro story, or *décima*, or prayer song—may have been composed by one Natividad Leyva, who sang it in 1942. But an account from musicologist John Robb's research contends that an earlier version of La Tañita "was composed by the late Joaquin Chávez, asking for help with Indian raids in the village's earliest days."[79] *Tañita*, or "little Tano woman," was the fond name for a painting of the Virgin in the Galisteo church, who was petitioned for help with land grants. Scholar Enrique Lamadrid dates this painting around the "mid territorial period," or around the time of the 1871 Cadial trial. In the song, the Virgin mother is called la patrona del Cadillal; there is a reference to "the year fourteen" (the 1814 founding of the village and the disputed Galisteo grant).[80] There are specific references in the 1942 version to the 1908–09 Cadial trial and to the lawyer Clancy, who represented the Galisteo defendants: "San José is a good lawyer / he has aided Clansy [*sic*]. It ends with a reference to "Panty" (Pankey). San José, alas, failed to win the case.

Robert Brewer, *Interior of Nuestra Señora de los Remedios*, Galisteo, 1975. The two hide paintings, copied from earlier works, flank the altar; the possible Tañita Virgin painting is hidden behind the chandelier. In a 1921 photograph of the church interior, both the hide paintings and the Virgin are absent, suggesting that the works were still in the possession of Josefa Ortiz y Davis. (Palace of the Governors Photo Archives, NMHM/DCA neg. no. 065149.)

This story emphasizes a factor often disregarded in New Mexico histories, which is the generally acknowledged but rarely explored *mestizaje*, or Indo-Hispano heritage, of a large part of the population. In the early days many vecinos intermarried with Pueblo people. In the late 1980s, during the second wave of struggle over the Tierra Amarilla land grant in Rio Arriba County, activist Pedro Archuleta famously responded to a *New York Times* reporter who questioned Spanish rights to land taken from Native peoples: "¿Pero, quién es mi mamá? (But who is my mother?)"[81] Galisteo censuses include people identified as from "Navajo Country" and "Apache Country" or just "Indian." The land grant heritage, especially in those areas, like Abiquiú, where genizaros had settled, was understood to be as complex as the centuries of interaction between conquerors and conquered: Indian, Spanish, and Anglo. *Querencia*, or deep rootedness and love of place, is as integral a part of land grant culture as the acequias that continue to bind residents to the land in the north.[82] Galisteo, on the other hand, has lost both its acequias and its ties to the Tanos.

In many brief accounts and histories of Galisteo, the Ortiz y Pino family dominates through the 1940s.[83] Less is made of other prominent Galisteo families—the Anayas, Senas, Chávezes, and Sandovals, who were among the very first settlers. Most of their properties were lost over a century of land grabs and economic depressions. Their descendants still live in the village, but few of these local families have had access to much historical or genealogical research. Oral histories have survived, but families are often reluctant to tell them to those not related, and they often conflict with the stories of other family members or other families. Fortunately, Anna Cárdenas, of Galisteo's middle-aged generation, indignant that the histories of working families are so rarely mentioned in New Mexico's schools, is delving into the archives and recording family stories. While it is impossible in this book to explore the lives of each individual or even each family in any depth, the following fragments offer some sense of what village life was like for *la gente* in the early twentieth century.

In 1905 Carmelita Chávez (1885–1981) was married to Serapio Anaya. The bridge across the river was washed out, and the groom's father carried the bride across the stream in his wagon to the church. The couple had eleven children, seven of whom survived. They owned a rancho of some 300 acres behind Cerro Pelón on the old road to Cerrillos (a portion of José Antonio Anaya's spread) but were forced to sell it before 1935. Carmelita (Mayita) never learned English because the school she attended through the second grade was Spanish speaking. She promised her grandfather she would never cut her hair and she never did. She remembered her mother cooking in a big outdoor *horno*. Whenever Indians came through town, the children were hidden in a back room. Carmelita was a *partera* (midwife) in the village, and as there was no doctor, she tended to injuries, as well as delivering babies. She also cooked at the WPA schoolhouse and then worked in Santa Fe around 1945.[84] A villager recalls that "Mayita was nice to everybody."

Simona Baros García (1909–2008) was born to Matilda Sena (daughter of Refugio Madrid Sena and Agapito Sena) and Eugenio Baros (son of Marcelino Baros and Teodora Sandoval). She was the only one in her family born in Moriarty. ("Over there with the hill-

Clara Anaya, *Carmelita Chávez y Anaya*, ca. 1930s–40s. (Courtesy of Kenny M. Chávez.)

billies!" she told me.) She lived in Galisteo until 1923, when the family, now landless, moved to Santa Fe, although her ties with Galisteo were never broken.[85] Simona was a treasured friend, a marvelous storyteller with a memory sharp as a tack: "No se me van mis cabritos" (Thank God for my little goats upstairs), or "I still have all my marbles," she would say gleefully as she reeled off detailed genealogies of practically everyone in the village. "Who doesn't Simona know!"

The Baros family lived on the creek next to the old bridge. Eugenio Baros built a little separate room by the road, where he had two chairs, one for shoe repair and the other for barbering. At one point it was also the post office, run by Simona's sister Adelicia. Simona loved to reminisce about her childhood:

> There was a well out back. It was nice water. They would put a bucket with meat on a rope down into the well to keep it cool, so we could have fresh milk andeverything else. When we had a watermelon, my daddy used to go to the river, make a little hole there, and put the watermelon so it would get cold. And my mother and the other ladies who lived by the river, they used to wash all their blankets, mattresses and pillows, both made of brown and gray sheep fleece, load everything into the wheelbarrow and before San Juan day would go to the river to rinse all the clothes out there in nice water so they didn't use much water from the well. My mother had one of those little hornos. My God, my mother

> used to bake a lot in there. She made *bolillos* with anise, *pan*, and tortillas in there. She pulled the bread out with a wooden shovel. Then my daddy had a little barn on the back of the house and by the barn a little room, just a little window with a screen so they could hang the meat that they killed to dry. They hung sacks of flour and had lots of bones to make soup and stuff like that, you know.[86]

Next to the Baroses' pens, she recalled, were "the *corrales* of the Ortizes, a big yard almost down to the river. Across the road [now La Vega] lived the Mendozas, who were Portuguese; they had a lot of sheep." (One of Remedios Peña Chávez's sisters married a Mendoza.) Next door to them was Gumercindo García, who worked for Pankey at San Cristóbal, then a little house (now a ruin) where Bluebell lived later. ("Before her was an old lady by the name of Asención.") The window on the west side of Simona's house faced the schoolhouse next door, a fence between them. The Sánchezes lived nearby; they bought their house "from a little old couple. He was blind. His name was Jesús and his wife was Philomena. We used to come with him every evening because he would sing the rosary in the little organ [probably an accordion] that he had."

Simona's sister Romalda Baros (who died in childbirth in 1933) and her husband did very well cooking and selling their food in a little stand by La Sala. Fred Vigil and Eugenio Baros sold ice cream, candy, watermelon, oranges, and chewing gum at dances at La Sala on El Día de Santiago. Across from the Davis hacienda was a vacant field (now owned by the community) where villagers gathered wild spinach (*quelites*). "All Galisteo was clean and no one was hungry," Simona recalled. "We had a cow, a pig, lots of milk, got butter and eggs from my uncle. The Ortizes wouldn't give anyone stuff from the orchards. They were stingy people. We never needed them and they gave us *nothing*. Every time my mother cooked, she

Lucy R. Lippard, *Ruin of Bluebell Hurtado Home*, 2010.

gave some to the neighbors and they did the same. When someone killed a sheep they shared, came with a leg of lamb. That's the way it used to be in Galisteo. Everything was good then, hon. When we came to Santa Fe it was much harder. We had to buy everything."

The apple and pear trees in the Ortiz y Davis orchard are said to be some 120 years old. "When I got the property," recalls John Benjamin, "this was called 'the forbidden orchard,' and I heard stories that there was broken glass on top of the wall to keep bums out in the 1930s."[87] Simona García remembered that when local children raided the Ortiz y Pino orchards for an apple or pear, Ricardo Castro, who worked for the patrón, took pity on them and let them fill their "little buckets" and run before he chased them out. But other employees did not. (Castro was better known locally as an outstanding musician.)

Paulita Peña (1905–2000) was the only one in her family to graduate from ninth grade. She was raised on La Otra Vanda and recalled that her carpenter father (Pedro Peña) earned one dollar a day, while also dryland-farming with a horse-drawn plow on Cadial land belonging to her uncle Apolonio Chávez. She and her sisters would get up very early to plant, hoe, and harvest and then go to school. Groceries and fabrics came from Henry Pick's market in Lamy. "We also traded at Juan Ortiz's store in Galisteo," she recalled. "Times were better then, although we did not have the conveniences of today. We lived happily, families were closer and attended church services together. Wages were very low, but everything was cheaper then. . . . Mr. José Ortiz y Pino was the owner of the largest parcels of land, and he never got along with people. He made the poor people miserable."[88] Paulita married Felipe P. Chávez in November 1930 at the Galisteo church. The custom was that the groom's parents wrote a letter (*prendario*) asking for the bride, whose dowry often came in a trunk.[89] The groom might leave the community for a few months in order to earn enough to pay for wedding costs, and wedding receptions were followed by a dance in La Sala.

Sisters Paulita and Annie Peña, 1920s. (Courtesy of Antonio Chávez.)

A story reflecting changes in cultural mores was reported on July 14, 1902, when the *New Mexican* announced the marriage, the next day, of a fourteen-year-old Galisteo girl to a sixty-five-year-old Santa Fe man. Three days later, the paper noted that the marriage had been "indefinitely postponed" because no priest or minister could be found to perform the ceremony. (Though girls were often married at that age, the age disparity apparently offended both Spanish and Americans.)

The village had its share of tragedy. A corrido by Luisito Antonio Sánchez begins: "The 23 of November / I was there / Lolita Chávez died / Andrés Mora killed her."[90] Lola Chávez was the daughter of Luz Peña and former probate judge Apolonio Chávez. In 1917, she was "running around with" Simona García's cousin Antonio Anaya. Mora, who "was in love with her, met her on the bridge on her way to school, and shot her" in a jealous rage, then shot himself.[91] Both died within two days. In the fall of 1918 the terrible Spanish flu, brought home by returning veterans of World War I, struck New Mexico, leaving five thousand dead in a month. Little medical help was available. Simona García was the only member of her family to come down with influenza. She recalled that her mother rubbed her with lard, salt, and pepper to bring down her fever. Other folk remedies included wearing a red ribbon on the left arm and drinking hot water with chile pods and garlic.[92]

World War I offered a chance for the new state to make its mark. Some 14,000 New Mexicans joined up. Whole football teams went to war. The average draftee had a second or third grade education and was used to hard work. University students were given leave to farm their lands and were not drafted if they were deemed indispensable for agriculture. The Women's Land Army pitched in to increase productivity. Fifty-four percent of all soldiers died.[93]

Although they had more resources than many others, the Ortiz, Davis, and Pino families also suffered personal tragedies in the 1920s. In 1921, Don José's younger brother Pedro Ortiz y Pino (1882–1923), who lived in a hacienda on the east side of the creek (probably his grandfather Nicolás Pino's home), was committed to the Las Vegas insane asylum as "non compos mentis" and died there. He had lost his first wife, Carolina Granito, to consumption only months after their marriage, and his second wife, Agueda Rael de Aguilar, mother of daughters Reynalda and Virginia and son Pedrito/Pete, also died. His third wife, Guadalupe C de Baca de Ortiz, and her infant son, Arturo, moved back to her home in Las Vegas after his death. Simona García, a friend of his two daughters, remembered Pedro Ortiz y Pino fondly. He would send the children and a maid with his chauffeur to the Harvey House in Lamy to buy them ice cream. "How do you like that?" she recalled. "He was not like these other ones over here. He was a good man, Pedro Ortiz y Pino." Gerald Ortiz y Pino, one of his great-grandsons, is a longtime progressive state senator.

When their stepmother returned to Las Vegas, Pedro Ortiz y Pino's older children were taken under the wing of his sister, Manuela Ortiz. Her first husband, José Gonzales (of the wealthy Nazario Gonzales mining family), was killed when his car was run down by a train, and he is buried in the Galisteo cemetery.[94] She later married José Sena ("one of us," as Simona García put it) on her family's advice; he had been in the military, so he paid no taxes. Manuela owned the ranch called Chaquako in the western Galisteo Basin, where around

Lucy R. Lippard, *Two Petroglyphs in Open Land near Galisteo*, made by sheepherders Luis Chávez (1938) and Arturo Anaya (1939).

1927–28 Felipe Chávez worked. (He drove the school bus, a truck, to bring the children to Galisteo on a now defunct road.) Around that time, "Tia Manuela" took five-year-old Luis Chávez, whose mother, Manuelita, had died when he was three, to Santa Fe for three years, where he attended St. Francis School. When she moved back to Galisteo, he ran away to his father, up The Hill.

Photographer unknown, *Cantina Leyba/La Salita de el Coruco de San Antonio*, 1930s. On the back of the photo, "bartender Luis Chávez, customer Torosio Chávez." (Courtesy of the Montoya and Anaya families.)

"The village was very different then," Luis recalled. "There were more old houses and ruins." Firewood was gathered on San Cristóbal, "but when butane came they didn't let us go there any more, around 1959, so we got the gas." In 1947 he married Remedios Peña, Paulita's sister. Luis's father, Felipe Chávez (who married Demasia Anaya after the death of Luis's mother), was employed by the Piedra Lumbre Ranch—"by Cañon Blanco on the road to White Lakes"—a few miles from Galisteo, where his stepson Joe D. Anaya also worked. In the 1940s, Luis Chávez worked for Don José, "then with Frankie Anaya at Cerro Pelón" from 1940 to 1945, then with José Ortiz y Pino III, and for the railroad in Kennedy, El Paso, Kansas City, and Denver.[95] Felipe Chávez was injured in a fall from a windmill and eventually returned to his home on The Hill in Galisteo. He died at the age of 102, survived by sixty great-great-grandchildren.

The Leyba bar on present-day CR 42 (Camino los Abuelos) was the best known of Galisteo's several cantinas.[96] A photograph from around 1913 shows the bartender (another Luis Chávez, Antonio Chávez's great-uncle) and a well-dressed customer said to be Torosio (Toribio?) Chávez. A handwritten note on the photo reads: "Don Justo Leyba. . . . After 1913 no liquor was sold." Sarapio Montoya disputed the story that there were once eight bars in Galisteo but conceded there was a lot of bootlegging in the 1920s. He remembered the Leyba place, where his mother once lived, as "the prettiest in Galisteo." It was a wide, rectangular, U-shaped building "with a big portal all around and a wall across the front, a zaguan and a courtyard and a well in the center. A wagon entrance was closed at night."[97]

By the early 1900s, the old church on The Hill was already a ruin. The new church was the center of the village.[98] Religious ceremonies, deeply embedded in the land and culture, were the beating heart of norteño villages, unifying events that brought neighbors together in a common cause. Mela Anaya Montoya recalled that during her childhood in the 1930s and 1940s, "Galisteo was very community oriented; there were *matanzas* [communal slaughters of a sheep or cow for food] and fiestas, all centered on the church and growing season." Key to

Former Justo Leyba Bar, ca. 1940. (Palace of the Governors Photo Archives, NMHM/DCA neg. no. 59245.)

Ruin of the First Church on The Hill, ca. 1910. (Courtesy of the Concha Ortiz y Pino de Kleven Photograph Collection, Center for Southwest Research, University Libraries, University of New Mexico, neg. no. 000-457-0110B.)

this unity were the *sociedades* formed around the church, which have survived to this day. One small society is dedicated to San Antonio, and another is the mostly women's Sociedad de el Sagrado Corazon, first recorded in 1925. Members were sold *devisas* (badges) and its *cuotas* (dues) paid the church insurance, "an unbelievable $1 per year."[99]

The largest group was the Sociedad de San José, founded in 1895 and soon headquartered in La Sala de San José, the new dance hall next to the church. Women were not allowed as members and rules were strict. Cuotas were ten cents; they paid for fuel costs and upkeep of the church and La Sala. (Dues are now five dollars, and women help the members with their luncheons.) A warranty deed dated January 19, 1899, documents the sale of land adjacent to the church to the Sociedad de San José by Marcelino Baros and wife Teodora Sandoval for

Ernest Knee, *La Sala de San José de Galisteo*, 1938. Next door is part of the former Mora/Fenten/Scholder home. (Courtesy Ernest Knee Photographic Trust.)

thirty-two dollars.[100] It was bounded on the north by "the wall of a *gallinero* [chicken coop] that is the property of Alejandro Mora, south by Marcelino Baros, east by el Camino Real [NM 41] and west along the wall . . . owned by the seller." Soon La Sala de San José de Galisteo was constructed as a dance hall and community/church gathering place.[101] People came from as far as Pecos and Santa Fe for bailes at La Sala, and it could be rented for family occasions such as *casorios* (weddings) or *bautismos* (baptisms) with permission from a notary public in Lamy. In her nineties, Simona García dreamed about dancing the waltz and La Marcha at weddings: "Everyone liked the way I danced it." Anna Montoya Cárdenas, recounting stories told by her parents, writes of La Sala in her mother's youth: "Kerosene lamps were lit, or for an extra fee, carbide lights were primed and lit. A *bastonero* [bouncer] was hired. Liquor was not allowed inside the Sala. . . . Picture the young ladies as they sat patiently on the wooden bancos along the wall, waiting for the handsome young men in their best attire to come and ask them to dance. Meanwhile the *colector* interrupts each couple dancing and asks the gentleman for ten cents" (which paid for the musicians playing violin, accordion, and guitar).[102]

Special masses called *funciones* celebrated saints' days and sociedad meetings and were often accompanied by processions. Simona García recalled the Día de San Juan (June 24) procession, when a bulto of the saint was carried out into the fields to pray for water, a ritual similar to that performed in other northern New Mexico villages, although it was more common to do so with San Isidro Labrador, patron saint of farmers.[103] Clarita Anaya remembered walking to the Cadial with the Sacred Heart of Jesus statue. Concha Ortiz y Pino de Kleven recalled that when she was a girl in Galisteo, the older women bathed in the river at sunrise on Día de San Juan and washed their hair to make it grow or cut "the tip of their hair with an axe," a tradition performed in Mexico with a machete. (Marc Simmons suggests this was a reference to the beheading of John the Baptist.[104]) In some villages, those whose first name was Juan or John were serenaded in honor of San Juan's feast day. (The white primroses that spot the fields in that season are called Flores de San Juan.)

Mela [Manuela] Ortiz y Pino Martin, one of Don José's daughters, recalled: "When I was young and there was a drought, my mother would wash the saints in the Galisteo church. Then they would be carried through the town's streets, as people sang alabados—hymns of praise—and prayed for rain . . . the church bell clanging the entire time. Then my father would take the priest out to the ranch [Las Marias] to pray for rain there . . . it always rained."[105] Around 1912, her mother, who, like many family members, had problems with her eyesight, commissioned a stained-glass window above the church entrance dedicated to Santa Lucia, "patroness of the laboring classes and against distress of the eyes." When in pain, she'd call Galisteo and ask to have the lights turned on behind Santa Lucia. Mela Martin also prayed to Saint Lucy (who is represented holding her eyeballs on a platter).[106]

Mela Montoya recalled the performances of *Las posadas* and *Los pastores* in the village on Christmas Eve. Each village had its own version of *Los pastores,* which may have come to New Mexico from old Mexico around the mid-nineteenth century. Natividad Sena is credited with initiating Galisteo's version of the play, recorded in the 1960s. Sara Peña Sena recalled it being performed when she was a child, and it continued until 1964, in La Sala.[107] Before the play, *Las posadas* was performed at the homes of those who had been invited by letter to participate. After "Humilde a su aldea" was sung at each home, "Abranse las puertas" was sung at La Sala, and the players, led by Mary and Joseph, would enter singing "Caminando va José."

Wakes took place at the home of the deceased. After two days, the body was taken to church for a funeral mass and then in a horse-drawn wagon to the cemetery. "Only the Ortizes had a big funeral. Others just had the body blessed and put in the grave."[108] Around 1910–13 Galisteo's old cemetery had reached capacity and a new one was consecrated across the road.

Headquarters of Don José Ortiz y Pino Sheep Empire (Now Quartermill Farm), early 1920s. The steel truss bridge in the background was destroyed by floods around 1923. (Courtesy of Denise Lynch.)

Los Pastores, ca. 1940. *Front, left to right*: Cesario Chávez, Inez Sena (Montoya) as the Virgin, Mela Anaya (Montoya) as Gila, Ernesto Sena (?), Manuel Anaya as San José. *Back*: Clemente Chávez, Ralph Vigil, and several others, including Simón and Daniel Chávez as shepherds, Natividad Sena as Lucifer, and Frank Sandoval as the Hermit. (Courtesy of Anna Cárdenas and the Anaya and Montoya families.)

Los Pastores, 1940s. Pedro Peña is fourth from the left. (Courtesy of the Duran/Peña families.)

The two Catholic cemeteries (non-Catholics cannot be buried there) stand appropriately on Camino los Abuelos, or Grandparents' Road. Researching the old families, I was told that there were many "strangers" buried there because it cost only $200—cheaper than in other communities.[109] Many early grave markers were wooden, and they rotted or were taken for firewood. Newer, more elaborately carved, wooden markers are said to have been stolen sometimes and sold to antique dealers. Many New Mexico communities have harbored Crypto Jews—Hispano converso families descended from the Jews who emigrated from Spain in the 1500s after being forced to convert to Catholicism and who maintained certain Judaic traditions in secret. If this took place in Galisteo, it was indeed kept a secret. However, a photograph of a stone laid on top of a gravestone in the old cemetery, a Jewish tradition, has been cited as possible evidence of Crypto Jews in the village. Some common family names have been associated with both Hebraic and Arabic origins, among them Rael, Leyba, and Anaya.[110]

Northern New Mexico villages faced the Depression almost a decade before the rest of the country. When livestock and wool prices dropped after World War I and many Galisteños left to find work, Kennedy became a real ghost town, and prolonged drought in the 1920s caused many small farmers (among them Simona García's father and uncle, Eugenio and Ventura Baros) to lose their ranchitos to the few larger landowners who kept their heads above water. As they were forced off their lands, jobs became scarce. Indicative of changing economies, vocations in the 1920 census included "retail salesman" and other "salesmen" and a "carpenter for private homes," although there were still many "herders" and farmers.

From the late 1920s, one disaster followed another in the Galisteo Basin, including the 1926 flood that destroyed the last of the village's acequias. The Lamy/Santa Fe rail link was temporarily abandoned at the same time that El Central at Kennedy was cut off.[111] The winter of 1928 was catastrophic in New Mexico. Hispano ranchers all over the state lost half their sheep. Another ruinous drought struck in 1931 and lasted through 1934. Livestock perished and the land was ever more heavily gullied. Many cattle ranchers lost their fortunes. The Taylor Grazing Act, "which was supposed to increase the grazing lands available to villagers,

H. Sage Goodwin, *Campo Santo [Oratorio]*, ca. 1929. (Palace of the Governors Photo Archives, NMHM/DCA neg. no. 119565.)

Lucy R. Lippard, *The "New" Cemetery (ca. 1913)*, 2011. The recent white metal cross was donated by the Christian Brothers, facilitated by María Ortiz y Pino when it was discarded by the defunct Santa Fe University of Art and Design.

actually had the reverse effect of strengthening the hold of corporate livestock interests on the range."[112] Only those with livestock and deep wells (and deep pockets) survived.

In 1929, the patriarch Juan Ortiz died, having handed over all his business matters to his son Don José years earlier. His house was bequeathed to his loyal servant Pino Villanueva, who was "half Indian, half Spanish."[113] The same year, his granddaughter, the redoubtable Concepción ("Concha") Ortiz y Pino, whose rebellious personality had already been revealed when she was studying at the Loretto Academy in Santa Fe (they told her family she would never amount to anything), dropped out of college at age nineteen because she felt it was irrelevant. Her father lent her a "large house," and with some expert help, she established the Colonial Hispanic Crafts Society/School of Galisteo to sustain the village economically and revive traditions that were being lost, such as weaving, furniture making, tinwork, colcha embroidery, and wood carving.[114] "Our equipment," she recalled, "consisted of tanning vats, looms, and carpenter's tools. Original items were separated for our own use; the remainder was marketed."[115] She taught weaving and her sister Mela (Martin) taught embroidery.

Threshing Wheat with Sheep and Goats near Galisteo, ca. 1918. (Palace of the Governors Photo Archives, NMHM/DCA neg. no. 021583.)

The New Mexico Department of Vocational Training sent six students. Although the school failed to attract tourists and seems to have lasted only a year, it served as a model for the state's long-lasting vocational education program.[116] Many proud villagers, however, rejected "charity" from a family resented for its success on the backs of the poor. Concha's claims that she would take in twenty village children at a time to fatten them up, then get another batch, that she lent dresses to Galisteo ladies so that they could go to dances, and so forth, were angrily denied to me by one prominent local woman who grew up in Galisteo in the 1930s and 1940s.

In October 1933, Concha revived the Corrida de Gallo and fiesta. The festivities included a *rosario* in the church and two *gran bailes* in La Sala, featuring the "dance of the broom" and La Varsoviana, a schottische. The rooster pull, in the plaza in front of the church, featured "Galisteo Boys vs. Santo Domingo [and San Felipe] Indians" in an ironic echo from the past.[117] A live rooster was buried in the sand with only head and neck showing. Riders competed by taking turns swooping down on the poor bird. Finally someone made off with it, "the rest of the horsemen in furious pursuit," according to Mary Coan's contemporary account: "The fortunate fellow's teammates surround him, fending off the opposing teams' effort to secure the hapless rooster," which was used as a weapon.[118] By sunset, the team in possession of the now deceased bird was the winner. And in a still more curious chronological compression, the Comanches came roaring back into the Galisteo Basin in 1935, in a spectacular performance sponsored by "local boosters" and the Taos Lions Club. Staged to attract tourists, some "real Indians" and actors as soldiers battled on "the plains of Galisteo," presenting "such a realistic scene, to the accompaniment of rifle shots and arrows, that the visitors took cover, thinking that real warfare had broken out."[119]

Josefa Ortiz y Davis's granddaughter, George and Angelita Davis's daughter Victoria Davis de Sánchez (who described herself as "dark skinned and Indian looking"), began teaching in 1923, in her teens, to help her family during the Depression.[120] In 1932, before receiving her high school diploma, she taught upper grades in Galisteo for three years, describing the village school as "very attractive" with high adobe walls and a schoolyard so small that recesses had to be scheduled at different times. Fuel for the wood stoves was provided by the community. There were three classrooms for three teachers, each with around thirty students, mostly Hispano, who had to learn English in school. When not yet twenty, Sánchez was a school principal in Lamy.[121]

Victoria Davis married Leveo Sánchez from a Presbyterian Galisteo family, horrifying Josefa. (They were married in Willard, not Galisteo, implying some family resistance, though he converted to Catholicism.) Leveo had worked in Terrero Coal Mines in northern New Mexico and, through Don José ("Uncle Joe Ortiz y Pino"), got a job in Moriarty with the Highway Department. He bought a small ranch a few miles from Galisteo, and the couple planned to raise a family there. However, on July 28, 1930, after only thirteen months of marriage, he was killed in an automobile accident while Victoria was pregnant with their son, Leveo. (From 1939 to 1945 she was married to her deceased husband's brother Atilano; her brother John Davis married Leveo's sister Tablita Sánchez.) Victoria became a respected international educator, and her son followed in her footsteps.[122] Today he is on the Board of Regents at New Mexico Highlands University in Las Vegas, where a building is named after his mother.

T. Harmon Parkhurst, *[Sheriff Jesús Baca at] La Corrido de Gallo (Chicken Pull)*, Día de San Juan on Today's Via La Puente, 1933. (Palace of the Governors Photo Archives, NMHM/DCA neg. no. 9322.)

Lucy R. Lippard, *"Ghost House," Portal of Fremont Ellis House at San Sebastián,* 2002.

Two of Galisteo's most significant historic homes are still standing, but not in Galisteo. In the late 1930s, or around 1940, the impressive Pedro Ortiz y Pino hacienda on the east side of the creek was dismantled and carted away adobe brick by adobe brick by Fremont Ellis, a famous local artist.[123] Simona García recalled that "it was a very nice home," large with a zaguan (grand hallway) facing west to the creek and bedrooms to the sides. In the twenty years since Pedro's death it had deteriorated, having been rented out and used for storage, although the farming plots, sheep pens, and splendid orchards along the creek were still maintained. (They are all gone now. Only a few crumbling rock walls remain.) The Ellises were familiar with Galisteo because Fremont's wife, Lorenzita (Lencha) Gonzales, had rela-

The Destroyed Peña de Chávez House, 1880. (Courtesy of Antonio Chávez.)

tives there, among them Simona García's maternal grandparents, Refugio and Agapito Sena, who lived next door and farmed on La Joya. Since the 1920s, the Ellis family had enjoyed moonlight picnics in Galisteo, and when they decided to expand their cabin off what was then Old Route 66, they bought the vigas from the old house. The way the wood had been softly stained by water coming down from the roof captured the artist's eye: "Dad noticed that the adobes were still intact and he bought the place room by room," recalled his son Fred. In the process they found that several of the rooms were stone rather than adobe; Salvador Gonzales, who drove the truck, refused to take such a heavy load. Fremont and Fred reconstituted the building up the road in San Sebastian, off Old Las Vegas Highway.[124]

In 1941, Ellis added a number of elements to his reconstructed home from the nearby Luz Peña and Apolonio Chávez hacienda that once stood on La Otra Vanda, built around 1880.[125] Mae Peña recalled its long hall, with Victrola and piano, which was used as a community gathering place, the four large bedrooms, each with a fireplace, and the kitchen in a wing of its own. Sheep were brought in from faraway grazing areas to be sheared there. She recalled how "the thick adobe walls, the high windows, and the protective wall projected a feeling of security and permanence."[126] After the death of her uncle in 1935, the house stood empty, and in 1940 it was sold to Ellis for only $300 in taxes. The Chávez house mound and midden are still faintly visible. All that remain of the Ortiz y Pino hacienda in Galisteo are traces of the foundation, an ornamental metal fence, a big cement irrigation tank where water was pumped from the creek (Daniel Anaya remembers swimming in it with other local kids), and the ruin of a small adobe outbuilding, where Pedro and Adolfo Sandoval lived into the mid-twentieth century. Its front door lintel threatens to collapse but never does—a metaphor, perhaps, for the hardy old Hispano village. In the early 1990s, the strip was subdivided and several homes were built there (the first was my own in 1993).

Don Antonio Anaya (1836–1900) was mentioned in the Santa Fe newspaper in 1900 as one of the largest sheep owners of Galisteo, "understood to own more than 40,000 head of the fleecy fellows."[127] In the 1930s, his son José Antonio Anaya (1857–1942) owned a large property to the west of the village, across the railroad tracks on both sides of what is now CR 42—"thousands of acres from Lamy to the Southern Creston," according to family.[128] His compound on The Hill in Galisteo is still occupied by some of his descendants, and several others live elsewhere in the village. The Rancho Grande encompassed several ranchitos, each one circa 650 acres, with a few little buildings, each used at a different season for a specific function of the livestock business—one for lambing (*borreguito* or *hijadero*), which took place in March, and others for branding, horn docking, castration of lambs, and shearing of adult sheep (tresquilando las ovejas) in May.

One ranchito, Las Arrugas (folds, hilly), was just west of the railroad tracks on the south side of CR 42. (It was inherited by Serapio Anaya, Sr.; his younger brother Francisco [Pancho] worked it.) Another, El Chante (shack, shanty; aka Rancho de Arriba), inherited by Crescencio and Catalina Anaya, was on the north side, and another, Rancho de Abajo, was near the Garden of the Gods off NM 14. (Roads in a residential development off CR 42 are

José Antonio Anaya, Sitting Next to His Home on The Hill, ca. 1940. (Courtesy of Anna Cárdenas and the Montoya and Anaya families.)

called Anaya Springs and Don José Loop, presumably after José Antonio.) Each ranchito had a garden/small farm when there was enough rain, and at one time the family ran cattle, as well as sheep. Cedar posts were cut by the villagers on land identified as Cession de Escuela (by the State Land Office). Villagers may also have taken advantage of the Ortiz Mine grant being opened in 1940 for drywashing for gold—only to the people of Cerrillos, Madrid, Golden, and San Pedro. Joe D. Anaya recalls that they were not allowed to work there full-time, but some made "over $4.00 per day," a handsome sum at the time. Wood hauling (dead wood only) for residents of Cerrillos was also free, with a permit.

Until the early 1940s, José Antonio Anaya's family would live in the village in winter, and in the spring the children were taken out of school to help at the ranch from April through August. Serapio Anaya Jr. (1925–2016, the youngest of José Antonio Anaya's grandsons) described life in Galisteo for those clinging to their lands in the 1930s and 1940s:

> We used to have a hard time when we were young at [grandfather José Antonio Anaya's] ranch. . . . When school started we moved over here [to their house on The Hill]. In the month of May my dad [Serapio Anaya, Sr.] used to take me out of school before school was over and he would give me to the sheepherders at lambing time. My Dad was over there too. After May I'd be a sheepherder helper with an old man and the rest of the sheep. A cook was the one that carried our bedrolls and supplies on a burro up to Cerro Pelón. It took us about two days to get up there, with the little lambs. And then they used to bring the sheep back again and take them with that same man over to those mountains over there, near Ojo de la Vaca. I tell people my first automobile was a donkey. An old man said to me take your clothes so your mother can wash them. I came

Sheep Shearing, ca. 1930s–40s. Large bands of sheep shearers traveled the area to service huge flocks. (Courtesy of Yolanda and María Ortiz y Pino.)

> all the way on the *burrito*, to the Black Mountain [northern creston], no bridle, just a couple of sticks. I sat in the back and if I wanted to turn this way, I'd hit him here, the other way, hit him there. I came over to my mother's, tied the burro up in the corral—where Mary Alice [Anaya] lives, my grandfather's house. Then I went back on my burro. I made it ok. I didn't have to put gas. It was hard, you know. Sometimes I used to cry. I was too young. But my father had me out there. OK. He had to.
>
> I kept on going to school, my first school was here [on La Vega]. Then they moved us up there [to the WPA school] on The Hill. I was about 15. The school was new. I hardly had any education at all. I just passed through the sixth grade and because of that I had a hard time. . . . When my grandfather got sick, he couldn't take care of the sheep, he sold them, "not much money too, at that time."[129]

In the early 2000s, I visited El Chante with two of José Antonio's granddaughters, Mela Montoya and Rosina Anaya. In an isolated location, the house and dilapidated corrals and sheds remain. A chicken coop, an old stove, a chopping block, a wooden trunk with a flowery stamped metal lock, and a wooden feed trough are poignant reminders of what was lost. "There was a well and a little dam," recalled Mela. The sisters agreed that there were more trees then and a bridge over the watering hole; a flash flood took it out. Meat was dried on a line under an oak tree. Men who came to help with the sheep slept in tents. A covered buggy with about three seats—a *caratela*—was kept there. On a hill above the ranchito were big corrals. The stone and adobe house partly fell in a few years ago. One room was a bedroom for the seven girls; their father slept in the one used for living and cooking. There were two doors for each room but no door between the rooms. "Everything came in big tin cans"; baking powder cans figure in several stories. The sisters remember finding petrified wood on the property, not uncommon in the Galisteo Basin.

The Chante house's walls and ceiling were papered with mail order catalogues. Mela and Rosina made their own toys, but they remember "ceiling shopping; at night we'd look up and say, 'I like this one or that one.' We didn't have dolls; we cut paper dolls from the catalogues. We played cooking and ate *jawari*" (a made-up word). Their mother, Catalina Sandoval, died young in 1934, so in the 1930s Mela helped cook for the herders: "[I] took lunch to my grandfather in the fields. We fed the lambs with bottles. When we were small, at shearing, we'd jump from an eight-foot-high platform into huge gunny sacks to press the wool down."[130] The bags would be sown up and brought down by wagon to Kennedy and sent off to wool companies. Don José Antonio Anaya feuded with the Ortiz y Pinos and refused to sell stock or land to the patrón, who was not allowed on his property. But ties to the Ortiz family were unavoidable. Most of the men in Galisteo worked for them. Onésimo Montoya, who would marry Mela Anaya, herded sheep for her uncle Serapio, but also for the Ortizes, and as a child was paid to play at boxing with José Ortiz y Pino III.

By this time the patrón system was being recognized for the feudal exploitation it was, and individual expectations were higher. Some employers charged the workers so much at company stores and cantinas that they were continually in debt.[131] When asked about his relationship to Don José Ortiz y Pino, Serapio Anaya jokingly replied, "He used to be the *patrón* here. Well, he was my daddy! He was my great great great great great grandpa I guess. He used to be the boss around here in Galisteo. At his store the clerk had a big book: Serapio Anaya owes $2.50. I was a sheepherder, no? I'd come back, Serapio Anaya owes $3.50. So that number would never come down. You got a pair of shoes? No, I can't. It was hard, you know. Here my dad would go in, I can't get a pair of shoes for my *hijo*? Well, there's a lot of good tires there on the dump. You can take them and make good soles."[132]

Packing Wool, ca. 1930s–40s. (Courtesy María and Yolanda Ortiz y Pino.)

Many New Mexicans were forced to hire out as farmworkers in Wyoming or in Colorado, in fields of sugar beets, onions, and other crops. They boarded trains in Las Vegas. Some took their families. This migration was known as *el renganche* (to hook, or recruit).[133] For two weeks in 1936, in an eerie foreshadowing of today's cruel immigration policies, Colorado governor Edwin Johnson blockaded his state against "alien" and "indigent" New Mexicans seeking work; if they had no money, they were turned back.[134] Even those who returned home often had to leave for months at a time to find wage work.[135] Some did not survive. When I moved to Galisteo in 1993, the village men who had been forced to migrate were still alive to tell their tales. Serapio Anaya recalls, "In 1942 my father went to [Alamosa,] Colorado, sheepherding. They had him by himself over there with the sheep; over here they had two men. He wrote a letter to my mother [Carmelita] he didn't like it out there, he wanted to come back. But he died [in a hospital in Trinidad]. They brought him in the train to Lamy. They didn't know what he died of; they said he had drank some bad water when he was with the sheep. I don't know. In places like that, you don't know. He was 57, in 1942. I was 16 years old."[136]

Kay Matthews explains: "It's important to remember that during the many years men had to leave the villages of northern New Mexico to make a living in the mines of Colorado or the factories of California, their wives took care of all the household and outside needs, which were extensive. In those days kitchen gardens provided much of the food consumed by the family, hay fields provided forage for the cows, sheep, and goats that had to be herded and cared for on a daily basis, village *molinos* ground wheat into flour, and firewood had to be brought in from the common lands to be cut and split."[137]

Galisteo struggled to remain a traditional Hispano farming and ranching village. Joe D. Anaya, ninety-three years old at this writing, recalls that during the Depression in Galisteo "everyone had pigs, cows, they all died. There was no water. To survive people had to steal, they were desperate. Then the good president Franklin Roosevelt was elected."[138] In 1933, FDR came through Lamy on a train, the closest a US president has come to the Galisteo Basin, though he probably never set foot in it. Like much of rural America, Galisteo was resurrected in the later 1930s and early 1940s by the New Deal. In 1938, New Mexico, which remains one of the poorest states in the nation, was 52 percent Hispano. Santa Fe County was 67 percent; Taos and Rio Arriba Counties were 93 percent. The WPA, called "El diablo a pie" (the devil on foot) because that's what it sounded like in Spanish, came just in time. Although every northern village had a chapter of La Liga Obrera de Hable Español or a Unión Protectiva, there seems to have been none in conservative Galisteo. However, some local men were lucky enough to be hired by the Civilian Conservation Corps (CCC), among them one villager who lied about his age and used another name, an act that became a legal nightmare years later when he was found to have two names and two social security numbers.

In 1939 the WPA leased its local headquarters at the hacienda from Josefa Ortiz y Davis and set up a factory where mattresses were stuffed with wool, in an old Montoya home on Avenida Vieja, administered by the National Youth Administration Vocational Schools. (Serapio and Julia Anaya received a mattress made there as a wedding gift.) The WPA also dismantled what was left of the old church on The Hill. It had been abandoned for some fifty

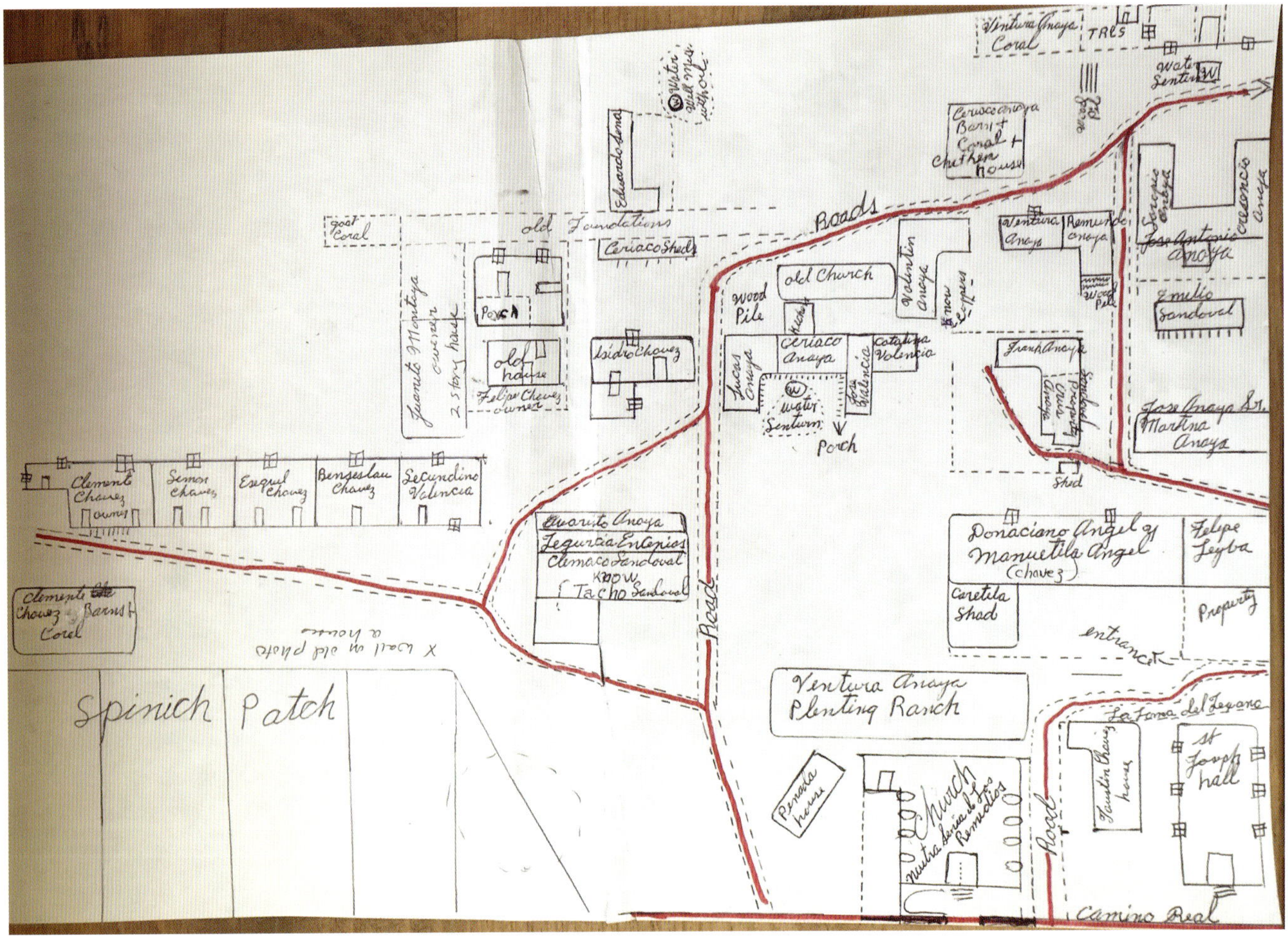

Joe D. Anaya, *Map of Galisteo in the Old Days*, 2014.

years, and its vigas had already been spirited away to homes in Galisteo and Santa Fe. Galisteo (described in a WPA guidebook as altitude 6,400, population 300, "a typical New Mexico farming village in the center of a stock-raising area"[139]) became one of the first towns in the state to receive a New Deal school when the old schoolhouse on La Vega was replaced in the mid 1930s.[140] Elegantly constructed in Pueblo Revival style, the new school west of The Hill had four rooms and a detached teacherage (both are now private homes, as is the earlier school). Local men made the adobes and the women plastered. (Galisteña Marcelina Montoya Mares was a well-known *enjarradora.*) Mary Mora, later the proprietor of Mary's Bar in Cerrillos, taught in Galisteo and lived at the teacherage. It only functioned for some twenty years.[141]

The war years saw radical change in New Mexico, and in Galisteo. Except for a few later skirmishes, the land grant battles in the Galisteo Basin were over. The local Hispano populace moved from centuries of self-sustaining agriculture to a wage-based economy, a process

Gene Garriote, *Former WPA Schoolhouse*, oil painting on board, 1983. This rendering of the original building, built in 1938, was given to the current owners when they purchased it. Water for construction was hauled up from the creek. The double adobe walls are twenty-four inches thick. (Courtesy of Joette O'Connor and Nicolas Trofimuk.)

already underway in the early 1940s. In 1941, a large number of young New Mexicans, including many farmers, ranchers, and shepherds, joined the military to fight in World War II. In 1942, sixteen-year-old Serapio Anaya heard about jobs on the railroad that sounded a lot better than sheepherding. Pedro Peña and other boys from the area were working at Kennedy. He went over but was told they had enough help. ("But I ate breakfast anyway!") Soon he and Tony Sena found work near the Lamy stockyard:

> It was hard, but better than sheepherding. Tony didn't want to go when the camp moved to Colorado. He said they're going to call me for the Army. He was a little older than me. I went all the way to Colorado, later I came back. . . . We told them we're going to back to school. So we came back on the train to Lamy and got a ride over here. My *padrino* and my *madrino* and my *tío* told me where you going? I'm going home. Your mother's not there. She had to move. There was no help then, like welfare now. She used to work as a cook in the school up here. Now she was working with people, cleaning, in Santa Fe, and I worked as a laborer building the veterans' general hospital there for two months and then I went to the Army in 1944.[142]

Joe D. Anaya as a Boy, with Karakul Lamb at the Ortiz y Pino Ranch, 1939. (Palace of the Governors Photo Archives, NMHM/DCA neg. no. 059019.)

Galisteo, New Mexico, ca. 1945. (Palace of the Governors Photo Archives, NMHM/DCA neg. no. 36455.)

FIVE

New Blood, a Sense of Loss (1945–1990)

El que pierde su tierra pierde su memoria.
—Juan Estevan Arellano[1]

Its spirit is still there, but a sense of loss.
—Don Usner[2]

I'll live in Galisteo 'til the day that I die.
—Burl Ives, "Galisteo"[3]

From the outside, Galisteo in the 1940s and 1950s was seen almost as a ghost town, although strong local families remained to carry on with their lives.[4] When Mary Alice Anaya moved to the village from Santa Fe to live with her husband, Pancho, in the compound of his father, José Antonio Anaya, "there was hardly anyone [t]here. They were all in Santa Fe."[5] The population had shrunk to around two hundred as military service opened up a new world to rural youth. When the veterans returned, they took courses in modern agriculture and sheep husbandry under the GI Bill but found little productive land and few opportunities available locally. Better jobs existed beyond Galisteo, often out of state, especially in California.

The last straw was a long and devastating drought in the 1950s—the worst since the 1600s—that made small-scale dry farming almost impossible. As they were sold off, the smaller farms and ranches were consolidated by a second Ortiz y Pino generation. José Ortiz y Pino III told me, "When I got back from the army I bought up all the old houses for sale, so they say I stole it."[6] The family's acquisition of abandoned homes in Galisteo, and the blatant economic disparities between the patrón family and their less fortunate neighbors, fueled a long-standing resentment among villagers who had been forced by economic circumstances to sell their ancestral homes and lands. Serapio Anaya's story exemplifies the plight of some Galisteños:

> When I went to the army my mother still had a ranch up there. This man said your husband owes me $200 would you let me have the ranch. So they make some kind of deal without paper. OK just give me fifty dollars and keep your ranch. My mother gave him the papers. The man turned around and sold it. . . . They wanted to get an abstract and the real estate company called me and told me I had given my uncle some property. I said no . . . and I saw the date, June 1944. I told the girl no, I was in Abilene Texas in the service. . . . So two hundred and something acres. . . . All the houses up there my grandfather used to own. I don't know how they did it . . . I told the real estate company the property is supposed to be mine.[7]

Mary Branham, *José Ortiz y Pino III Repairing Coyote Fence*, 1959. (Palace of the Governors Photo Archives, NMHM/DCA neg. no. 111675.)

Meanwhile, changing demographics were transforming the state itself and contributing to the social fragmentation of villages like Galisteo, which lies on the border of the subtly different cultures of the Rio Abajo and Rio Arriba (Lower and Upper River) and is not easily categorized within either one. Galisteo is something of an anomaly even in central New Mexico. In the mid-twentieth century, the village became increasingly distanced—culturally, economically, and even politically—from the harsher, better watered, but poorer mountain villages farther north, while continuing to share their religious base, devotion to the land, and contentiousness. Thanks to its proximity to the state capital, Galisteo was more gentrified and less parochial than similar towns in the north, but it differed from southern New Mexico too, and not just in chile recipes and the names for bagged Christmas candles and bonfires, *farolitos* vs. *luminarias*.

The last militant confrontations in the area between Anglos, Mexican/Spanish Americans, and Native peoples—the raids by the Gorras Blancas and La Mano Negro—took place in the nineteenth century. But to this day cultural clashes and coalitions are a significant undercurrent to life in New Mexico. Cultural stress, poverty, resentment, addiction, and grief are often attributed to a century marked by the wholesale loss of land. Taoseña scholar Sylvia Rodríguez observes, "The Hispano landscape of identity or ethnoscape combines themes of rupture, displacement, and a deep longing to remain on the land." The key word is *querencia,* loosely defined as love of place, of roots, bringing a sense of safety and belonging.[8]

Josefa Ortiz y Davis, whose life defined an era of Galisteo history, died Christmas 1940.[9] The end of a shorter, but even more influential, era was marked by the death in December 1951 of her nephew and son-in-law Don José Ortiz y Pino, a victim of Parkinson's disease and a stroke. The "Last Patrón" of his namesake's elegiac book, his empire was breaking up on the shoals of falling wool prices and family discord. When Don José was ill, he charged his daughter Concepción (Concha) Ortiz y Pino de Kleven with the responsibility for the huge Agua Verde Ranch, which stretched all the way to Clines Corners, and a herd of black Karakul sheep. The fact that Don José handed this job to Concha and not to Frank was a sore point, but the ranch had fallen into debt under the son's management and the family dispute was resolved in court.[10] Don José spent his last years in Santa Fe, where he was buried. Frank Ortiz was appointed his father's executor, only to be legally disempowered by his mother and sisters.[11]

Concha (as she was known statewide) was by then a veteran of the state legislature and the first woman in the nation to be majority whip. In April 1943 she married University of New Mexico professor Victor E. Kleven, but she often lived on Agua Verde with the local men who were helping her restore the ranch house and get the ranch back on its feet. (As a youth in the 1940s, Galisteño Rudy Sena worked for Concha at Agua Verde as an "indentured servant" because his father owed Don José money. He was committed to working there for three years for nothing. One day he took a ranch truck to a dance in Galisteo, stayed the weekend, and was fired.)[12] In 1956, the day Concha's herculean task at Agua Verde was completed and just as her husband was to join her, he died of a heart attack.

Concha returned to her active civic career and died in 2006. Her sisters Mela (Martin) and Josefita (Gómez) lived in Santa Fe. Don José's widow, Pablita, sold the Agua Verde

Robert Martin, *Bluebell Jackson Hurtado and Antonio (Felipe?) Chávez Dance while sisters Concha Ortiz y Pino and Mela Martin Look On*, ca. 1950. A party at the Ortiz y Pino Santa Fe home. (Courtesy of La Herencia Archive.)

Frank Ortiz y Davis Museum, 1950s. (Courtesy of Yolanda and Maria Ortiz y Pino.)

Ranch to Robert O. Anderson, a Roswell oil millionaire. Frank Ortiz y Davis, Don José's only surviving son, was the sole member of the patrón's family still based to some extent in Galisteo, though he and his wife María (Mary) García lived in a fashionable home in Santa Fe, where they raised their children José Ortiz y Pino III, Frank Ortiz y Davis Jr., Juan Ortiz y Davis, María (Catanach), and Margaret Ortiz y Davis (Truscott).

Frank Ortiz Sr.'s fortunes were somewhat diminished, though he inherited a good deal of land around Galisteo. In 1970, he was still "the boss" of 33,000 acres, extending fourteen miles from the village, including Piedra Lumbre and the "ghost town" of Ojo de la Vaca.[13] Las Marías remained the ranch headquarters. Reportedly a jovial and outgoing man, Frank ran a gas station, bar, and "historical museum" in the old Davis hacienda, as well as operating a livestock business out of the ranch headquarters (later incorporated into the Vista Clara Spa, now the Qigong or Chi Center). In the late 1950s Frank Ortiz was joined by his son José Ortiz y Pino III.[14]

The six-year drought that began in 1950 marked the turnover of virtually all the large ranches in the east central Galisteo Basin. In 1948 San Cristóbal was sold to the Farr Brothers and the Sawyer Cattle Co. of Texas, which was dissolved in 1955. Ranch managers Harper and Elsie McFarland were to remain through other owners for almost fifty years.[15] Fences were built, wells with windmills were drilled, and in 1955 the ranch was sold again, to Texas senator William A. Blakley and his wife, Villa. In 1960 they revived the 1924 and 1944 searches for oil, gas, and minerals on San Cristóbal, leasing 39,000 acres of the ranch to the Fullerton Dobson heirs for fuel exploration that proved unsuccessful. A planned subdivision also failed.

The villagers' use of the Cadial's common lands for grazing persisted into the 1960s despite their loss in the courts. Cattle could wander into the village, and when horses were rounded up in the fall, they galloped past homes to corrals in the bosque. Onésimo Montoya recalled that suertes on the Cadial were marked with rods or axles from old buggies, and that there was nothing left of houses there, which were "too far from the river"—either the Rio Galisteo or the San Cristóbal/Atascoso Arroyo, which produced terrible water. Boggy on the east side, it was, according to Montoya, "shallower than now [2000], almost flat across." Pankey had permitted use by villagers "rather than getting into a fight about it."[16] But in 1965 M.W. "Buddy" and Betty Jo Branum of Midland, Texas, acquired San Cristóbal and finally fenced the west side of the San Cristóbal Ranch, cutting it off from villagers' homes and grazing, delivering yet another lethal blow to small-scale ranching.[17]

In 1956, farther away but in the area of influence on Galisteo, Alva A. Simpson Jr., and his wife, Anneliese, (with the proceeds from a uranium sale) bought the former Onderdonk Ranch/Lamy grant, from Frank and Carolyn Teal for $12.50 per acre. The 27,000-acre property extended up the mesas to Lower Cañoncito. However, as Simpson's nephew Robert Dobyn later explained, the wells at the Lamy ranch were a problem, and the drought wasso bad that trees died when their roots in or near rocks got deadly hot and junipers took all the water from the grasses. There were other drawbacks: "The rancher is so dependent on the natural grasses which are non-existent and, of course, the moisture you get in the air which is basically non-existent in this part of the country. Las Cruces, an agricultural college, paid Alva $20,000 or $30,000 if they could come up here for a couple of years and bulldoze all the trees down and do a study on the increase of grazing. What happened [was that] the trees were replaced by cactus. No trees came back, no grass came back. It was a total failure."[18] Thus the ground was laid for repurposing this major ranching property, which was to become the vast subdivisions of "El Dorado at Santa Fe," north of Galisteo.

In 1949, Haworth Thornton, from Payote, Texas, bought some 20,000 acres in the northern Galisteo Basin for $9 an acre. His son Bluford ("Blue") Thornton ran it for many years. The new ranch bordered Galisteo in several places, absorbing the holdings of José Antonio Anaya east and west of CR 42. When they were first married, Bluford's daughter Genora and her husband, Sarge Moore, had worked as ranch hands for the adjacent Simpson Ranch and knew the area well. In the late 1950s Bluford Thornton hired Galisteño Sarapio Montoya, a diminutive but consummate cowboy, who had worked in Colorado, at the Simpson Ranch, and as foreman on the McKee Ranch. Montoya was highly respected in the area. Genora Moore called him *Abuelo* and eloquently recalled ranch life in those days: "There are fewer of us now, hardly any who remember the open range, like Sarapio. So many of the ranches I remember as a kid are sold, cut up, and developed." (Her own family ranch would meet the same fate.) She described the Spiess siding, next to the railroad near the intersection of US 285 and NM 41: "There was a set of livestock scales and loading ramps, a lot of cattle still went out by train. The local ranchers used these pens to hold and sort their cattle and load them on cattle cars. It was quite a sight on a fall morning to see the rolling hills around that corner fill up with cattle."[19] Rancher and ranch hand Archie West, from the western basin

Renowned Vaquero Sarapio Montoya at Thornton Ranch, mid 1970s. Born in Leyba in 1914, Montoya earned $12.50 a month as a ten-year-old sheepherder, walking behind the flock (and occasionally traveling by train) to Laramie, Wyoming. He went to work for the Thornton Ranch in 1959 and was foreman there for twenty-five years. He died in Galisteo in 1999. (Courtesy of the Montoya and Thornton families.)

(brother of artist Jerry West), famed as a cowboy and the best dancer in the county, worked at the Simpson Ranch around 1965 breaking horses.[20] "Archie spent the night and left before dawn, with a new string of colts to break," recalled Moore. "It had snowed in the night and the ground that morning was glistening white and trackless. It was cold and silent, with a streak of pomegranate across the horizon and the world was empty as far as you could see, except for the lone figure, his hat pulled low and his collar turned up, riding away to the west."[21]

Finally, and most significant for the village of Galisteo, in the mid 1950s Robert McKee of El Paso—owner of a construction company that was once the largest in the world, builder of Los Alamos, the Nevada Test site, the Los Angeles and Dallas–Fort Worth airports, among other major projects—started shopping for a ranch for his son Philip, who was about to graduate from New Mexico State University in Las Cruces, where he and his young wife, Jean, were studying ranch management and animal husbandry. Robert McKee was willing to pay up to $300,000 for ranch and cattle. Although the Galisteo Basin property was not Philip's first choice, his father bought some Ortiz y Pino land from Frank Ortiz, as well as other parcels, eventually cobbling together a large spread where he wanted Philip to run four hundred cattle.[22]

The property was described by Realtor F. W. LaRouche as 23,000 acres (some of it leased from the State Land Trust),[23] "water ample at 15–22 ft. depth, plus large amounts of level land. . . . Ten wells and windmills, many stock tanks. c. 15,000 sq. ft. of buildings . . . five separate pastures and a holding pasture on the railroad."[24] The "historic José Ortiz y Pino Ranch" was purported to have been "in the family's contiguous [*sic*] possession for 250 years, having been presented to the original owner by the King of Spain. This ranch has never been sold before—one of the most colorful and historic in the Southwest. Site of two ancient Indian pueblos. Could be one of the showpieces of the country. Price $160,000."[25]

That was impressive, if inaccurate.[26] Abstracts reveal that what is now called the Cerro Pelón Ranch (or Rancho Cerro Pelón) was a more interesting patchwork of smaller parcels that had been land grants, homesteaded, sold, and resold for more than a hundred years before the McKee family had them from 1954 to 1960. A large part had been acquired in the twentieth century by Don José Ortiz y Pino. By 1957 the McKee Ranch was up and running. In 1959 Robert McKee, whose letters testify that he continued for years to micromanage his son's affairs, was still expanding it.[27] At its largest the McKee Ranch comprised 27,000 acres, including a state lease, spread over three townships and three ranges.

There was no headquarters on the acquired land; the prospectus noted, "[The] historic village is Ranch Headquarters," meaning Don José's deteriorating compound in the village center (which had once consisted of a cantina, a store, a house, corrals, and orchards). Philip and Jean McKee lived there while the ranch was being established, and then her parents, the Hovers, occupied it for a decade or so.[28] McKee built his own ranch headquarters (now La Jara Ranch) southwest of town on the far side of the Arroyo de Los Angeles. The village of Galisteo also figured in the deal as the source of "ample male and female help, competent and low priced."[29]

The unforgiving drought paved the way for more home sales and residential land use. In the 1950s, Galisteo began to be perceived as a hub for Anglos "of a special kind," who began

Joan Myers, *Gate to the Old Garrison at Ortiz Hacienda/John Benjamin Home*, 2018. Around 1992, Benjamin restored the gate based on old photographs.

to buy up inexpensive old adobes, a trend that took off in the 1960s and has barely faltered since, although prices have risen exponentially.[30] Consider, for instance, Father Stanley's romanticized description of Galisteo: "A quaint, ancient place . . . a photographer's delight. It is the past rubbing elbows with the present; it is Spain on American soil; it is New Mexico. It is magic. The world stands and waits. In fact, it doesn't exist in this timeless town. It is the glory of the past in the joy of the present."[31]

This kind of effusive journalistic prose ignored the struggles of the longtime residents and provided a magnet for newcomers who were to change the character of the "timeless" Hispano farming village. The old families' hard work and hard lives on the land they were losing were invisible. Remedios Chávez recounted a conversation with Natividad Sena. She bemoaned, "This world has changed so much." Sena replied, "No, *hermana*, the world is still round. It's the people that have changed."[32]

Despite the postwar exodus of many older families, Galisteo remained a stronghold of the Anayas, Chávezes, Montoyas, Sandovals, Senas, and their relations. Onésimo Montoya's (1929–2012) immediate family had moved around but returned to Galisteo from Lamy when

Wedding of Mela Anaya Montoya and Onésimo Montoya, Galisteo, April 1950. *Left to right*: Ines Sena Montoya, Best Man Sarapio Montoya, Onésimo Montoya, Mela Anaya Montoya, Maid of Honor Pablita Montoya, Conrada Anaya, and Flower Girl Viola Anaya. (Courtesy of Anna Cárdenas and the Montoya family.)

he was nine years old.[33] In 1950, he married Mela Anaya (1929–2010), José Antonio's granddaughter, who had graduated from Stanley High the valedictorian of her class. The couple built a home on CR 42 on land bought from the Leybas.[34] Five of the Montoyas' nine children remain in the village, and the family has maintained invaluable ties to its past.

Rural electrification finally arrived in Galisteo in the early 1950s, though a community water system was still a decade away. J. B. Jackson's memories of rural life in La Cienega at the time are probably applicable to Galisteo: "We still had the remnants of rural services. There was a dilapidated bus twice a day, took people to Santa Fe," as well as bread and meat deliveries. Election candidates appeared in old cars, loudspeakers on the roof: "He'd sit on the roof in the back, telling all about himself." With the reduction of livestock and the arrival of natural gas, recounted Jackson, the trees had come back: "They don't cut them for firewood. When I first arrived this little valley was practically naked of trees. Now it's almost like New England" (much of which was also "naked" until the mid-twentieth century). Jackson's neighbor, Facundo Pino, plowed the fallow fields even though he no longer planted them, saying, "It was just so that 'all the germs and evil forces in the earth, I want them to leave the earth.'"[35]

Mela Anaya Montoya ran the last Galisteo post office out of her house from around 1947 (under her father's name at first, because she was underage), preceded by her older sister Josefina Anaya de Anaya and by Remedios Chávez (also underage). It was closed March 31, 1959. After that, the closest post office was in Lamy, where Postmaster Carmen McGuiness (whose mother was a Valencia from Galisteo) ran it from a shelf in her walled-in front porch

Tourist Map of Galisteo, September 1960 (*El Puente*, Nov. 2002).

until November 2000, when it, too, was closed. Local USPS service is now run out of Santa Fe. The school was also closed, and children were sent to Stanley (and later to El Dorado). Anna Montoya Cárdenas remembers getting on the school bus in Galisteo at 5:30 a.m.

In 1959 Mary Branham reported in *New Mexico Magazine* that the new people coming in and restoring the old adobes were bringing commerce to the once destitute village.[36] In the 1960s, Galisteo was not the quiet residential community it is today, but home to a number of younger families and commercial ventures. Blazoned across the hacienda's façade was a sign reading "Historical Trading Post Frank Ortiz y Davis and Sons." In addition, Anglo businesses had sprung up, some operating out of La Sala de San José next to the church: "Spanish and Mexican Imports, Gay and Glittering Gifts, Elita Wilson's Southwest Dresses" and La Vela, "Candles, Ceramics, Baskets, Gifts," run by Jeannie McKee and her mother, Helen Hover; "Hacienda de San Francisco," southwestern painter María Salazar's studio; the Blue Bulto,"Something Old, Something New," proprietors Henry and Virginia Wicks. Next door was Major Felten's Galisteo Craftsmen, offering "the most beautiful custom-made furniture in the Southwest," some of it made by Onésimo Montoya.[37] The phone numbers were Galisteo 1, Galisteo 2, Galisteo 3, and so forth.

All of this was part of a major push to "revitalize" Galisteo as a tourist destination, although a 1962 *Westways* article warned, "Business is rotten in Galisteo."[38] The village was still being described as "a green farming oasis amid a stockman's huge domain," a "ranching town," surrounded as it was by three large ranches, all owned by Texans: San Cristóbal to the east, Thornton to the northwest, and McKee to the southwest. While sheep had so long been the sign of prosperity for old Hispano families (their descendants often mention that their forebears owned many sheep), few had survived the droughts, but many locals continued to own some livestock and horses for personal use.

Lamy was recommended as another stop for "Wild West atmosphere." It boasted a reconstruction of the Legal Tender bar and restaurant. An undated report (probably from the 1960s) calls on the state to establish a visitor center for the Galisteo Basin in Galisteo

Tyler Dingee, *Leo D. Pick General Merchandise, Lamy, with Photographer*, ca. 1950. Nearby was the saloon first known as the Pink Garter and since 1968, the Legal Tender. It boasts a stunning old wooden bar. (Palace of the Governors Photo Archives, NMHM/DCA neg. no. 073809.)

and to acquire "certain points of interest such as the Galisteo Pueblo, the San Cristóbal ruins, petroglyph sites, picnic and rest areas, along with reconstructed hotels, craft shops, horseback riding facilities, and similar establishments"—an idea that has surfaced in various guises ever since but never succeeded.

In a typical trajectory, Henry (Hank) Wicks, with his second wife, Virginia, researched and restored an old adobe (El Retiro) on La Vega that he had bought in 1950 with his first wife, Mabel Hart. Since 1934, it had been occupied by the Villanueva family, described as "loyal workers," to whom Juan Ortiz had bequeathed the house.[39] It came back into the family in

Lucy R. Lippard, *El Retiro from La Vega*, 2018. José Ortiz y Pino III contended that this was Nicolás Pino's home, built in the 1830s, although documentation points to Nicolás living on the east side of the creek and no homes being constructed on the west side until perhaps the 1840s.

December 1960, when it was purchased by José and Yolanda Ortiz y Pino, with their children José and María.[40] Before that, they had lived at Las Marías Ranch headquarters (aka Las Tres Marías, named after José's mother, sister, and daughter), then at the 1860s former home of Antonio Ortiz and his wife, Liz Durán, where they ran the flourishing La Mancha restaurant in 1960. Until 1972 guests could down a famous margarita at Frank Ortiz's museum bar in the Ortiz y Davis hacienda—eventually overseen by a stuffed deer's head boasting a red bandanna that John Wayne had tied around its neck one night in the 1970s when he was filming *The Cowboys* on the San Cristóbal Ranch—then walk along a lighted path through Ortiz property to dine at La Mancha.[41]

After Frank Ortiz y Davis's death in 1973, José Ortiz y Pino III closed his father's museum "because the locals did not respect it," sold the ancestral Ortiz y Davis hacienda, and donated some of its collection to the "living history museum" at Las Golondrinas near La Ciénega.[42] Following his family's longtime tradition of entering politics, he was a two-term county commissioner, a state senator, chairman of the State Parks Commission, and special assistant to Governor David Cargo. In 1972 he self-published, with Libriano (Larry) Anaya, *The Herbs of Galisteo and Their Power,* followed in 1981 by *Don José: The Last Patrón*, an entertaining, if often historically inaccurate, account of the commercial exploits of his grandfather Don José Ortiz y Pino in Galisteo.[43] On his retirement from civic life, José III became a self-styled curandero. Until his death in 2016 he worked out of his "office" in a little adobe on ancestral property, distinguished by a cow skull, cross, and strange figure that appeared to be a mummy, with a sign announcing Yerbas y Remedios.

Lucy R. Lippard, *José Ortiz y Pino's Curandero "Office,"* ca. 2006.

The larger properties around Galisteo village are rich in water rights.[44] Actual wet water is harder to come by. The history of Santa Fe County planning over the last few decades indicates increased concern and more regulations (not always effective, monitored, or enforced) on water use, but the water rights attached to tangled land grants and changing titles often prove too much for modern bureaucracies. Water rights in the Galisteo Basin, where the hydrology remains bewildering even to experts, are excruciatingly complicated and unequally distributed. Wells on the east side of the Galisteo Creek and the Arroyos San Cristóbal and La Jara have traditionally produced very bad water, thanks to patches of Mancos shale that produce a sulphurous, rotten-egg odor.

Elita Wilson, *"Picturesque, Yes; But Not Practical,"* 1962. (Courtesy of Remy and Luis Chávez.) This picture accompanied a brief article headlined "Old Village to Get New Aqua System": "This ancient village is finally going to get running water . . . a group of local citizens have formed a corporation to supply water. Two-thirds of the cost of the project will be borne by the state and the remaining third by the village. A well has already been dug and preparations are being made for digging the trench and the installation of the water main in it."

In 1960, Galisteans had neither irrigation ditches nor running water infrastructure. Those without wells who could afford his service paid Tobías Anaya twenty-five cents to deliver water in metal drums by horse-drawn wagon from the creek to their cement-lined, backyard cisterns on The Hill. Anna Montoya Cárdenas remembers when "Tobias came driving very early in the morning with water splashing from the barrels." For those who could not afford this service, the women carried water up The Hill on their heads. Joe D. Anaya recalls lugging it up in buckets as a child. In 1962, the *Santa Fe New Mexican* published a photograph by Elita Wilson of Tobías hauling water from the creek in a wagon, with Johnny Anaya as a boy in the foreground. It was captioned "Picturesque, Yes; But Not Practical."[45]

The establishment of the Galisteo Mutual Domestic Water Consumers and Mutual Sewage Works Association promised a more communal approach. On April 21, 1961, nineteen residents signed a paper to incorporate it with a loan from the state. Allotted to the village were 42.56 acre feet.[46] From November 1961 through March 1962, the men of Galisteo, led by Joe M. (José Manuel) Anaya—"a recent graduate of St. Michael's College," who was president of the "mutual domestic" until 1981—worked to build the system, which for years remained homemade

Lucy R. Lippard, *Agua Es Vida: Village Water Tanks and the Old Cemetery*, ca. 2000.

and high-maintenance. (On the advice of engineers, the wrong-sized pipe had been initially installed, raising perennial problems.) Pipes run under paved highways NM 41 and CR 42, making repairs extremely expensive. The sewage system never got off the ground, and septic tanks remain the norm. People were initially encouraged to buy more than one hookup to meet the state quota for a Mutual Domestic Water Consumers Association. The shallow village well on the west side, on land formerly owned by the patrón, however, is of good quality and produces plentifully. It was donated to the new communal system by then owner Philip McKee, who also owned a bulldozer and trenched at cost; an anonymous donor filled the gaps.[47]

The first foreman, or mayordomo, of these new buried ditches was Felipe Chávez y Chávez; then came the vaquero Sarapio Montoya, and then Roman Attenberger (b. 1919), who served from the mid 1970s almost to his death in 2003. The more or less homemade system

Joe M. Anaya and Family in Their Galisteo Home, Easter Sunday, 1970. Joe, his parents, Miquelita and Basilio Anaya, his wife, Mary Ann, and his children, JoAnn, Robert, Michael, Mark, Dora Jean, and Joseph Richard. (Courtesy of the Anaya Family.)

Four Generations of Chávez Men, ca. 1986. *Left to right*: Antonio holding his son Angelo, Felipe, and Luis. (Courtesy of Antonio Chávez.)

leaked constantly, and the stalwart Roman, a former Wisconsin farmer in his seventies, could be seen digging beside the road in all weathers, up to his hips in mud. Today's longtime foreman is Antonio Chávez, Felipe's grandson.[48]

At the outset, the Water Association served twenty-six members. By 1987, there were forty-five members and there was a waiting list. Expansion of the system was necessary, but the state refused to give the association a loan because the fees were too low ($10 per month). Galisteans considered raising the dues to $25 too much of a hardship for some residents, so the community decided to go it alone. Funds were raised by selling more hookups, and there are various stories based in intricate village and family politics about who got the available hookups, how many, and why. A longtime resident who was deprived of a hookup when he arrived in town at the founding of the water system told me, "[The way] water is used to control growth here is classist. People with hookups use all the water they want and keep poorer people and kids of old families from getting it." It was not that directly Machiavellian, but the cost of installing a hookup today ($10,000) remains prohibitive for many families whose children have land and would like to live here, although the money is increasingly necessary for the association to fund maintenance and improvements.

Brothers Tobías and Antonio (Tony) Anaya, as well as their sister and brother-in-law Clarita and Manuel Anaya, lived on The Hill. Tobías (1909–89), a self-taught artist, made inventive wooden sculptures, which he sold by the old cemetery, where a *descanso* is dedicated to him. Tony (1916–97) traveled all over the state making paintings of New Mexico churches.[49] For decades, his depiction of the first Galisteo church stood with a small wooden cross on the remaining mound. It was mounted on a discarded real estate sign—an ironic touch given Galisteo's gentrification; decades later it faded away and has been replaced by a photograph of the old church.

The patrón's home and compound saw a downward trajectory. After Philip McKee's divorce, it changed hands a couple of times. In the late 1960s or early 1970s, "Linley Tonkin Solari bought it from some people named Maytag and leased it to a bunch of hippies and to some priests and some different people, and they used what is now [a] riding arena for a

Tobías Anaya Selling His Art at the Old Cemetery, ca. 1970s. (Courtesy of Kenny M. Chávez.)

Lucy R. Lippard, *Descanso for Tobías Anaya at the Site Where He Displayed and Sold His Art*, ca. 1998.

garbage dump. . . . It was more of a hippie commune," recalled owner Priscilla Hoback (artist-daughter of Rosalea Murphy of Pink Adobe restaurant fame in Santa Fe). "When I bought the place [in 1978 Linley] had it on the market for like three years, and it was empty" except for an old German caretaker named Bruno, "who was kind of crazy." "There was no heat, no plumbing, no water." A root cellar under Hoback's studio (Don José's former store) had a big lock and bars on the door. One of the little structures next to the big house was an old cantina. The land extended to the southern highway bridge, much of which has since been sold and is the site of several houses. Hoback named her new home, stable, studio, and gallery Quartermill Farm (the price she estimated to restore it). As she has noted in her memoirs, some of the buildings might date to the 1860s, but most were built around the turn of the twentieth century during the heyday of the last patrón. "By the end of the 1980s, there were several houses being remodeled in Galisteo, and I bought all the old boards and doors and windows and fireplace tops, posts."[50] Despite these major changes in the area, in 1970, travel writers were still producing saccharine descriptions of the "primitive" village: "The Indians are gone from the Galisteo Basin . . . but the rustling cottonwoods along the creek and the quiet serenity of the undeveloped plain still provide a primitive picture for travelers along State Highway 41."[51]

Lucy R. Lippard, *Painting of Old Galisteo Church* by Tony Anaya, ca. 1996. This painting eventually faded to illegibility. It was recently replaced by a photograph of the old church on the mound where it once stood.

During the 1970s, a new population of Anglos discovered Galisteo. Joining or replacing the more prosperous artists, entrepreneurs, and Old Santa Fe antiquity dealers of the 1950s and '60s, young middle-class hippies and emerging artists rented, bought, or just moved into crumbling adobes, sometimes camping on empty land. Relations between these young newcomers and their Hispano peers were for the most part casual and friendly as they shared a pot and partying scene. Some stayed in Galisteo, raised families, and forty years later are pillars of the community. One of them thrived for years by growing marijuana on nearby ranchland.

Barbara Gluck, *Party in Florence Sohn's and Scott Diffrient's Teepee*, 1983. (Palace of the Governors Photo Archives, NMHM/DCA neg. no. 122459.)

Christina and Richard Griscom arrived in Galisteo in 1970. For a few summers she ran a summer camp: "We'd go to the grandmothers' houses, they'd talk about herbs and tell us stories, because I wanted the children to really respect their history."[52] After they divorced and Richard married mezzo soprano Janice Felty, Christina became a spiritual guru—to Shirley MacLaine, among others—and in the early 1980s founded the Light Institute in her home (the former Chávez house, now Durán, at the dead end of Avenida Vieja). In 1988 she added the Nizhoni School for Global Consciousness, which acquired land and built some domed structures just north of the northern creston. Dick Griscom was the first president of the Galisteo Community Association and was a dedicated environmentalist and community member for the rest of his life.

Over the years, Rod Hall, who arrived in 1972, renovated the old Clemente Chávez house on the southern slope of The Hill, while David van Dyk lived in the ruin of a once substantial family compound that had been connected to Hall's. Charlie and Barbara Holloway lived at the McKee Ranch line camp in 1974 before buying land in the village from the Community Association in 1979 and building a passive solar home on Avenida Vieja, where they pursue their businesses in passive solar construction and fine weaving. Jeweler Scott Diffrient and artist Florence Sohn came in later, rehabbing a crumbling adobe near the church that is attached to the old compound occupied by the late Anastacio (Tacho) and Libby Sandoval and their children. They continue to add studios and extensive gardens.

In the summer of 1974, local initiative did for tourism what the state did not. Rudy Sena (one of several sons of Natividad Sena and Sara Peña Sena), who for many years had led trail rides for Santa Fe Detours, built an arena on his inherited land on the southern bank of the San Cristóbal Arroyo and created the Rodeo de Galisteo. With the help of his family (offspring Audra Baca, Amy Gallegos, and Clint Sena), the rodeo on the last weekend in July

Barbara Seiler, *Thirty-First Galisteo Rodeo*, 2001.

Michael Datoli, *Cowboys*, 1987. *Back row*: Lester van Norman and Antonio Chávez; *front row*: Jack Caffrey, Sean Caffrey, Rudy Sena, and Park Dutton Hofer. (Courtesy of John Benjamin.)

became an annual tradition that lasted until 2014, when it became economically unviable. Each year, an opening parade through the village, featuring local floats and (later) fire trucks, was led by the rodeo queen (María Ortiz y Pino in 1979). The small-town rodeo was "open," meaning that local participants didn't have to be members of a national association to enter. It featured bronc riding, bull riding, team roping, calf roping, barrel racing, calf scrambles, and the ever popular "mutton busters," in which small children try to stay mounted on small sheep for six seconds.

In 1972 artist Fritz Scholder (part Luiseño Indian), who is credited with helping to revive Native American contemporary art in his year of teaching at the Institute of American Indian Arts in Santa Fe, bought the old Mora home from Major Fenten and his wife Elita

Juan Ortiz Store/Galisteo Inn, 1954. (Courtesy of Joanna Kaufmann and Wayne Aarniokoski.)

Worker (*Tobías Anaya?*) *at Fenten/ Scholder House*, 1970s. (Courtesy of Romona Scholder.)

Wilson. It is now the most elegant property in the village. When the parents of Fritz's wife, Romona, came to help them move, Romona's father, Roman Attenberger, bought from the Villanuevas/Begays the house by the old bridge where Simona García was raised, beginning a long process of restoration. (When Roman and his wife moved in, only one room had a working roof.) Attenberger became an active member of the community. Before he died in 2005, he funded the replastering of the church exterior (without ecclesiastical permission) as a final gift to the village. (Soon after, the positive karma of that home was passed on to two more active community members, Hopi tribal member and geodesist Phillip Tuwaletstiwa and his artist wife, Judy.)

Jay Raymond, *Simona Baros García, Age 91, Visiting with Roman Attenberger at Her Childhood Home (His Current Home)*, 2000.

Romona Scholder, *Three-Legged Race at the First Annual Galisteo Fiesta de Santiago*, 1974. Mary Alice Anaya is second from left, Walter Scott Perry and Eric Engheben on right. From *Viva* (Sunday magazine of the *New Mexican*), Aug. 4, 1974. The article, by Scholder, is titled "Galisteo Is a Quiet Little Village." (Courtesy of Romona Scholder.)

In August 1974, villagers revived the fiesta tradition, moribund for twenty years. The "first annual Fiesta de Santiago," which began in the church with a Mariachi Mass, was, as Romona Scholder wrote, "one of those rare moments when the church was truly catholic. Under its roof and spilling out of the door was the entire village—people with names like Montoya, Rosenwald, Attenberger and Anaya. The remainder of the day was a melange of sack races and watermelon eating contests, magicians and puppeteers, gossip and laughter . . . [the fiesta] had about it an air of family that urban strategists vainly try to incorporate into their city master plans."[53]

The event was a fundraiser for the new Community Center Corporation, founded in 1973, which became the Galisteo Community Association, still the administrative heart of the village. The burgeoning Anglo population spearheaded the construction of a passive solar

Lucy R. Lippard, *Galisteo Community Center*, ca. 2015. The fire station is next door, at right.

Lucy R. Lippard, *Former Lamy Train Depot (Ferneau House)*, 1998.

building, intended to provide young people with a place to meet and play. The Gledhills, then residents of the old Pantaleón Montoya (now Watson-Jones) house on Avenida Vieja, donated land for the center and for a future fire station. In 1973 newcomer Rod Hall spearheaded the eventful construction of the Galisteo Community Center, with Rudy Sena as foreman.[54] The center, complete with pool table, was initially open to all at all times, resulting in some wild parties, although vandalism eventually necessitated stricter policies. A basketball court was to become an ice-skating rink in the winter. (This never happened, but a county-funded outdoor basketball court was constructed in the 1990s.)

In 1975, Elmer (Doc) and Marie Ferneau bought the old yellow Lamy railroad depot for $2,500 and paid another $2,500 to have it moved to their land on the southern boundary of Galisteo. "The station was solid as the Rock of Gibraltar, with the tensile strength of Noah's Ark," wrote Marie. Built in the 1880s, it had been moved once before in Lamy, to make room for the extant depot, and became a dormitory for railroad workers, as well as a community center. "People came in wagons, buggies, on horseback, on foot for gatherings that could last several days. They camped around the station and at night whooped it up in the waiting room [the Ferneau living room]. Perhaps things got a little wild at times." While the Ferneaus were pleased with the low cost, renovation was painful. Counting their considerable sweat equity, they estimated it cost them "about 12 billion dollars."[55]

While Anglos were remodeling old adobes, younger Nuevo Mexicanos were giving them up for new, clean, modern double-wides, often placed next door to their parents' old adobes, kept so that "even after the children had left . . . the young people would have a place to live 'when they got tired of California.'"[56] Hart, Rhodes, and Morgan; Alvar Carlson; and J. B. Jackson all studied this phenomenon in the West.[57] They found that in some northern New Mexican villages, over half the homes were manufactured. Some critics deplore the boxy shapes, industrial materials, and colors that can be disharmonious in the bare New Mexico landscape, so unlike the rounded, mud-colored houses they replace, not to mention the planned obsolescence that leaves them on site forever, long after they have been abandoned. There are beige trailers with fake plastic vigas on the market, but one sees few of them. It is a mystery to me

John Benjamin, *Galisteo from the West*, ca. 1992.

why socially engaged New Mexican designers have not yet come up with ways to make affordable, movable housing with the virtues of the manufactured home and the inventiveness of contemporary southwestern architecture, along the lines of Samuel Mockbee's pioneering Rural Studio in Hale County, Alabama.[58]

The end of another era came in 1976 when the Homestead Act was rescinded. The same year, Teledyne Inc.—a corporate conglomerate founded and chaired by Texan Henry Singleton from 1960 to 1990 (he was also a trustee of Ronald Reagan's "blind trust")—was still searching for minerals on San Cristóbal. But the biggest change on the northeastern side of the Galisteo Basin had begun in August 1969 when Alva Simpson sold his vast ranch to the developers known as Rio Rancho Estates, or AMREP (American Realty and Petroleum Corporation) for $3.2 million. Sad as it is to see ranches replaced by subdivisions, the land had been exhausted by overgrazing. Over the next decade or so, it was subdivided to become "El Dorado at Santa Fe"—some twelve miles north of Galisteo, half way to Santa Fe. Our once isolated village was about to be overshadowed by this vast development. Originally planned for 25,000 homes, El Dorado was conceived as a twin of AMREP's Rio Rancho farther south—now the third largest city in New Mexico. But Santa Fe County planners restricted the corporation to some 2,100 homes and struck a deal to counteract the density by creating a green belt, the Eldorado Wilderness Area on the mesas above Lamy. The Teal Ranch House, designed by artist/architect and solar pioneer Bill Lumpkins, is now the El Dorado Community Center. It was a golden opportunity for AMREP, although around 1970, its directors ended up in federal prison for fraud and were forced to sell some of their holdings to other subdividers.[59] El Dorado took off in 1974 with eight occupied houses. By 2010 there were 2,887 households. Before 1971–72, said Robert Dobyn, "all you had to do was have an engineer stake it, then you filed it and that became the subdivision. There were no hydro regulations and it could be anything you wanted. . . . There was nothing out there. No roads out the sides, just little pathways."[60]

If the 1950s saw the formation of the large ranches, the 1980s began the story of their breakups. Nature played a grim game with the area by providing abnormally wet years just as the world seemed to be discovering north central New Mexico, when not-so-smart growth and optimism ruled. During this auspiciously (but ultimately disastrous) wet period, the calamitous drought of the 1950s was forgotten. With the ensuing real estate boom, Santa Fe and environs became not only an international tourist destination but also a lifestyle option. Each of the three large ranches that surround Galisteo village—Thornton, Cerro Pelón, and the venerable San Cristóbal—provides its own lessons about current and future land use.

The land sale that was to have the most impact on the village of Galisteo was on December 31, 1981, when most of the McKee Ranch changed hands. After an acrimonious and expensive divorce from his second wife in 1979, and less than thirty years after his father had created the McKee Ranch for him, Philip McKee (1931–96) was forced to break his holdings into several parts, beginning another wave of wholesale partitioning of the eastern basin. Malicious scuttlebutt had it that he had frittered away his fortune on divorce settlements, horses, wine, and women. (José Ortiz y Pino III insisted, "It was not me that sold out Galisteo. It was Philip McKee."[61])

Lucy R. Lippard, *Looking North from the Northern Creston at Nizhoni and Goose Downs*, ca. 2009.

The official story (from a book on Robert McKee) states: "Gradually Philip repaid his father for the ranch, but as he himself aged, he had less time and less need for that much land. By 1981 he had sold most of the property except 300 acres, retaining that to preserve his sense of freedom and isolation."[62] The bulk of the McKee Ranch was sold to Lew Wilkins (Bill) Cook of California and Scottsdale, Arizona, who owned several other ranches around the West; his wife, Marian, was a prizewinning developer. The list price was $4.3 million for the roughly 24,000 acres of the McKee Ranch proper, including a grazing lease on State Trust Land. McKee had run three hundred head of cattle. Cook planned to run perhaps as many as six hundred under the "Rhodesian" or "Savory" system of moving stock continually from one small pasture after another, divided in a pie-shaped circle around a central water hole and corral.[63]

McKee sold two large parcels of land north on NM 41 to the Nizhoni School for Global Consciousness and to Goose Downs, a prestigious equestrian facility run by Jeffray Ryding and Tom Angle. The ranch headquarters and substantial acreage went to Texans Ralph and Heidi Tingle, to become the La Jara Ranch, named after the arroyo that runs through it. On his 300 acres north of CR 42, McKee re-established himself, and he and his third wife, Linda, became more integrated into village life. He died suddenly of a stroke in 1996, and his then remarried widow died several years later of a heart attack, tragically alone with her beloved dogs.[64]

Most significantly, in 1981–82, a large section of the McKee Ranch, adjoining the village to the west, became an upscale subdivision called Ranchitos de Galisteo—an ironic, if unintended, homage to the small subsistence ranches lost by Galisteo villagers over the last century. Ranchitos has its own covenants, water system, and architectural committee. Some residents consider themselves part of the old village and are active in community activities, though for many years local elders did not consider Ranchitos part of Galisteo at all.

The eastern Galisteo Basin had long been a film set. In 1955, *Man from Laramie*, starring Jimmy Stewart, was shot at the Sawyer Ranch (San Cristóbal), where the set for John Wayne's *The Cowboys* (1972), complete with windmill and rundown barn, remains visible from the highway. In 1984, Lew Cook accepted an offer from film director Lawrence Kasdan for what seemed a modest movie set for *Silverado*, starring Kevin Costner and Kevin Kline. Filming took ninety-six days from November 1984 to March 1985 and became a big deal. From then on, the Cook Movie Ranch, aka the Silverado Set, was in business, eventually becoming the largest set in the western United States. The Cooks were absentee landlords and the movie business was facilitated by ranch managers Don and Trixie Pope, who raised their own cattle there. In 1999 Cook was reported to be rebuilding the movie set in Idaho (to be shipped down to New Mexico, depriving locals of jobs). This proved a lucrative way to maintain a tax-break ranching enterprise, later coinciding with New Mexico governor Bill Richardson's tax-incentive outreach to the film industry, which has proved a boon to this poor state.[65]

The 1980s marked another stage in the erosion of traditional Galisteo, though vestiges survive. While small stores were crucial in the days when the road to Santa Fe was dirt and wagons were the prime transportation, the automobile speeded things up and these little ventures became barely feasible economically. La Tienda Anaya, across from the church, run

Ray Belcher, *Church on the Silverado Movie Set*, 1985.

Susan Crocker, *La Tienda de Anaya*, mid 1990s.

by Andrés (1920–2003) and Josefina (1925–2004) Anaya, sold gas, groceries, and Indian jewelry and once housed the village's only pay phone.[66] (They had previously run a small store on The Hill.) By the 1990s, "the Country Store" was selling only a sparse selection of groceries, catering primarily to workmen passing through the village. Josefina, whose tamales were famous, angrily quoted to me a magazine article that said the wares on her shelves looked as though they'd been there since statehood. When the couple passed away, the store was sold to art dealer Tim Willms, owner of the Talus Winds Ranch near Cerro Pelón. Despite hopeful plans for a much needed coffee shop and local gathering place, so far ideas for new uses have fallen through, though the tienda briefly served as a summer showcase for House of Ancestors Antiques owned by Jim Godman and Teresa Bohn, who have remodeled the WPA mattress factory.

While most of the small shops in the village had closed, larger enterprises were hovering. In 1988 the County Development Review Committee (CDRC) tabled requests for two new businesses near Galisteo, pending further reviews. In regard to Chris and Carmen Partridge's proposal "to build and operate a health retreat" (six guest rooms plus the existing 1,350-square-foot Las Marías ranch house) on eighty-two acres north of the village, the CDRC wanted more information on water use and discharge of waste. The plan finally came to pass once these problems were negotiated.[67] Later the property was significantly expanded to become the Vista Clara Ranch and Spa, which closed in 2004.

Gene Thornton's application in the late 1980s to "operate a sand and gravel operation" on two sites, circa 700 acres of the "16,000 acre ranch he own[ed]," required creation of a new mining district. Seventy-five Galisteo residents concerned with truck traffic attended the Board of County Commissioners hearing, applauded when the request was tabled, and

The Galisteo Inn, 1987. (Courtesy of Joanna Kaufmann and Wayne Aarniokoski.)

Jean Anaya Moya, *Feast Day of San José*, straw appliqué, 2008. The fiesta is traditionally March 19, organized by the Sociedad de San José. This piece won the E. Boyd Award at Spanish Market in 2008. (Photo by Firefly Studio, courtesy of Jean Anaya Moya.)

Woody Gwyn, detail of *285 South (Lamy Pass)*, 1990. Oil on canvas, 9 × 66 feet. Many of us, when driving down the Lamy Hill from Santa Fe, find ourselves smiling at the familiar sight of the Galisteo Basin unfolding before us.

succeeded in killing the venture. However, developer Joe Miller still operates a large gravel-mining operation below Cerro Colorado in Lamy, within the bed of the Galisteo Creek and adjacent to Coalition Period pueblo ruins and County Open Space.

In 1984 Elizabeth Luster opened Willows Southwest—The Galisteo Inn as a women's retreat in the old Juan Ortiz store. She sold it in 1989 to Galisteans Wayne Aarnokoski and Joanna Kauffman, and it thrived as a destination for locals and savvy Santa Feans. The upscale inn's dining room was named after the Ortiz y Pinos' restaurant La Mancha. In 2000 it was sold to Christina Griscom, and in 2008 her daughter and son-in-law sold it again. By selling the liquor license separately, they pretty much guaranteed that it would never be an inn again, leaving Galisteo with no social meeting place or commercial employment. Even today, as we walk through the village, we are sometimes stopped by out-of-state cars looking for the inn. The current owners, a physician and a horticulturist, have embarked on a remodeling process of the historic building.

When the town gained the reputation of an artists' community in the 1970s, the Anglos who moved in tended to be young, poor, and/or creative types. By the late 1980s, the demographics were slanting toward older and upscale. Increasingly better known and better-off artists continued to be attracted to Galisteo. Marion Steele noted proudly in the 1980s that two of the village artists were "world known—one's work hanging in the Museum of Modern Art." I assume he referred to Fritz Scholder and Agnes Martin, who lived in Galisteo from 1978 to 1992.[68] Other Galisteans or former residents hanging in the Museum of Modern Art include Richard Tuttle (who briefly lived in Ranchitos), the late Nancy Holt, Harmony Hammond, and international art stars Bruce Nauman and Susan Rothenberg, who built a sprawling home, studios, and stables on land north of the village acquired from the Ortiz y

Donald Woodman, *The Former Galisteo Property of Donald Woodman, with His Tipi and Agnes Martin's Structures*, ca. 1982.

Harmony Hammond, *Farm Ghosts*, 1990. Oil on canvas, metal and wood, 97 × 189 feet. (Courtesy of the artist and Alexander Gray Associates, New York. Art © Harmony Hammond/Licensed by VAGA at ARS, NY.)

Florence Sohn, *Jim Sloan's Paintings Mounted on Quartermill Farm Wall on Via La Puente for the Studio Tour*, 2012. (Courtesy of Florence Sohn.)

Pinos that includes the sites of the ancient Tano pueblos of Las Madres and Tanuge. In 1989, Hammond—artist, writer, and LGBTQ activist—used her Guggenheim fellowship to build a large, barn-like studio above the creek next to her home at La Lanera, the former wool warehouse. A number of other accomplished artists and writers moved here and are working from their village homes.[69] The best known local artist is Jean Anaya Moya, descendant of Galisteo's early settlers, who has won the Governor's Award and first prizes at Spanish Market for her crosses, bultos, and narratives in straw inlay.

The very successful annual Galisteo Studio Tour was initiated in 1987, cementing the village's image as an "artist's town." Held in the last weekend in October, when the golden hues of the bosque cottonwoods are at their most striking, it is still going strong, providing an economic staple for local artists. A few women from the old families offer embroideries, hot pads, pillows, and empanadas. The long life of Cocina de Mela is now commemorated by a carved plaque in the Community Center in honor of the Montoya matriarch's famous cooking for Studio Tours and other local gatherings, continued after her death by several of her daughters, who come from as far away as Ohio for the event.

Place names tell their own stories. Like the landscape itself, names have changed over the centuries. Lost names have thrown many land rights cases into limbo when landmarks cannot be identified. But at one time every field and feature was most certainly named and recognizable to locals. J. B. Jackson recalled that the father of his twentieth-century La Ciénega neighbor Facundo Pino "drew a little map, a profile of all the hills around here and named them. Every one of the hills had a name. The fields all had a name. It was the White Field or the Square Field. That's gone."[70] Today we are now at least one generation too distant, and many once well-known names are forgotten, even by the elders. Luis Chávez told me that some of the Galisteo names I asked about were "very far away"—less in miles, it turned out, than in familiarity.

There is no question that Pueblo people had names for every feature in the Galisteo Basin, but these are mostly lost to historians. Even the eminent ethnographer J. P. Harrington, working in the early twentieth century, struck out. Places are tied to belief systems. Contemporary Pueblo peoples are justifiably reluctant to divulge such information to outsiders. One nearby hill on County Open Space, religiously significant to several local tribes, was unfortunately dubbed Petroglyph Hill by rock art enthusiasts and is now the subject of intense discussions with Pueblo representatives about renaming it and banning visitation without their consent.[71] Native names also denote resources (medicinal herbs, flint, dyes) or describe past events, evoking stories about place.[72]

The Spanish preferred descriptive or religious names (Cerro Pelón, Ojo Hedionda, San Cristóbal, San Lázaro, San Marcos) within a very different political and economic system, but their attachment to land was equally powerful. Like Americans, they named places after prominent people (Ortiz Mountains)[73] or Old World places, like Galisteo itself, the name of which, unlike many New Mexican towns, dates from the sixteenth century.[74] The earliest Spanish explorers renamed Tanuge for a town in Caceres, Spain. For some reason, it survived the centuries, though serially elaborated with religious names: San Lucas, Santa María de la Gracia, and Nuestra Señora de los Remedios. By naming places, the earliest Spanish settlers acquired a precarious sense of communal control over these new and strange lands.

A few Native names were adopted by settlers. Mount Chalchihuitl in the redundantly dubbed Cerrillos Hills, is Nahuatl for "turquoise," inherited from the Tlascalans—Mexican Indians who arrived with Spanish conquistadors.[75] In some cases, Native names were Hispanicized. In others, the conquerors understood, according to the Jesuit scholar Thomas J. Steele, that "the function of a name is not merely to denominate, it is also to dominate." The saints' names given the little isolated *capillas* (chapels) required for each settlement legitimized foreign places, inserting them into "the ultimate order that is sacred time."[76]

Lucy R. Lippard, *Black Mountain*, 2018. Many villagers called the northern creston (aka the hogback) Black Mountain.

Lucy R. Lippard, *El Puente (The Old Bridge)*, ca. 2016. In December 2011, El Puente was dedicated to Corporal George Michael Anaya (son of Josefina and Andrés Anaya), killed in Vietnam in 1970 at the age of 18, only three months into his tour of duty. As a kid, he and his friends hung out under the bridge listening to AM radio. He was one of many in his family who served—and some died—in the military. An embroidery in the church listed the names of those who served in foreign wars.

Some Galisteo names speak for themselves, like Wild Horse Mesa and Mesa de Cabreros (where goats grazed) or Loma Montosa (Wooded Hill) and Loma Molina (Mill Hill). The lower part of the San Cristóbal Arroyo was originally Arroyo Atascoso (boggy; *atascar* means "to get stuck"). Ojo Hedionda is Stinking Spring, probably after the sulphur produced by the ubiquitous Mancos shale. Piedra Lumbre (a chert used for striking sparks to light a fire) takes its name from a thirteenth-century pueblo on a high gravel-covered outcrop on San Cristóbal, known by the invading Americans as Kearny Gap.[77] Chapatalito, a little pointed hill below Cerro Pelón, may be named for the Mexican sombrero it closely resembles.

Other names tantalize, suggesting lost stories, like Rincón del Padre (Priest's Corner) on the Eaton grant map. Does it relate to a scratched petroglyph of a possible priest at the nearby ruins of Pueblo Colorado, probably executed in the seventeenth century? And why was the usually dry lake (La Laguna or Las Lagunitas) also called Laguna del Doche (Dutch Lake)? I've been told that La Loma Tejana is the place villagers watched retreating Texans in the 1850s or 1860s. Another story has it that Ezekiel Chávez shot a Tejano there. The park behind the Galisteo church is named for Phillip Watts II, a troubled local boy from an old family who died from a fall. The old bridge is named after George Michael Anaya, killed in Vietnam.

What archaeologists call Comanche Gap in the southern creston takes its name from the descent of Clark Hill, known as La Bajada de los Comanches and La Bajada de los Salados (it led south to the Salinas). However, the actual Bajada de los Comanches was farther to

Nicolas Trofimuk, *Highway 41 to North*, 2014.

the east on old maps, and what is called Clark Hill after a railway stop was once La Ceja, or the Summit. La Ceja was another generic term, applied to several crests of hills to the north and south of the village. La Joya (The Jewel, or fertile watered land) was an earlier name for Avenida Vieja, the road that ran through the then irrigated strip paralleling the east bank of the Rio Galisteo, belonging to Nicolás Pino and then Pedro Ortiz y Pino—sometimes described as San Cristóbal's western boundary. The name also appears in other places in the basin, such as a vast pasture west of Cerro Pelón. Peñolcito (low rock outcropping) connotes several local sites. A floodplain was *vega del agua*. The names of springs were also repeated; there seems to have been more than one Galisteo Spring, another stumbling block for land grant boundaries.

Trails, ancient and new, can be seen as ur-maps, drawn full scale on the ground, urging us onward, suggesting that the visualized goal is within reach. The story of roads in and out of Galisteo could roughly encapsulate much of the tricultural history buried in a landscape that seems both welcoming to and dismissive of passers through. What follows is a generalized version of the roads in the immediate vicinity of the village, gathered from histories, maps, and hearsay.[78]

Pre-European Pueblo peoples walked long distances and constantly traveled between settlements, even after some had been depopulated. Ancient trails cut across the basin in several places, connecting the local Tano pueblos to Pecos Pueblo and the plains to the east; other pueblos in the north; the Rio Grande settlements; Acoma, Laguna, Zuni, and Hopi to the west; and the Tiwa/Piro/Tompiro Pueblos to the south. Early settlers followed Indian trails that became wagon roads and occasionally superhighways. Until widespread fencing in the twentieth century, the basin was crisscrossed by paths, ranch roads, and horse, sheep, and cattle paths wherever expedient. Many of those roads were short-lived, accessing long-gone fields or houses. All created visible dents in the delicate landscape, remaining only as traces illuminated by aerial photography or the late afternoon sun.

From at least the 1850s (as on the 1853 Marcy map), there was a major trail from Anton Chico to Santa Fe that passed through Galisteo. CR 33, for instance, which once ran across a corner of the San Cristóbal grant to Lamy, was an open route through San Cristóbal to Ojo de la Vaca and all the way to Las Vegas; it now begins in the village and continues on private ranchland.[79] Roads to the west have varied drastically. Military maps from the 1860s show a road from Galisteo to La Ciénega that followed the river. The Madrid road went past the railroad tracks and crossed the river over to Cerrillos. Another ran behind Cerro Pelón, and there were several "shortcuts" to Cerrillos. Pino Villanueva told Onésimo Montoya that when the Omara (Romero or O'Meara) coal mine on the current Cerro Pelón Ranch was still working, the road to it went west before NM 41.

The Wheeler Survey maps of the 1880s show tracks from all directions leading to and from Galisteo's plaza. Those from Galisteo to present-day Golden, Albuquerque, and the Ortiz Mountain mines have vanished, though traces are still visible from the air. The road from Santa Fe to the Galisteo plaza changed routes over time, passing first through the wide gateway, or puerto, through the northern creston, skirting around it to the north, crossing to the Ojito de Galisteo, a convenient spring for travelers, now on state land at Thornton Ranch.[80] From there, it eventually met Old Galisteo Road and Galisteo Street in Santa Fe. Probably in the 1970s, when I-25 cut across it, the main road to Santa Fe shifted toward Lamy and Old Las Vegas Highway.

Avenida Vieja, the "Old Road" east of the river, more or less paralleled the irrigated fields called La Joya, which was apparently the name of the road before it was "old." It has been slightly rerouted westward over the years, affected by property rights and legal struggles. As it went south of the village, it proceeded roughly on present NM 41 up Clark Hill and on to Stanley, Moriarty, Estancia, and Willard. As early as 1912, NM 41 first ran down Avenida Vieja from the south, taking a right angle to the west (between what is now La Otra Vanda and Via La Puente) to the old bridge, arriving at the Santa Fe road in front of the church. The road from there north was called El Camino Real—the vernacular term for any main road, not to be confused with the historic royal route from Mexico, farther west.

Juan Ortiz's mercantile was on La Vega, and the influential family made sure the earlier main road ran by it to the bridge. NM 41 had been recognized state highway since 1912, but when the modern road barged through the church plaza in 1935–36, thanks to the WPA, Don José Ortiz y Pino was chairman of the Road Commission, and the highway passed near his store on what was then Calle Grande, now Via La Puente. (Across the bridge, a house was deemed too close to the highway, and the family was paid $50 to move it across La Otra Vanda.) Abandoning the old route from the east, the new highway, with concrete bridges over the San Cristóbal Arroyo and Galisteo Creek, cut through Ortiz y Pino orchards and fields and destroyed the roughly defined, dirt plaza, splitting the village center in two. Some of the current fences lie *on* the right of ways, which were set very wide, enough for four lanes, which fortunately have not yet arrived.

Mela Montoya recalled that CR 42/Camino Los Abuelos was there in the 1930s, but very narrow. Until recently it was a plain dirt county road—rutted and rocky, running up and down hill and around curves through beautiful ranchland between the two paved state highways 41 and 14. As development crept in at the turn of the twenty-first century, the first two miles of CR 42 on each end were paved, luring unwary strangers to zoom along before abruptly slamming into the malevolent washboard dirt or glass-smooth, wet clay. A county dump (once landfill, now transfer station) is located about midway on a bucolic site, once marked by sculptures made from recycled trash by dumpmaster Reyes. When surveyed, one stretch of CR 42 just west of the village turned out to be the property of a local landowner and not the county's at all, so it could theoretically be shut down at her request.

In the 1980s, as part of the nationwide 911 labeling for emergency services, street signs were required for the dirt roads that crisscross the village. Obligatory green-and-white signs went up across the state. Some names were misspelled, some newly invented, others remembered by elders. Residents John Benjamin and Moira Walden took charge of the program, with José Ortiz y Pino III advising. Some names are clear: La Vega is named for the meadow

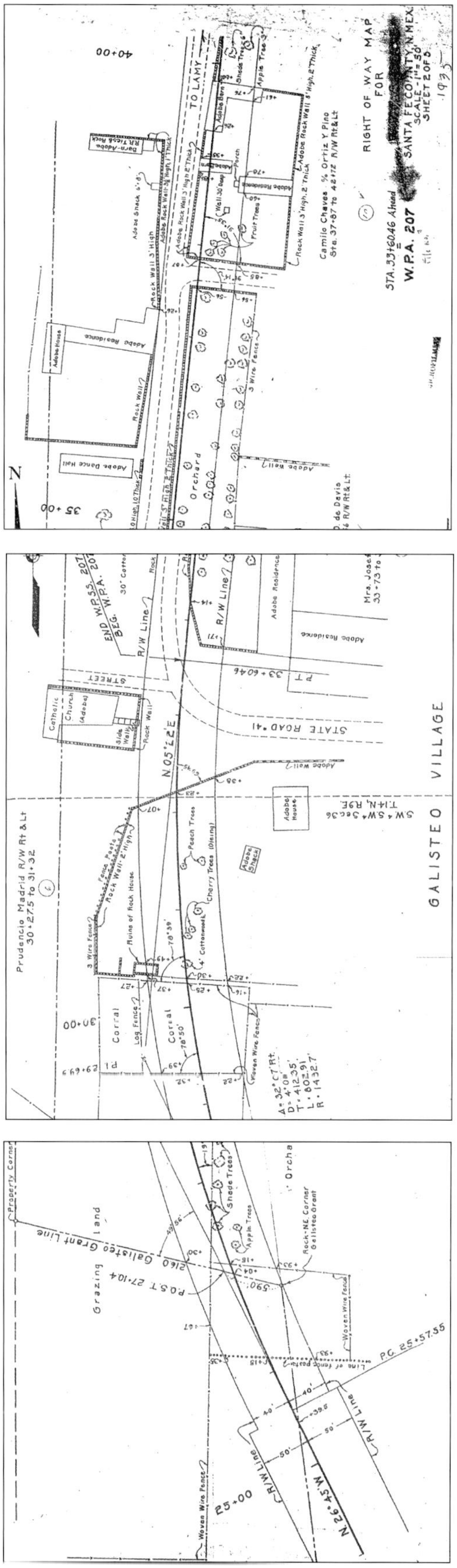

Highway 41 map, ca. 1935.
This map shows the fields and orchards in the path of the new highway route through Ortiz y Pino property. (Courtesy of John Benjamin.)

Lucy R. Lippard, *Street Sign*, 2018.

bordering the creek; Marcellina Lane (*sic*) is named after Marcelina Montoya Mares, an independent woman who recently passed away at an advanced age. Magdalena Lane was probably José Ortiz y Pino III's idea; it leads to his home. Via La Puente, once Calle Grande, starts from the church, crosses the old bridge, and then bears right. The straightaway, once just an arroyo, is called, as it was for many years, La Otra Vanda—the Other Side. (Originally, Onésimo Montoya told me, La Otra Vanda was *either* side of the river, depending on where you stood.) Across the highway, The Hill rises to the site of the earliest settlement and the old cemetery. The short lanes south of CR 42 are Los Anayas Lane, Via Si, Tobias Lane, and Chevy Lane (named for Dave Montoya's auto body business).

The newer roads within the 1980s Ranchitos de Galisteo subdivision were named by former owner Philip McKee: Camino Cabreros (the name of a mesa to the west; for years this sign wrongly read "Caberos"), Camino San Cristóbal, Camino Los Angelitos (presumably named for nearby Arroyo Los Angeles), and Camino Libre. Farther out of town before the railroad tracks that form the village's western boundary is McKee Lane, La Jara Ranch Trail (leading to the old McKee ranch headquarters), and Las Tres (for the three large homes built there). North of town the roads are named after commercial establishments—Calle Nizhoni (the former Nizhoni School for Global Consciousness), Goose Downs Road (for the equestrian facility), Camino Vista Clara (the former spa), and Entrada Tranquilas (*sic*) leading into the failed subdivision Hacienda Tranquillas (*sic*). Cerro Pelón is called The Wave by some longtime Anglos, El Cerro by some locals, and its original names are unknown. In the county's naming contest for CR 42 (now Camino los Abuelos), someone suggested Mad Gal Road (for Madrid and Galisteo) but was told by the county that "those feminists wouldn't like it." (A Galisteo feminist had suggested it.)

Over the centuries, as properties are divided and subdivided, little thought is given to the effect of careless and multiple placement of roads on the increasingly eroded and gullied lands. (These days the roads to widely spaced "ranchettes" in new subdivisions do similar damage.) As cultural groups and social classes move on, are displaced, or vanish, the meanings of former boundaries and the stories they once told are left for us to ponder.

And here is where I arrive as an active witness to more than two decades of land use victories and losses, and the subtle social upheavals that have affected Galisteo since 1990. The next chapter is something of a fond and sometimes frustrated memoir. (A friend suggests that I should publish this book posthumously so that I don't get run out of town.) I first saw Galisteo around midnight in 1985, when Donald Woodman was building a rammed earth house in the shadow of the northern creston. With his wife, artist Judy Chicago, Romona Scholder, and Patrick Mehaffy, I climbed up over invisible petroglyphs to see Halley's Comet. In 1987 I returned with some Colorado friends to hike the southern creston, which boasted still more impressive rock art. (In those days you could hike, or trespass, relatively freely on both crestons.) My old friend Harmony Hammond was preparing to buy La Lanera. Stopping to see it, I walked through the village in daylight for the first time, across the old bridge and along the creek in the bosque. Galisteo seemed totally unfamiliar, even "foreign," especially the east side of the creek, where I was to settle a few years later.

Edward Ranney, *Manuel Anaya Watering His Garden*, 1999.

SIX

These Days (1990–2018)

Lucero de mañana, alumbre mi día.
—Mathilda Sera Baros, morning prayer[1]

People only die when no one tells their story any longer.
—Patricia Marina Trujillo[2]

History never really says goodbye. History says see you later.
—Eduardo Galeano[3]

These days, more than two centuries after its beginnings, the eastern Galisteo Basin would be unrecognizable to its earlier inhabitants. For over 150 years, in the face of bad odds, the village—isolated by Indian attacks, then by treacherous roads, harsh topography, poverty, droughts, land loss, and official neglect—was forced to be self-sustaining. Today the lush grasses for which the basin was known in colonial and territorial days are short, patchy, and dry. The acequias that nourished the farms are long gone. Streams, footpaths, livestock and animal tracks—even light-footed coyote trails—erode into gullies. Piñons and junipers have crept down to lower ground because the grasslands can't hold their own any longer and because trees are no longer cut down in large quantities for building materials and firewood. The land may have changed in the last half century, but Galisteo is still embroiled in battles over land and water. Today the quarrels are less often about individual/family rights and more often about a small community opposing large-scale development and the extraction industry, fueled by local political machinations. Through it all, the land remains, the land that newcomers may see as dusty, infertile, featureless, rock hard, the land that once provided for many people, whose spirits remain to haunt us.

Lucy R. Lippard, *View of the Basin from South of Cerro Pelón*, ca. 2010.

Lucy R. Lippard, *No Trespassing Sign in the Bosque*, ca. 2014.

In Navajo the word for one's home is *naagháhígi*, "the place where that individual is walking around." When I first began to explore the Galisteo Basin, before I moved there, I vowed to walk every inch of it, in search of the historical record written on the land itself but also for personal, sensuous satisfaction. I wanted to know the place I had fallen for, with all its idiosyncrasies in all its seasons, the way only walkers and lovers can. Like all relationships this one has been rocky (pun intended); I've lost a lot of earrings and nicked a lot of jeans and jackets ducking through barbed wire. The "discoveries" have been personal as well as historical, and I'm always aware of how many others have "discovered" these places before me. The pleasures of walking the map remain, but I expected to be able to trek cross-country for the rest of my life, with relative caution, responsibly closing gates, not letting the dog chase livestock, taking nothing but pictures. I'd been well trained living on an English farm in the 1970s. I envisioned rattlesnakes, flash floods, and lightning strikes as the greatest dangers. Not cowboys traveling in pickups, armed with guns and ominous reputations, or Vietnam vets in Chevy Blazers brandishing Uzis, who were rumored to be guarding the Zorro Ranch. I hadn't counted on the increasing hostility of ranchers and their surrogates toward local trespassers, who had for years been reluctantly tolerated. Nor had I counted on the increasing intrusion of new fences, driveways, and "ranchettes" straddling familiar trails. I still walk the land where I have access, where I won't be arrested or shot at, but I can no longer look out my window after work and wonder what's up there or out there and decide that's where I'll hike today.

I can, however, continue to learn about my immediate environs from those who were raised here. I've talked to old men who herded sheep for the patrón as children. I've found their drawings and initials carved into rocks next to pre-European petroglyphs. Serapio Anaya recalled camping on top of Cerro Pelón in the early 1930s and crying, because from there he could see his village home, so near and yet so far, not to be visited for another month, when

Joan Myers, *Loma Tejana Today*, 2018.

he took his laundry down to his mother. Tacho Sandoval had similar memories. For me the Cerro is a place to hike, another world. I've tromped through the snow there, but I haven't had to sleep in it. For me it's a site of pleasure; for them it was a memory of hardship.

While it still nestles amid shrinking ranchlands, the village of Galisteo is no longer rural, no longer a working landscape in any authentic sense. The fields where beans and alfalfa once grew when there was more water and the creek was still accessible to the acequias, have gone back to drought-stricken nature—weeds and cholla, cheatgrass and goatheads. There are no small farms or ranches. The few old men who maintained chile patches have passed on, although there are sporadic waves of interest in communal gardening among newer residents. Grazing is difficult even on the big surrounding ranches—now all tax-break spreads, ripe for future development. A cow-calf pair can require as much as 160 acres. In my time, there have been no sheep in the area, but I've seen an occasional steer being fattened up, a pet pig, goats, a few chickens, a pair of peacocks, a lot of outdoor dogs and doomed cats (coyotes and owls get them). Fewer and fewer horses pace small paddocks and fields in the village proper, some kept perhaps as valued tokens of the old days when the people still had their ranchitos, although some current villagers, male and female, Hispano and Anglo, still cut fine figures on their steeds.

The demographics of the Galisteo Basin and Santa Fe County have also been changing, although New Mexico's is proportionally the largest Latino population in the nation,[4] and Hispanos have been described as legally white but socially nonwhite: "Hispano identity has mutated over the course of several centuries from vecino through Mexican, Spanish American, Chicano/Indo Hispano/Nuevomexicano phases, always in interaction and co-formation with other self-identified neighboring populations, including Pueblos, Navajos, Apaches, Utes, Comanches, Genizaros (detribalized Indians), Anglo Americans, Mexican nationals, other Mexican Americans and Latinos," writes Sylvia Rodríguez.[5]

Richard A. Shuff, *Music at the Community Holiday Breakfast*, Dec. 15, 2002. *Left to right*: Patricia Heller, Yolanda Herrera, Lucy Lippard, Onésimo Montoya, Martha Anaya Delgado, Mela Montoya, Anna Montoya Cárdenas, Tana Cárdenas, and unidentified children. For a more detailed account of music in Galisteo in the 1940s and later, see the interview with Onésimo by Margarita Cordero (aka Nacha Mendez) and Tacho Sandoval's reminiscences, *El Puente*, March 2002.

As the rest of the country becomes browner, this often insular Indo Hispano village has become whiter. Galisteo is now majority Anglo (a term that includes Caucasians, African Americans, Jews—anyone who is not Indian or Hispano), and Hispanos make up only around a quarter of the population. "There has always been a connection to land, but the nature of that relationship," as Rodríguez notes, changed through time."[6] The old families maintain a profound attachment to their lost ranches, as do the Pueblo people who once inhabited the Galisteo Basin and consider none of their ancient homes "abandoned." The younger Nuevo Mexicanos, like all North Americans, seem less attached to their roots.

Richard A. Shuff, *Tacho and Libby Sandoval*, 2002. Tacho composed the "Galisteo Polka" and played a traditional accordion. Libby sang and played the tambourine. He reminisced about how important music was in his Galisteo childhood; later he and his friends played in Santa Fe, other local towns, and at church. On New Year's Eve they serenaded los Manueles (everyone named Manuel) with accordion and guitars.

Language disparities are also disappearing. Unlike their elders, who spoke English as a second language, Galisteo's younger generations often know little Spanish. Most of us Anglos, of course, speak Spanish poorly, if at all. (Simona García in her nineties called me La Americana to her friends, as she might have in 1848 when the Americans arrived in force; later she began to call me "ILoveLucy," all run together, citing a shared popular culture.) The advent of many contemporary Mexicans and Central Americans to the city of Santa Fe means even more Spanish is spoken in the supermarkets and everywhere around the capital, but the distinctions between Mexicano and Nuevo Mexicano are sharp. A Chicana neighbor raised in El Paso found most New Mexicans standoffish. A local man asked me if she was Spanish (*hispano*) or Mexican (*mexicano*)?

In the mid-1980s, Marion Steele wrote of Galisteo, "there are practically no community activities."[7] By the time I moved to the village a few years later, this was not the case. Community gatherings were changing but still centered around the old local families. I arrived on the cusp of the change, best defined by community meetings, then still crowded and diverse. I remember an informal "receiving line." Men in cowboy hats—members of the family most affected by the issues to be decided, usually the Anayas, the most politically involved and genealogically interconnected family—met us at the door to shake hands.[8] I didn't know any of them yet, but the welcome seemed genuine. The Hispano population turned out for issues involving land, water, and unwelcome change. At social gatherings, Onésimo and Mela

Richard A. Shuff, *The Cuervo Wranglers Playing at La Sala for the Studio Tour after Party*, 1998. The lead singer is former county commissioner Michael D. Anaya.

Richard A. Shuff, *Remedios and Luis Chávez Dancing at La Sala after Studio Tour*, 1998.

Lucy R. Lippard, *Gathering at the Community Center*, 2017.

Montoya or Libby and Tacho Sandoval would provide traditional guitar, vocal, and accordion music, or Martha Anaya Chávez Delgado would sing, or the Cuervo Wranglers (the Anaya boys) would play country rock. Watching expert dancers like Remy and Luis Chávez was one of the joys of local celebrations, along with abundant food. Handshakes are the standard greeting; a brief, formal embrace is an acknowledgment of respect or fondness.

Within a few years of my arrival, many of the elders had passed away or were too frail to come to functions, and the character of meetings and gatherings, now dominated by Anglos, had subtly changed. The Community Center is used primarily for meetings, rentals, community breakfasts and book exchanges, and traditional potlucks after local graduations, christenings, weddings, and funerals. The annual Chile & Margarita Cook-Off is the liveliest and most inclusive party of the year. Constant improvements are made to the aging building, including a small meeting and "Archive Room" featuring Onésimo Montoya's handsome carpentry.

Over the decades, as the transition was made from rural to bedroom community, the proudly traditional village has become an increasingly wealthy residential town. At community meetings, the pendulum has shifted from very local politics toward broader issues of planning, environmentalism, and maintaining the village's "character," which no one knows better than the old families, nostalgic for the days of closer community despite a harsher economy. Not yet a suburb of Santa Fe (thanks to the ranchland that separates us from the 285 corridor), Galisteo maintains its own identity despite the influx of out-of-state retirees.[9] Old houses are gutted to adapt to different lifestyles; new houses are rarely built in the traditional village center. Both tend to bring high prices on the market. A population of around 260, which includes children and elders and the Ranchitos subdivision with its high percentage of second homes, is hard put to provide the human power necessary to support the village's volunteer civic institutions: The Galisteo Community Association (GCA), the Volunteer Fire Department (GVFR), the Mutual Domestic Water Association, Community Planning committees, La Sala Art Center,

Philip Pfeiffer, *Winners of the Chile and Margarita Cook-Off*, 2011. *Left to right*: David Maestas, Richard Fenker, Craig Moya, Barbara Pfeiffer, and Roger Taylor.

Tom Martinelli, *Procession Celebrating the 125th Anniversary of Nuestra Señora de los Remedios*, 2009. María Ortiz y Pino carries the bulto of Nuestra Señora.

Caroline Hinkley, *Former Isake Montoya House and WPA Mattress Factory*, 1930s. It has been radically remodeled and is once again a private home.

Studio Tour, and the monthly newsletter, *El Puente de Galisteo*. New arrivals are greedily recruited for the eternally opening slots on the various boards that operate these organizations. For instance, the advent of Roger Taylor, an energetic former insurance executive who came first in 2002 and settled here permanently in 2009, has been a boon to the village, the GCA, planning committees, La Sala, the Ranchitos Water Association, and further afield into the county. He has taken on many of the onerous tasks of attending meetings, fundraising for ecological projects, representing our community in the county and state at a time when many dedicated villagers, Anglo and Hispano alike, were burning out.

When I began researching local history—first out of curiosity, then for the newsletter, and finally for this book—the village elders, courteous, reserved, and often secretive, were bewildered as to why I would care about their family histories. Was it really any of my business? When asked why I was so interested in their families rather than my own, I tried to explain that my focus was on people *in place* and my family had never stayed long enough in one place to be interesting in that context. Sarapio Montoya kindly responded, "When you get old and sick, you may want to go back to your own country." He may have meant my *patria chica*, my own little country—all you can see from the nearest high point—or just home. I consider Galisteo my home, but I did indeed come from "another country"—the lofts of Lower Manhattan.

There are local Galisteans who welcome the flood of newcomers from "away." There are those who are resigned to it, those who abhor it, and those who are convinced that they will outlast it. Rudy Sena told me he likes seeing Galisteo get bigger again so long as new people treat him with respect and know he's lived here all his life. When I was new to the village, the late José Ortiz y Pino III told me, "We don't worry about gringos. They come and they go. They don't stay. They get old and there's no one to take care of them, and they go back to their roots even though they've sworn they'll stay here forever. We sit and watch them. No one's a threat to me. I know them better than they know me."[10] (Actually, in my time in Galisteo a number of longtime Anglo residents have died here, many of whom were very active in the community.)

Five Generations of Anayas, ca. 1998. *Left to right*: Clarita Anaya de Anaya with her daughter Martha Anaya Delgado, granddaughter Yolanda Herrera, and great-granddaughter Monica Herrera and her baby Gabriel. (Courtesy of Martha Anaya Delgado and Kenny M. Chávez.)

Ortiz y Pino was the prime informant for the past few decades of Galisteo histories, and his tight grasp on his family's and village's story has rarely been challenged. But the descendants of the other, often older, families, la gente, are stepping up to reveal their own family histories. New obstacles arise. A friend who has been researching her genealogy found that some elderly male relatives were reluctant to tell their stories to a woman. Some people I have interviewed about the past like the idea of their histories being written down, for the future. Others are fearful of what that means—a throwback to the times when the legal process in New Mexico changed languages and bilked so many out of their common lands and their cultural inheritances. Nothing good has come to them in writing, although *telling* is a different matter, generously proffered. "Most educated people say, 'Where is it written?' Our people say, 'Where is it *lived*?'" A native Nuevo Mexicano said this to an artist working in another part of the state.[11] And Patricia L. Price writes: "The landscapes shaped by narratives are as real as those sculpted by the action of wind, waves, and glaciers."[12] Because lived experience, my own and others', is important to me, I was able to interview many elders before they passed on, though unfortunately I often did not yet know the right questions to ask. It was harder than I had imagined, not because of ill will, but for lack of common ground. Native Hispanos and one rich and powerful old family, struggling and successful artists, wealthy newcomers who often don't last long—we all live in the same place, attend the same community gatherings, are often friendly, though our life experiences can be miles apart. Historian Ernst Bloch called this "non-synchronism," meaning that people from different backgrounds and social classes can exist contemporaneously while actually living within very different cultural contexts.[13] But everyone has stories.

Some scholars don't trust oral history because of its tendency to favor stories overspecific dates and places, which can be frustrating for researchers. The sense of time is flexible. The old Galisteo families adamantly prefer their own family histories, which often conflict with those of their neighbors, their relatives, and the few extant documents. Because New Mexico is a poor state and was slow to acquire the amenities of modern life, I have met villagers who remembered customs, beliefs, and lifestyles that elsewhere had disappeared in the nineteenth

or early twentieth century. I spoke to those who survived the Depression. I spoke to women who bore many children and worked as hard as the men. I spoke to those who were children in the 1920s and 1930s and could remember a tight, supportive, culturally homogenous community. And I have spoken to those who are disenchanted with present-day Galisteo, so unlike that of their childhoods. We all love "our village," but its "ownership" is an issue.

We outsiders move to the Galisteo Basin thinking romantically of the past while ignoring its lessons and our own impact on the present and future. Those who were raised in Galisteo can feel what is called "primary nostalgia . . . felt for something once actually experienced," whereas "imagined nostalgia," according to Arjun Appadurai, is when "consumers are induced to 'miss' things they have never lost."[14] Rodríguez adds: "Nostalgia, one supposes, did not color how vecinos felt or talked about their fields, gardens, pastures, acequias, buildings, placitas, forests, arroyos, or mountains—more likely a mix of fear, aggression, and aspiration."[15] "Galisteo is very different from what we wanted it to be," said Mela Montoya. One middle-aged woman who was raised here and lives in Albuquerque told me she hated Galisteo and would never come back, even if she could have her parents' house. "The place ha[s] changed too much. It's too sad. It used to be just our own people. . . . We worked things out. Now there are too many rules, and all these new houses." Another woman her age told me she "hated" living in Galisteo now: "New people have ruined Galisteo, all those rules and regulations. Why can't they just *live* here?" An older man said more bluntly, "Galisteo's no good for nothing now." I'm not clear about what these despised rules are, aside from the community's contributions to the county's new Sustainable Land Development Code, based

Bill Mitchell, *Luminarias at Nuestra Señora de los Remedios*, 2007; *The Old Bridge with Farolitos, Christmas Eve*, 2007.

Lucy R. Lippard, *The Old and the New: Old Cemetery and New "Portal" Construction on John and Tanya Young's Home*, ca. 2015.

on endless deliberations by a volunteer planning committee and public community meetings. But the old families are justly proprietary. In a public meeting about land-use planning, the son-in-law of one local family, speaking, he said, for the Hispano constituency as a whole, wondered why Anglo "newcomers" (residents in the village from zero to forty years) had any right at all to plan "our village." Years later, he perceived a plot to "get rid of the brown people." Although these conversations were relatively cordial, the changes referred to were clearly perceived for the worse, and the changers, of course, were me and my ilk.[16]

These comments reflect an ambivalence that is an integral part of New Mexican cultural exchanges. An old *dicho* warns, "Pueblo chico, infierno grande" (Small town, big hell). Many complaints stem from the painful experience of becoming a minority in one's ancestral place and from historical divisions that are the legacy of the 1600s and the 1840s. Others are the product of ancient internal feuds. "Galisteo is usually a warm and generous little community, with occasional mean-spirited moments," said a local woman raised in Santa Fe but married into Galisteo, where she has lived for most of her life. "They can be so nice and they can be so terrible."

To live in such a village for a while is to understand how stubbornly tradition is embraced, even as it seems to be disappearing with TV and ATVs, social media, smart phones, and video games, on top of old enmities and new scandals and the ever-present threat of outside invasion, met with anger or resignation. Resentment stemming from income inequities and losses of land and tradition surfaces from time to time. There have been occasional rashes of vandalism. In 2005 the target was the new bank of locked mailboxes; eggs were splattered on them and firecrackers tossed into the "outgoing mail" slots. Around the same time, two of the tall windows of the Community Center were smashed; repairs cost some $1,200. Later a grass fire was started near an Anglo artist's studio (perhaps just an accidental result of fireworks). A fence was destroyed by a drunken teenager who drove his truck through it. Although youths from a struggling family were once blamed for everything bad that happens, in 2018 Anglos were known to deface local signs and try (unsuccessfully) to bully a ninety-one-year-old

Lucy R. Lippard, *Remains of Old Car below Agnes Martin House*, ca. 2015. Once carefully hidden by a cover of branches.

Anna Cárdenas, *Los Pastores at La Sala*, 2017. Savannah Gallegos is Mary, Jason Montoya is Joseph, with the Gran Pastorela de Belen.

Alice Kruse, *El Demonio*, 2017.

woman. Such events signal a deeper rip in the social fabric. However, although the elders are passing on and there are few young people and children living in Galisteo, there is still a village within the village. Hispano life, bolstered by tight family ties, flows on like an unseen current below the general civic surface.[17]

Most of my neighbors are, like me, refugees from "back East," or Texas, or California, or the Midwest. Some stay a few years and move on, having discovered, as someone put it, that "Galisteo is not La Jolla." Many newcomers never expected any change at all in and around Galisteo and are incredulous at its rapid rate. Some move away when their views are blocked by another dream house, much like their own, illustrating the textbook "drawbridge syndrome": everyone wants to be the last to move in. Yet despite the generally congenial co-existence, lively community events, and hardworking, relatively uncontentious planning meetings that characterize village life, it is not utopia. The late Bernard Pomerance, author of *Elephant Man* and a Galisteo resident for decades, wrote an unpublished series of whimsical short stories à clef about "the world's most difficult village."

There is an assumption that all Anglos are transient, while members of the old families maintain contact with the village through the church and family gatherings, even when they live elsewhere in the area. A local woman grudgingly acknowledged to me that if *they* stayed ten years, *they* tended to stay. Yet many of us newcomers also have a fierce affection for this place. It is what we have been searching for. A number of Anglo families have been here thirty or forty years, even if their parents and children are elsewhere, while the founding families have, of course, been here "forever."

After I'd lived in Galisteo for over a decade, I was told, with casual frankness rather than hostility, that I would never belong here. This was not news. Having written extensively about what constituted the "local," I knew that I could never fully belong to a place I had come to so late, a place that differed so drastically from my own lived experience. Most contemporary North Americans move so often, we're constantly trespassing in one another's homeplaces. In New Mexico, in Maine, and other poor states where persistence and fortitude have been so important, you'll always be "from away" or "just off the bus," as Debbie Jaramillo, the forthright former mayor of Santa Fe, liked to say. A telling aspect of the mini-diaspora shared by many of us who live where we weren't raised is the transitional phases. Over the years we slowly morph from tourist to visitor to optimistic newcomer to busy local, a transition marked by that moment when you realize you're staying, you're stuck, you'd better get to work. My favorite definition of a local is "someone who gives more than they take." The last stage, the "neo-native," includes building memories.

Even if the bonds to place are very different, many of us outsiders become deeply involved in the community, settle, and hope to die here. An elderly Hispana neighbor told me, "I shouldn't say bad things about gringos. Without them we wouldn't have a community center, a fire department, a water system . . . or a newsletter." (Of course, these things were accomplished through the instigation, input, and participation of the shrinking Hispano community as well, even when gringo labor and gringo money tend to keep them going.) Most residents try to practice what has been identified as three types of social capital important for collective

Lucy R. Lippard, *Rodeo Parade*, 2008.

Tom Morin, "*Galisteo Garden Club" Float in Rodeo Parade*, 2007.

GALISTEO
GARDEN
CLUB

Lucy R. Lippard, *El Tanque Viejo*, 2018. The Anaya compound; the barn is a new addition to downtown Galisteo.

action: "trustworthiness, networks, formal and informal rules and institutions," or the local equivalent, described by Sylvia Rodríguez as ayuda mutual, respeto, y confianza (mutual support, respect, and confidence).[18]

"Change and growth cannot be controlled," writes Christina Nealson, "but they can be directed. Let towns define who they are and proclaim such. Then newcomers will know who they attempt to join."[19] An attempt to explain who we were joining was made by Michael D. Anaya before he was county commissioner. While living on the family ranch in Stanley, he adapted a "Code of the West" to explain to rural newcomers "just how things work around here." Some of the advice was helpful: New Mexico is still a fence-out state; it's your job to fence cows out of your yard, not the rancher's to fence them in. Other advice was somewhat ominous: A dog chasing cows can be shot. Digging a well is no guarantee you'll find water. Urban services like garbage collection and neighborhood police patrols are not available.[20]

"You can't fight progress" is a popular, if inaccurate, assumption. All change is not progress and much change is contentious. Many native New Mexicans are resigned to change even as they deplore it. Where should the line be drawn between "progress" that benefits all and a rush to change for the worse? Or can that line even be drawn? I find myself going case by case. A local woman told me that since Ranchitos was settled, "people don't wave when they drive by. You respond by not being as friendly anymore." In community meetings, one often finds oneself allied with virulent opponents on some previous issue, or vice versa. Listening to each other isn't always easy. Another community activist with whom I am often at odds once called me to say, "Well, hell has frozen over. We agree on something." Her call did break some ice.

One of the hardest parts of joining a historic community is seeing its flaws but respecting its identity enough not to try to change everything. Graciela Esperanza, a community organizer from San Antonio, Texas, has commented on the "outsider's agenda." The community, she said, takes tradition and goes on a political route with it; the outsider walks away with what the community has developed. Many communities have suffered, or enjoyed, a sequence of outsiders who arrive and announce, "Here's what you need or should do. Lucky you, we can do it for you." The initial response, she observed, "tends to be, 'Don't do us any favors.'"[21] A poster in my workroom backs this up: "*Nothing About Us Without Us Is for Us.*"[22]

Lack of understanding about how people choose to live, or are forced to live, has at times exacerbated the social divide in Galisteo village. Yet this mobile population must take responsibility, even temporarily, for the land on which we find ourselves living together. We are all part of a cultural continuum that goes back over a thousand years to varying Native tribes, Pueblo peoples, Spanish and then Mexican explorers and settlers intermarrying with local indigenous populations, and finally American entrepreneurs and homesteaders. It's a continuum with a lot of rough edges, or torn seams. The future of development in Galisteo may or may not obliterate the varied senses of place that exist today among the old families and more recent arrivals.

When it finally became possible for me to move from New York City to the West, where my maternal grandparents were raised, I knew exactly where I wanted to settle for the rest of my life. Living in New Mexico was an idea that had been incubating since my first visit in December 1972. Twenty years later, when my ties to the East were partially severed, the twenty-three-acre strip of overgrazed pasture across the creek from my frequent refuge at La Lanera—the Nicolas and Pedro Ortiz y Pino property—had been subdivided into four lots, initially offered by a wealthy admirer to the famous Buddhist teacher Thich Nhat Hanh, who already had a retreat in France and declined her offer. I chose the lot closest to the highway so that I could

Lucy R. Lippard, *The Shack by the Creek*, 1993.

Richard A. Shuff, *Lippard House from the North*, early 2000s.

enjoy the view across rangeland to the mountains and would not have to worry about what was built in front of me. When my one-room house went up in 1993—sixteen by twenty-four feet, stucco/pseudo adobe on frame (the real thing was too expensive) with its pitched tin roof and sleeping loft—it resembled a child's drawing. An absentee rancher patronizingly called it "the shack by the creek," and I found out later that villagers called it the Smurf House.

I was alone on the strip for several years and was often asked if I had a gun and a dog. (Like a proper bruja, I had a little black cat.) Remedios Chávez, an elderly neighbor, complimented me on my house but said it was "too bad about the trees." Since I'd chosen to build too close to the creek because of the trees, I asked her why. "Snakes live under trees," she said firmly. Her own yard was traditionally bare ground. At first, my little house rested in a sea of dust or mud, now saltbush and range grasses. Some of the tiny locust saplings I found at a nursery sale survived and have produced a volunteer forest of drought-resistant offspring. I've added a big workroom and other bits and pieces over the years. Off the grid from the onset, I first plugged my house into my car and tried to read by dim oil lamps and a gas lamp donated by my then neighbor Bill Kastle, who felt sorry for me. I graduated to a golf cart battery and a couple of solar panels leaning against the house and finally to a tracker and roof-mounted panels that have proved sufficient for my minimal needs (no TV, no washer or dryer, no microwave).

When I settled in Galisteo, in a very dry year, I was astonished at the sensation of grass crackling under my feet in springtime. It's become a familiar experience. Now and then we get enough rain to fill the tanks and make everybody feel safe wasting water again. Annual rainfall for Santa Fe in 2016 was 14.21 inches, and Galisteo often receives less. From my house-building notebook in November 1992: "When the dowser comes, he finds enough water (140 feet and 40 gallons per minute) and no nitrates, lead, copper, or clay." He was wrong, but he had just acquired a pacemaker, which may have disturbed the transmission of magnetic energies. Years later I saw a geological map and realized I had drilled 400 feet into Mancos shale, also known as hell.[23] After ten years, my well produced so much sulphur, a grime of black barillium, and who knows what else that the house smelled of rotten eggs and the copper pipes were corroding. I had to close down the well. For years I paid to have water hauled to a cistern while I waited for the town system to expand in my direction (I was about seventeenth on the waiting list when I signed up) or for the county to enter the fray and construct a countywide water system. In 1998 the Galisteo Mutual Domestic Water Consumers Association's Board announced that we were very close to our allotted usage of 42.58 acre feet, or 13,874,735 gallons: "We regret to inform those of you who are on a waiting list for a hookup that there can be no new hookups."

However, around the same time, a local man and his nonresident partners in an electrician's business headquartered in Galisteo were permitted to transfer a domestic water hookup to a planned (but never executed) commercial venture. The County Development Review Committee (CDRC) approved his request for 1.39 acre feet, despite a petition signed by 32 of the 57 members of the Galisteo MDWCA asking that his project be limited to the .53 acre feet per year then recommended for each domestic hookup.[24] This case sparked the decision to meter the village's water uses and also to question whether our Water Association was autonomous and to what extent the CDRC or the Board of County Commissioners (BCC) controlled our water systems.

The twenty-five miles to Santa Fe have shrunk since the early 1990s, when the drive out of town was a soothing and (in winter, adventurous) ride. There were few lights in the nocturnal landscape. The subdivisions composing El Dorado were hidden in a dip, their presence betrayed by a pale glow. Lamy made little dent on the vast night sky. Kamikaze cottontails and an occasional deer, pronghorn, coyote, or bobcat dashed across the headlights. Galisteo appeared, dimly lit, out of the darkness. Few lights were still on by 9:00 p.m. Darkness, the Milky Way, and a startling starry sky ruled. There was so little traffic on NM 41 that I woke up when headlights swept across my ceiling. Today there are two traffic lights, streetlights, and security lights almost all the way from Santa Fe. In the village itself, a few locals had security lights and some newcomers began to leave bright lights on all night. (When the house next door to me was empty, I would go over and unscrew the porch bulb.) I spoke to the changing tenants of the prime perpetrator, who sometimes complied. I wrote to their landlady—doyenne, ironically, of the Light Institute. As a member of the Volunteer Fire Department, I complained about the light on the American flag by the station and was teased by the chief, who told me it was a federal law, so it was fine if I wanted to come over every night and take the flag down and raise it again every morning. (I demurred.) An editorial in the village newsletter touted the New Mexico Heritage Alliance's choice of the New Mexico Night Sky as the most endangered historical monument in the state. I hoped this would make some impression on my neighbors. It did. Some twenty years later, the east side of the village is mostly dark again.

Today my once empty strip of land is shared with three congenial neighbors, some of whom work hard to support the community. Together we have imposed the ecological weight of four homes on the once empty agricultural strip: a house, a studio/casita, and a two-horse barn; a handsome modernist four-part compound built of rastra (recycled soda bottles) that was wisely designed by well-known local architect Beverley Spears as four small units, maintaining a scale commensurate with its neighbors; it is now graced by a vast bank of ground-based solar panels. The third-story cupola and carport solar-paneled for hot water heating of the newest structure is the home of our state representative, environmental lawyer Matthew McQueen and his young family. Galisteo east of the river also boasts a mobile home, a couple of inhabited near-ruins, little houses, elegant renovated adobes, new structures, scattered old and new vehicles, RVs, and horses. This kind of mixed-use, mixed-taste village is where I want to live.

I moved to Galisteo rather than to the more isolated areas I was drawn to, not only because I was in my mid-fifties and didn't want to move ever again, but also because I wanted to be part of a community. I knew a few people in the village. After trying for a couple of years to find a way to contribute, to find my place here, I came upon a flyer asking for help in building the new fire station. I spent a little time making, hauling, and laying adobe bricks and meeting people. Someone asked me to write something about helping the fire department,

EL PUENTE DE GALISTEO

ISSUE #50 DECEMBER 2001

MERRY CHRISTMAS AND HAPPY HOLIDAYS

THIS IS THE 50th ISSUE OF EL PUENTE, marking 5 full years of publishing. It's a good time not only to sponsor an issue (a $75 check made out to GCA with note that it's for El Puente) but also to let the editor know what you like and hate about the paper. For once, I'll even welcome anonymous comments (though prefer signed ones), and will take it all to heart. What do you want more of? Less of? Any features you love or hate? Story suggestions? General direction? Get it off your chest. This is a community paper and *you* are the community!

AND A HAPPY NEW YEAR TOO... Margarita and Melanie will be away for New Year's, so the "traditional" New Year's Eve party at the Community Center won't happen unless somebody else would like to organize it. Call M & M if you're up for it (466-6696).

TOBIAS ANAYA, ARTIST: FROM GALISTEO'S ROOTS

If you're lucky, you've lived here long enough to have known Tobias Anaya, and you had the sense to buy one or more of his sculptures. A Galisteo icon and one of its greatest artists, Tobias sold his wares next to the old cemetery, where a well-tended cross and text in his memory still stands. Tobias Lane, on the Hill, is named for him.

Tobias's sculptures were assembled, or transformed, from found objects —what most people think of as junk. He scavenged the Galisteo roadsides daily, a familiar figure in his black coat, on crutches, or two canes. David van Dyk, who enjoyed his company, remembers that when the family clothesline was raided by the wind, the children's socks would turn up in Tobias's art. He displayed his works on an old bedframe, and later made a whole cage, or *cerquito,* for them.

Tobias was born in Galisteo in October 1909 and lived here for most of his life, dying sadly in a house fire on November 29, 1989. He was Clarita and Serapio Anaya's older brother, Michael D. Anaya's uncle, and was related to many other *(cont. p.2)*

Above: Tobias Anaya,1986. Right: Tobias Anaya, Three Musicians, Collection David van Dyk (photo: Richard Shuff)

EL PUENTE DECEMBER 2001 - 1

EL PUENTE DE GALISTEO

ISSUE #66 SUMMER 2003

*** SUMMER CALENDAR ***

JUNE 23rd: 6:30PM at the Community Center: **COMMUNITY MEETING WITH THE SANTA FE COUNTY PROJECTS AND FACILITIES DEPARTMENT** regarding the Infrastructure Capitol Improvement Plan (ICIP). The County is asking for input from residents about what items we would like added to the list sent to the legislature for funding. County Commissioner Mike Anaya will be present. Please plan to attend this important meeting and come with ideas!

JULY 19-20: RODEO DE GALISTEO. Parade through village on Saturday morning before events begin at the Rodeo Grounds.

AUGUST 23 6PM at the Community Center: **GALISTEO'S FIRST ANNUAL CHILI FESTIVAL.** Prizes for best Chili, Cornbread, and Margaritas; music, arts and crafts, fun for the family and dinner too! Sign up now for competitions and arts/crafts: Victoria Prewitt, 466-6359 or Mela Montoya, 466-1430. Sponsored by the GCA.

JULY 6, AUGUST 3, SEPT. 7: BOOK/VIDEO SWAPS 2-4PM, Community Center. Community survey will be on display.

NEXT ISSUE OF EL PUENTE, MID-SEPTEMBER

HAVE A GREAT SUMMER

CRITTER CORNER

A new column by Isabella Gonzales (and anyone else who steps up)

VITAL STATISTICS: Full name: Desdemona; **Nickname:** Mona; **Species:** Canine; **Age:** 11; **Astrological Sign:** Pisces; **Breed:** Classic New Mexican Mutt; **Hobbies:** Chasing rabbits, chasing rabbits, and chasing rabbits. **People:** Linda Rice and Grace; **Long Term Love Interest:** Boris (his person is Nancy Helle); **Favorite Toy:** Prefers not to play with "dog toys" because of the stigma attached.

Mona considers her greatest adventure as the time she was running errands with Linda in Santa Fe and got lost. Mona tells us, "Linda ran in to get a cup of Joe and suddenly I felt as if I left my body. I watched myself jump out of the truck window toward a bright light in the shape of a bunny. I still can't explain what happened."

An hour later (at her next job) Linda noticed that Mona was missing (*hey, she was really busy and she hadn't* (cont. p.2)

INSIDE: SPECIAL SUPPLEMENT ON RESULTS OF COMMUNITY SURVEY

NOTICE: GALISTEO STUDIO TOUR IS ACTIVELY RECRUITING A FOOD VENDOR ON THE WEST SIDE OF TOWN. Call Victoria Prewitt, 466-6359.

Mona Comes Home (Photo: Richard Shuff)

EL PUENTE SUMMER 2003 - 1

El Puente de Galisteo, December 2001.

El Puente de Galisteo, Summer 2003.

and when my New York friends asked what I was working on, I told them excitedly that I had just written a piece for the *Galisteo Fire Flyer,* a single-page occasional newsletter. A few months later I heard that a village newsletter was being considered. Activist Michael Datoli, who intended to edit it, was ill and could take on no more causes, so I grabbed my chance. It seemed important to provide a vehicle with which to bond and inform the community. Land and water issues crucial to communal health were rarely brought to the attention of the general population, although there was always a hard core of activists keeping an eye on external affairs and calling community meetings when necessary. Word of mouth thrives in small communities, but newcomers tend to be out of the loop. Finally I'd found something I could do well, as I had edited small activist art papers and written and copyedited many books. There was a brief set-to when a Community Board member from an old family wanted to know if I was "some kind of radical or community activist." I pleaded guilty but explained that I had other outlets for my left politics and was committed to a monthly *community* newsletter in which all voices would be heard. My critic also contended that local history was the last thing we needed: "All the old people are already at each others' throats about things that happened a hundred years ago and this just stirs things up again." (At the time, this sounded absurd to me; later I learned better.)

A small, all-Anglo editorial committee began to meet, and we named the new enterprise after the old bridge that bisects the village. Although we knew correct Spanish was *El Puente*, we decided to be colloquially correct, according to a dictionary of New Mexican Spanish, and call it *La Puente,* after the village's main street.[25] Artist Cara Lee drew a striking logo. The first issue appeared in January 1997 as *La Puente de Galisteo.* A storm of protest ensued, a taste of what was to come. We hastily changed it to *El Puente.* Then other community members insisted that we should have kept *La Puente.* The solution came when Anna Cárdenas pointed out that the street called Via La Puente meant "the way to the bridge" and *el puente* meant the bridge itself. And I began to practice what I had preached in a book I was about to publish called *The Lure of the Local. El Puente de Galisteo* has allowed me for twenty-three years to be nosy, to collect stories, to put my foot in my mouth while attempting to cross cultural boundaries, and to begin to get a grip on the bewildering maze of local genealogies, the long-held grudges, and the lay of the lands. I have learned a great deal about Galisteo and about the pitfalls of publishing in a pueblo chico. I have been privy to the gossip, rumors, and hearsay on which small towns thrive, although I'm often told, "But that's not for the newspaper." I've become very fond of certain evasive phrases: "I'm told" (hearsay) or "according to so and so" (passing the buck), or "it is said that" and "rumor has it" (local stories impossible to document)—all those phrases used by insecure historians, who are the best kind.

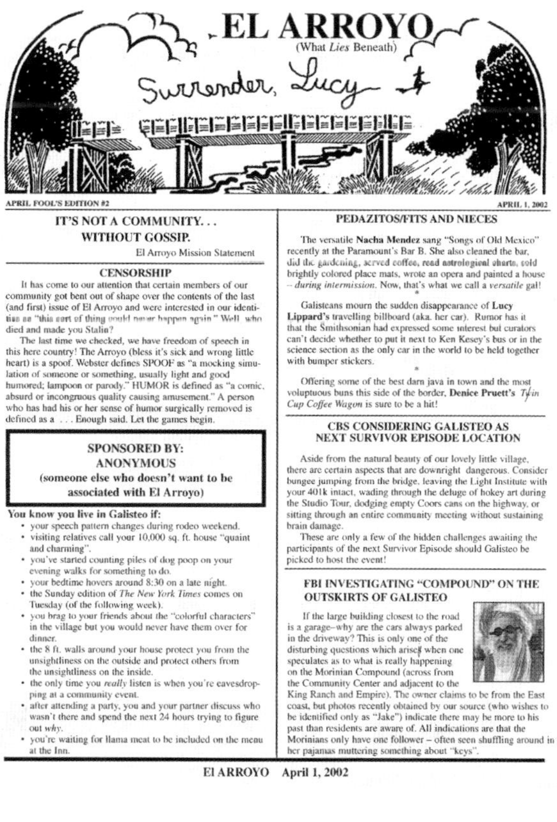

EL ARROYO
(What *Lies* Beneath)
Surrender, Lucy

APRIL FOOL'S EDITION #2 — APRIL 1, 2002

IT'S NOT A COMMUNITY . . . WITHOUT GOSSIP.
El Arroyo Mission Statement

CENSORSHIP

It has come to our attention that certain members of our community got bent out of shape over the contents of the last (and first) issue of El Arroyo and were interested in our identities as "this sort of thing could never happen again." Well, who died and made you Stalin?

The last time we checked, we have freedom of speech in this here country! The Arroyo (bless it's sick and wrong little heart) is a spoof. Webster defines SPOOF as "a mocking simulation of someone or something, usually light and good humored; lampoon or parody." HUMOR is defined as "a comic, absurd or incongruous quality causing amusement." A person who has had his or her sense of humor surgically removed is defined as a . . . Enough said. Let the games begin.

SPONSORED BY: ANONYMOUS (someone else who doesn't want to be associated with El Arroyo)

You know you live in Galisteo if:

- your speech pattern changes during rodeo weekend.
- visiting relatives call your 10,000 sq. ft. house "quaint and charming".
- you've started counting piles of dog poop on your evening walks for something to do.
- your bedtime hovers around 8:30 on a late night.
- the Sunday edition of *The New York Times* comes on Tuesday (of the following week).
- you brag to your friends about the "colorful characters" in the village but you would never have them over for dinner.
- the 8 ft. walls around your house protect you from the unsightliness on the outside and protect others from the unsightliness on the inside.
- the only time you *really* listen is when you're eavesdropping at a community event.
- after attending a party, you and your partner discuss who wasn't there and spend the next 24 hours trying to figure out *why*.
- you're waiting for llama meat to be included on the menu at the Inn.

PEDAZITOS/FITS AND NIECES

The versatile **Nacha Mendez** sang "Songs of Old Mexico" recently at the Paramount's Bar B. She also cleaned the bar, did the gardening, served coffee, read astrological charts, sold brightly colored place mats, wrote an opera and painted a house – *during intermission*. Now, that's what we call a *versatile* gal!

*

Galisteans mourn the sudden disappearance of **Lucy Lippard's** travelling billboard (aka. her car). Rumor has it that the Smithsonian had expressed some interest but curators can't decide whether to put it next to Ken Kesey's bus or in the science section as the only car in the world to be held together with bumper stickers.

*

Offering some of the best darn java in town and the most voluptuous buns this side of the border, **Denice Pruett's** *Twin Cup Coffee Wagon* is sure to be a hit!

CBS CONSIDERING GALISTEO AS NEXT SURVIVOR EPISODE LOCATION

Aside from the natural beauty of our lovely little village, there are certain aspects that are downright dangerous. Consider bungee jumping from the bridge, leaving the Light Institute with your 401k intact, wading through the deluge of hokey art during the Studio Tour, dodging empty Coors cans on the highway, or sitting through an entire community meeting without sustaining brain damage.

These are only a few of the hidden challenges awaiting the participants of the next Survivor Episode should Galisteo be picked to host the event!

FBI INVESTIGATING "COMPOUND" ON THE OUTSKIRTS OF GALISTEO

If the large building closest to the road is a garage–why are the cars always parked in the driveway? This is only one of the disturbing questions which arise when one speculates as to what is really happening on the Morinian Compound (across from the Community Center and adjacent to the King Ranch and Empire). The owner claims to be from the East coast, but photos recently obtained by our source (who wishes to be identified only as "Jake") indicate there may be more to his past than residents are aware of. All indications are that the Morinians only have one follower – often seen shuffling around in her pajamas muttering something about "keys".

El ARROYO April 1, 2002

April Fools Page of *El Puente*, April 2002.

STOP
90
22
11
LOVE

There's never a dull moment in sleepy Galisteo. Two longtime Anglo residents, since departed for other states, wanted me to run a down-and-dirty gossip column but were unwilling to write it. I thought a "Milestones" column would be less risky. I'd seen two new burials in the cemetery and called the family home to get material for obituaries. The woman I spoke to said I should talk to her husband, because they were his nephews. He said I should talk to his niece because they were her brothers. She had no phone. I was told later that both deaths were drug involved. Births sounded uncomplicated, so I called a woman I knew slightly and asked if she knew of any births. "Noooo," she said thoughtfully. I called another woman who said the first one had a new grandchild. I wondered why she hadn't told me. "Well, they aren't married." I gave up on the milestones idea, clearly too sensitive for an outside meddler. Eventually I compromised on "Pedacitos/Bits and Pieces," a monthly roundup of events and individual accomplishments.

I wanted to be involved in the village, but I should have watched out for what I wished for. Little did I know how much of my life could be swallowed up by this little patch of place (this book being the logical outcome). And my overeager outsider ignorance often got me in trouble. Once I published the name of a local man who had told the sheriff about a car leaving a burgled home. He was horrified; only then did I realize I could have endangered him. Another time the printer misplaced a paragraph that interrupted an elder's obituary and I got an enraged call from his son's girlfriend. It had not occurred to me that I might have to write most of *El Puente*'s copy forever. A younger woman raised in the village told me after a few months that people really liked the newsletter. "Great," I said. "And when do you think they'll start sending me stories?" "That'll take a long time," she replied. (It did.) For several years Jan Saunders contributed a bird and nature column, later compiled for El Puente Press's first booklet.[26] For a few years Isabella Gonzales came up with an anonymous April Fool's page: "El Arroyo, What *Lies* Beneath [the bridge]."[27] The "mission statement" was, "It's not a community without gossip," and the column was wickedly funny. While I reluctantly edited her wit, it was still controversial. More recently, Stella Maestas, descendant of Sandovals and Moras, has regularly contributed touching childhood reminiscences.

For years we illegally delivered *El Puente* into all the village mailboxes with the kind disregard of our longtime postman. In 2005 we were forced by the US Postal Service to forego the scattered, incoherently organized, and quaintly decorated rural mailboxes that had become a village trademark. They were replaced by an impersonal metal bank of locked boxes behind the church. Now everything has to be mailed through the post office, which makes *El Puente* far more expensive to produce. However, it's an ill wind that blows no good. Midafternoon, the mailboxes become a meeting place where one can chat with neighbors otherwise unseen, around the bulletin board of notices and the occasional sandwich board announcing pending community events.

The "newspaper," as some of the older people called it, is not always popular, and a community email now announces events immediately. It still seems worthwhile to provide a vehicle to examine the issues in more depth and continuity. Over the years, *El Puente* has offered an overview of some aspects of the place that remain stubbornly hidden from the

Lucy R. Lippard, *Old Village Mailboxes* and *Bulletin Board at New Mailboxes*, 2009. The Ramada was built when the park was remodeled. In 2011, a sign was added to commemorate Philip Watts III (son of Ramona and Philip Watts), who died young in an accident.

Lucy R. Lippard, *El Davez*, 2017. David Montoya's auto body repair shop on Chevy Lane is the only business left in Galisteo. It opened in 1970 when he was 24 years old and has become a mainstay for village residents.

dominant systems of control, ownership, and representation. When writing about one's own place, one sees or begins to understand something new each week, and the learning never ends. I've resisted putting it on line as some residents don't use email or the Internet and I'm personally devoted to hard copy. I like to think that *El Puente* fulfills the mission described in the first issue: "a way to keep in touch with each other, a forum to discuss issues affecting the community's present and future, and to inform ourselves about its past."

Today's Galisteo is outwardly a very quiet place, with little street life except for those of us walking our dogs or picking up the mail. There is no longer a store, a post office, or a school, no coffee shop, no cantina. In 1990 the only commerce in the village consisted of La Tienda Anaya, El Davez Automotive, the Galisteo Inn, and the Vista Clara Spa north of town. In 2018, El Davez is the only survivor. The church is usually open only for Sunday Mass and christenings, weddings, or funerals; there is no resident priest. The Community Center is open only for meetings, near-monthly breakfasts, and infrequent events. The busiest civic structure in town is the fire station. Of the few middle-aged Hispano families that remain, some are successful and some are struggling. A still younger generation may inherit land but be unable to build on it (county zoning regulations impose a minimum lot size of three-quarters of an acre) or to manage the expense of a hookup to the water system. Some Galisteans work for state, county, or federal government, or work on the ranches, or sell firewood, clean houses, and pick up work as handymen when they can. Others teach, work in retail, or are self-employed in a cottage industry or retirement vocation. A few long-standing artistic home industries flourished, such as Antonio Chávez's fine woodworking, Priscilla Hoback's ceramic murals, and Barbara Holloway's custom weaving. The annual Galisteo Studio Tour boasts twenty to thirty art stops and several food venues, including church ladies selling cookies.

Cindy Lux, *Volunteers at La Sala de San José de Galisteo*, April 2011. The Sociedad had leased the building to the newly formed community arts group, and restoration was just beginning.

In the early 2000s, a resurgence of interest in making the arts central to Galisteo's economy inspired the long, painstaking restoration of La Sala de San José de Galisteo, the century-old dance hall next to the church, on long lease to the community from the Sociedad de San José. With the aid of many grants and local contributions, the crucial support of Cornerstones Community Partnerships, and an extraordinary amount of hard work by those committed to its transformation into a community arts center, including local youth, it is now open as the Galisteo Arts Center. The lovely one-room building forms the centerpiece of a potential Galisteo Revitalization Plan, in collaboration with Main Street, Frontiers, and Santa Fe County. Members of the community have been meeting off and on with these groups to

Richard Shuff, *Tony Anaya's Truck*, ca. 2000.

Bob Christensen, *Felipa Lucero House ("Galisteo Trash and Treasures")*, 1977. This now vanished structure facing the west side of the old bridge was very briefly the first Galisteo Fire Department, as well as an ongoing garage sale. Felipa Lucero was a Native woman who worked for the Ortiz y Pinos earlier in the century. (Courtesy of the Galisteo Volunteer Fire and Rescue.)

plan for possible parking, restrooms, and a coffee shop at the former Tienda Anaya, all stalled at this writing. Most residents are hoping for a local meeting place, as well as amenities that will offer jobs for local youth and lure tourists to La Sala and open studios. A wine bar, once suggested for the former La Tienda, would be difficult as alcohol cannot be served so close to a church.

Despite strong ties to the village, it is rare that younger members of displaced families are able to move back home, but there are two notable exceptions. In 2002–03, Teresa Vásquez, a nurse, daughter of Tony Anaya and Juanita Chávez, returned to Galisteo to renovate their deteriorating adobe on The Hill, through pure willpower and hard labor. Next door is a tiny lot where her uncle Tobías Anaya lived and eventually died in a house fire. On its other side (once they were all a connected structure) was the home of her late aunt and uncle Clarita and Manuel Anaya, who had both lived on The Hill since birth. (Their home is now the studio of Jim Sloan, an artist/earthmover who has lived and often worked in the village for decades.) And the compound that was the Light Institute for years has been reclaimed by Sandy and Danny Durán; she is a descendant of the Chávez family that built it. Her parents, Clyde and Mary Peña, have a home nearby.

The Galisteo Volunteer Fire and Rescue (GVFR) has been the cross-cultural center of town, where the civic mix is alive and well, despite an aging population. After a couple of false starts in the 1970s and 1980s, the GVFR was reestablished in 1992 by Chief John Benjamin.[28] Although he resigned after a year or so during bitter disputes with a local family, he cajoled a 1953 brush truck out of the county. A 1948 Army tanker, hose and reel, two handheld radios, and a 1971 truck were inherited from other county departments. GVFR members were given standard-issue jackets, but not the pants, and the local paper published a pantsless picture of them. But by 2001 a fine solid fire station with water catchment (an innovation at the time) was built. At the inauguration it was dedicated to the memory of Joe M. Anaya for a lifetime

Members of the Galisteo Volunteer Fire and Rescue, before they were issued pants. The picture was published in the *Santa Fe New Mexican* (June 29, 1993) after the GVFR had finally received full gear. (Courtesy of the Galisteo Volunteer Fire and Rescue.)

of service to Galisteo. The building was traditionally wet down with fire hoses, and professional mezzo-soprano Janice Felty sang a stunning *Star Spangled Banner*. (Among other feats, she has performed with John Harbison and Philip Glass in New York. "Only in Galisteo," we muttered proudly.)[29] Sirens and applause followed—topped by a spectacular rainbow. In 2004 we were the only department in the county to have elected women as both chief and assistant chief (Jean Anaya Moya and her then sister-in-law Linda Anaya). At this writing, Jean is still chief and has served nine of the last ten years as president of the County Chiefs' Association. A fitness room and a new bay to accommodate a new truck were added in 2018. As village residents age and trainings and regulations get increasingly demanding, liability laws can scare away potential volunteers. The stalwart GVFR periodically suffers from attrition, then recovers as new blood comes to town.

Richard A. Shuff, *GVFR Station Inaugural Wetting Down*, 2001.

Downtown Galisteo, the Church and Felten/Scholder Home, 1950s. (Courtesy of Alan Wilson.)

In 1969 José Ortiz y Pino III applied to the State Historical Preservation Department (HPD) to create a historic district for the village of Galisteo. It was approved, but the required "narrative" was not provided until thirty years later when historian David Kammer was commissioned to write it. Specific boundaries of the "traditional village" had never been determined. It was demarcated on county maps as an arbitrary square around the church and village center. HPD decrees that structures fifty years and older in a historic district are "contributing properties," and owners may qualify for a tax break if the home has not been too drastically altered. Many Galisteo houses qualified, although some, equally old and significant to village history, are not included because their architectural footprints have been changed. Kammer did much valuable research, although in most cases he was only authorized to examine the exteriors of homes.

Through the Galisteo Community Association, the unincorporated village administers without governing—a role reserved for the elected BCC. The list of GCA presidents is a cross section of residents, Hispano and Anglo. The push for a Galisteo Community Plan began with an article by Richard Griscom in the January 1998 issue of *El Puente*. As a result, an "ad hoc committee to get going on a Community Plan" was formed.[30] Eventually we were finally given a chance to control a small part of our destiny by the creation of a Traditional Community Land Use Plan with Santa Fe County. It would allow us to customize some of the county's general ordinances to our own needs within our own defined boundaries. By January 2002 we were having serious conversations with the county and had begun to work with Professor David Henkel of the University of New Mexico Planning Program, who volunteered a class's semester to help us. By 2003 we had already done much of the preparatory research and were holding community meetings with county staff.

Henkel and his students saved the nascent Galisteo Steering Committee a good deal of time and energy by designing a community survey that was inserted in *El Puente* in Spring 2003. Fifty-four percent of village residents replied, far more than the predictable 5–15 percent. Among the respondents, 23 percent were residents for 0–3 years; 23 percent, 4–9 years; 30 percent, 10–20 years; and 14 percent over 30 years; 87 percent were first–generation residents.[31] Ninety percent owned their homes and 96 percent were primary residents, with 4 percent second homes. Sixty-five percent worked in Galisteo and 35 percent did not. The four things most liked about Galisteo were its small size, open space, rural character, culture, and history. Least liked were "litter/trash/junk," inadequate water system, lack of affordable housing, and lack of access to the Community Center. Growth and development concerned 73 percent (55 percent wanted "slow growth," 38 percent no growth, and 18 percent agricultural growth). Increasing traffic through the village worried 78 percent, 75 percent approved of adopting a community plan, and 55 percent were willing to participate in its development. Everyone wanted to maintain the village's "rural character"—something of an illusion and a phrase that seldom included the manufactured homes and yards of retired vehicles that are rural trademarks.

The UNM students also tracked down relevant hydrology reports and put together a computerized map of all wells and hookups and the 117 structures within the rectangle that marked the vague historic village boundary before our plan.[32] Henkel, like then county planner Jack Kolkmeyer, favored long-term thinking and a regional approach. But we were still not on the understaffed County Planning Department's formal waiting list for aid in creating the required plan, map, and ordinance that could be incorporated into the new Sustainable Land Use and Development Plan.

In June 2006 the Planning Committee was finally under way. We crafted a vision statement declaring our intention to promote "a strong land and energy conservation ethic," preserve our history and shared values, and "strive for autonomy by implementing effective land and natural resource conservation measures."[33] The list began, naturally, with water. The first three of eight bullet points demanded an efficient water utility, effective water conservation methods, and appropriate residential density/lot size with regard to water availability. The remaining points covered the concentration of residential growth in and adjacent to the village center, affordable housing, access to open space through a trail network, control of traffic flow, and definition of public gathering spaces. We agreed that we wanted to maintain the quiet, historic character of Galisteo but we did not want to see it become moribund, static, Disneyized, or resistant to positive change. Jobs for Galisteo youth were on the wish list, and self-determination was a high priority. While acknowledging the possibility that we might eventually be subsumed by regional planning, residents were worried about the ever-present "threats from outside interests," informed by the fact that small villages all over the West were being swallowed up by sprawl like that surrounding El Dorado.

Our land-use planning committee redrew the village boundaries from the 1969 arbitrary square to an irregular shape, determined in part by the preferences of individual owners. Residents on the edges of the traditional village were allowed to "zone" their own properties. Everything on the east side of Avenida Vieja is a five-acre minimum, but on my side of the road, two of us opted for three-quarter-acre minimums and two for five acres. (My own rationale was the hope that if the village grew, there would be small lots available to encourage affordable housing.) These are written into the County Sustainable Land Development Code. The devil, of course, was in the details. Should our plan include the old Galisteo grants? Land north of the creston where the pueblo once thrived? Old families worried about regulations against family lot splits below the county-determined, three-quarters-of-an-acre minimum. As we worked, we identified three separate categories: the "traditional village," the "historical district," and the "planning district," showing areas for commercial activity and areas we hoped to preserve, trying to mediate between those who hate double-wides and those who hate oversized mansions.

I frequently wonder how such a mobile population can plan for the future and how regionalism and the bioregions are affected by our mobility. Perhaps the most difficult issue—still not addressed—is the tragic lack of affordable housing for young people, laborers, and artists. Mobile and manufactured homes constitute affordable housing for much of the lower-income population of New Mexico. With the encroachment of development on rural land, traditionally low property taxes are rising. For those moving out of crumbling adobes beyond restoration, double-wides can provide clean, convenient dwellings. (On the other hand, run-down or abandoned mobile homes and trailers can be dangerous, and some harbor illegal or unwelcome commerce.) For the incoming wealthier class, they are seen as eyesores. In the 1980s, Galisteo's first attempt at a community land-use plan foundered on demands that mobile homes be off their wheels. (A local man told a new couple that if they wanted to live in a country club, they should get out of Galisteo.) Once again, in the early 2000s, some newer residents called for "design standards" along the lines of Santa Fe's dreaded Historical Review Board that would eliminate mobile homes, but this time the issue was avoided.

For decades it was up to community activists to keep an eye on county permissions and land sales. Real estate in Santa Fe County was out of control before the 2008 crash. The prices of homes and land kept rising. El Dorado's various developments, boasting a 2016 population of 6,130, include two shopping malls and a 24/7 gas station. Developmental juggernauts were coming at Galisteo from the north and south. While the plan promised us increased control, we are still all too aware that we have no power to affect the two big absentee-owned ranches on either side of the village, which could have the greatest impact on our future. In February 2012 the Galisteo Community Plan was finally approved by the BCC, although members continue to be called back to the drawing board, first to work on ordinances for the final code and then for possible amendments to permitted commercial uses.[34] In 2016, thanks to our county-designated status as a CO (Community Organization) and an RO (Regional Organization), Galisteo is now supposed to be legally notified of new development applications instead of having to chase them down in county documents.

John Wesley Powell's recommendation in the 1880s that watersheds (bioregions) rather than political boundaries should determine the boundaries of states in arid lands was unfortunately not taken seriously. Nevertheless the idea was reintroduced a century later by Daniel Kemmis, former mayor of Missoula, Montana, who suggested that the future of the arid West is a trans-state Watershed Democracy. I like the idea, but when I think about the tangle of legal and historical complexities in our tiny village, I shudder to think of the bureaucratic pitfalls of such an expansive plan. Paula García, president of the New Mexico Acequia Association and a native of Mora County, to our northeast, is more optimistic. Writing about New Mexico's water-sharing history, she cites her grandfather's "fierce optimism that the changes and exploitation brought by capitalism could be overcome with unity and collective effort."[35] Yet climate change is already wreaking havoc with the Southwest, and it is not inconceivable that a time could come when New Mexico—already losing population—has to close its borders because there is not enough water to sustain increased population. We are reminded of the fifteenth-to-sixteenth-century exodus of Ancestral Pueblo populations that had outgrown their resources in the Galisteo Basin and become unsustainable. It was once conventional wisdom to note that more people lived in the basin in pre-European times than today, but early population estimates are changing, and current tentacles of growth are reaching toward us at an unexpected speed. Just as it was then and in the homesteading era, development is inextricably tied to water. Currently, water is seen as both an instrument of growth and a tool for slowing it down, since shrinking resources and falling aquifers affect all property values. New roads and infrastructure encourage development and damage fragile land. Backcountry becomes battleground.

All water rights in New Mexico are overseen by the Office of the State Engineer (OSE), which permits domestic wells and Mutual Domestic Water Consumers Associations.[36] The new (2016) Santa Fe County Sustainable Land Development Code (SLDC) specifies one-quarter acre foot per house and strongly recommends that if there is a nearby water system, the lot owner should connect to that rather than drill a well. Although the OSE has to allocate water rights for a well (also restricted to one-quarter acre foot), it can pressure homeowners to connect to a nearby system. While there is no current program to monitor well usage, the county is slowly implementing meters at wells, and lot size is no longer a factor. There are separate county hydrologic zones, based on a far-from-thorough knowledge of local aquifers and long-term potential. When a subdivision is larger than twenty-five lots, the developers have to prove water for 100 years (so they often limit their projects to twenty-four lots). But such "proving" is also pretty hypothetical. "It's under there," the optimists and the developers say. "We just haven't found it yet." Hydrologic modelers are more cautious. And the building goes on, acre after acre dotted with houses, so visible in this treeless valley.[37]

In the early 1980s a classic long-running water case began when El Dorado Utilities Inc. (EUI) illegally altered the Lamy Megawell, located close to the Galisteo Creek upstream from the village. This huge well threatened to deplete the village's riparian water supply. In 1995 it pumped enough water to supply 30–40 percent of EUI's total needs. Galisteo sued to have the well shut down and won the case in District Court, the State Court of Appeals, and the State

Supreme Court. In 1993 the state engineer ordered EUI to stop pumping. It appealed and kept pumping, apparently believing that if it could keep tiny Galisteo in court long enough, we would run out of steam and money. They were wrong. The lawsuit was funded through many large and small private contributions to the GCA. In 1997 it had already cost the GCA and village supporters around $55,000. In 1996 the BCC declared a water emergency in Eldorado and placed a moratorium on development. At the same time, the EUI announced that it had pumped the Lamy Megawell dry. Then it backtracked; the well had recharged. In March 1997 the state engineer finally declared the well illegal, the District Court agreed, and the well was shut down. Joe Cooper, the Galisteo resident who led the charge for a decade along with environmental attorney Grove Burnett, concluded that our victory "helped force Santa Fe County to consider future developments in terms of water availability."[38]

The larger properties beyond the purview of the GMDWCA appeared to have water to waste. In April 1998, then owner of the Vista Clara Ranch/Spa was considering a donation from its thirty-two acre feet of water rights to the village (which would have allowed the number of hookups to be expanded), but the president of the Water Board turned the offer down, perhaps because it would facilitate growth. The offer was promised again *if* there were still "extra" water when and if Vista Clara finished its grandiose planned expansion. (It didn't, and no more was heard of the gifted water rights.)

In October 1998, not for the first or last time, the GMDWCA's annual meeting could not raise the required quorum of fifteen out of fifty-seven members. Calls were made to neighbors to fill the gap, one of whom said, "I don't have time." This provoked a finger-shaking *El Puente* editorial: "Too many of us take for granted the time and energy . . . of the many volunteers who keep the village running. . . . We don't have our priorities straight when people just don't have time to support those who provide our services. In Galisteo there is an (almost) free lunch. But it's offered in exchange for mutual communal responsibility." This sentiment was supported when Water Board president Steve Moya, citing the immense amount of time he was spending on the association, said when his term was up, "I ain't doing it again."[39] Rod Hall took over the presidency in March 1999 and hung in until 2016, aided by officers Scott Diffrient and Richard Patton, bookkeeper Romona Scholder, and archivist/all-round associate Florence Sohn, among other changing board members elected at annual meetings.

The GMDWCA has evolved over the years. In 1999, a pump and a new storage tank adding 54,000 gallons to the old tank's 15,000 were approved and installed, with some help from the state, next to the old cemetery (confirming the adage "Water is life"). Fiber optic cables were laid beneath the paved roads, which could no longer be dug up with impunity. Replacement of the main four-inch pipe with the required eight-inch pipe was obligatory. If the fiber optic broke, repairs would cost $10,000 a minute. This ticklish job was performed by JVS construction company, owned by villager Jim Sloan, who said if the fiber optic broke, he'd just "leave the keys in the machine and start walking to Amarillo."[40]

Despite moderate growth, Galisteo's water budget remains at 42.58 acre feet, distributed to members lucky enough to have a hookup, or several, for domestic use and landscaping. Charges are now determined by a tiered system based on the amount of water used, with a

Lucy R. Lippard, *Water Tanks for Ranchitos de Galisteo, from the Northern Creston*, 1999.

basic charge of around $30 per month. (For years it was only $15, far below the state average.) Water usage swings across the spectrum. Some members never use their system water so long as their wells provide for all needs. One member goes way over the apportioned amount and casually pays the fine. Others cannot or do not pay the monthly fee, although as the board points out, you pay for your cable TV, cell phone, and electricity. Is water less important?

The Ranchitos de Galisteo subdivision has its own newer and more efficient water system: thirty-two acre feet for fifty-nine lots. Meters were installed a decade ago and records show improvements in water conservation. Grants to local Mutual Domestics are unavailable unless they are metered, so the village finally followed suit. Meters are monitored by the Water Association foreman. In 2012, thanks to the need for a new flush line down Avenida Vieja, the system was finally expanded to include my neighbors and me. We bit the bullet, but the price for a hookup remains out of reach for many villagers. It was a long wait, and I am now on the GMDWCA Board. In 2016, under the leadership of Phillip Tuwaletstiwa and Michael Golino, Galisteo's water system was "modernized," introducing electronically read meters, a tiered system of billing, and revised bylaws. A major loan/grant with many requirements was awarded us by the state in 2018. But the income inequities and perceived slights that plague the village on other levels too have not yet been resolved; negotiation of leaks at private homes continues to be a bone of contention. Public money cannot be spent fixing pipes on private land, and many of the system's weakest points are connections to houses owned by those who do not have the disposable income to permanently correct their leaks, which of course wastes a lot of water and affects the whole system. While those in arrears are threatened with cutoffs, attempts are made to deal compassionately with hardship cases and a fund is proposed to help out, backed by an anonymous villager. The Water Board's dilemma lies in how to balance the state's increasingly complex regulations, demands for expansion of the system to outlying areas, and the social complications of a pueblo chico.

In the late 1990s, writer and environmental activist William deBuys mentioned to me something called the Galisteo Watershed Restoration Project (GWRP). I was surprised that I had never heard of it, nor had anyone else in the village. I called Leslie Barclay, founder of

Earth Works Institute (EWI), under whose aegis the project was born, and entered the loop of this admirable (now defunct) organization, which owed much of its successes to Dutch-born Jan Willem Jansens, veteran of ecological work in the African Sahel and with New Mexico Pueblos.[41] For a few years, GWRP was a major player in the ecological planning process for the Rio Galisteo's 735-square-mile watershed. Its mission was to rewater the river, which requires "restoring its tributary channels and the vegetative cover of its hillsides, managing stormflows, and managing the reservoirs to keep a trickle in the river"—which, in turn will recharge city wells.[42] In collaboration with the GWRP and the stalwart Quivira Coalition, Bill Zeedyk, master of the induced meander as a way of coaxing rivers back into their healthier original curves, worked against head cuts and gullying at various degraded locations on the Galisteo Creek. My own house, built dangerously close to the steeply eroded creek banks, was one of EWI's initial reclamation projects.[43] (Realtors and builders should be given classes in local ecology and sustainability before they pass on the responsibility to ignorant newcomers like me.) We had to haul off all the brush and chunks of concrete I had for years begged people to dump in my gullies to slow down the erosion. They were replaced by gentle hills covered with green erosion cloth, river-rock-lined drains, and later a straw-bale mini-amphitheater. Today it all looks entirely natural, and so far my house has not collapsed into the creek, even during an extraordinary "tornadic event" in October 2017, when the creek blew up to sixty-five feet wide and six feet deep for a few wild nocturnal hours.

The view from my window seat, where for years my cat and I sat obsessed with the never-ending cloud shows, stretches across the Cerro Pelón Ranch to the distant mountain ranges, with only one house visible to remind me that humans affect every inch of the Galisteo Basin and that I am part of the process, or problem, try as I may to be part of some as yet undiscov-

Lucy R. Lippard, *View toward Mountains in Snow*, ca. 2012.

ered solution. The concept of the local, which literally lured me into this whole enterprise, has to include cosmopolitan restlessness and the tremendous challenges of cross-cultural communication. Although New Mexico remains culturally unique, in the twenty-first century the Galisteo Basin is a microcosm of the ills and beauties of the entire New West, with the bloated prices of unreal estate producing increasing gentrification, income inequality, and loss of agrarian lands and values. Rural gentrification (a cousin of sprawl) doesn't get much attention yet, but having been one of its agents, I think about it a lot. It is multifaceted: sprawl, ranchettes, shrinking open space, some insensitive newcomers, water shortages, ingestion of agricultural lands and traditional lifeways, lack of long-term planning, political greed and incompetence, and cultural clashes that sometimes verge on class war. The rolling landscape, surrounded by forested ridges and rutted mountains, is a double-edged sword. Its beauty attracts growth, and growth detracts from its beauty. Here is a note from my window seat, February 7, 1996: "The wind blows the grasses, the sun rises and reddens the flank of Cerro Pelón. Everything seems 'normal.' But somewhere in banks and corporate offices, machinations are under way that will affect our lives. We wait, keeping a wary eye out for the telltale stakes with Day-Glo tape, the SUVs parked beside the road, women in business garb and heels wandering the fields, the dreaded pale green metal transformers that herald development."

Ranchers often insist that they care more deeply about the land and what happens to it than their environmentalist opponents, but when push comes to shove, if profits are lost in the process, there's rarely enough love (or money) to place the land in conservation

Lucy R. Lippard, *Transformer, Herald of Development*, ca. 2000.

Joan Myers, *Two Houses in Ranchitos*, 2018.

easements or agricultural security areas. Despite occasional disputes, no one in Galisteo wants San Cristóbal or Cerro Pelón to break up. We know that the ranches could be subdivided and become upscale developments of luxury ranchettes or archaeological theme parks. Neither prospect appeals to anyone. With the example of El Dorado over the hill, "Better ranches than ranchettes" has been an environmental motto for decades. As the ranches surrounding the village change hands or break up, the Galisteo Basin is advertised in real-estate hyperbole as quaint and inviting, another "new frontier" for those escaping downtown Santa Fe's tourist culture. The names of subdivisions and roads (Spirit Wind, Cosmic Way) reflect imported notions about the Land of Enchantment. Some properties are touted as housing "ancient ruins" with "Indian picture writing"—flashing a red light to preservationists who predict new hazards to cultural resources.

Some of the "dream houses" are built and then abandoned and resold at a rapid rate. Their owners appear to be initially charmed by the place and then disillusioned—by the dry wind, by the isolation. But, like Burl Ives, the next comers are also convinced they will stay forever and need to build their own dream house, so an increasing number of large houses on large acreage, some unoccupied most of the year, dot a landscape that only forty years ago was still rangeland. The long view exemplified by the Pueblo dictum "Look to the mountain" is being reconceived. Across the vast openness, every house is visible, especially those with bright-colored Pro-Panel roofs. Landscape-sensitive architects can try to employ the topography to screen new buildings from each other, but people like to build high, which provides spectacular views and allows them to look down on other homes, a trope as old as civilization. The choices made can seem bizarre. In the Ranchitos subdivision, two large houses, side by side on a sandstone ridge, provide an interesting comparison. One is low and flat-roofed. Despite its size, it almost melts into its site. (The incongruous green lawn within is not visible from beyond.) Next door is a two-story house with awkward arches that stands out like the proverbial sore thumb.

In November 1998, a general obligation bond was approved to form a County Open Lands and Trails Planning and Advisory Committee (COLTPAC). I served on the committee's first incarnation, arguing in *El Puente,* "The Open Space in the Galisteo Basin is strictly visual. It would be nice if we got a piece of this pie so we could walk into our views."[44] In September 1999, I presented to the county a proposal for the "Galisteo River Park" on a 355.35-acre parcel north of the creek, a 1991 lot split for sale by Cerro Pelón Ranch owner Lew Cook. It included the 260.79-acre, reduced Galisteo grant of 1898 and would have provided a buffer of open space for the traditional village and almost two miles of trails, as well as protection for the river and its riparian environment.

When he sold his ranch to Cook, Philip McKee deliberately denied him access to the strip north of the creek adjacent to NM 41 by keeping part of Small Holding Claim 2490 and donating ten acres along the highway to the GCA.[45] In 1990 Cook went crossways with the village when he claimed a right of way across this land to the 355 or so acres north of the creek where we were proposing the park. When it went to court, he claimed he needed access only to tend his cattle, but the community suspected him of paving the way for development.

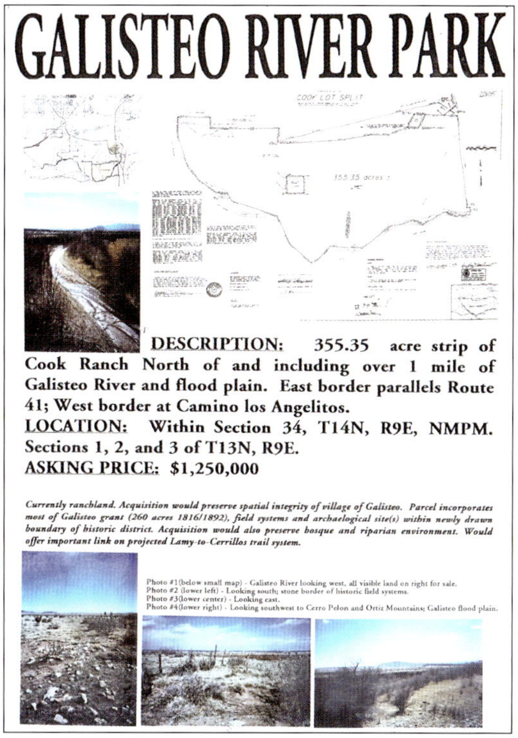

Caroline Hinkley, *Galisteo River Park Poster.* Produced by the author, Richard Shuff, and Cara Lee and presented by COLTPAC to the Board of County Commissioners, October 1999.

The issue divided Galisteo residents.[46] A 1994 fact sheet from the GCA observed, "If we grant him this easement, we make this land extremely attractive to any developer. There will be easy access from the highway. . . . Given the development going on all around us, it is safe to assume he will find a buyer very quickly under these conditions. . . . Mr. Cook is not a rancher and he is not our neighbor. He comes to Galisteo for a few days several times a year. He has had the entire ranch on the market several times." In 1995, after detailed discussions of water law and the quality of the bunch grass and how hard it was to drive through, Cook was granted only an agricultural easement to reach a well on his property by Judge Edwin Felter, a canny New Mexican who, when invited to come out and view the property, said dryly, "No thanks, I've seen plenty of fences."[47]

COLTPAC rated the Galisteo River Park proposal as the third priority out of eighteen, and the Santa Fe County BCC approved its purchase for the asking price of $1,250 million. But in the end, after months of negotiation and despite community support, Cook refused to negotiate with the county or the Trust for Public Land (TPL), which was acting as intermediary. Not long after this, he put the whole property, now called Rancho Cerro Pelón, up for sale: "24 square miles of privacy. . . . Significant pre-Columbian sites, location for epic Western films [plus 3,743 acres state lease and 790 acres BLM lease; 140 acre feet of water rights, a 4,000-foot grass airstrip and hangar, 2.5 miles of Galisteo River frontage] '2 High Intensity/Short Duration grazing centers (Savory Center),' twenty separate pastures, 'historically interesting pueblo ruins and petroglyphs.'" The proposed Galisteo River Park land was swallowed up by the rest of the ranch and thereby lost to the community.[48] This was the first big struggle in recent years to pit the village against potential development, but it was not the last.

Commonweal Conservancy's Galisteo Basin Preserve and the plan for an accompanying town was a poster child for obstacles to sustainable development on former ranches. Proposed by Ted Harrison of the TPL as an innovative "conservation cluster development," it was carved out of the 20,000-acre, family-owned Thornton Ranch to Galisteo's north and west. Initially, the Thorntons planned to subdivide the ranch and sold off a few lots piecemeal. (This was legal because a big chunk of the property had already been sliced into homesteads.) However, around 2000, through a series of happy coincidences, the infant COLTPAC, with the assistance of TPL, optioned some 13,000 acres of the Thornton Ranch, to be acquired in phases. (These were the funds originally intended for the Galisteo River Park.) When TPL decided it didn't want to go into development, it gave its blessing to Harrison, who founded the Commonweal Conservancy to continue the project, which was also admirably supported by the Thornton family, who kept the ranch headquarters and 500 acres. The rest—stretching from US 285 just below Lamy Hill to border on Galisteo properties in several places, crossing CR 42 to include what is now County Open Space—encompassed significant archaeological sites and the remains of Kennedy Station.

It was an ambitious (probably overambitious) project. When the Master Plan application was presented, it included 965 residential units and 150,000 square feet of civic and commercial uses in a 300-acre development envelope. Lots ranged from .3 to 3 acres, plus a 21-acre Community Parcel (village market, café, community center, live/work spaces for artists, office suites, childcare center, guest casitas, and swimming pool), 8 acres for ranching with barns and stables, plus rental units and agricultural space. A fire substation and post office were also envisioned, as were a bilingual environment-based charter school and a green burial site. Sustainable density was to be concentrated at the center. The residential development was initially called The Village at the Galisteo Basin Preserve, but the name provoked opposition in the actual village of Galisteo and eventually it was changed to Trenza (Braid).[49]

Initially, there were high hopes for the Commonweal project. If the cluster village was too large for many to swallow, it was far more sustainable than the same number of scattered ranchettes, with their roads and accompanying infrastructure, and the project was considered a national model for conserving water and natural resources.[50] Commonweal was planned for 100 acre feet of water with the hope of getting all water rights under contract in five years.[51] At first, things seemed to be moving forward smoothly, but the basin itself was fighting back. A hydrologist's report demonstrated unpredictable water resources, a much less "dynamic" water situation than in Santa Fe or Albuquerque, with a much lower rate of long-term replenishment. In addition, every step of the way the project was contested—by the county, by local residents, and at times by the village of Galisteo, where some feared for our own riparian water supply, not directly connected to the Commonweal sources.

The now diminished project to which Ted Harrison had devoted almost twenty years was devastated by the 2008 recession and never recovered. More large lots at the margins

Richard A. Shuff, *Sioux Village on Highway 41*, 2005. Set for the TV miniseries *Into The West*.

(Half Moon, West Basin Preserve) have been sold off separately for conservation-oriented private residences to finance ongoing efforts. Slowly working its way through the bureaucracy (water being, as usual, the biggest obstacle), Commonweal preserved and provided public access to 1,300 acres of stunning open space with extensive scenic hiking and riding trails—the only way most basin residents can "walk into their views." In early 2018 it was reported that Commonweal could be in foreclosure, that the preserve was endangered, and that the village plan had been abandoned. By the end of the year, some hefty donations seemed to have saved the Galisteo Basin Preserve, the most valuable and popular amenity in the eastern basin, for the time being. Its value is all the more obvious as a thirty-nine-unit subdivision right across US 285 from the preserve's entrance is being built out with "ranchettes."

Only a barbed wire fence, occasionally breached by adventurous bovines, separates San Cristóbal Ranch from the village of Galisteo, but it demarks two very different worlds. In June 1997, ranch owner Henry Singleton was the largest (absentee) landowner in New Mexico, with close to one and a half million acres on over twenty ranches in eight New Mexico counties, beating out even Ted Turner. By the early 2000s, San Cristóbal was the only remaining working ranch adjacent to the village. The Singleton family inherited the ongoing problems of the original grant and its proximity to Galisteo. Although for years some local horse owners had permission to ride and even to hunt on the ranch, relations with the village have not always been the best. In 1997 an overzealous San Cristóbal cowboy shot a Galisteo family's pregnant golden retriever, though she was chasing pronghorns, not cows. He was cited for cruelty to animals, but the dog's owner was also cited for trespassing. The ranch foreman declared the pasture paralleling the village was the best place on all of his 81,000 acres to run calves and that Galisteo dogs were his biggest problem. Most local ranchers once turned a blind eye to minor trespassing, but as the county's population grew, the numbers reached a tipping point. Today there is zero tolerance for neighbors, hikers, or rock art researchers ducking through fences and pursuing their passions.

Lucy R. Lippard, *Central City Billboard*, 2009. Movie set on NM 41.

Notes from my window seat in February 1996 as I looked out toward Cerro Pelón: "The movie set is very busy. Two dilapidated antique wagons, or facsimiles thereof, just went by on a flatbed truck. A huge white moving van, several pickups. It's too early in the morning for the stretch limos bearing stars. They come later." My view of the Silverado set provides a perfect postmodern illustration, a temporal vignette within the view, surreal glimpses of the Old West, including, in 2005, a Sioux village of tipis next to NM 41. Right there on the cusp of the next hill, myths are being woven that have already affected the future of the beautiful but unproductive ranchland surrounding them. Just over that hill, Kevin Costner is posturing, the Apaches are lurking, a captive maiden is plotting her escape. When we travel through a "primal" landscape like the American West, we populate it with vicarious nostalgia for imagined wildness and wildernesses, justifications for the violence in today's society.

In the twenty-first century, the film industry has become a major player in the state's economy, urged on by former governor Bill Richardson's tax incentives, almost sunk by his successor, Susana Martínez, then revived when their profitability was proved beyond doubt.

Lucy R. Lippard, *No Trespassing on Cerro Pelon Ranch*, ca. 2012. The author's dog Chino is illiterate.

Among the movies made on the Cerro Pelón Ranch were *Wild Wild West*, which burned down a fake town with an overzealous train fire that could have been lethal for the infant Galisteo fire department, tasked with oversight.[52] Others were *Lazarus Man, Last Man Standing, Hi LoCountry, John Carpenter's Vampires, Into the West, No Country for Old Men, Lonesome Dove, 3:10 to Yuma, Thor, Crazy Heart, Appaloosa,* and *The Homesman.* My own little house, disguised as a "modest ranch house in Marfa, Texas," was used as a set for *Crazy Heart;* the film company contributed $1,000 to our campaign to keep oil and gas out of the Galisteo Basin and paid several neighbors for minor tasks. The scene was cut from the final film.

San Cristóbal has gotten back into the movie and TV business as well, and one minor film was shot at Vista Clara Spa. The village center sometimes serves as a location, raising a welcome amount of cash for the Community Association.[53] Filming brings to Galisteo literally heavy traffic (I looked up from my desk one day and saw a real locomotive on a flatbed crossing the 1936 highway bridge with a fifteen-ton capacity), huge white tents, and occasional military-style lights at night, for a couple of months at a time. Film companies also have to put up with the ornery, independent citizens of Galisteo. Once, Priscilla Hoback and her daughter Denise Lynch, finding their driveway blocked by filming, got on their horses and rode up and down the set uninvited until they were allowed out. The fall of 2016 was particularly busy, with Netflix creating an old-fashioned market on Via La Puente and other sets on Cerro Pelón and San Cristóbal. A series called *Godless* ran into an obstacle when its title almost prohibited the film company's use of the village church's parking lot.

The Cook Ranch didn't sell until 2001, when it was bought by designer Tom Ford and his longtime partner Rich McCauley. The Silverado set continues to thrive, despite the fact that Ford initially swore to close it down. He soon reconsidered, perhaps in view of his own ambition to direct films (his first was nominated for an Academy Award). Ford painted his tractors black and mounted stylishly lettered, charcoal gray No Trespassing signs. Proving the adage "all hat, no cows," aimed at absentee ranch owners, he got rid of cattle on the ranch, though initially he wanted to stock his property with some longhorns because he liked their

Caroline Hinkley, *Hacienda Tranquilla* (sic) *on NM 41*, 2018. Also incorrect, the street sign reads Entrada Tranquilas.

Lucy R. Lippard, *Gate to Saddleback*, ca. 2016. The sign reads "Keep Out."

looks; it turned out they were too hard to transport (those *long* horns). Around 2014, cattle were welcomed back to the range when the new foreman leased grazing land from the owner. West of the old line camp, where he could see no one and no one could see him, Ford built a large equestrian facility and a relatively small, modern house (only 10,000 square feet) with a wide moat around it, designed by Tadao Ando.[54] In the meantime, to maintain his agricultural water rights, Ford put a number of acres into vineyards and orchards.[55] At a 2003 meeting with some members of the community, the bare fields provoked complaints from residents of Ranchitos, who objected that the mobile homes brought in for workers marred the views from their "million-dollar homes." Ford's then agricultural advisor, a professor at NMSU, replied that he himself objected to all the Pro-Panel roofs on those million-dollar homes and found it interesting that people moved to rural areas only to be offended by agriculture. Both orchard and vineyard failed. The ranch went up for sale again in 2016, for a reported $75 million, since reduced to $48 million. The ad in a glossy Realtors' magazine described it as "a sparkling sanctuary in the vast American Southwest . . . with the allure of ancient petroglyphs, pottery shards and Pueblo ruins juxtaposed with Tadao Ando's dramatic contemporary compound."[56]

Villagers are particularly concerned with the future of the northern approach through open rangelands on NM 41. Sprawling subdivisions would end Galisteo's visual isolation. Local activists are aware of the threat but are often powerless to combat it, although a longtime coalition of concerned citizens along the 285 corridor (now named the Max Coll Corridor after a progressive legislator) has been an effective monitor. Around 2001, a new sign appeared on NM 41: "COMING SOON: Hacienda Tranquilas. 23 proposed 12.5 acre home-sites. Community water. Incredible Views!"[57] The land had been for sale for so long that none of our local development watchdogs was paying much attention when the deal was sealed. The subdivision was approved with little protest. (I had been told by a state employee that the property lacked water; a guerrilla action to alter the sign to read "Haciendas Sin Agua" was contemplated.) Some unlovely gates were installed to guard the only extant "hacienda," which cost $2.5

million and remains for sale to this day. So far, there has been no further building. In 2007, developer Victor Ballas (known as "Ballas from Dallas") sued the architect, landscape architect, and all concerned for the new home's disintegration. He lost.

But in 2005, along came the sale of the approximately 200-acre Saddleback Ranch on the other side of NM 41, asking price $14.5 million. (Like so many "ranches" in the area, it is not a working venture, but it includes part of the Galisteo Pueblo site.)[58] The property of art-world-connected New Yorker Emily Fisher-Landau, who constructed two handsome homes and at one point ran a few shaggy Scottish Highland cattle, it was bought by Texas developers just in time for the great recession and then foreclosed. It will have to be re-permitted if a new development is proposed; in the meantime, a stricter new county code has been put in place—another disaster narrowly, and probably temporarily, avoided. Near Saddleback and Hacienda Tranquilas is Las Madres, the unostentatious home and studios of two famous artists who breed horses and also own a working ranch in Santa Rosa. Farther south, across NM 41, is Nizhoni (Navajo for "beauty and order"), heir to Chris Griscom's Light Institute.[59] Its peculiar dome-shaped huts are now abandoned and the enterprise exists primarily in cyberspace. Both of these properties represent "appropriate land use" for the Galisteo area.

Development juggernauts are also coming at us from the south. Up Clark Hill, on the plain overlooking the southernmost edge of the basin, a sprawling estate called the Zorro Ranch gives notice of what could happen in the north. Its palace is an architectural anomaly of no apparent design (not even imperial Santa Fe Style) poised on the brink of a ridge high above the highway, near the spot from which the Teyas, Apaches, and Comanches once poured down to raid the basin's pueblos. Overlooking both the plains above and the basin below, epitomizing the late twentieth-century ridgetop trophy house, this gigantic edifice belligerently separates itself from the surrounding landscape and habitations. Purportedly the largest (second) home in New Mexico, it is the haven of a notorious celebrity and convicted child molester and trafficker. (Rumor garnered from construction workers has it that when the owner heard he did not have the largest *kitchen* in the state, he tore down a wall and added 3,000 feet.) A private airfield is hidden below the ridge to the south. On the plains across NM 41 is another unsuccessful Ballas project, first called Pine Canyon Estates and now dubbed Green Ranch. As far as I can tell, one lot has sold, the only one boasting an exquisite view overlooking the Basin and the southern creston.

To the west, the modern Galisteo Basin is embraced by the "scenic byway" of NM 14, or the Turquoise Trail, and on the east by US 285, the WIPP route for transporting nuclear waste—a fragment of our state's nuke-friendly history. (An accident there, or at nearby Los Alamos, would bring us peremptorily into the nuclear age, and our volunteer fire department takes "hazmat" training for handling hazardous materials.) One of the village's ongoing struggles has been with the State Department of Transportation (NMDOT). The advent of an oil refinery and industrial-scale gravel pits in Moriarty, half an hour to the south, engenders an estimated thirty-four gravel trucks a day and an oil tanker an hour passing my house on NM 41. Despite a 35 mph speed limit, they rattle the bones of the village's old adobes, built close to the once narrow dirt road. At endless meetings with the community, there was little

Lucy R. Lippard, *The "OK Corral,"* 2005.

evidence that DOT was listening as we expressed our road rage. LED signs announcing the speed limit were installed at the village edges, along with plans for a wider road, which would actually encourage speeding.[60] Sometimes community members take things in their own hands. In early 2004, Denice Pruitt and Isabella Gonzales stood on the highway with a hairdryer and pretended to be monitoring speeds. Traffic slowed.

In 2015 an ugly little median was installed and the two WPA bridges, dating to the mid 1930s, with weight limits of fifteen tons, were replaced by new bridges after a year and a half of jackhammers and beeping machines. But it was worth it. If one of the decrepit old bridges had given way under a forty-ton tanker, the bosque (and my house) would have gone up in flames. As I write, a $22 million project is straightening the curves and flattening the low hills on NM 41 from the village to Clark Hill, making the trip to I-40 faster and more dangerous.

In the last decades, the old internal land struggles have also resurfaced. Over centuries of deals and transactions, bits and pieces of property along the Galisteo bosque and creek and within the eastern part of the village have floated loose from their legally described tracts or have been found to be extralegal. Fences arbitrarily constructed to contain livestock had become de facto boundaries, leaving vulnerable slivers of no man's land. Buyers and sellers had learned to shrug this off, since the creek offers a favorite local walking path and was assumed to be in the public domain. Actually, in the old deeds, properties on either bank went to "the middle of the river," which shifts constantly, perhaps as much as a half-mile in the last century, so this is a literally fluid premise. In the late 1990s, however, a title search revealed that some tracts (my own included) were platted only to the arroyo edge and not to the river.

In 1997, Richard Griscom, a lawyer, an environmentalist, and a community activist who had been in the village for almost thirty years, ran up against the Galisteo Community Association, over which he had once presided, when he quiet-titled roughly one acre leading into the bosque from his property on the southeast side of the old bridge. There were no recorded deeds. The GCA opposition, funded by local resident Moira Walden, was based on historic communal use. Eventually a solution was more or less equably hammered out, though not without acrimony: Griscom would own the land, but the community would have "an irrevocable easement for its use."[61] It would be open to walkers, an informal parking area would be maintained, and the easement would be a legal attachment for any deed to the property. (The Community Association has at times seemed reluctant to own the bosque outright, in part because the ever-changing members of the board could be liable for accidents there.) Griscom died in 2011, and a stone memorial and wooden bench in the bosque were installed by his widow. A sturdy metal gate has also been installed by the GCA to protect fragile ecosystems and ban all motorized traffic, after havoc was wreaked upon the riparian area by ATVs.

In 2004, a new and more threatening land dispute galvanized the entire village. At its center was a fenced four-acre lot on the east side of the village that came to be known locally as the "OK Corral." It was just another patch of poor pasture where a local family grazed their horses on land once owned by their forebears, with permission from Concha Ortiz y Pino, who was assumed to own it.[62] But the ramifications were grander. For almost a century, the fact that the San Cristóbal grant included the eastern part of the long-established village of Galisteo and its common lands was never fully addressed. The "250-acre exception" of 1907 had purportedly been made to acknowledge residents ("settlers") of the village, though its boundaries and legality were never satisfactorily defined. The OK Corral became ground zero for a contemporary micro-land struggle that echoes and epitomizes the history of the basin itself.

The cast of this melodrama was augmented when suddenly the five acres was claimed by three Anglos. The key actor, a longtime Galisteo resident I'll call Moreland, a foxy, affable, and unstable Texan who worked several years with Agnes Martin, had long been scouring the county records to identify unclaimed Galisteo land. In the process he made quitclaims to 4.5 acres of gaps between properties along the bosque and to the 4.1 acres of the OK Corral, bordered by La Otra Vanda, Avenida Vieja, Singleton Ranch, and private properties. Moreland contended that a quitclaim deed to the tract was given to him by Buddy Branum, former owner of the San Cristóbal Ranch, who hailed from his own hometown of Midland, Texas. In a fit of temporary generosity, Moreland deeded over the land to Richard Shuff, an Anglo

Joan Myers, *San Cristóbal Ranch Gate*, 2018. Access to the old Cadial common lands is closed off.

Lucy R. Lippard, *Hogan and Tipi*, 2018.

photographer and a jack of all trades who didn't have the resources to buy land, although he and his wife were for a decade integral participants in village activities. Then Moreland took it back and gave it to an untrustworthy cowboy briefly married to a local woman. Although Shuff had already registered the deed in his own name, the cowboy put a heavy chain on the gate and deposited a rusty piece of old farm machinery within as proof of occupation. In December 2007 a No Trespassing sign from "Pankey Co." was posted there in an unexplained blast from the past. Nearby is another No Trespassing sign on the red-and-white gate of San Cristóbal with *S* for Singleton, a logo evoking a dollar sign.[63]

At first, the OK Corral saga seemed to be an isolated instance, not exactly a joke, because land is always serious business, but subject to a certain amount of eye rolling. Things heated up when Moreland partnered with "Purse," a newly licensed Realtor/schoolteacher from El Dorado, who went so far as to claim El Puente (the old wooden bridge) and the county road that traverses it—patently absurd since the county had maintained bridge and road for so long, it was indisputably eminent domain. Between Moreland and Purse, they claimed not only the OK Corral but virtually everything in the village that wasn't nailed down—a considerable amount of property (around eighteen acres), especially those slivers in the bosque along the creek, affecting a large number of villagers, old and new.[64]

This got everybody's attention. Much of the land claimed was unbuildable and seemed worthless, but subpoenas were delivered to some twenty landowners. One of the largest community meetings in years was convened. Newcomers worried about their property values. Community activists worried about the co-optation of the river. Old people from Galisteo's original families who had lost their farmlands worried that now their homes would be taken from them, given the fact that insecure historic titles were coming to light. The land grabbers claimed that they wanted to give all of what they call the "abandoned" creek lands to the community to protect the bosque—a process already in the works by the GCA for almost a decade. They claimed they tried to inform the community of their good intentions but no one would listen and they felt threatened. (It was often remarked that the two were lucky they didn't live in a more violent norteño village.) Rumors and epithets flew. The Community Association hired a lawyer on behalf of those who couldn't afford one, and set up a legal defense fund. The bills climbed.

Untangling the deeds from people who had been living on the lands for at least 100 years was a legal nightmare. The County Assessor's Office, trying to get a grip on the situation, gave up when it discovered that some twenty-six owners were listed for the original San Cristóbal grant, producing a number of heirs that has since multiplied exponentially. In October 2004, County Assessor Benito Martínez spoke to the Galisteo community about such cases: "Accessors' maps cannot be deemed accurate . . . this is happening everywhere in the County. It's the nature of our land grants." He told how one man successfully claimed the entire town of Golden and was selling land back to those who thought they already owned it: "He's sitting on his porch with a shotgun."[65] County map specialist Shawn Thornton researched the Galisteo case for a while, finding that a deed to T. B. Catron in the early 1900s did not mention the infamous 250-acre exception. But he was not given the time to track down its origins. However, in 2005, the assessor found an August 13, 1907, Quit Claim Deed from Benjamin Pankey to Thomas Catron, reserving the 250-acre exception outside the ranch's barbed wire fence "for the use and benefit [of] Settlers at Galisteo."[66] When Branum sold the ranch to Singleton in 1986, he signed a separate quitclaim for the 250 acres, although apparently he had never received this plot in his original purchase. He filed a second quitclaim to give land to Moreland, whose claims therefore appear to be preceded by Singleton's, *if* Branum ever actually owned the 250 acres.

In 2006, Judge Daniel Sánchez upheld a motion for a summary judgment dismissal of the "Moreland" case. In the "Purse" case, a frustrated District Judge Jim Hall declared that trying to quiet-title with no proof of ownership "put the process all out of whack. How am I supposed to know where the land is?" He advised Purse to get a lawyer and respond with the full chain of title.[67] Moreland's case was dismissed first. On January 2, 2007, Judge Hall dismissed Purse's claim to two tracts in the bosque (and County Rd 33A and the old bridge).[68] A summary judgment was granted the defendants—the whole village, via the GCA. Judge Hall advised, "A Quiet Title Action means establishing a good title, not just something with your name on it." Purse declared that he had bought the land from Moreland on the basis of his "all-purpose deed" and that he could build on it or sell it "today," apparently based on the notion that although he never lived in the village, he could count himself one of those "settlers" of the 250-acre exception. Both claimants were "dumfounded" by the adverse decision and on notion that although he never lived in the village, he cold count himself on of those "settlers" of the 250-acre exception. Both claimants were "dumbfounded" by the adverse decision and on January 31, against all reason, they appealed. The case stumbled on and eventually the community triumphed, although the battle to recover legal costs continutes. Some things never change. The ambiguities of nineteenth-century land grants will continue to create new legal struggles as they crawl through political labyrinths.

John Young, *Community Cleanup*, 2013. Michael J. Anaya and son Jerry Anaya at the home of John and Tanya Young, sponsors of the cleanup.

In a Galisteo community meeting a few years ago, local developer Joe Miller advised landowners who discovered archaeological sites on their property to destroy them immediately or those danged experts would come in and ruin their plans. (I had never before seen the articulate director of the New Mexico Office of Archaeological Studies almost speechless in response.) Fleeting traces of our distant predecessors' lives on the land are everywhere above and below the surface, including my own property. Washed up into plain view after heavy rains are potsherds, stone tools, chert, quartizite and obsidian flakes from tool and weapon making.[69] There are purpling and blue-greening fragments of glass, ancient and more recent redware. There are odd metal fragments, rusted tin cans, and twisted enamel coffee pots, remnants of ranchers' and shepherds' campsites. And increasingly there are plastic bags and Styrofoam cups, Coors Lite cans, roofing paper, and other detritus from the construction boom—new middens, litter in the process of becoming artifacts.

Surface finds are not much respected by archaeologists unless they are guaranteed to be in or near their original context, but artifacts have long been casually collected by local residents, led to believe (as I once did) that taking one sherd from public land as a souvenir will do no harm. Multiply their numbers and one sherd becomes hundreds. And the one sherd in the pocket, destined for a dusty pile on someone's desk or mantel, might have been key to a whole new view of the place. For me, the click came one afternoon at a Pueblo village site near Lamy, when two Tewa women, both cultural scholars, found an uncommon bit of pottery. An archaeologist scrutinized it and said, "Well, this takes the history back a hundred years." If it had been picked up by a curious collector and removed from its original context, we might never have known. Remote sensing, Lidar, even drones, are proving effective archaeological tools in many areas. But technology is a mixed blessing. With the aid of GPS, detailed old topo maps, and Google Earth, anyone can track down archaeological sites. Ubiquitous looting/pothunting craters are visible in aerial photographs. Thanks to the vandalism resulting from growing populations and the Internet, there is a pressing need for monitoring sites, a task taken on by the Site Watch organization, whose volunteers patrol sites for disturbance and evidence.[70]

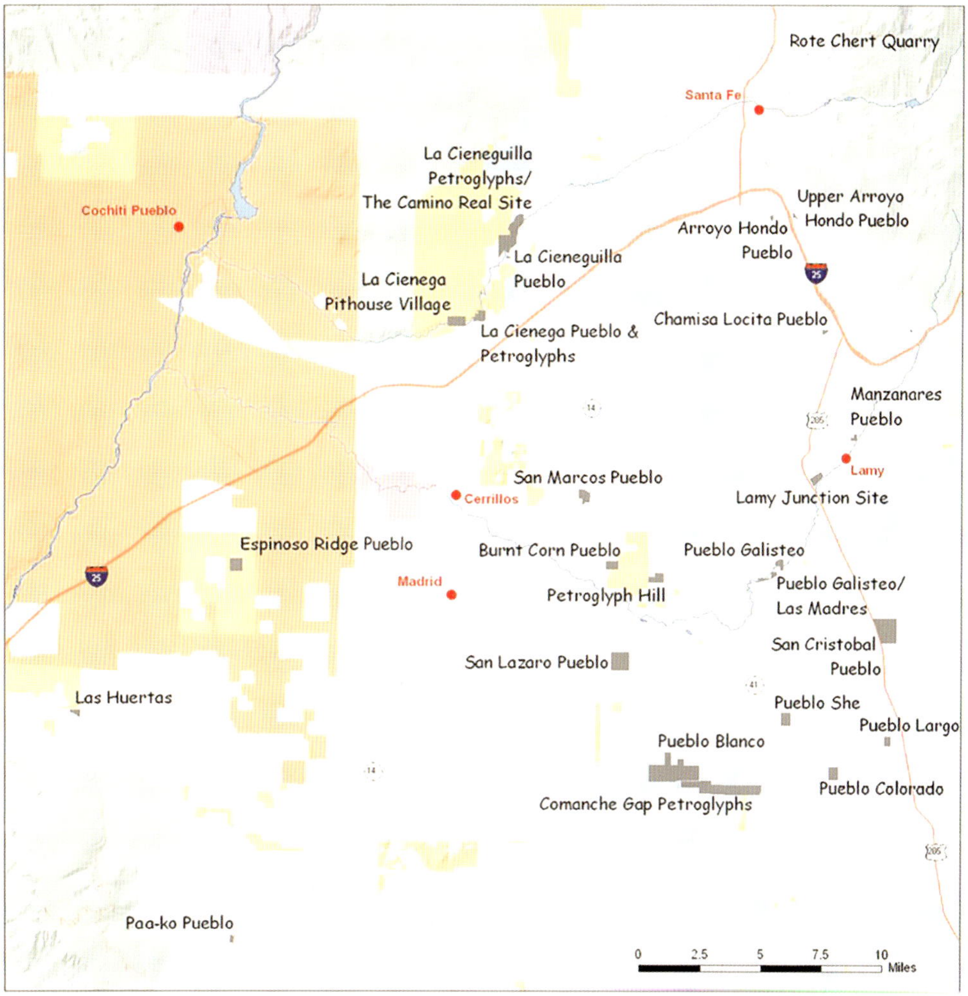

Map of Sites Included in the Galisteo Basin Archaeological Sites Protection Act, 2008. (Courtesy of the New Mexico Office of Archaeological Studies.)

In 1999 the Galisteo Basin Archaeological Sites Protection Act (GBASPA) was proposed for federal legislation by Senator Jeff Bingaman, sponsored by the Albuquerque-based Archaeological Conservancy, to protect twenty-six ancient sites in and around the Galisteo Basin. In September 2000, GBASPA went down to defeat, thanks to Senator Pete Domenici, who killed it in the Energy Committee, citing property rights, although the bill was explicit in its provisions that private landowners' participation would be entirely voluntary. New Mexico law states clearly that landowners can do anything they want with their archaeological sites (with the exception of human remains), including, alas, wrecking them for any future scholarship by amateur excavation or extraction. Domenici got on board to support the act when it was reintroduced in weakened form, allowing landowners to renege on their commitment to cultural resource protection. In March 2004, it was finally passed, though unappropriated. Even in this toothless condition, it was a significant beginning. Planning began with volunteers working with a State Site Watch program and several agencies—BLM, NPS, County Open Space and Planning, Office of Archaeological Studies (OAS), and the State Land Office—

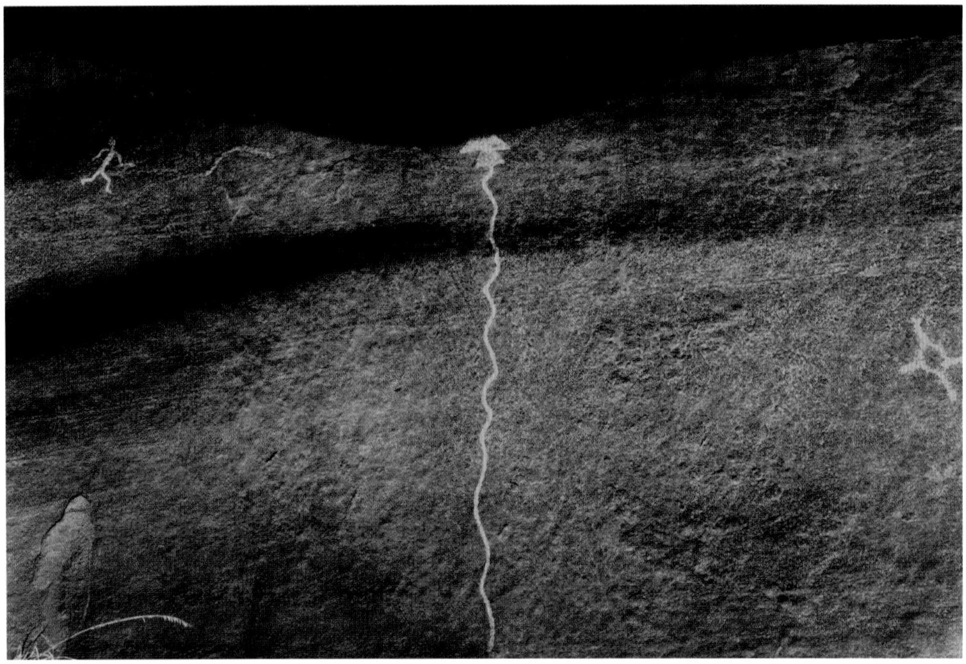

Edward Ranney, *Rock Art at San Cristóbal Pueblo*, 1999.

collaborating in hopes of funding, which eventually arrived, although in 2006 Governor Bill Richardson vetoed state money for the act. A volunteer working group was set up to administer some of the details and advise on a thorough management plan, under the auspices of the Taos BLM district and OAS. The group continues to function in an informal advisory and support role, with the crucial participation of tribal partners. It reflects the fact that by the 1980s archaeologists were moving away from a focus on artifacts and architecture that tended to neglect the interconnections between sites. Their views have expanded via drainages and valleys into broader regional concepts that illuminate a shared cultural landscape—more appropriate to Pueblo beliefs and also contrary to the dominant culture's devotion to private property.

Four of the major pueblo ruins, hundreds of related sites, and some particularly stunning rock art lie on the San Cristóbal Ranch. Thanks to the unsuccessful searches for mineral resources, an archaeological report was commissioned to investigate the Galisteo Basin's seismic potential. In 1977, an exhaustive survey of San Cristóbal's archaeological sites by Charles Lange renewed momentum in Galisteo archaeology. In 1996, with the cooperation of the OAS, the ranch owner's daughter, Christina Singleton Mednick, published *San Cristóbal: Voices and Visions from the Galisteo Basin.* In it she announced, "The Singleton family is making plans to create a conservancy to protect San Cristóbal Pueblo and its petroglyph site. The land will remain in its natural state, but the area will be fenced and protected. Visitors will be welcome, but they will be asked to sign in and out, and pay a token fee toward the preservation of the site. In this way the rock art may be saved from the harm some other sites have suffered."[71] Alas, this never came to be. Henry Singleton died in 1999 and GBASPA has not been able to confirm official protection for the numerable significant sites on the San

Cristóbal Ranch. Infrequent tours and hikes are organized by OAS and Santa Fe museums whenever the ranchers/landowners agree. Amateur archaeologists and rock art enthusiasts (cultural trespassers), who had taken such jaunts for granted over the decades, began to be forcibly discouraged in the mid 1990s. Today, sites that were once regularly visited by aficionados (as well as those who looted and vandalized) are now firmly out of bounds. Trespassers have been shouted at, shot at, and arrested.

The Galisteo Pueblo, a historical and archaeological site with deep connections to its village namesake, is one of two local sites protected by an easement with the Archaeological Conservancy (though not before the owners had carefully, lovingly, but unfortunately unearthed a great many artifacts). Easement of course does not mean public access. Elaborate management plans must be in place before visitation begins, if ever, and that process can take years. Only Pueblo Blanco, on State Trust land, and part of the smaller Burnt Corn Pueblo, on federal (BLM) land, are public lands, though they are not publicly accessible either. State Trust land is mandated to raise money to support state schools, so Pueblo Blanco was leased for grazing, and cattle have long been tromping over fragile sites and artifacts. A major petroglyph area associated with Burnt Corn is now owned by the County Open Space Program, which is trying to create a management plan that both meets the county's mandate for public access and, at the behest of several tribes, denies access to the rock art.

Pueblo Blanco has its own village-related history and serves here as a case study for land use around all the archaeological sites that are related to the village but lie beyond it. The cultural landscape has undergone many transformations since the Pueblos departed around 1525. The rough hills and chaotic topography can seem bleak and wild (cougars, deer,

Edward Ranney, *Pueblo Blanco*, 1999.

and antelope play), but traces of human ambition are everywhere. Never part of a Spanish or Mexican grant, the land was informally homesteaded by local Hispanos and Anglo newcomers. One small adobe ruin keeps watch over old cottonwoods and a human-made stock tank that probably dates to the late nineteenth or early twentieth century. It may be related to the extensive coal mine just to the west, which has left great scars on the land, as well as remnants of a sizable miners' camp, where stone outbuildings and piles of debris remain.[72]

For years, Galisteo rancher Frank Anaya, who settled about 291 acres bordering Pueblo Blanco and the McKee/Cook/Ford Ranch, thought he owned the pueblo ruin; once he offered to sell it to the Archaeological Conservancy. I've been told that even the State Land Commission didn't know it was the guardian of such an important site. After Pueblo Blanco had been identified as one of many archaeological sites on state land suffering from vandalism, weather, and years of neglect, $50,000 was made available in 2005 by state land commissioner Jim Baca to protect it. A major reclamation project ensued under the direction of State Land Commission archaeologist David Eck. Exposed human remains were reburied and ancient rooms that were crumbling into the arroyo were protected by a massive earthen barrier constructed to hold back erosion.

Most of the lands surrounding the pueblo are privately owned. The several tomes of title abstracts for the McKee Ranch reveal a complex history of land use—a microcosm of most areas of New Mexico. Deeds and grants are lost, inaccurate, or nonexistent. Anaya sold his ranch to a surgeon who tried and failed to cultivate orchards there. It was on the market again in 1996, touting "petroglyphs, Indian ruins." Tim Willms, an art dealer and a purveyor of meats to Santa Fe's upscale restaurants, bought it and transformed the modest adobe spread into Talus Winds Ranch, complete with a flagstoned patio and a customized swimming pool, where he once

Edward Ranney, *Hot Sauce Ad on Abandoned Structure, Frank Anaya Ranch Road*, 1999.

Lucy R. Lippard, *Former Industrial Brick Pit near Pueblo Blanco in Process of Restoration by Priscilla Hoback and Family*, ca. 2008.

raised miniature horses. A different kind of settler is artist and longtime New Mexican Sina Brush, who bought eighty acres of treeless ranchland on the road out to Cerro Pelón from Joe Miller, who had acquired it from Frank Anaya. Off the grid on solar, with some dogs, a stable, four handsome horses, and a locked gate, she hauls water in her pickup to her small adobe. So far, the only other new home near Pueblo Blanco was built off the grid, tucked unobtrusively up against Cerro Pelón in the 1990s by a practitioner of Chinese medicine. Adjacent lots are owned but not yet exploited. Along the same dusty road lies an unremarkable, gray-stuccoed adobe box that, when scrutinized, turns out to boast some uncommon attributes—two false windows with shredded plastic curtains and, painted on the west end, a giant tilted bottle of hot sauce. Once a two-room habitation, this bleak little edifice was the site of a twentieth-century TV commercial. I'd always wondered about it and was enlightened when I was driving past it with a friend, who mentioned that he'd been asked to act in that commercial years before.

Close to the border of the State Trust land (which incidentally is not fenced according to surveyed boundaries and encroaches on an adjacent property) is a small-scale clay source where the pueblo residents probably dug for their pottery. (Appropriately hidden in a cleft in a nearby outcrop is a petroglyph of the deity of the underworld.) After centuries of disuse, it became an industrial clay pit when the land was sold to the New Mexico Brick Partnership in 1981 by Philip and Robert McKee. In 1986 it was transferred to Ladrillo Brick Co., which divided it into three tracts for sale. The huge pit passed to Priscilla Hoback, a Galisteo clay-mural artist who made an effort to restore it (and set up a tipi) to create a wildlife refuge.

One adjacent parcel was donated to the Archaeological Conservancy by Robert Ryman, a New York artist internationally known for his white (*blanco*) paintings, and his former wife. To the west are tracts that have been owned by two Galisteo residents, both coincidentally named Sloan, though unrelated. The eastern boundary of the pueblo (including much of the most significant rock art) belongs to a part-time resident of Galisteo who also hopes to conserve the land.

The secrets of Pueblo Blanco are protected by both culture and nature. The artifacts uncovered by Nels Nelson in the early 1900s are buried in the basement of the American Museum of Natural History in New York, while millions of others lie hidden beneath the mounds.[73] Today the ruins are fortunately isolated and unmarked, under the care of devoted Site Watch volunteers. They can be reached only by rutted and often impassable ranch roads through a series of locked gates. Blanco is a world in itself, still strewn with artifacts, despite the fact that the site has been picked over not only by archaeologists but also by centuries of cowboys, sheepherders, an increasing number of amateur visitors (some taking nothing, some only a handful of sherds, others bagsful), and professional pot hunters absconding with major finds we will never know about.[74] The winds blowing across high mounds covered with cholla and prickly pear cactus expose the sherds underfoot—especially in the pueblo's plazas, trampled by people and livestock—and the remarkable rock art, which extends across the countryside in unexpected crannies, rock overhangs, on exposed, southeast-facing basalt outcrops, and on low boulders and natural stone walls almost underfoot. Eventually the ancient pueblo will share whatever fate has in store for the Galisteo Basin as a whole. If the area is developed (the King Cattle Company once got as far as installing transformers on nearby lots before that venture collapsed), it could be tragically advertised as a treasure trove for amateur archaeologists.[75] Despite all this activity around the Ancestral Pueblo sites, historical archaeology of Galisteo village itself is non-existent. Conventional excavation with modern standards is prohibitively expensive. Today's archaeological credo is to leave it alone for future archaeologists, who will have still better tools. The remains of stone walls, property lines, and acequias on the Galisteo and Cadial grants and traces of the first settlement on The Hill, as well as the history of the Ortiz y Davis hacienda, await attention.

The literature is full of well-deserved encomiums to Native ingenuity and intimate knowledge of the unforgiving conditions in which the Tanos and Keres peoples lived during their five-hundred-year tenure in the Galisteo Basin. They had a far greater scope than their successors in land and climate management, given that they could and did move frequently, as often as every generation or two, as a spiritual directive and in order to better utilize stressed resources. These moves were voluntary and communally determined, without the hardships they would cause today in our private-property-and-commodity-ridden society. Nevertheless, the Pueblo relationship to specific place was powerful, in part because of the belief that the spirits of their habitations, shrines, burials, and artifacts all lived on after their departures. Native belief systems fostered what Gregory Cajete, from Santa Clara Pueblo, has called a "theology of place," extending to all of nature. He quotes an elder: "It is this place that holds our memories and the bones of our people. . . . This is the place that made us . . . Indigenous people felt responsibility not only for themselves, but also for the entire world around them."[76] In indigenous and folk stories, chronology is far less significant than location. Concepts and experiences of time, distance, and proximity vary, dependent in part on the means of transportation—on foot, horse, wagon, and finally, by mid twentieth century, automobile.

Two controversies define the first decades of the twenty-first century: the OK Corral was local, sparked by past land use and ownership; climate change is global, sparked by the future. "Sustainability" is a battle cry for return to a resiliency that Americans may already have lost forever. Ecologists and those seeking a sustainable lifestyle that goes beyond the countercultural back-to-the-land movement of the 1960s are learning from indigenous models to take a long view. However, Cajete writes, "as we change our landscape and allow the self-serving will of materialist economic systems to have sway over our view of the land, we also allow the natural landscape of mind and soul to be altered. Each generation of Americans has become significantly more impoverished in terms of collective and individual connection to places that form the biological and geographic tapestry of America."[77] We all live in what he calls a schizophrenic state, *pingeh heh.* The cycles have been broken and it will be a long, hard job, even for modern indigenous people with devoted allies, to resurrect them.

Since the railroads and World War II, Galisteo, like many small New Mexico communities, has been forced to shift from self-sustaining agriculture to wage-based economies. The lurking threat of fracking, oil, and gas intrusions in the Galisteo Basin is alarming, given the fact that the extraction industry (along with the military) is a mainstay of the economy of the "Land of Enchantment"—one of the poorest states in the nation and the site of some 240 nuclear weapons sites. Across the New West, this is another pervasive and divisive issue, especially given western laws of split estate, wherein mineral rights are owned separately from surface rights, meaning that unbeknownst to a property buyer, the land beneath her home could be drilled or

Harmony Hammond, *Galisteans Protesting Oil and Gas Development in the Galisteo Basin*, Santa Fe Plaza, December 2007. *Left to right*: the author, Anna Cárdenas, Amy Tremper, and Wendy Chase.

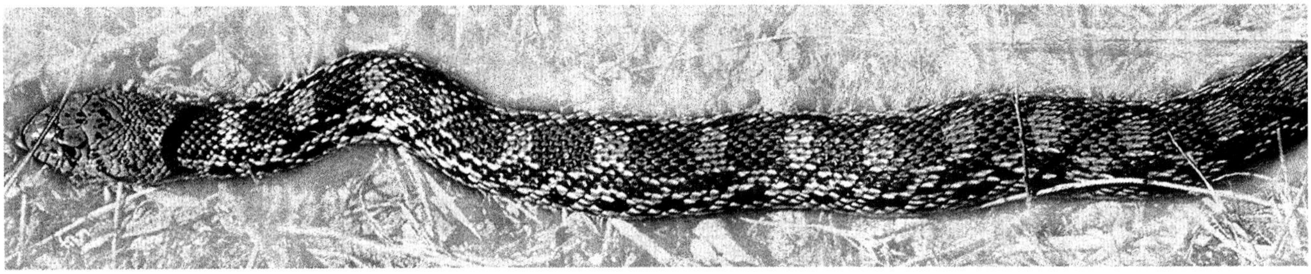

mined without her permission. Fossil fuel explorations over the years on San Cristóbal came up with nothing profitable, and as far as I know, there is only one oil well in the Galisteo Basin: the Black Ferrill on the former Hazel Cash Ranch in the west. Nevertheless, in 2007, a Texas corporation announced its intention to explore the possibility of fuels in the Galisteo. Communities across the basin and in the capital fired up a wave of protest, and in 2008 the Santa Fe County Commissioners hired a Los Angeles lawyer to fashion an ordinance that has been effective, so far, in making the permitting process too onerous for most to pursue. However, we know we have not seen the last of this particular threat to the local environment. If fossil fuels are ever phased out in favor of renewable energies, one of the more hopeful scenarios is that life could once again become sustainably local. Permaculture is providing a bridge between indigenous and modern growing strategies. Based on recognition of interdependence between humans and nature, it "could be described as a reintroduction to how the planet we live on really works," says Joel Glanzberg, who writes of his childhood experience of the woods as "one big life woven out of many."[78] Over the years, various Galisteo residents have occasionally suggested a community garden, and villager Ken Kuhne has made a successful business from his double-covered, hooped, raised beds, which he calls Grow Y'Own, inspired in part by another Galistean, writer Deborah Madison, internationally famous for her farm-to-table cookbooks.

Mark Fiege has written about the concept of an ecological commons (and a hydrological commons) in the West, a "Third Space" where ecology and culture intersect. Amid the No Trespassing signs, in "a land of rigid property boundaries," he writes, lies "a greater world of fluid ecological relationships and the social conflicts and compromises that emerge from their interaction. . . . Even parts of nature that humans do not want, and which they seek to destroy (weeds, diseases, animal pests) easily cross boundaries and so compel humans to view otherwise privatized landscapes in collective and public terms."[79] Citizens and groups such as the Sierra Club are working to create and protect wildlife corridors through the Galisteo Basin, a crucial passage for many species moving north and south across the continent (if they survive the crossing of I-40, thirty miles south of Galisteo). We often hear the nocturnal songs and ecstatic yelps of coyotes, the great survivors of the Anthropocene. The more they are poisoned and killed by bloodthirsty citizens and government agencies, the more they retaliate with increased reproduction.[80] Other frequently spotted denizens are the deer that dash across our fields between the creek and their diurnal hideouts, leaping the barbed wire fences. The legs of our pronghorns, imported from Wyoming and often incorrectly called antelopes, are too fragile to do this successfully; they are best off crawling under the wire, though they can get trapped there. Cougars are present but rarely sighted. Bobcats are more visible. Black bears come down into the arroyos when drought deprives them of sustenance in the mountains. When I first moved here, I saw porcupines, skunks, and raccoons, but they are few and far between now.[81] Rodents flourish—mice, pack rats, and pocket gophers, the banes of rural life.[82] Rabbits bound and abound, to the point where our dogs barely glance at them.

New Mexico's light is famous, even now, when its clarity is blurred by urban pollution (and forest fires) by day and the glow of Albuquerque and Santa Fe by night. The yellow-tan of winter and drought is most common. But in a wet spring or during a healthy monsoon

Jane Perry, *Doe Visiting Nancy Holt House in Ranchitos*, 2017.

Phillip Tuwaletstiwa, *Prowling Bear Caught by Wildlife Camera in the Wee Hours*, 2018.

Richard A. Shuff, *Six-Foot Bull Snake*, 2005.

Catherine Ferguson, *Coyote*, 2011.

Jan Saunders, *Coopers Hawk Banded in October*, 1997.

Richard A. Shuff, *Vultures in Their Favored Tree off Avenida Vieja*, 2006. The birds were unfazed and, according to workmen, quite entertained by the construction of the adjacent McQueen home.

Richard A. Shuff, *Goat Intervention in SoGal*, December 2002. Two hundred ewes, one weary ram, and a wether (gelding) were recruited by Earth Works Institute to fill up on the weeds and aerate the soil along the east bank of the creek. They were moved around with portable electric fences.

Roger Taylor, *Bobcat Visitor*, ca. 2016.

season, the land bursts into downright lushness, overlaid with a green scrim, tiny wildflowers everywhere underfoot. Descent into shallow canyons reveals natural and cultural oases. The basin's gently rolling landscape, an ancient seabed, harbors arroyos and gullies, precarious wetlands, springs and seeps that sustain delicate ecosystems and invisible wildlife, hardy piñons and junipers, cholla, yucca, prickly pear, and other resilient cacti. Draining the precious water in the Galisteo Creek are the insidious imported salt cedar (tamarisk) and Russian olive.[83] As hardy as coyotes, these trees suck up and even poison water, depriving the native cottonwoods, while tougher willows tend to survive.

Beneath the Galisteo Basin's tumbled rocks, impermeable clay, and hardy vegetation lie traces of the botanical lives once lived here and harbingers of losses to come. In June 1993 I found thirteen different wildflowers in my field between the two roads. In June 2000 I found none. In the summer of 2007 I counted perhaps five. In June 2016 there was a healthy greenish vetch and some other bedraggled drought survivors (globe mallow, verbena, thistle, goatsbeard, perky sue, the pretty but prickly wild potato or horse nettle, Mexican hats, varieties of wild sunflowers, and white primroses that look like discarded Kleenexes). In June 2018, only the vetch was thriving. Some blooms wait, above the river-laid clay, to emerge when the rains come. But how many are gone forever? The soil around my house is dusty and depleted, and a few inches down it turns rock/clay hard, deterring deep roots and water infiltration. I can barely coax hardy locusts and chamisa to survive in the yard. In addition, pocket gophers, rarely seen but all too present, burrow under the soil to chew on roots, sending up telltale piles of dirt. When the droughts are particularly insidious, the ground squirrels get so desperate that they eat the blossoms off my potted flowers.

Birders love the Galisteo Creek and birds should love Galisteo, since so many of us feed them. I have striking spotted towhees, colorful finches, and migratory exotics that visit my feeders, daily raided by two kinds of doves. Hawks hover on the fence hoping to lure the little birds from their hideouts in the four-wing saltbush. Ravens and crows perch on fence posts to converse with passersby, competing with their sculpted brethren on local gates. Waves of red-winged blackbirds sail through in late winter, consuming everything in sight. Persistent hummingbirds arrive each year in mid April, demanding sugar water until mid-September. Meadowlarks nest perilously in ground cover, betraying their presence with haunting song. I rarely see piñon jays, which are common a quarter-mile higher. The occasional roadrunner (the state bird) and ferruginous hawks are exciting to see even for those, like me, who are more into seeing than identifying. The advent of the vultures (*zopolotes,* or turkey buzzards) in mid March and their departure in mid October are local events; one year some neighbors with young children held a one-truck parade to welcome them. Classically ugly up close, vultures are sheer elegance overhead as they ride the thermal currents with wide, white-undercoated wings shining. They roost in the bosque and in the mornings are often found perched on a dead tree nearby, wings spread to dry and warm.

The insects that feed the birds are changing with the climate. (When I first moved here, I was told that the increasingly maddening mosquitos were imported from Africa by a long-

Judy Tuwaletstiwa, *Dancing at Bicentennial Party at La Sala*, October 2014. *Left to right*: Freddie and Anna Cárdenas, Mary Alice Anaya, and Dorothy Victor.

time resident's trade in art objects.) Horseflies invade from the stable next door. Once, and only once in twenty-six years, I saw a pale scorpion in my front yard. More recently a fuzzy tarantula invaded a friend's patio. I have never seen one, though they are common in nearby areas.

Several years ago I was pleased to see my cat jump backwards from a large bull/gopher snake—beneficent scourge of rodents—that was disappearing into a hole in my yard. Occasional sightings and ghostly, transparent skins attest to reptilian omnipresence. Given the thriving rodent population and occasional cases of the plague, West Nile virus, and hantavirus, snakes are decidedly beneficial in this environment. I have caught glimpses of brilliant red racers, or coachwhips—lithe, long, and lightning fast, streaking through the high grasses. (They also hang from trees, but I've been spared.) For all the tramping around the countryside I've done, I've seen few rattlesnakes, though I try to keep in mind the stories of those who have almost stepped on one, reached over a ledge to find one coiled, or found one in their closet. Curious dogs are particularly vulnerable. In the bosque where I walk almost daily, I have seen only one rattler in all these years, and it was being killed by a local man. But in the spring, still groggy, they get run over on the roads. They are supposed to hibernate in the winter, but a veteran westerner says the biggest one she ever saw was in February. Once, in May, she yelled a warning as I was rushing toward an ancient petroglyph on the northern creston. I stopped short to see a yellow and black diamondback majestically reared up against the black basalt. I was mesmerized, not by fear, but by beauty. It ruled its place and I paid homage, as had those who made the petroglyphs, so many of which depict snakes—coiled snakes as springs, running snakes as lightning, snakes as symbolic connectors between earth and sky, bringers of water.

Judy Tuwaletstiwa, *Denise Lynch and Friends at the Bicentennial Parade*, 2014.

On October 4, 2014, the whole village and many former residents from old families (as well as some spectators from Santa Fe) gathered to celebrate Galisteo's bicentennial, headed up by Anna Cárdenas. La Sala displayed documents, letters, art, photographs, and artifacts contributed by local families. El Puente Press published two booklets—a historical timeline from 1814 to 2014 and Wayne King's *Speculations on the Economy and Roads at Galisteo*. Locals and relatives brought mementoes and scrapbooks of family photographs to exhibit. The celebration boasted a parade, a car show organized by David Montoya, and burgers courtesy of the GVFR. The parade was led by two men on horseback, followed by two pickups with waving children, family crests, and a guitar player, the Galisteo Morning Walkers carrying a banner, a candidate for the state legislature pushing his baby in a carriage, and GVFR vehicles. Bringing up the rear was Denise Lynch perched precariously on a bicycle, leading a skittish horse in one hand and a nervous saluki in the other. Then the crowd, including many elders, climbed The Hill to the old church mound, where Terry Anaya Vásquez, with her grandson Seth Griego, descendants of the original settlers, looked out over the old suertes and spoke movingly about the courage of her forebears. At the end of the day, after most spectators had departed, a dance was held in La Sala to the strains of a youthful rock-and-roll band from Pecos. Cousins danced with cousins, neighbors danced with neighbors, grandmothers danced with grandchildren. Cakes in the form of La Sala, made by sisters Priscilla Montoya and Lisa Griego, were admired and consumed. A good time was had by all. The village founders would have been confounded, and proud.

Judy Tuwaletstiwa, *Terry Anaya Vásquez and Grandson Seth Griego Recall Their Ancestors from the Old Church Site on The Hill*, 2014.

Anna Cárdenas, *Lisa Griego, Emily Montoya, and Priscilla Montoya with Bicentennial La Sala Cakes*, 2014.

La Sala

The story of Galisteo's vortex of land and lives is full of unheeded warnings. "History . . . happens to you while you're doing the dishes," wrote Grace Paley.[84] It is everyday life, and in Galisteo, as in so many other pueblos chicos in the southwest, the land or memories of the land are still where everyday life takes place. The next years of the Galisteo story will be no less fraught with conflict and struggle than the past two centuries. The land-and-lives lens through which I am gazing at these histories belongs to individuals and groups—friendly, hostile, and neutral. History is a living and changing narrative, written, it is said, by the victors but often revised and challenged by newly powerful voices. It will always be fluid and unsettling. Its tentacles reach into the present, which is where I work and where I look at history—as a great tangle of stories from different points of view.

¡Qué viva Galisteo!

Nicolas Trofimuk, *Rain Cloud over Galisteo*, ca. 2013.

NOTES

Acknowledgments

1. *1909–17 Proceedings of Case #6470, "Benjamin Pankey v. Juan Ortiz et al."* in the District Court, Santa Fe County, typescript (bound copy in the possession of a Galistean villager, referred to in the text as the "Cadial book"). In nineteenth-century documents, the Cadial (cocklebur pasture) was often spelled Cadillal, as Anglo recorders struggled with Spanish names such as Analla (Anaya), Sandobal (Sandoval), and Chaves (Chávez). Since then, spelling has been standardized to modern usage.

Note on Spanish Accents

1. Personal communication, February 26, 2019.

Introduction

1. Rael-Gálvez, "Testifying to the Silence of Servitude," 291.
2. Jackson, *Discovering the Vernacular Landscape*, 5. The term *cultural landscape* was coined in 1925 by Carl Sauer, who defined it: "Culture is the agent, the natural area is the medium, the cultural landscape is the result" (*The Morphology of Landscape*, 31). The term was illuminated for New Mexico by Jackson, who also noted that the history of New Mexico's villages was "largely unrecorded; all we usually know about them is roughly the decade of their settlement, the date of the first church, and the place of origin of their first settlers. . . . What is lacking is any picture of the villages in their prime" (Jackson, *A Sense of Place, A Sense of Time*, 19).
3. Henderson, "What (Else) We Talk About When We Talk About Landscape," 195.
4. Simmons, *Coronado's Land*, 114–15.

Chapter 1

1. Kenner, *The Comanchero Frontier*, 77.
2. At the onset of the Pueblo Revolt, the Tanos abandoned their Galisteo mission to colonize the Casas Reales, or royal headquarters (Governor's Palace) in Santa Fe, which they remodeled into a large multistoried pueblo.
3. These intriguing documents are still being investigated. See Ebright, Hendricks, and Hughes, *Four Square Leagues*, chapter 8.
4. A league was then 2.6 miles, so the four square leagues would have covered the village site of Galisteo to the south (Ebright, Hendricks, and Hughes, 225, 395 n100).
5. The Tano/Tewa had fled to other pueblos and to Hopi First Mesa. David Snow tells me that there is a mid-eighteenth-century request from a Galisteo Pueblo resident for permission to go to Hopi to visit relatives (personal communication, 2018).
6. For instance, in 1794 there were no non-Indians living at Pecos Pueblo, but five years later, as the pueblo shrank and lost strength, the settler invasion had begun, and by 1838 the survivors moved to join fellow Towa speakers at Jemez Pueblo.

7. There was no Protector of Indians from 1717 to ca. 1810; the office was abolished by the Spanish king in 1821 (Ebright, Hendricks, and Hughes, 343 n25, 363 n146).
8. Meinig, *Southwest*, 9–16.
9. Twitchell, *The Spanish Archives of New Mexico*, 30. Chaquaco is a ranch northeast of San Marcos now owned by the photographer Edward Ranney. In 1810 the San Marcos Grant was open again and "denied to Francisco Ortiz," who, along with Captain Manuel Delgado, was admonished not to graze his herds on this and adjoining pastures because the San Marcos tract was reserved for the poor of Santa Fe to graze their cattle. In 1891 the Antonio Urban Montaño grant went to Lehman and Willie Spiegelberg with Sally Arunheim of New York.
10. Pino's claim was based on a copy of the grant made at Aragón's request to replace the original, which had been water-damaged. This led to the Pino version of the grant being identified as a forgery by the US government. When the case came up in November 1896, he dropped his suit (Bowden, "Private Land Claims in the Southwest," 300).
11. Reconocida (Familiar) and Cuchillas Pedrogosas (Stony or Rocky Sharp Ridges) are not familiar names today, and I have found them on no maps; this is the only instance I have found where "del Monte" is appended to San Cristóbal.
12. Bowden, "Private Land Claims in the Southwest," 300–301.
13. Simmons, *Spanish Government in New Mexico*, 180. For a thorough account of New Mexico in 1803, see Governor Fernando de Chacón's "Report of Governor Chacón, 1803" in Simmons, *Coronado*'s *Land*, 162–72.
14. The still unresolved issue of Spanish grants establishing the rights of Pueblo people to their traditional lands has been considered in depth by Ebright, Hendricks, and Hughes, *Four Square Leagues*. The study area covers all of northern New Mexico, as far west as Acoma, but unfortunately cuts off east of Santa Fe, just above the Galisteo Basin.
15. Gutiérrez, *When Jesus Came, the Corn Mothers Went Away*, 105.
16. A vara roughly equaled a yard, officially measured by a "vara stick" of heavy oak divided by brass studs into four sections, or hand breadths, and then into two-fingers breadths. In the late 1800s there was a legal question about the length of the vara, which impacted the size of people's grants. It was either 33 1/3 or just 33 inches. The vara system was discarded by the Americans soon after 1846, but since it appears in all the old documents, it continued to be a staple in legal cases and was used in New Mexico until the 1890s. The long, usually narrow strips of land called *suertes* or *solares* were perpendicular to the bottomlands along a river or an acequia in a system called *lineas* See Shultz, "A Case for Revising the History of Chupadero and Rio en Medio."
17. Gutiérrez, *When Jesus Came, the Corn Mothers Went Away*, 106.
18. Spanish Archives of New Mexico [SANM] II, doc. 1830, "Census reports for several New Mexico jurisdictions," May 19–29, 1805, Reel-frame 15:608, New Mexico State Records Center and Archives, Santa Fe.
19. Archaeologists concede that the stone stock pens built by Hispano or Indian herders at the prehistoric pueblos are difficult to distinguish from Pueblo shrines and structures. Hispano herders often used "tipi-like tents," so the stone rings archaeologist Richard Lange discovered in the area could have been made by herders, or they could be evidence of portable Apache dwellings. Archaeologist Steve Post has studied the colonial ruins at Pueblo She in detail and considers them to be probable traces of shelters for soldiers grazing their horses and livestock (personal communication, 2018).
20. Swadesh, *Los Primeros Pobladores*, 17.
21. Twitchell, *The Leading Facts of New Mexican History*, 311. Along with the Cabeza de Baca and Gonzales families the Pinos were the wealthiest landowners in La Cienega at the end of the 1800s.

22. Marc Simmons, "'The Abraham of New Mexico,' Don Pedro traveled in luxurious style," *Santa Fe New Mexican*, May 1, 2004, B1, B3. (He may have moved as early as 1768.)
23. Chávez, *My Penitente Land*, 223.
24. Córdova, *¡Concha!*, 5.
25. Pino, *The Exposition on the Province of New Mexico, 1812*.
26. Gilberto Espinosa letter (Concha Ortiz y Pino de Kleven Papers): "Apparently the Report was not written but dictated to a writer who adroitly arranged the first letter of each of the first Paragraphs, to spell his name," which is not identified. It was first published in Puebla, Mexico, in 1823, under Pino's name, though it has also been suggested that he never got to Cadiz at all and that the report was written by someone else using information he provided. In 1839 Pino's report was republished "with additions" by Antonio de Barriero, a Mexican lawyer assigned to New Mexico as advisor to Governor Espinosa (translated by Lansing B. Bloom, "Barreiro's Ojeada sobre Nuevo-México").
27. In 1815 he was a founder of modern Socorro, alcalde mayor and *regidor* of Santa Fe, and a commissioner for the settlement of Pecos valley. Pino was re-elected in 1820 as deputy for a new cortes but received only enough money to get him to Mexico, where he gave up the trip. The cortes was dissolved in 1814, when King Ferdinand was freed after Napoleon's defeat, and its good intentions were forgotten. Before returning home, Pino visited Paris and London, where he bought a fancy landau that was knocked down into pieces, sent back to Veracruz, and driven on a wagon to Mexico City and up the Camino Real to Santa Fe "over the frightful roads of New Mexico."
28. He was first married to Manuela Gabaldón (in 1772), then to a widow, Lugarda Lucero (in 1781), both of whom died. Baca had been married to Manuel Delgado two years earlier, and after Pino's death she married Gregorio Sánchez in 1830.
29. María Guadalupe de la Trinidad (b. 1818), Nicolás de Jesús (b. 1819), Miguel Estanislao (b. May 6, 1821), José Facundo, called Facundo (b. Nov. 27, 1823), and Germán, who is mentioned in Galisteo accounts but seems to have settled in La Cienega.
30. W. H. H. Allison, in Horgan, *Great River*, 420. According to Linda Tigges, official grazing in the eighteenth century was limited to the western basin, excluding the San Cristóbal Pueblo (soon to be a grant) and the Galisteo Pueblo.
31. José Ortiz y Pino III, personal communication, 1997.
32. According to architectural historian David Kammer, nothing in Galisteo village is this old. The reference may be to the Sitio de los Cerrillos, a grant of 1,479 acres in the far western basin made to Cleto de Miera and Pedro Bautista Pino on Feb. 11, 1788, or the Sitio de Juana López in the same area (a *sitio* was a small farm). A century later, in the 1870 census Nicolás Pino is listed as the first postmaster of Juana López, Santa Fe County, beginning Dec. 10, 1866 (Dike, *The Territorial Post Offices of NM*).
33. His descendant José Ortiz y Pino III contended that Pedro Bautista lived in Galisteo, in El Retiro, the house he himself bought in 1960. He hoped to prove that Don Pedro was buried in the Galisteo cemetery. However, unless new documentation emerges, it is safe to say that Pino never lived in or near Galisteo, though he may have claimed some land in the area.
34. Twitchell, *Spanish Archives*, 410.
35. Kammer, *Application for Registration*, sec. 12, 18 (citing SANM II, doc. 2114). Another reference announces the mustering out of one destacamento at Pecos and the reduction of that of Galisteo, ordering "relief for the present force of Galisteo."
36. Seven leagues seems to put it nearer the old pueblo as the village was said to be eight leagues south. But the league had flexible measurements in the colonial periods. It has also been suggested

that the garrison was on top of the hill next to the eventually settled Hill, now the property of John and Tanya Young. There are purportedly archaeological remains beneath this house.

37. Bandelier, *The Southwestern Journals of Adolph F. Bandelier, 1880–1882*, vol. 1, 377.
38. Bainbridge Bunting Manuscript Collection, Center for Southwest Research, University of New Mexico, Albuquerque (cited in Kammer, *Application for Registration*).
39. Harrington, *The Ethnography of the Tewa Indians,* 485.
40. Bandelier, *Southwestern Journals*, vol. 1, 377.
41. Snow, *Archaeological and Historical Investigations*, 22. According to Father Stanley, whose booklet on Galisteo disdains sources and references, when the pueblo was abandoned, "others came in from Santa Fe, Peña Blanca, and surrounding towns to establish the Galisteo of today." He mentions Peña Blanca twice; the only connection would be its proximity to Santo Domingo, where the Galisteo Tanos had fled; they may have been the first to know the pueblo was deserted (Father Stanley [Stanley Crocciola], *The Galisteo, New Mexico Story*, 11).
42. Snow, *Archaeological and Historical Investigations*, 2. ARMS Survey #27253 Santa Fe County, Sept. 1989, for Jim Sloan, concerning a little ruin on the northeast side of The Hill, assumes "that the new Galisteo was established between 1821 and 1846" and dates the ruin 1821–24; it was standing until at least the first quarter of the twentieth century.
43. Steve Post, personal communication, 2018.
44. Cadial book, 343ff. Vigil (1802–77) was Secretary of Military "Commandancy" of New Mexico under the Mexican regime and secretary of state under the Americans, as well as an acting governor and then governor (Dec. 1847–Oct. 1848) of New Mexico Territory. He was born and lived in Santa Fe; Galisteo is not mentioned in his biographies.
45. Juan Cristóbal Vigil was listed on an 1818 petition for the Galisteo grant, so he may have been an actual grantee.
46. An 1822 document cited at a trial almost a century later noted that one Don Francisco Trujillo at the Ojito de Galisteo was to maintain the reservoir. It is elsewhere referred to as the "grazing permit" for the first Hispano settler, Juan Aragón.
47. Elkus, "Galisteo: 1500–1900," 65.
48. Kammer, *Application for Registration*, section 12, 21. For instance, in 1821, Matías Sandoval sold land to Gregorio Chávez "on the *otra vanda* of the river" according to Francisco Sandobal in 1849. This implies that the Galisteo grant spanned the river, important in the later trials concerning the Cadial grant (see chapter 2). According to Frances Swadesh (*Los Primeros Pobladores*, 160), "until 1824 *vecinos* could settle a grant for four years, fulfill all requirements for receiving full title, then sell their allotments at a profit and request new grants."
49. An *hijuela* was an inventory of an estate done by government officials and appeared in wills, but not a formal deed.
50. Twitchell (*Spanish Archives*, vol. 1, 266) mentions two 1822 documents, part of the 1814 Galisteo grant to Matías Sandoval, Rafael Sena, and Felipe Sandoval—all denied decades later.
51. Kammer, *Application for Registration*, sec. 12, 19.
52. Eventually, American courts (on the basis of some local accounts) decided that it was never a town or community grant; it was said to be sufficient land and water to support twenty families.
53. More rudimentary techniques such as vertical poles and adobe plaster, or jacales, may also have been common.
54. Kammer, *Application for Registration*, sec. 12, 19.
55. Cadial book, 348. These names are all on the 1821 census except Felipe Sandoval, although there is a Francisco Sandoval.
56. Anastacio Sandoval, Cadial book, 200. Warfare resumed in the 1820s with these tribes after an earlier peace.

57. Anastacio Sandoval, Cadial book, 182.
58. Swadesh, *Los Primeros Pobladores*, 133.
59. In the 1821 census, "parv" refers to children under eight; those over eight are "single."
60. Simmons, *Spanish Government*, 187–88. He observes that the alcalde was often a corrupt and dreaded figure.
61. Lecompte, "The Independent Women of Hispanic New Mexico, 1821–1846," 29. John Kessell (in conversation) suggested that he may have been banished to the garrison and forced to serve as a soldier.
62. Evidence that some of the houses were also jacal emerged when artist Jim Sloan recently bought an old adobe on The Hill from the heirs of Manuel and Clarita Anaya and discovered an underlayer of vertical sticks.
63. No historical archaeology has been executed on or around Galisteo's earliest settlements. With the advent of a new home being built in early 2018, archaeologists Mike Marshall and Steve Post examined rock remains on the west side of The Hill, finding primarily evidence of an 1880s residence (probably that of Eduardo Sena). They suspect that earlier occupation could be found beneath it.
64. Kammer says ca. 1825. Bandelier was told by Ramón Cháves in Galisteo in the 1880s that the church was built around 1834–35, which seems late (Bandelier, *Southwestern Journals*, vol. 1, 377). It is not, as is sometimes assumed, the seventeenth-century church at Tanuge to the north.
65. Dunbar-Ortiz, *Roots of Resistance*, 94.
66. Hall, *Four Leagues of Pecos*, 21. This was the same Domingo Fernández (1788 or 1792–1854) who was a custodian of the Church's Lamy grant. He was on the *deputación* that made the grants and was also a historian who indexed all grants in New Mexico.
67. Baxter, "Cerrillos Area Names Database," 638.
68. Domingo Fernández, Reel 14, Land Grants, New Mexico State Records Center and Archives, Santa Fe. The Church itself seems not to have been involved. Five years later, in 1827, all "Iberians" were ordered out of the Republic of Mexico, presumably to forestall Spanish rebellions, though some Iberian priests remained since clergy were so scarce. There were fewer than twenty priests in the whole territory during the Mexican period.
69. Ibid.
70. Presumably Don Julián Lucero, lieutenant (*alcalde teniente*) of Galisteo.
71. Mednick, *San Cristóbal*, 136. (See chapter 4.)
72. Ibid. This promise was later repeated under Eaton. This time Fernández's fourteen co-grantees (all given the honorific title of Don) are Francisco Fernández, Antonio Sena, Juan Jesús Rivera, Miguel Rivera, José María Rivera, Ignacio and José Ortiz, Miguel Lobato, Pablo and Florentine Ortiz, José Trugillo, Meriano Baca, Miguel Rodríguez, José de Jesús Chávez, and "natives of this city" (Santa Fe).
73. Mednick, *San Cristóbal*, 137.
74. Ibid.
75. Bowden, "Private Land Claims," 276. The western boundary was "a point opposite the middle creston." (This is the *en medio,* the location of which causes trouble later.)
76. In one document, grantees were admonished by the Santa Fe ayuntamiento to "love Fernández as a brother" and give him preference in water rights (Baxter, "Cerrillos Area Names Database," 638; Ebright, personal communication, 3/2/05).
77. Mednick, *San Cristóbal*, 138.
78. Ibid., 139.
79. Walker, reporting on research done by Michael Olsen and Harry Myers on the Gallego diary, "Diary Opens Another Page," 50.

80. Townley, "Mining in the Ortiz Mine Grant Area," 54.
81. Ibid., 59; see also 43–51, Townley writes of José Francisco Ortiz: "His way of life was not uncommon for members of the wealthier families in that day. . . . [He] was a member of the Santa Fe Company of the militia, and spent his adult life as an officer commanding various garrisons and on field service against the Indians." In 1840 he moved to Santa Fe. There was also a Francisco Ortiz who lived in Dolores in 1838; both owned stores, and they were probably related.
82. A village elder told me that the Galisteo Ortizes were not Ortizes, but Garcías, who had killed Ortiz to get the gold. (See chapter 2 for more on the Ortiz lineage.)
83. Gregg, *Commerce of the Prairies*, 135.
84. The term itself was banned in 1821, although a friend who grew up in Alamogordo in the 1950s recalls "genizaro" being used as an insult. There has been a recent resurgence of interest in genizaro heritage. (In 2016, Sylvia Rodríguez organized the lecture series "Transformative Events and Process in New Mexico's Colonial History"; on Oct. 6, Gregorio Gonzales of the University of Texas, Austin, spoke on genizaro identity.) See also Rita Younis, "Genizaro Servants," *Santa Fe New Mexican*, July 30, 2007; Dunbar-Ortiz, *Roots of Resistance*.
85. On May 18, 1830, seven citizens of Santa Fe—Juan de Díos Peña, Ignacio Ortiz, Teodoro Quintana, Jesús M. Alarid, Román Brito, Jesus María Peña, and Juan Lovato—took possession of 500- and 100-vara tracts on a grant called La Gotera, which usually means "drop" or "leak" of water, but also "out-of-the-way place." It was open land along the Galisteo Creek between present-day Galisteo and Cerrillos. Grantees were charged with "activating the soil and occupying the tract with their livestock from year to year as the hostilities of the Indians permitted." Possession of La Gotera grant was given at a place called Nuestra Señora del Pilar de Zaragosa (Snow, *Archaeological and Historical Investigations*, 23, 27–29, appendix). Among the heirs were Remedios Padia Peña and Pedro Peña, probably from Galisteo.
86. Dunbar-Ortiz, *Roots of Resistance*, 73, 84. After 1831, however, taxes on American trade made the Santa Fe Trail less profitable.
87. Meinig, *Southwest*, 17.

CHAPTER 2

1. Frank Waters, *People of the Valley*, 88. An alabado is a Spanish hymn.
2. Ebright, Hendricks, and Hughes, *Four Square Leagues*, 118.
3. José Francisco Baca y Terrus (b. ca. 1776–79 at Las Golondrinas near La Cienega, which was the Baca y Terrus hacienda, north of the ranch called El Guic; in 1816 he married Manuela Delgado; in 1821 he lived in La Ciénega). The grant appears in Bowden's thesis ("Private Land Claims in the Southwest," 463–67) as the Cañada de San Francisco grant, including an undated "sketch" map of it, obviously made post 1846, as some of the notations are in English. Domingo Fernández was involved. According to David Snow, the Baca y Terrus grant was 1,300 acres; there are still building foundations on the site (personal communication, 2018).
4. In 1826 the Santo Domingo de Maragua grant was attributed to Francisco Baca y Terrus (according to an 1855 map). Tigges describes the Maragua grant of 1840 as located from "'brow to brow' on both sides of the Galisteo Creek west of the settlers of Galisteo."
5. The Hills of Matadero (Slaughter) are said to be south and west of the village. Snow (*Archaeological and Historical Investigations*, 29ff) says they are behind Cerro Pelón. Local resident Michael J. Anaya believes that they are the double-peaked hill on County Open Space known until recently as Petroglyph Hill. In a later trial the same boundaries were described by Tomás Roybal of Galisteo, and in his testimony the Hills of Matadero extend over about three miles and are compared to similar hills in the north, which suggests the two crestons.

6. One commonly identified site for "the ceja" is the southern ridge of the basin, now called Clark Hill. But *ceja* is a generic term for summit; this double ceja could be the northern and southern crestons or Clark and Lamy hills, or any other summits. This description resembles another grant in 1840–41 to several of the grantees, with the addition of the ubiquitous Domingo Fernández. On May 16, 1871, the petitioners were Baca, Juan Benavides, José Ma. Benavides, Cruz Cháves, José Lucero, José Maria Padilla, Miguel Rodríguez, Esteban Sena, Manuel Baca, Nasario Gonzales, Ignacio Baca, P[edro] Baca [y Terrus], José Durán, José Baca, Vicente Anaya, Califas(?) Sena, and Leonides (?) Baca.
7. According to Bowden ("Private Land Claims in the Southwest") it was denied by the CPLC to claimant Nazario Gonzales in 1894.
8. "Said grant" must be the Ojito/Galisteo grant as it is too early to be the Cadial (see below). It is unclear what "ford" that would be. The obvious interpretation is the one crossed by today's El Puente, the old village bridge. But this one seems to be farther north, where a "pool" is located on an old map, next to the northern creston. Two houses are marked on another map, from the US Surveyor General's Office, dated 1900: "stone house" is right up against the northern side of the creston. "House of Juan Sandoval" is to the west, near the break in the creston through which the Arroyo de los Angeles flows, although on this map it is called "Sandy Arroyo." "East of the Santa Fe road used to be a house of Pedro Madril" (Cadial book, 169).
9. Elkus ("Galisteo: 1500–1900") says this grant was never decided.
10. A Bureau of Ethnology map of the San Cristóbal/Eaton grant patented in 1880 and published by J. P. Harrington shows the puertocito as the gap farther east than on the site of the current road, which explains later controversy about which hump of the creston is "en medio." Just to further confuse things, it was noted at the 1909–17 Cadial trial that there had been another Juan Ortiz in Galisteo, (Juan J. or Juan José Ortiz), an old man who had died long before and also had "another name" (Cadial book, 132).
11. In the Cadial trials, Juan Ortiz said, "[The Loma Gavilán is] above; it isn't close to the arroyo at all and not in the Cadial" (Cadial book, 174). Elsewhere it is noted as a boundary on Domingo Fernández's land, so it is somewhere on the western San Cristóbal Ranch.
12. The best guess at the location of Mesita Blanca is a "Mesa Blanca" marked on the Bureau of Ethnology map near the current San Cristóbal Ranch headquarters, just south of the San Cristóbal Arroyo. However, there is also a strikingly white hill farther south above the ruins of Pueblo Colorado.
13. This appears to be the same grant petitioned in Jan. 1841 to a different group of seven individuals (Ignacio Chávez, Miguel Archuleta, María de Jesus Luján, Joaquin Chávez, Nicanor Hidalgo, José de la Cruz Chávez, and "latecomer" Tomas Rafael Sais) for portions of the Galisteo grant "upstream from the earlier settlers." Alcalde Anastacio Sandoval awarded each 200 varas (SANM I, Twitchell no. 398, "Luis Griego and others, Petition for Land around San Cristobal," 1843, Reel-frame 34:052, New Mexico State Records Center and Archives, Santa Fe).
14. SANM I, Case #159, cited by Bowden ("Private Land Claims," 281), notes the description as bounded "on the north, by an arroyo and a cross; on the east, by the lands of Domingo Fernández; on the south, by the point of a white bluff and a cross; and on the west, by the upper point of a hill known as the Gavilanes." Antonio Baca, Jesús Griego, Francisco Provincio, Juan Silva, Francisco de Garza, Vicente Roibal, Benito Varela, and Marcelino Ortiz were the ones who filed suit in 1893, but when it came up for trial in 1897, the grant was rejected (SANM I, Series V: Surveyor General/Court of Private Land Claims Records, Sub-series 5.4: Court of Private Land Claims Case Files, PLC Case 159, Mesita Blanca Grant, Reel-frame 49:729, New Mexico State Records Center and Archives, Santa Fe).
15. "The population of the first 18 settlers having increased . . . Don Ignacio Chávez petitioned the Cadial for them [in the 1840s]" (Anastacio Sandoval, Cadial book, 182).

16. It was lent to me by the late Mela Anaya Montoya of Galisteo and her daughter Anna Cárdenas, descendants of José Antonio Anaya, who was one of the defendants.
17. Anastacio Sandoval says the San Cristóbal arroyo marked the center of the land (Cadial book, 150). The younger Juan Ortiz said the Cadial was bounded on the north "by the foot of the heighth [Cañada de en Medio]" and on the south by "the foot of the crest of the *Creston La Jara* heighth [Alto de la Jara]" (169). Librado Valencia said the southern Cadial fence was "just north" of the Galisteo Lake (58). According to Apolonio Chávez (116–17), the fence went right into the lake at or near Loma Gavilán.
18. Ibid., 278, 260
19. Ibid., 126–27. In 1895, José Manuel Sandoval testified that he knew the Cadial lands before they were all allotted under the Mexican government, suggesting that they were already used for grazing.
20. Ibid., 174, 200, 221. Quite recently Avenida Vieja (La Joya) lay east of its present path.
21. Ibid., 220–21. Anastacio Sandoval says he "never owned an inch of land at Galisteo" (meaning farmland) but built a house north of one of the "first donations." He was born "in a house on top of that hill and afterwards I married and was living down on the plains" (179).
22. Anastacio Sandoval testified that the road east from Galisteo to San Cristóbal came through part of cultivated land toward Loma Parda. The old road to San Cristóbal, now cut off by ranch fence, was used before the Cadial was fenced.
23. Cadial book, 58.
24. A little house below San Cristóbal built by Don Joaquín Chávez is mentioned, possibly the ruin behind the present-day Durán home, formerly the Light Institute; the crops were close to it (ibid., 164). There were also "the ruins of old houses some 200–300 yards from Tacubaya's east boundary," possibly those still visible near Pueblo She.
25. Ibid., 120. Juan Ortiz (88) says his father left a will and that it was probated and "disappeared." His mother, Paublita, who died in 1880, had given him the hijuela for Ignacio Chávez's Cadial land in 1866–67. His brothers Susano and Calletano allotted their shares to him (Cadial book, 119, 133).
26. Attorney Catron argued that Ortiz had "no direct title in writing. . . . You simply claim the two strips covered by the hijuelas given to Juan Ortiz and to Juaquin [*sic*] Chávez through verbal transfers from your mother and brothers and sisters." Ortiz replied that one was given and the other bought in 1869 from Martín Gallegos, who lived at Dolores (ibid., 134, 127).
27. Marc Simmons, "Trail Dust: New Mexico's Bulls," *Santa Fe Reporter*, February 25–March 3, 1998, 18.
28. King, *Speculations on the Economy and Roads at Galisteo*, pages not numbered.
29. Nicolás Pino was born Dec. 4, 1819, to Pedro Bautista Pino and Ana María Baca, was baptized Dec. 6, 1819, in Santa Fe, and died in 1896.
30. Marc Simmons, "Trail Dust: Settlers, towns, often subjected to raids in early New Mexico," *Santa Fe New Mexican*, Oct. 5, 2002, 9.
31. Clarita Anaya told this story from her mother, Carmelita (b. 1885). Similar tales were told all over the north; either it happened often or the story spread. Relations between Indians and Hispanos were different in each northern village.
32. Madrid, "Ciria's Tale and the Long Walk," 29.
33. See Kendall, *Narrative of the Texan Santa Fe Expedition*.
34. José Ortiz y Pino III, personal communication, 10/15/03. Another local version has La Loma Tejana named after a Texan who was killed there.
35. See Meketa, ed., *Legacy of Honor*. See also account in Sides, *Blood and Thunder*, with its unforgiving portrait of an obese and ethically challenged Armijo. Kearny's Gap was another name for the Piedra Lumbre Canyon.

36. Elliott, *Notes Taken in Sixty Years*, 241–42 n61, 243. These guns were found by Kearny's men and are now said to be in the collection of the Palace of the Governors in Santa Fe. A fourth "little cannon," dubbed "the Lone Star of Texas," had been presented to the State of Texas by "patriotic ladies" and was brought to New Mexico in 1841. It has since disappeared.
37. Ibid., 73.
38. State historian Rick Hendricks, personal communication, 2017. Sandoval was alcalde in 1841, but Hendricks could not say how long he served. His son Anastacio Sandoval (b. 1840) recalled that his father was in charge of Cadial crops and was paid "one *costal* of corn for each 50 varas of land [each grant]" in 1848–51 (Cadial book, 178–80).
39. Pancoast, *A Quaker Forty-Niner*, 214.
40. Elkus, "Galisteo: 1500–1900," 76, citing Stanley, *Galisteo, New Mexico Story*, 12. The protest was addressed to the governor, John Calhoun.
41. Turner, *The Original Journals of Henry Smith Turner*, 74–75. On August 28, Turner noted the arrival of "a large deputation of Mexicans" to swear allegiance to the United States. He deemed them "more respectable" than others—"less of the Indian tinge in their complexion."
42. Hughes, *Doniphan's Expedition*. He also observes (220) that Kearny imposed a tax collected at Galisteo on "each wagon or carriage." Elliott (*Notes Taken in Sixty Years*, 77), on the way to Galisteo, notes finding "four pieces of the petrified trunk of a tree, each piece about four feet long and eighteen inches in diameter, and the fractures apparently caused by the same violent effort of nature which has disturbed everything else in the neighborhood." This suggests that he was in the western Galisteo Basin, where years later, whole logs on the Sweet Ranch became something of a tourist destination. Petrified wood has also been found in Pueblo shrines in the Galisteo Basin (e.g., San Lázaro) from centuries earlier. See also Marc Simmons, "Petrified forests were spectacular findings for N.M. explorers," *Santa Fe New Mexican,* July 19, 2008.
43. Del Gardo (Delgado) is mentioned by several of these travelers; it was probably the ranch near Cerrillos owned by the Delgados, one of the families dominating the mining scene until 1879.
44. Ruxton, *Adventures in Mexico and the Rocky Mountains*, 185–93.
45. This probably referred to the southern creston near which coal mines were later established.
46. The story goes that it was the old Exchange Hotel, but Pino was more likely to be sitting in front of the Missouri House, a hotel he owned with John Abel in 1847; the Exchange was not so named until 1850.
47. Don Clemente Ortiz quoted in Twitchell, *Leading Facts of New Mexico*, 317.
48. Brooks, *Captives and Cousins*, 282.
49. In 1869 Nicolás Pino is listed as "a prosperous Galisteo landowner," and he is still living in Galisteo in 1884, though he is also consistently associated with La Ciénega.
50. Meinig, *Southwest*, 31.
51. Pancoast, *A Quaker Forty-Niner*, 212ff.
52. Meinig, *Southwest*, 37.
53. Pino was out and about during this period. In July 1857, he took a 5,375-mile steamship trip from San Francisco to New York, via Panama, carefully logging on a single page the ports (including Acapulco, Santo Domingo, and Cuba) and the distances traveled each day, but with no commentary.
54. In the abstracts for the McKee Ranch (124), there is a reference to Don Juan (Esteban) Pino, Nicolás's half-brother, having built two large houses on the Galisteo grant in 1856.
55. Vigil, "The Legacy of Our Land Grants," 8.
56. Kammer, *Application for Registration*, sec. 12, 20.
57. Andelecio (last name never mentioned), quoted in Graña, *Begoso Cabin*, 47.

58. Westphall, *Public Domain,* 20.
59. Ibid., 42.
60. Vigil, "The Legacy of Our Land Grants."
61. Marc Simmons, "Col. George McCall comes to the wild, unknown New Mexico Territory," *Santa Fe New Mexican*, May 3, 2003, 9, 11.
62. Diary of William Anderson Thornton (Baxter, "Cerrillos Area Names Database").
63. See McNitt, *Navajo Wars.*
64. See Bowden, "Private Land Claims in the Southwest," 276; and Westphall, *Mercedes*, 232, for more detailed and complex accounts of this deal. The property stretched from Las Lagunitas to Ojo de la Baca, southwest to the Bajada de los Comanches, then from "La Lagunita" to "a ledge of rocks known as the creston, on the north, and from said ledge . . . to Ojo de la Baca (including the spring) to the Bajada."
65. Juan Ortiz was a compadre of Ethan Eaton's, godfather of one of his children. Eaton was a colonel in the Civil War and captain in the New Mexico Volunteers, was involved with mining claims, and moved to Socorro when he sold San Cristóbal in 1874. In 1880 he was involved in a vigilante posse and lynching after a murder in Socorro. It has been suggested that he was a member of the Santa Fe Ring.
66. Anastacio Sandoval in 1909–15 legal proceedings (Cadial book, 222). Cañada de la Casita is where part owner of San Cristóbal Saron Laughlin built a house. In the early twentieth century, Benjamin Pankey, by then owner of San Cristóbal, bought a house and lands in Tacubaya from Agapito Sena.
67. Bowden, "Private Land Claims in the Southwest," 277.
68. Boundaries are arable lands "from the Mesita de las Lagunitas upward as far as the spring of La Vaca, the remainder of said arable lands in the same bottom and adjoining the said Mesita distributed in strips of 100 varas each from east to west." The settlers' lands "form a narrow strip not exceeding in any part ½ mile in width." This contradicts other descriptions of the Cadial as much larger (Cadial book, 291).
69. An October 20, 1940, letter from Don José Ortiz y Pino to Charles E. Minton (WPA #229) says that Lamy built "a church in 1854" four miles below Cañoncito/Ornas, which must be this "convent." Don José claimed to have a wooden cross made by the carpenter, Juan Lucero, who built this "church." Beams from the building were used in El Ortiz Harvey House.
70. See Kammer (*Application for Registration*, sec. 9, 6–10) for detailed descriptions of each contributing property in the village.
71. Agnew, *Garrisons of the Regular US Army, New Mexico, 1846–1899.*
72. Mednick, *San Cristóbal*, 157, quoting Anonymous, *An Illustrated History of New Mexico*, 1895, 268–69.
73. This is presumably the same "government post" mentioned in Galisteo in 1856–57 (Kammer, *Application for Registration*, 20, 23).
74. Elder and Weber, eds., *Trading in Santa Fe*, 262–63.
75. See Brugge, *Navajos in the Catholic Church Records of New Mexico, 1694–1875*. See also Reséndez; Brooks; Rael-Gálvez, *Identifying Captivity and Capturing Identity.*
76. However, as late as the 1960s, peonage was alive and well in isolated areas of the state (Marc Simmons, "Peonage lingered after its abolition in New Mexico," *Santa Fe New Mexican*, Feb. 20, 2016).
77. Joe Martínez, in a discussion organized by Anna Cárdenas at La Sala de Galisteo, July 12, 2015; personal communication, 2015.
78. Marc Simmons, "The celebrated 'ciboleros' hunted buffalo," *Santa Fe New Mexican*, Oct. 22, 2004.
79. Meinig, *Southwest*, 33. In 1870 the territorial government abolished the Comanchero trade, but it continued for several years, during which Texans took the law into their own hands, reclaim-

ing cattle from New Mexicans (Marc Simmons, "Texans' 1872 raid reclaimed stolen cattle from N.M.," *Santa Fe New Mexican*, March 5, 2016).

80. Brooks, *Captives and Cousins*, 315–16. See also Brown, *Hispano Folklife*, 49.
81. Meinig, *Southwest*, 37.
82. Marcy, *The Prairie Traveler*. The late Charles Hagerman told me that this route led past the Ojito de Galisteo (personal communication, 2008).
83. Marc Simmons, "Salt adds flavor to New Mexico's history," *Santa Fe New Mexican*, March 24, 2001, 13.
84. Elkus, "Galisteo: 1500–1900," 76.
85. Marc Simmons, "Salt adds flavor to New Mexico's history," *Santa Fe New Mexican*, March 24, 2001, 13.
86. According to John Benjamin, former owner of the main building at the Ortiz y Davis hacienda, personal communication, 2016.
87. Peticolas, *Rebels on the Rio Grande*, 74–75. By 1884, the date of the first photograph of the old church, it bears little resemblance to the Peticolas drawing. The window under the bell tower had been added. The façade appears to have been remodeled in the intervening twenty-two years. The side buildings were altered and crumbling. Peticolas's comment on the Battle of Glorieta Pass: "With few exceptions, including Col. Pino, they had little further interest in defending the territory" (53 n18).
88. John Benjamin tells me that he found "a Texan's account that drunken Sibley was in Galisteo until word of the battle came and then he hightailed it back to Albuquerque in the ambulance," personal communication, 2016.
89. Baxter, "Cerrillos Area Names Database," 1649. The Pino letter was estimated to be written in late 1860.
90. Ibid.
91. Sánchez, *In the Footsteps of an Educator*, 2–3. Josefa had a local reputation for exaggeration.
92. Cadial book, 119, 120.
93. John Benjamin (personal communications over the years and email, 6/8/18). This is still a possibility as the site of the later Galisteo is marked on an undated map as "azienda." When remodeling the hacienda, which he bought in 1987, Benjamin did a detailed analysis of the structure's walls, determining that the 28-foot west stone wall is a Spanish original, as are the lintels, which he contends could mean that the building was much earlier than the garrison. He estimates that the large front room, also apparently Spanish, had 12-foot ceilings, while one bedroom was part of the original zaguan. The east wall of the front room of the hacienda, which he believes could be ca. 1846, is 18-inch adobe and has ax-cut vigas. Kammer locates it "ca. 1800–1870," noting the possible late-eighteenth-century barracks and the possibility that "subsequent construction may have added to that defensive nucleus over the next half century. Many of the details apparent today, particularly the pedimented windows and doors and transoms, suggest the influence of American builders [after 1846]" (Kammer, *Application for Registration*, sec. 9, 9).
94. Another possible scenario was reported by Mary W. Coan ("La Corrida del Gallo in Galisteo," 16). She was told by Josefa Davis that "as a shy young bride of fourteen, she came to the house built for her by the American from Boston." She was not yet a bride when the family moved to Galisteo in 1865.
95. John Benjamin, personal communication, 2016. He has also found what he believes to be Masonic symbolism in and around the compound.
96. José Francisco (son of Juan Antonio Ortiz and María de Loreto de Ribera, baptized July 22, 1787) was said to be a fifth-generation descendant of Mariana Coronado and Nicolas Ortiz I. On Feb. 20, 1808, Ortiz married María Ynes/Inez Montoya, aka Maraquita Montoya. In 1812, he was an officer in a campaign against the Navajo in retaliation for the depredation of farms and ranches

in the Rio Grande valley. He was said to own five houses, a ranch at Abiquiú, and at least 14,000 pesos, as well as the Ortiz land grant. He is also occasionally referred to as José Francisco Juan Nepomuceno Ortiz. Deceased siblings' names were sometimes added to those still living, and he appears to have had a brother named Juan Nepomuceno (baptized May 1805, also the son of Juan Antonio de Jesús Ortiz and María Loreta Ribera).

97. José Francisco's wife was the sole beneficiary of his estate, and vice versa (Townley, "Mining in the Ortiz Mine," 58 n22, citing Gildersleeve v. NM Mining Co., 307). "No living heirs" is repeated several times in other documents (Baxter, *Gold and the Ortiz Mine Grant*, 4). Nancy Ligon de Ita's Ortiz y Pino genealogy notes the lack of a son but suggests that "perhaps the sudden riches caused family problems."
98. The Olmsted Ortiz y Pino genealogy says Juan (no birthdate) is son of José Francisco Juan Nepomuceno Ortiz and María Ygnes Montoya and he had a sister who died as an infant. The 1850 census lists a Juan Ortiz, "servant, 35 years old, illiterate, b. ca. 1815," living in Santa Fe with Maraquita Montoya Ortiz, José Francisco's widow, b. ca. 1800, illiterate, and worth $11,000. But our Juan Grande (also in the 1850 census) is a "farmer" age 34, married to Paula, age 23, with children Antonio José, age 7, and Cayetano, age 3 (Olmsted, *The Ortiz Family of New Mexico*, 13, 19, 43).
99. María Paula Ortiz y Martín (aka Paubla Ortiz de Ortiz or Paula Ortiz y Martinez de Ortiz, 33 in 1860 census but baptized in 1821), daughter of Ygnacio Ortiz and Lus Martín (ibid., 43).
100. Luz (b. ca. 1848) may not have lived. Susano Ortiz, who lived in San Pedro and Golden, had a checkered history. He was appointed a judge in 1884, and in 1891 he made a profitable gold strike. But in 1894–95 he (or someone with the same name) was described as "a known criminal," twice convicted of sheep stealing, and "a character who ha[d] long infested Santa Fe County" (Baxter, "Cerrillos Area Names Database," 2248–49).
101. Birth dates differ in different censuses and documents. John Benjamin believes Cayetano lived in the back of the hacienda in a sort of "dungeon" with a latrine, which he has identified.
102. Córdova, *¡Concha!*, 13.
103. According to one descendant, Concepción was the "only recognized wife" of Juan Ortiz. But he refers in a trial testimony to his wife Margarita.
104. José Ortiz y Pino III, *Curandero*, 13.
105. The marriage announcement also said that Davis had been living in Galisteo for three years, e.g., 1865.
106. The Native blood could have been from her father, Juan Grande, or from further back.
107. Sánchez, *In the Footsteps*, 1.
108. Córdova, *¡Concha!*, 9.
109. The records are contradictory; 1838 is another purported birth date, and his birthplace is variously listed as Concord, MA; Manchester, NH; and Missouri.
110. Sánchez, *In the Footsteps*, 2. One pair of "Spanish" earrings designed by her grandmother was in Victoria Davis de Sánchez's possession. There is a photograph of Josefa's young daughter Pablita Davis wearing "the first gold necklace from the Ortiz Mountains mine," a mine owned by Josefa's putative grandfather.
111. George married Angelita Chávez from the Pecos area. Victoria Sánchez was one of their children and they had two sons named Sylvester; one died at 8 months and the other at age 28.
112. Branches of the Ortizes and Pinos had intermarried for generations, but it seems no one had previously adopted the name Ortiz y Pino.
113. Davis, *Diary of Sylvester Davis*, 413, 415. "Captain" Davis apparently did not fight in the Civil War, having come west before it began. One source labels him a deserter, while another claims he served in "regiment 98." Although it is sometimes assumed that Captain Davis Mountain to the

west of Galisteo was named after Sylvester, the actual namesake was Captain Nathan S. Davis, who built railroads in the Ortiz mining district.

114. Another account says that Davis passed through Galisteo en route to Chilili, where he built and ran a sawmill (Baxter, "Cerrillos Area Names Database," 5019). He was recorded as living in Chilili in 1859.
115. According to John Benjamin's notes on conversations with his granddaughter, Audrey Phillips, Manuel Stevens (aka Stevenson, see ch. 4, n6; the census spelling may have been inaccurate) was an overseer at the Ortiz y Davis hacienda. He carried a white cane and owned gold mines and lots of property. When he died in 1913, Josefa refused to let Bluebell notify his family and burned letters he wrote.
116. King, *Speculations on the Economy,* pages not numbered. By 1864 there was a military freight route running from Galisteo to Fort Stanton via the Estancia Basin.

Chapter 3

1. Cannon, "The Perils of the Humanities or How I Became Human," 36.
2. Quoted in García, "La Lucha Es Tu Herencia (The Struggle Is Your Inheritance)."
3. Swadesh, *Los Primeros Pobladores*, 69.
4. In 1998/2001, Senator Jeff Bingaman and Representative Tom Udall introduced legislation to establish a presidential commission to evaluate the validity of the Guadalupe Hidalgo land claims, but it failed to pass.
5. Swadesh, *Los Primeros Pobladores*, 69. 6.
6. Elkus, "Galisteo: 1500–1900," 68.
7. Testimony of Agapito Sena, Nov. 20, 1877 (Baca y Terrus file; Case #57, file 136; claim May 16, 1841).
8. See Benavides, "Lawyer-Induced Partitioning of New Mexico Land Grants," 9.
9. Swadesh, *Los Primeros Pobladores*, 70.
10. Westphall, *Public Domain*, 50. Congress could take as long as 36 years to clarify land titles (ibid., 51).
11. Ibid.
12. Elkus, "Galisteo: 1500–1900," 68.
13. Westphall, *Public Domain,* 53ff.
14. Vioalle Heffernan, quoted in Quintana, *Pobladores II*, 91. Between 1869 and 1917 Catron was the New Mexico attorney general, a state legislator, a US attorney, and a US senator.
15. Westphall, *Mercedes Reales*, 236
16. Lummis, *Letters from the Southwest,* 146.
17. Ibid., 103.
18. Otero, in his memoir, *My Life on the Frontier,* quoted in Marc Simmons, "Santa Fe Ring Remains an Enigma," *Santa Fe New Mexican*, Nov. 3, 2007. His father, prominent merchant M. A. Otero, was also an enemy of the Ring.
19. Lew Wallace, 1897 letter, quoted in Baxter, *Gold and the Ortiz Mine*, 106.
20. Westphall, *Public Domain*, 24ff. Among the suspects was Antonio Ortiz y Salazar, who owned a ranch on the Arroyo "Chora" (probably the Arroyo Chorro, near San Lázaro Pueblo in the western Galisteo Basin).
21. Ibid., 112–13.
22. Baxter, "Cerrillos Area Names Database," 1926.
23. Westphall, *Public Domain*, 31.
24. Quoted in Vigil, "The Legacy of Our Land Grants," 8.
25. Westphall, *Public Domain*, 33.

26. Frank Springer, quoted in a review of David Caffey's *Frank Springer and New Mexico* in the *Santa Fe New Mexican*, April 6, 2006.
27. Marc Simmons, "Vigilante movement began in Socorro," *Santa Fe New Mexican*, Aug. 5, 2006. During the Civil War, Eaton was a colonel in charge of Fort Wingate.
28. By 1885 the census for the combined villages of Galisteo and Cerrillos counted only 349 people, which may simply have been due to a lazy census taker.
29. Elkus, "Galisteo: 1500–1900," 77–78. The 1880 Production of Agriculture Census listed 34 farm owners in the Galisteo District with only 5 of them worth over $1,000. Nine farmers owned flocks of sheep between 500 and 1,500 and all listed high losses.
30. From 1866 to 1870 he was postmaster of the Juana López grant in the western Galisteo Basin, where the Pinos also owned land.
31. Elkus, "Galisteo: 1500–1900," 78. There is no information on how it was water powered on a creek as small and usually slow moving as the Galisteo, although in those days conditions may have been better. See Marc Simmons, "Technology grounds millers' job into history," *Santa Fe New Mexican*, May 21, 2016.
32. Ambrocio Pino, baptized Dec. 8, 1834, was the son of María Josefa Ortiz and Manuel Doroteo Pino. He married Trinidad de Pino and died young. Don Miguel E. Pino, who was also involved in the Pecos land grants and mining around Dolores, was called in his obituary "the greatest statesman of his day." He died of stomach cancer in 1867, at age 45, leaving no children. Facundo, married to Virgina Pino, died Jan. 28, 1863, "aged about forty years." Another son, Germán, is mentioned but was in La Ciénega and less involved in Galisteo, although he apparently owned land in the Cadial at some point.
33. Steele, "Galisteo," 27–28.
34. Coan, 16. According to a typescript by Lorin W. Brown dated 1939, "October 22nd [was] the date of the annual feast day observed by the villagers of Galisteo to honor their patron saint, Nuestra Señora de los Remedios." The festivities traditionally featured a *corrida del gallo*, or rooster pull.
35. Cadial book, 352.
36. Five Acts of Possession were filed: #58, 616, 892, 893, and 894. Twitchell (*Spanish Archives*, vol. 1, 266) mentions two 1822 documents, part of the 1814 Galisteo grant to Matías Sandoval, Rafael Sena, and Felipe Sandoval, all denied because of Maynez dates. Donaciano Vigil testified that the town had been there since 1790 or 1795, when a house for troops was built; the military left in 1814 when the grant was made by Governor Alberto Maynez to individuals he then named. Vigil, who was also a political player, testified that he knew Maynes personally in 1814 when he made the grant to Galisteo (though he was only around 12 years old), and he claimed to have seen the original grant in 1831–32 in the ayuntamiento office when he worked there. However, he testified that the document offered by the claimants was not identical to the one he had seen; it was only a copy of the "alleged original." And Trinidad Barcelo held no office until 1846.
37. According to the remaining documents, Maynes was *gobernador interino* (acting governor) in 1808 when the position was taken over by José Manrique. One Ysidro Rey was briefly governor in 1814, but by the end of the year he is again just "Captain." There is an incomprehensible reference to Maynes in November 1814 and by February 1815 he is again interim governor. Some sources say he was governor in 1814, and others contradict it. Clearly there was a good deal of switching around in 1814 and it is certainly plausible that Maynes had the power to award the Galisteo grant, at least verbally. Agustín Durán testified that Maynez (maybe) succeeded Alencaster and was governor about the year 1814 or 1815 (Cadial book, 351).
38. Cadial book, 350.

39. Case #16, approved by an Act of Congress June 21, 1860.
40. Surveyor General's Records, file 1318, Case 16, microfilm roll 19, July 20, 1871.
41. Mednick, *San Cristóbal*, 196.
42. Though the AT&SF changed its corporate composition many times over the years, this railroad held various rights and interests to the coal at Madrid from 1892 to at least 1938. (See Baxter, *Gold and the Ortiz Mine.*) To the west of Kennedy, after 1881, was Ortiz Station—a sheep-loading corral and siding platform near La Gotera grant—and the elusive "town" of Ortiz, 2.5 miles north of San Lázaro Pueblo. In 1925 it had a chapel that was a mission of Peña Blanca and a schoolhouse patented by Antonio Ortiz y Salazar. Some schoolteachers in the 1920s were said to be from Galisteo. Two village elders have recalled lending the Galisteo church's bulto of San José to the chapel at Ortiz for religious occasions.
43. Tórrez, *UFOs Over Galisteo and Other Stories of New Mexico's History*, 112–14.
44. *New Mexican*, Nov. 9, 1880. For a detailed account, see Stanley (*Galisteo, New Mexico Story*, 16), who mistakenly places the wreck at Galisteo rather than Galisteo Junction.
45. Mednick, *San Cristóbal*, 163.
46. Baxter, "Cerrillos Area Names Database," 83.
47. Ibid., 1090, 262. These rocks may have been garnered from Pueblo ruins at both sites.
48. Mednick, *San Cristóbal*, 163.
49. There seems to have been little or no Asian population until the railroad and its Chinese workers came through; after 1880 there were several Asians living in the railroad towns of Cerrillos, Santa Fe, and Las Vegas, but not in Galisteo.
50. In May 1880, during the Boomtown era, a hotel was built in Carbonateville (aka Turquesa, settled 1879); water was brought five miles from Bonanza. "The long-established control of the Cerrillos galena mines by the Delgado and Pino families was shaken in 1869 when their claim of a Mexican Land Grant was disallowed" (Baxter, "Cerrillos Area Names Database," 305, 342).
51. Baxter, "Cerrillos Area Names Database," 1884.
52. *The Cerrillos Rustler*, owned by M. D. Lattia, was edited for ten years by F. C. Russell. In November 1893, Lattia started the short-lived *Galisteo Valley Democrat*.
53. Bandelier, *Southwestern Journals 1880–1882*, vol. 2, 254.
54. Baxter, "Cerrillos Area Names Database," 171 (Bennett), 173 n264 (Brown), and 449 (Craycraft).
55. Marc Simmons, "Estancia Valley land fight led to fatal shooting," *Santa Fe New Mexican*, June 7, 2014. This joke is ubiquitous in Western folklore.
56. Baxter, "Cerrillos Area Names Database," 364.
57. Ibid., 1243.
58. Ibid., 1549.
59. *New Mexican*, June 24, 1903; July 28, 1903.
60. Thanks to Luis Chávez. Sarapio Montoya told me that the man was not from Galisteo (personal communication, 1993). La Sociedad de Bandidos de Nuevo México, with thirty to forty members, had a hideout in the mountains of Santa Fe. The Ojo del Monte Largo gang broke up when Silva stabbed his wife.
61. "The Story of Galisteo Church," Sept. 11, 1983, file #137.
62. Bandelier, *Southwestern Journals*, vol. 2.
63. Unattributed, undated, typed sheet about Nuestra Señora de los Remedios, Archdiocese of Santa Fe, Office of Historic-Artistic Patrimony and Archives. Josefa Ortiz y Davis also claimed that the painting had been in the seventeenth-century Galisteo Pueblo church and was taken to Santo Domingo, then brought back to Galisteo in 1706. This seems doubtful, as it confuses the Tano

people's final exodus to Santo Domingo in 1782 with their resettlement of Tanuge after the Reconquest. A 1921 photo of the church interior shows none of these images, so Josefa Ortiz y Davis presumably still had them in "safe keeping." (See chapter 4.)

64. The crucifixion shows cattails and reeds at one side, a column at the left with a cock on top of it, a sacred heart under a cross, a hand and an arm reaching from the left. Nuestra Señora de la Begoña was the patron saint of Bilbao in Vizcaya, Spain, painted by the Franciscans in the late 1700s after a 1608 engraving of her statue. See Boyd, *Popular Arts of Spanish New Mexico*, 121, 130, 132.
65. José Ortiz y Pino III, personal communication, ca. 1998.
66. Chris Wilson, interview on KUNM FM (Albuquerque), Feb. 10, 2012; Wilson and Polyzoides, *The Plazas of New Mexico*, 3, 5.
67. Current brochure for Cerrillos Hills Park; see also Baxter, *Gold and the Ortiz Mine* and *The Gold of the Ortiz*; Patricia McGraw, *Tiffany Blue*.
68. Westphall, *Public Domain*, 75. In 1891 the Timber Culture Act, which was very unsuccessful in New Mexico, was repealed.
69. Ibid., 24, 51ff.
70. Ibid., 81. In 1885–87 livestock losses were as high as 90 percent (Merlan, *Historic Homesteads and Ranches in New Mexico*, 12).
71. Nicolás Pino, quoted in "Galisteo's Prosperity," *New Mexican,* June 18, 1884, 4.
72. Bandelier, *Southwestern Journals 1889–1892*, vol. 4, 84.
73. Marc Simmons, "N.M. Fence Varieties Grew from Necessity," *Santa Fe New Mexican*, July 28, 2007.
74. Merlan, *Historic Homesteads and Ranches in New Mexico*, ix. Merlan's report is an invaluable compendium of information on agriculture, ranching, and settlement.
75. Mass production of barbed wire began in 1873; in 1877, use was fifteen times that of 1876 and usage doubled in every subsequent year. See Razac, *Barbed Wire*.
76. Arellano, "The Never-Ending Land Grant Struggle," 16. See also Larson, "The White Caps of New Mexico." Lloyd Rivera, another Gorras Blancas scholar, from Mora County, informs me that Juan José Herrera was a captain in the Union Army and an Indian agent: "Around 1864 or so . . . he became aware of Captain William Quantrill's C.S.A. riders, who donned white hoods to conceal their identities on daytime raids. . . . By 1880 the A.T.S.F. Railway of Kansas had reached Las Vegas! Herrera was shocked that open grazing lands, forests, and waterways were fenced off by barbed wire! He mobilized 1,800 riders from San Miguel and Mora Counties in defense of their homelands and land grants. From Pecos to Galisteo and Bernalillo, *los gorrones* conducted raids, and at La Cueva by Mora they cut seven miles of barbwire fences at the Phoenix Ranch & Cattle Company. Up by Roy, they destroyed several miles of fencing at the Wilson Waddingham Ranch, plus others cut fences at the village of San Geronimo near Las Vegas. . . . They were and are resistance fighters and are omitted from history, have been down-trodden, when in reality are true heroes! LAND! Tierra y Justicia! is still our heart! Their struggles have freed the entanglements of newcomers. They are LAND-BASED FREEDOM FIGHTERS" (Lloyd Rivera, personal communication, 12/20/18).
77. Bandelier, *Southwestern Journals*, vol. 4, 125, 525 n800.
78. Reprinted in Spanish in Arellano, "The Never-Ending Land Grant Struggle," 16, author's translation. See also Graybill, "A Shot in the Dark."
79. Ambrocio Pino was postmaster from 1876 and Davis took over in 1879. Josefa may have inherited the post when he died in 1913. In 1882 there were complaints that there was no post office at Galisteo; the closest one was in Glorieta, fourteen miles away.
80. Sánchez, *In the Footsteps*, 2.
81. Photos from the 1930s show a low picket fence around the hacienda; the earlier adobe wall was reinstated by later owners.

82. Córdova, *¡Concha!*, 29. According to the Assessment lists, many local Hispano families were wealthier than the Davises. In the 1870 census the Davis land was worth $600, and their personal property $500. Francisco Leyva, age 23, owned land worth $500 and personal property worth $2,000. It is not clear when the Leybas, whose fortunes continued to be healthy, arrived in Galisteo, but they were also involved in business ventures in the western basin.
83. On legal documents, women's names were often given in the diminutive.
84. Córdova, *¡Concha!*, 29.
85. Kammer, *Application for Registration*, sec. 12, 21. The "Mayoralgo tract" owned by Don José may be the area on the south side of the current Via La Puente owned by Don José and eventually by Priscilla Hoback.
86. Ortiz y Pino, *Don José: The Last Patrón*, 40. Many homes were already built on the land.
87. Steele, "Galisteo," 29.
88. David Snow notes that a Pueblo man told him "that his grandma at Pecos remembered Santo Domingos with carts full of fruit and pots for sale as far as Las Vegas" (personal communication, 2018).
89. Córdova, *¡Concha!*, 28.
90. José Ortiz y Pino III, personal communication, ca. 1998. Twitchell (*History of Military Occupation*, 310) also says that he is buried in Galisteo.
91. Mednick, *San Cristóbal*, 166. Her book is the source for much of the following information.
92. N. B. Laughlin, grandfather of Santa Fe resident/Realtor Laughlin Barker, was headed to Colorado to mine gold after the Civil War but "ran out of money near Galisteo" and stayed in Santa Fe to become a landowner in the area.
93. See Westphall, *Mercedes Reales*, 233.
94. Bowden, "Private Land Claims in the Southwest," 279.
95. Mednick, *San Cristóbal*, 196. Tacubaya followed the same legal trajectory as the Cadial. In the early twentieth century, Agapito Sena and his wife, Refugio Madril, lived on Tacubaya.
96. Bowden, "Private Land Claims in the Southwest," 280ff.
97. Ibid.
98. Mednick, *San Cristóbal*, 168.
99. Cadial book, 232.
100. Ibid., 184, 219. Anastacio Sandoval was former alcalde and member of the Santa Fe ayuntamiento, then territorial adjutant general and auditor. There was an Anastacio in many Sandoval generations, including my late contemporary in Galisteo, whose nickname was Tacho.
101. Agapito Sena was a "principal witness." Those whose names led the petition were all relatively wealthy and powerful landowners.
102. Mednick, *San Cristóbal*, 168.
103. Ramon Chávez, Demetrio Leyba, Alexandro Mora, Franco Leyba, Juan Ortiz, Nicolás Pino, Juan Bta. Larranaga, Marcelino Varos, Silvestre Davis, Rafael Ortiz y Pineda, Juan José Silba, Canuto Leyba, Jesús Gil Sandoval, Agapito Sena, José Chávez, Juan Lucero, Jesús M. Sena y Baca, Pedro Peña, Antonio J. Ortiz, José de la Cruz Chávez, Luis Griego, and Ambrocio Pino (but not Luciano Cháves).
104. Cadial book, 490.
105. Ibid., 253.
106. Kammer, *Application for Registration*, sec. 12, 19.
107. José Manuel Sandoval stated four days later that he knew the Cadial strips "before they were allotted . . . under the Mexican government," suggesting that the settlers were farming there before the papers went through. Four Galisteo claims don't appear to be decided, even one to the powerful Nicolás Pino (Elkus, "Galisteo: 1500–1900," 70). Others were rejected out of hand despite evidence to the contrary (Elkus, 65ff).

108. José Ortiz y Pino testified in 1915 that there had been no crops in the preceding two years but they had cut hay every year (Cadial book, 98).
109. Ibid., 233, 152.
110. Ibid., 208.
111. Ibid., 51, 103, 191–96.
112. Ibid., 191–94.
113. Westphall, *Mercedes Reales*, 233.
114. Kammer, *Application for Registration*, sec. 12, 25.
115. Among them in 1893–94 were F. Chávez de Montoya, Apolonio Chávez, Ascención Chávez, M. Pino, and Sylvester Davis.
116. Baxter, "Cerrillos Area Names Database," 1182, 1183: Justiniano Leyba was listed in the 1905–06 business directory as proprietor of a general merchandise store and a saloon, ruins of which were visible until recently on CR 42.
117. Vigil, "The Legacy of Our Land Grants." Different figures have also been reported, but the gist is the same.
118. Swadesh, *Los Primeros Pobladores*, 68, 70.
119. Steele, "Galisteo," 32. Prince was governor from 1889 to 1893.
120. José Abel Anaya's first wife died; his second wife, Simona Baros (Simona García's aunt), inherited nine children and had four more of her own.
121. The original grant had nineteen grantees, and there is no explanation as to what happened to the other two.
122. The people living there in 1821 were Felipe Sandoval, Luis Lovato, Julian Lucero, José Antonio Sandoval (alias Bachicha) and others Durán could not recall in an 1871 trial. These are also among the names appearing both on the standard Galisteo grant map of 1899 (#1) and on the slightly different map (#2). Bachicha is on #2 and not others; Julian Lucero is José Lucero on map #1; other names and acreages diverge slightly. In the most common version of these conflicting maps, recorded names and acreages, reading from west to east: Pesa(?) Sandoval, 8.40 acres; Miguel Lovato, 13.44 acres; Jesús Benavides, 17.65 acres; José Baca, 17.85 acres; Manuel Trujillo, 17.34 acres; Rafael Sena, 16.53 acres; José Antonio Bachicha [noted elsewhere "aka Sandoval"], 16.29 acres; Miguel Roybal, 16.06 acres; Diego Pineda, 15.97 acres; José Antonio Alarid, 14.69 acres; Bartolo Lovato, 12.99 acres; José Lucero, 12.80 acres; Felipe Sandoval, 21.20 acres [on both sides of Galisteo Creek, as are the following]; Matías Sandoval, 17.54 acres; Luis Lovato, 17.56 acres; Ignacio Chávez, 17.55 acres; and Rafael Luján, 8.92 acres. (Most of these people were on the original 1814 grant and had been long deceased.) This drastically reduced remainder of the original grant excluded the plaza, spring, and shared grazing land—which would be the Cadial to the east, still confused and unconfirmed in the courts as part of the original Galisteo grant. No house sites on The Hill are included, although in various trial transcripts there are references to houses on the suertes below.
123. At one point the Loya/Miguel Pino Ranch is said to *be* the Galisteo grant, about 500 acres (McKee abstract, 121–25). In the 1870s it is called Rancho de Galisteo. In 1901 the court "inadvertently" determined that "the Galisteo Ranch is a part of the Galisteo Grant, when the fact is that the two names have at all times been interchangeably used and designate the same place."
124. Today the area between San Cristóbal Arroyo and Galisteo Creek is owned by Ferneau, Lippard, and the Cerro Pelón Ranch, with a sliver belonging to a McKee heir. In 1954, the boundaries were described as a stone in the southeast corner, and a stone in the northeast corner (on land across present-day NM 41, now owned by Quartermill Farm).
125. Steele ("Galisteo," 27) locates the Rancho de Galisteo as north of the village when purchased by Ambrocio Pino in 1846, but it is also identified as the Galisteo grant. Bergere was the daughter

of Don José Chávez y Castillo. Her first husband was Manuel B. Otero, who was shot in a land dispute, after which she married Alfred Bergere. They were represented by A. B. Renehan (1869–1928), a criminal lawyer from whose papers these accounts were taken (Eloisa Luna de Bergere v. Luciano Chávez, decided Dec. 8, 1913, Renehan-Gilbert Papers, papers 111 and 113, New Mexico State Records Center and Archives).

126. Chávez lost the case against De Bergere and in August 1906 he appealed. In 1913, the suit was still dragging on, with Renehan still the defense lawyer T. B. Catron was involved in a 1902 motion for a new trial. These cases aroused passions and feuds among the villagers. Scribbled in a different hand on a reference to the 1871 Cadial trial is "BIG FAT LIAR S.C. de la C." And it is noted that Jesús María Sena, known as "Crooked-Nose Jesus," was said to have frozen to death, drunk.

127. The documents, which go back to 1820, show a bewildering succession of sales of fragments of the tract to a parade of different people, many with similar names and most of them recognizably from Galisteo. Among them are tenants who owned or inherited thirds and halves of the property.

128. Territorial Supreme Court Records, Feb. 19, 1902.

129. The new tank was 500 feet wide and 8 or 9 feet high. Romberg owned two houses, one on The Hill and one below, which was formerly Luis Griego's at Tanque Viejo (ibid.). Control of floods from this no longer dammed arroyo remains an unsolved problem, as proven by a "tornadic event" in the fall of 2017 that flooded houses below. Members of the Anaya family own land that was once classified as floodplain, which did not allow buildings, but several houses exist there today.

Chapter 4

1. Decades later, when his fortunes ebbed, he opened a store and a cantina in his compound, where he also oversaw an extensive orchard.
2. King, *Speculations on the Economy* (pages not numbered). Goats were used to help with herding as they were smarter than sheep, and nanny goats would nurse orphan lambs.
3. Simmons, *Coronado's Land*, 95. He also writes that most herders were not educated and could not count beyond the fingers on their hands, a disadvantage when counting for buyers or patrons. Some used bags of stones for the count; others included one black goat as a *marcadero* (marker) for every 100 sheep.
4. King (*Speculations on the Economy*) cites a 1902 blueprint for the entire length of the Santa Fe Central showing homesteads (160, 143, and 80 acres) on each side of the track (now on La Jara and Cerro Pelón ranches) granted to Rafael Ortiz y Salazar, Abel Pino, Camito Leyba, George Howland, C. M. Cooke, and Anastacio Trujillo—none recognizably Galistean residents.
5. Among the culvert signatures, occasionally dated, are Sylvester Davis (1910), Audrey Stevens Phillips and Manuel Stevens (1924), L. Chávez, O. Gonzales, B. Mares, Tony Anaya (1947), and Pedro Peña. The Kennedy Depot was eventually moved to the Simpson Ranch and became the El Dorado Community Center.
6. José Ortiz y Pino III, *Curandero*, 39. La lanera's pitched roof, one of the earliest in the village, was added in the 1930s. The corrugated roof/ceiling of terne metal is marked in numerous places on the inside as American Sheet & Tin Co. Pittsburgh. Patented May 1915. La lanera was in use for storage until around 1950, and today is the home of painter Harmony Hammond, who has retained the ceiling signatures. See *El Puente*, Summer 2001, for details.
7. Fayette Jones in deBuys, *Enchantment and Exploitation*, 158.
8. Swadesh, *Los Primeros Pobladores*, 205.
9. Nelson, "Camp Life in New Mexico," 19. See also Mednick, *San Cristóbal*, 200.
10. See Lippard, *Down Country*, 41–42, 110.

11. Dutton awoke those slumbering sites in the 1950s, working in partnership with the Girl Scouts of America. In 1956 she discovered the site LA333, on US 285, believed to have been built as early as 1204–24. For a brief period she owned a home in Galisteo, on The Hill.
12. Nelson, "Camp Life in New Mexico," 21. I was hoping for some local names to surface in Nelson's letters and reports, but no luck, and no one in the village seems to remember anything about that period. Little is known of Nelson's relationship with his workers since even his foreman is unnamed in letters. My attempts to find Ethelyn's letters to her family from this period—on the assumption that women are more likely to talk about people—were unsuccessful.
13. Brown, *Hispano Folklife*, 91.
14. Ibid., 93.
15. Ibid. On Pankey, see also Burchill, *Lady of the Canyon*, 25–26. I do not know of any other documentation of this find. However, in the mid 2000s, Forrest Fenn, a Santa Fe art and antiquities dealer and owner of the San Lázaro Pueblo ruins, buried his own treasure with much fanfare. After several deaths and injuries, it has yet to be found. Among the buried valuables is a Spanish ring found at San Cristóbal.
16. Sánchez, *In the Footsteps*, 3.
17. José Ortiz y Pino III, *Curandero*, 22.
18. Córdova, *¡Concha!*, 12.
19. Simona García, personal communication, as in numerous following quotes. I interviewed García extensively for several years, from 1999 to her death. As a child, Concha lived in Santa Fe but spent time in Galisteo.
20. Sánchez (*In the Footsteps*, 26ff) called Bluebell her "grandmother's helper." (Córdova spells her name Bluebelle in *¡Concha!*, but I have chosen the spelling used by others.)
21. Her grandmother's "home was always open to everybody," Concha recalled, including a woman who was part Black and part Plains Indian (Dahl, "Concha Oriz y Pino de Kleven Interview," 7–9).
22. Two other African American girls were also apparently adopted by Pedro Ortiz y Pino. Adela is pictured at her 1926 wedding (Córdova, *¡Concha!*, 92, 95).
23. José Villanueva's family later lived in the Baros house next to the bosque. Martina Anaya Villanueva also taught at the school. In the early 1970s, Roman Attenberger bought the property from Emma Villanueva and Sophie Begay, daughters of Juanita and Pino Villanueva. The land was originally part of the San Cristóbal/Eaton grant.
24. Nicolás López to Lorin Brown, Aug. 11, 1937, in Weigle, *New Mexicans in Cameo and Camera*, 11.
25. I inaccurately cited this document in *El Puente*, Dec. 1998, as "a letter from Teddy Roosevelt." In a letter to the editor (*El Puente*, April 1999), then Galistean Patrick Mehaffy noted that it was a copy from the General Land Office Patent book; the president's signature was automatically attached to all such documents.
26. Santa Fe County Deed Book, vol. 776, 212. (See also Kammer, *Application for Registration*, sec. 12, 19–20.) Mehaffy estimated that the patent was bounded by "A) the north boundary of the Galisteo Grant, B) by the land west of a north-south line roughly along the back of the existing church, C) the land east [of] a north-south line near the eastern boundary of the Ranchitos de Galisteo subdivision, and D) everything south of a line somewhere near the Pattons' north boundary" (letter to the author, Feb. 22, 1997). John Benjamin (email to the author, 9/3/16) says this area included an acequia and some of the fields below The Hill.
27. Kammer, *Application for Registration*, sec. 12, 20.
28. Martínez was a "public official" (a probate judge in 1904 and 1908) and was known as "a professional witness" in mining cases in the 1880s. On Feb. 1, 1893, a Candelario Martínez was charged with adultery with a ten-year-old victim and was sentenced to three years in prison. But by 1895 he was running for district attorney. In 1899 he requested a military pension.

29. Patrick Mehaffy, personal communications, Feb. 1997. The Township 13 plot seems, perhaps coincidentally, to cover land now owned by the community.
30. Mednick, *San Cristóbal*, 169.
31. They all died between 1911 and 1913; this is testimony from the later trial.
32. Cadial book, 266–71.
33. Ibid., 270.
34. Ibid., 184.
35. Mednick, *San Cristóbal*, 193ff.
36. Ibid., 195–97, accounts of the disputes.
37. Anastacio Sandoval, Cadial book, 207. It was not until ca. 1946 that the "exception" was solved in favor of the villagers whose homes had been there for close to a century.
38. Cadial book, 37–38, 43, 40.
39. Librado Valencia testified that his father, Antonio, held a suerte on the Cadial and that he (Librado) was a member of the New Mexico legislature in 1884 when he received a petition from Galisteans asking that the Cadial be fenced to keep San Cristóbal stock away from their crops. Senator T. B. Catron backed this bill, and it passed.
40. In the introduction to the proceedings on April 30, 1909, it was noted that "within the out-boundary lines of the said Eaton Grant . . . said Cadial Tract was at some time prior to the final decree hereinbefore referred to, fenced, which said fence, through the course of time, ha[d] fallen down in parts" (Cadial book, 12–13.)
41. Cadial book, 93. Silva, who was eighty-five at the time, had lived in Galisteo forty-five years and was a major player in many of these grants and land sales. He was the son of José Ignacio Silva and related to the Lobatos. Pankey's interpreter on these occasions was Teodocio Montoya.
42. Ibid., 98.
43. Ibid., 97, 218.
44. Defendants were Antonio [José] Ortiz, Antonio Anaya, Juan José Silva, Apolonio Chávez, Luciano Chávez (who died that year), Sylvester Davis, Juan Ortiz, Donisiano Angel, José Ortiz y Pino, Pedro Chávez, and Antonio Sandoval.
45. Pankey's lawyer (Cadial book, 31) described the disputed area (Cadial) as 3,100 varas, 50 varas each to 62 grantees—around 9,300 feet from east to west. The location of the Cañada de en Medio became a key point of contention.
46. Case #6470, "Benjamin Pankey v. Juan Ortiz et al.," 1890, law firm of Catron, Knabel, and Clancy.
47. The Eaton grant patent has the Cadial tract east of its western boundary: "the west end of the Cadial tract is about one half on the east of that western surveyed line," around 7,500 total acres, according to the plaintiffs (Cadial book, 335).
48. Individual trials were not apparently followed up, although on April 2, 1915, a part of the trial was devoted to José Ortiz y Pino as defendant.
49. Ambrocio Pino to Juan Ortiz, 1910, eleven suertes (Cadial book, 31, 139). C. C. Catron says it was to raise money for this suit. Juan Ortiz also owned land in Puerto de Luna and noted in 1915, "my son José who is in charge of all my business" (ibid., 122).
50. Ibid., 23. There was also a controversy about "unknown heirs" of Ignacio Chávez and Ignacio Armenta.
51. Ibid., 98.
52. Ibid., "Conclusions of Law," 565–80. It is difficult to determine what the outcome really was, and I've seen no records of what happened when it was appealed. One current resident of Galisteo (in his sixties) says he remembers the Cadial being farmed.
53. Bowden, "Private Land Claims in the Southwest," 232.
54. Mednick, *San Cristóbal*, 197, 200. 53.

55. Ibid., 200–201.
56. Jan Willem Jansens, personal communication, 2016. One theory holds that the Río Galisteo may have run right through the center of the present town until a big flood in the late nineteenth century, although it fails to explain how the river avoided all the dwellings in its path. Citing an old map and "old meander patterns upstream," Jansens suggests that the creek moved from an alignment just east of where NM 41 is now to the current location farther east of the village. This must have been before the late eighteenth century, since the barracks and later the Ortiz y Davis hacienda would have been underwater.
57. He seems to have occupied the property, known locally as "el Rancho del Doctor," until the 1950s.
58. Rodríguez, "Acequias," 1. A ditch association consists of the parciantes, receivers of the water, who are obligated to clean the ditches and can access water at determined times, the mayordomo, who manages the distribution, and the comisionarios, who oversee the process. Rodríguez cites the distinction between "hydroscientific" and "hydrosocial" theories of water use, emphasizing the latter as the basis of New Mexico histories. See also Rivera, *Acequia Culture*.
59. Rodríguez, "History, Memory, and Querencia," 201.
60. For detailed accounts of two of the most notorious cases in northern New Mexico—Aamodt and Abeyta—see Rodríguez, "Acequias"; Matthews, *Culture Clash*, 187–90.
61. Rodríguez, "Acequias," 11.
62. Joe D. Anaya recalls that the plaza ditch's source was to the north. The pond now at Nizhoni was on Sena's ranch. (This is probably the Sena who prevented the railroad from coming to Galisteo.) Another possibility for the ditch's source is The Hill itself, an arroyo just to the north that intermittently drains down into the floodplain in the old plaza. The Sandovals had to build a wall to keep the water out, and Nick and Corinne Anaya have been flooded. (Joe D. Anaya, personal communication, 2017.)
63. Resident John Benjamin and archaeologist Mike Marshall generally agree on this path. In documents over the years, there are mentions of El Tanque Viejo "within the townsite of Galisteo," vestiges of which are visible today. On the 1899 Galisteo grant map a "reservoir" is the northernmost point of the grant. (Personal communications, 2015, 2018.)
64. Personal communications with Joe D. Anaya, 2016–17, and John Benjamin, 1999–2018.
65. Cadial book, 106; Jan Willem Jansens, personal communication, 2000.
66. Cadial book, 187–89. Apolonio Chávez, who had been a petitioner for the Galisteo grant in 1892, said he was also an heir to the larger San Cristóbal grant but didn't know the Cadial was on the same land they'd been granted before.
67. Cadial book, 106.
68. Ibid., 85. This was probably the long mesa now called "the Hub." Pankey did not prevent villagers from getting "dry wood" (dead wood) from the ranch, but they were not allowed to "cut trees or get rocks or brush or stone" or graze cattle and "trespass."
69. Ibid., 98.
70. Colorado, or "Coloradito," as one elder called it, was a short-lived community upriver from the village, on what is now Saddleback Ranch property.
71. Cooperrider and Hendricks, *Soil Erosion and Stream Flow*, 15–16.
72. Rodríguez, "History, Memory, and Querencia," 202. The 1889 census was the first to include irrigation records. The New Mexico Acequia Association was founded in 1989 and is not concerned with ditches that shut down long ago. My visit to the Office of the State Engineer came up empty despite welcome help from Meme Young.
73. William deBuys, personal communication, 2015.
74. Kammer, *Application for Registration*, sec. 12, 26.

75. This dam was large enough to be still very present, though breached long ago. It seems to have been part of an Anglo water scheme to sell water for irrigation. Linda McKee told me (10/23/2000) that during the Depression the owner could not pay his workers and lost his water rights. The next owner straightened it out with the state engineer. Philip McKee's transfer of water rights to the community well was protested, and it took Linda six years to clear it. In 1970, a major dam was built by the Army Corps of Engineers many miles downstream from the village, just east of where I-25 crosses the Rio Galisteo. It was constructed to control downstream flooding to Santo Domingo/Kewa Pueblo and to halt the flow of silt from the Rio Galisteo's excess of sediment, which was threatening to clog the Rio Grande itself. It also controls downstream flooding. See Weidemann, *Santa Fe New Mexican Real Estate Guide*, May 5, 2005, 22.
76. Bandelier, *Southwestern Journals*, vol. 1, 82.
77. Batchen, "El Indio viejo." The sources of her story were several Placitas residents in their seventies. Elsewhere, Batchen mentions some Tanos returning from Hopi in the eighteenth century to Abiquiú and then to Carnuel.
78. David Snow (personal communication, 2018) tells me of a "request by a Galisteo individual in mid-eighteenth century for permission to go to Hopi to visit relatives." Ciriaco Anaya, father of Andrés Anaya, proprietor of La Tienda Anaya, was friends with Pueblos from Santo Domingo and "helped them farm." As a youth, Andrés went with him and Monica Lovato, wife of a Pueblo man, and they stayed at Santo Domingo for a month. Andrés was also in the army in World War II with Domingos and remained friendly with them (personal communications with the Anayas, 6/18/99).
79. Francisco Leyva (b. ca. 1870), who takes credit for the last verse, was an informant for Robb. I'm assuming he was related (son?) to Natividad, who would have been alive in 1871 when the first Cadial trial took place. Even if he was not, he would have been familiar with this major event in Galisteans' lives. The version of La Tañita I have was kindly provided to me by Enrique R. Lamadrid (personal communication, 2018).
80. Lamadrid contends that this date refers to 1914 (ibid.), but the references to the 1909 trial suggest otherwise. If the Tanos cited here are the Galisteo settlers, 1814 is certainly the reference. Francisco Sandoval and Bachicha, cited at the end of the 1951 version, are both local names.
81. Quoted in Lamadrid, *La Geografia de Querencia*. In other words, he is not just Spanish, but also Native.
82. Ibid. See also Reséndez; Brooks; Rael-Gálvez, *Identifying Captivity and Capturing Identity*.
83. Notably by Father Stanley and Christina Mednick and in an unpublished manuscript by Marion A. Steele and a thesis by James Elkus.
84. "Remembering Carmelita Anaya," *El Puente*, Feb. 1997, from the author's interview with Clara and Manuel Anaya; a published interview with Carmelita by Mildred Beach, *Cerrillos Rustler*, March 8, 1975. At her death Carmelita had 41 grandchildren, 105 great-grandchildren, and 4 great-great-grandchildren. A villager told me that there were two other parteras in the 1930s, Epifana Sosa Almedes and Tiburcia Encinias.
85. All quotations from Simona Baros García are from several years of interviews we did together while she was living in Santa Fe on García Street and later at Casa Real nursing home. Although her immediate family had fallen on hard times, she was proud of the distinguished Baros family, which had owned many sheep. Her grandfather, Marcelino Baros, was known as an outstanding musician and horseman who won the 1878 corrida del gallo. She told a story about a carload of Anglos who drove by and asked a little boy what was going on. He said, "All I know is, all day long they're killing the rooster. And at night time they're having a revolution." (Presumably a baile, turning round and round.) As a founding member of the Sociedad de San José, Marcelino Baros (who lived for a while in the house on Loma Tejana) donated the land on which the Sala was built. His son Eugenio Baros, also a musician, was Simona García's father.

86. Simona García, excerpts from my interviews in *El Puente*, Jan. 2000. Her uncle Apolonio Chávez had a lot of sheep, and "who had sheep had money." Abel Anaya's storeroom was full of wood, food, flour, candy; "they had money."
87. John Benjamin, quoted in *El Puente*, Dec. 2004.
88. Excerpt from Paulita Peña's memoir, dictated in 1999 to an unknown oral historian, courtesy of Remedios and Antonio Chávez (*El Puente*, March 2007). Paulita was the daughter of Tomás Peña and Julianita Chávez. Her paternal grandparents were Pedro Peña and Francisca Chávez; maternal grandparents, José Silva and Julianita Chávez. Her siblings were Sara, Anne, Remedios, Magdalena, Pedro, José, Gavino, Leopoldo, and Juanito. She and Felipe lived in Galisteo until 1945.
89. Paulita's memoir includes a letter to her parents asking for her hand, her wedding invitation, and letters inviting sponsors for baptism. She and Felipe (d. 1980) had nine children: Leopoldo, Victor, Jimmy, María Gracia Consuelo, Julianita, Isabelita, Mercedes, Susana, and Margarita Viviana.
90. The entire corrido was published in *El Puente*, April 2007, translated by the author with Isabella Gonzales.
91. Simona García, personal communication, July 2002; "Youth Shoots 14-Year-Old Girl, Then Himself," *New Mexican*, Nov. 24, 1917. Chávez was fourteen and Mora was twenty. Soon after the shooting, he died in jail, and she died in the hospital.
92. Mack Sewell, "Everybody was sick," *Santa Fe New Mexican*, Oct. 16, 2005.
93. See Holtby, *Lest We Forget*.
94. Nazario Gonzales turns up occasionally in Galisteo documents; he also had interest in the 1782 Juana López grant. He gave Manuela Ortiz de Gonzales some agricultural land in La Ciénega.
95. Interviews by the author with Luis and Remedios Chávez, Feb. 1998. There was an unrelated Chávez family in Galisteo (and a Felipe Chávez in each family). Two unmarried sisters who lived behind the church and in summers crossed the Río to their other home (later the Light Institute, now the Durán home) were known as Las Chavezitas.
96. It was also known as La Salita del Coruco (red mite) or La Sala de San Antonio. Its ruins were accidentally bulldozed and destroyed quite recently.
97. Sarapio Montoya, personal communication, 1993.
98. The earliest image of the new church's interior I could find is dated 1921. The graceful arch framing the altar and a chandelier remain, enhanced by a lovely little carved fence. The painting of the Virgin holding the Christ child, flanked by two tall candles, is hung very high over the altar.
99. Anna Cárdenas, "Las Sociedades de Galisteo," *El Puente*, Summer 1997.
100. The deed was not recorded until 1904. In some accounts the land was donated by the Baroses, whose four sons were among the founders of the Sociedad. The sala is in Territorial style with mud adobe and a foundation of basalt and the extant original wood floor. The one room is focused on a stage at the west end, with bancos on the sides.
101. In the 1990s, La Sala served as a studio for artists Patrick Mehaffy, then Patrick McFarlin. It was renovated and transformed by a dedicated group of residents after an agreement with the Sociedad. Today, La Sala de San José de Galisteo is a thriving community art center.
102. Anna Cárdenas, "Me Acuerdo Cuando," *El Puente*, Sept. 2000.
103. A woodworker in the northern town of Córdova recalled the ritual last done there in 1932 and the alabado: "Saint Isidore the husbandman / Patron of husbandmen / Free our fields / from locusts and storms / Free our sowed fields." In those days they took San Isidro out into each field, chanting prayers and hymns. "I say that it was very dry in those days and when they took Saint Isidore and Saint Anthony of Padua . . . through the fields, where there were beans and wheat, everything And the rain came right away. . . . Well, if the rain didn't come that same day, [it came] the next

day. . . . And now nobody would take one of these images (*imagen*) around the fields" (Briggs, "A Conversation with Saint Isidore," 103–04).

104. Simmons, *Spanish Pathways*, 146.
105. Mela Martin, personal communications, phone interview, ca. 1993.
106. John Benjamin recalls the lovely light cast at night in the 1980s when the Santa Lucia window was lit up. Saint Lucy's Day is Dec. 13, near the winter solstice; it is celebrated in Scandinavia by girls with crowns of candles.
107. *Los pastores* was resurrected by Anna Cárdenas with La Gran Pastorela de Belén. In 2013 it was held in the church but since has been held in the newly remodeled Sala because some felt that the church was an inappropriate site. An elegant booklet was produced by Cárdenas in 2017 that includes the script, song lyrics, and history. See *El Puente*, Dec. 2013, 2014, 2015, 2016, 2017.
108. Simona García (personal communication, ca. 2006) said that the Baros monument in the cemetery was her cousin's: "We had no money for monuments." Today Rosario masses are held in Nuestra Señora de los Remedios the day before the funeral, after which congregants walk or drive up to the cemetery to gather around the grave for the burial. Despite the Church's disapproval, cremation is becoming common.
109. José Ortiz y Pino III (personal communication, 6/13/97): Father Otto, the reigning priest at the time, said the decision was up to the Archdiocese, not to the Galisteños, who often resented the invaders. José's father and grandfather didn't want to be buried here, preferring the National Cemetery in Santa Fe. But he is buried in Galisteo. I've been told that Phil McKee gave an easement for a road past the cemetery on town land—it was not his, but no one disputed it. Lew Cook, then owner of Cerro Pelón Ranch, was going to give land for a new cemetery, but the trade never happened because he didn't get an easement. Pecos church records, including Galisteo, burned with the church at the turn of the century. A few are rumored to have survived somewhere in Mexico, but they have never been found. In the late 1990s I recorded all the existing stones in both cemeteries and gave copies to the Archdiocese.
110. See Marc Simmons, "Traces of Moorish influence on Spain survive in N.M.," *Santa Fe New Mexican*, July 15, 2016.
111. Lamy suffered a terrible fire in 1907 and another in 1909, but that town actually grew a bit in the 1930s. The Pink Garter Saloon (later known as the Legal Tender), with its massively handsome wooden bar, remained a rousing center in the old mercantile building during World War II.
112. Swadesh, *Los Primeros Pobladores*, 125.
113. José Ortiz y Pino III, personal communication, 2004.
114. Elsewhere, Concha describes it as a "little house up there on The Hill." (See Dahl, "Concha Oriz y Pino de Kleven Interview," 14–17.)
115. "Personal Résumé," typescript by Concha Ortiz y Pino de Kleven, n.d. She hoped to "supply furniture, blankets, leather goods and some clothing for the trainees." The same year, 1929, the Spanish Colonial Arts Society was founded in Santa Fe. See Wroth, "New Hope in Hard Times."
116. Concha described her father closing it down but also said it lasted three years and was tremendously successful (Dahl, "Concha Oriz y Pino de Kleven Interview," 16). I have not found any villagers who were involved.
117. Although as far as I can tell the school was closed by 1933, the advertisement "Fiesta, Dinner and Baile . . . for Benefit of the New Galisteo Vocational Crafts School" implies that Concha hoped to revive it under a different name.
118. Coan, 16. See also *El Puente*, Oct. 1999. Coan reported that Miguel Anaya won the corrida, but Clarita Anaya corrected this, telling *El Puente* (Nov. 1999) that it was won by her brother-in-law Celso Anaya.

119. Folklorist Arthur Campa, quoted in Lamadrid, *Hermanitos Comanchitos*, 70.
120. In the foreword to her book, a fellow teacher describes her: "a little darker-skinned than the few Hispanics that I had seen 'pass.'" In her opening epigraph, Sánchez (*In the Footsteps*) notes: "My people were nourished by Spanish, Anglo and Native American bloodlines."
121. Sánchez, *In the Footsteps*, 38.
122. Ibid., 40–41. Victoria Davis de Sánchez later taught in Guatemala and Nicaragua. Her son, Leveo, was an administrator in the Peace Corps, where, coincidentally, he worked with attorney Richard Griscom, a resident of Galisteo since 1970. During the summer of 1942, at the age of eleven, Leveo Sánchez ran his mother's farm in Nambé alone on weekdays while she studied in Las Vegas.
123. Fred Ellis, who was a teenager when he helped his father move the buildings, says the year was 1940. However, Onésimo Montoya, who returned to Galisteo in 1937, insisted that the house was gone by then, and other villagers concur that this took place in the 1930s. All the photographs and records of the process were inadvertently discarded by Fred Ellis's sister Bambi.
124. *El Puente,* Dec. 2002, Jan. 2003. A two–part article on the "Ghost House" based on interviews with Fred and Bonnie Ellis.
125. The photograph of San Sebastián in *El Puente* was recognized by older villagers as a restoration of the old Chávez house on La Otra Vanda.
126. From an undated, unattributed typescript by or from Mae Pena Delgado (*El Puente*, Nov. 2010). She worked in the Ellis household as a teenager and recalled the home being dismantled.
127. *New Mexican,* March 18, 1900.
128. His wife was Martina Valencia (or "Martenez Chacón") from Pecos. His father was José Anaya (b. Santa Fe 1836, d. Galisteo 1/8/1900; buried in old Galisteo cemetery), also referred to as Antonio and José Antonio. The younger José Antonio testified that his mother was Martenez Chacón, grandmother, Tomasita Chávez, and paternal grandparents, Rafael Anaya and Rosalia (Cadial book, 96–97).
129. "Serapio Anaya: A Galisteo Memoir," *El Puente,* Sept. 2004. (English was Anaya's second language.) When José Antonio died in 1942, his children had to sell almost everything. The ranch went to Jack McKinley and later was divided up. Most of it was sold to the Thorntons; part of it was the Cash Ranch. Cresencio sold his part for 50 cents an acre to Leo Pick in Lamy, whose wife, Ada Pick, taught at the Galisteo school.
130. Mela Montoya and Rosina Anaya, personal communications, ca. 2001.
131. Anita Gonzales Thomas of Santa Fe recalled to John Pen La Farge: "Mother came home so mad, because José Ortiz y Pino, from Galisteo, wanted the money for the guys from Galisteo that were to get jobs [with a public relief agency], the money they owed him. She said, 'I won't pay you. I'm going to pay these people. They're the ones that did the work; they have to feed their families *now*'" (La Farge, *Turn Left at the Sleeping Dog*, 114). Ortiz y Pino's daughters had far fonder memories of his generosity (see Córdova, *¡Concha!*).
132. "Serapio Anaya," *El Puente*, Sept. 2004.
133. Korte, "En el Renganche," 45.
134. Andrew Oxford, "New Mexicans once cast as those to be kept out," *Santa Fe New Mexican*, Sept. 3, 2017.
135. Swadesh, *Los Primeros Pobladores*, 126.
136. "Serapio Anaya," *El Puente*, Sept. 2004.
137. Kay Matthews, "In Honor of #DayWithoutAWoman on #InternationalWomen'sDay" *La Jicarita News,* March 8, 2017.
138. Joe D. Anaya, personal communication, 2016.
139. Federal Writers' Project, *New Mexico*, quoted in *El Puente*, Jan. 2000.

140. Swadesh, *Los Primeros Pobladores*, 205: "Ever since George Sánchez wrote his immortal *Forgotten People* in 1940, there have been voices in the wilderness preaching the need for bilingual-bicultural education."
141. Mary Tappero Mora remembered that when she taught in Galisteo in the 1940s, the students "were all Anayas, Chávezes, Garcías, Sandovals, Senas . . . Tacho [Anastacio] Sandoval was one of the smartest kids. When parents tried to take local kids out of school in spring to herd sheep," she refused. "The Ortiz y Pino kids didn't go to school there. Nobody liked Don José or Frank Ortiz. . . . Bluebell was a wonderful person and went through hell for her children" (personal communication, 2003). She was the proprietor of Mary's Bar in Cerrillos, which was named on a movie set.
142. "Serapio Anaya," *El Puente*, Sept. 2004.

Chapter 5

1. Juan Estevan Arellano, quoted in Rodríguez, "History, Memory, and Querencia," 199.
2. Don Usner about the old Chimayó plaza, KUNM, *Raíces*, March 13, 2014.
3. From the song "Galisteo" by Burl Ives, who came to New Mexico in 1969 for the filming of *The McMasters* (partly shot in Galisteo) and bought several acres and an adobe ruin at the Arroyo de los Angeles just west of the village. There he and his wife built a "little brown adobe nestled warm in the sun, where the coyotes chase the rabbits and the roadrunners run," according to this song. It is still known as the Burl Ives house, though occupied by the Gilmore/Merrick family for close to thirty years. Ives left after two years, having divorced his wife (McGrath Morris, "A Mighty Balladeer").
4. At least one Anglo family lived in Galisteo: Ruth Hogan (her married name) "spent time in Galisteo as a child where her parents owned a bed and breakfast during World War II" (Museum of New Mexico Foundation newsletter, 2011).
5. Mary Alice Anaya, personal communication, 6/18/99.
6. José Ortiz y Pino II, personal communication, ca. 1998.
7. "Serapio Anaya," *El Puente*, Sept. 2004.
8. Rodríguez, "History, Memory, and Querencia," 198.
9. In her will the estate was divided between her living children: George, Frank, Pablita, and Rosario Davis de Leyba. She left her many grandchildren one dollar each.
10. Córdova, *¡Concha!*, 83–84; Dahl, "Concha Oriz y Pino de Kleven Interview," 32–34.
11. A 1953 court case found that there existed "extreme hostility" between Frank Ortiz y Davis and "the principal legatee," his mother, Pablita Ortiz y Pino. He was removed as executor. In the 1950s Don José Ortiz y Pino, then his son Frank Ortiz y Davis, owned "all lands within what is known as the 'Galisteo Grant'" except north of the reservoir, totaling 260.70 (*sic*) acres, which he also sold (McKee abstract, 121). Frank Ortiz told the McKees that he couldn't get along with his sisters but got along fine with his father. Grandson Frank Ortiz II married Lucas Anaya's daughter and inherited the Tres Marías Ranch, selling it to the Partridges, who made it into a spa (later sold to Kaye Sandford to become the Vista Clara Ranch and Spa, currently the Chi Center).
12. Rudy Sena, personal communication, 1997.
13. Zeke Scher, "The Dons of Galisteo," *Sunday Empire/Denver Post*, Oct. 25, 1970.
14. According to José Ortiz y Pino III, it is a "family tradition" that one son take the Ortiz y Pino name. In his father's generation, José Ortiz y Pino II died young. Jose III's son José Ortiz y Pino IV lives in Vermont; however, his sister María is also Ortiz y Pino, as are all the descendants of Don José's brother Pedro Ortiz y Pino.
15. See Mednick, *San Cristóbal*, 213–14.

16. Onésimo Montoya, personal communication, 2000.
17. Antonio Chávez recalls it happening "overnight," and there was no resistance. The eastern section along US 285 was already fenced. In the 1970s José Ortiz y Pino III claimed some of the fenced off area and his suit was not settled until 1972, out of court.
18. Eldorado Volunteers, *Windmills and Dreams*, 84.
19. See *El Puente*, Summer 1998, for Genora Moore's fond memories of her adopted abuelo and *El Puente*, May 1999, for his obituary. Charles Hagerman told me about bringing cattle up from his family ranch way down south to the Spiess siding (personal communication, 2006).
20. Archie and Jerry's father, Hal West, was hired by the Teal family to run the Pink Garter Saloon in Lamy in the mid 1950s.
21. Eldorado Volunteers, *Windmills and Dreams*, 74.
22. According to his third wife, Linda McKee, Philip had preferred a ranch near Cimarron with less unusable land (personal communication, 2002).
23. Elsewhere described as 21,000 acres, 5,000 leased from the state. In a 1954 Realtor's prospectus, the land was described as the "historic 27,000-acre" ranch. In 2016, two owners later, it went up for sale for $75 million, since reduced to $48 million.
24. F. W. LaRouche advertisement (McKee papers). Sarah Moody was another Realtor involved.
25. F. W. LaRouche advertisement (McKee papers).
26. In a letter dated Feb. 19, 1954, Robert McKee reported that descriptions of the "Ortiz Ranch" were "sadly mixed up." On March 9, he wrote that the patrón's son Frank Ortiz y Davis was "very nice" (McKee papers). The McKee correspondence and ranch papers are in the author's possession, given to me by Linda McKee's widower, John Pack. Upon publication of this book, they will be donated to the New Mexico State Library.
27. McKee mentions having bought the "Dooley, Frank Ortiz, and Gassman lands" (640 acres) on the same day. And he was still interested in the Dolores Springs Ranch to the west (at the foot of and including part of the Ortiz Mountains: 19,219 acres; 13 springs; 1 ½ miles off Galisteo Creek at the northwest corner), owned by Treva B. Speight, whose husband died while they were negotiating (McKee papers).
28. The banks of the creek, with its woven channels, were mostly bare and treeless at the time. In the 1950s, Helen Hover planted cottonwoods on the riverbanks around the old bridge to provide a "park" for Galisteo. The resulting bosque is one of the village's most appealing features.
29. F. W. LaRouche advertisement (McKee papers).
30. Sinclair, "Galisteo of the Remedies," 6.
31. Father Stanley, *Galisteo, New Mexico Story*, 19.
32. Remedios Chávez, personal communication, ca. 1999.
33. See Onésimo's obituary in *El Puente,* May 2012. He was born in Ilfeld to Isabel Baca ("maybe C de Baca") and Luis Montoya; the family moved to Lamy when he was a year old and to Galisteo in 1937. Luis Montoya was born at "Tequvalla" (Tacubaya), was raised in Ilfeld, and then lived in "a section in back of Galisteo—a group of families lived there—the Gómezes, Bacas, Chávezes." His grandfather Severo Montoya lived in what is now a ruin behind the Watts home on Avenida Vieja; his wife was a Mares from La Ciénega. Onésimo's uncle was Pantaleón Montoya, whose home (now Watson-Jones's) remains on Avenida Vieja. Isaake Montoya's former house, the WPA mattress factory, is farther down the road.
34. Anna Cárdenas's great-aunt Cruz Anaya lived in what is now a ruin across the road from her home on CR 42; its walls were still standing when Anna was little.
35. J. B. Jackson, quoted in La Farge, *Turn Left at the Sleeping Dog*, 277.
36. Mary Branham, *New Mexico Magazine,* quoted in *El Puente*, November 2002.
37. Sinclair, "Galisteo of the Remedies," 6.

38. Ibid.
39. I am told that it was once attached to the inn and that on Juan's death the place was dissected, the house being Juan Ortiz's home and the later Galisteo Inn his mercantile store. This building was owned in the 1950s by a Texan, Dr. Maldonado, a relative of Yolanda Ortiz y Pino; it was there she met her husband. The Villanuevas also owned the home by the old bridge where the Baroses lived, later Attenbergers and now Tuwaletstiwas.
40. José Ortiz y Pino III was raised in Santa Fe, graduated from the New Mexico Military Institute in Roswell and New Mexico State University, and spent two years in Germany in the military before settling in Galisteo with his Texan wife, Yolanda (Nella) Cárdenas. They married in 1951 and had two children, Jose IV and María. See obituary in *El Puente*, March 2016.
41. Yolanda Ortiz y Pino published a La Mancha–based cookbook: *Original Native New Mexican Cooking*, 1993. The building became the Linda Durham art gallery and is now a private home, for sale. The Ortiz y Davis hacienda also changed hands and is now split into two parts, owned by painter Woody Gwyn and his wife, Dianna, and by John Benjamin in the former barracks.
42. In the curious collection of antiques in the Galisteo History Museum was a huge wooden cross purportedly "from a Galisteo Indian Pueblo dating to 1610" (José Ortiz y Pino III, personal communication, ca. 1998). The cross is not at Las Golondrinas.
43. It was followed in 1983 by *Curandero: A Cuento*, a fictional account of life in the Galisteo hacienda. He also privately published a book of poems, *There is Another You* (n.d.).
44. Partridges's spa/Vista Clara Spa/Chi Center has 46 acre feet of water rights, more than the entire village system, some of it purchased from elsewhere.
45. See Walden, "Running Water for Galisteo," *La Puente de Galisteo*, Jan. 1997. Tobías's cousin Crescencio Anaya also delivered water at times.
46. In many accounts, the figure is 42.58 acre feet and sometimes other figures. The state engineer lists it simply as 42.5. It was apparently donated by Phil McKee, who transferred some water rights from his ranch.
47. Walden, "Running Water for Galisteo." The well was once touted as "Coronado's Well."
48. The first president of the Water Association was Alvaro López-Watermann, then Joe Anaya, Freddie Cárdenas, Maurice Dixon, Alvaro again, Tom Fitzpatrick, Patrick Mehaffy, Steve Moya, Rod Hall, Michael Golino, and, as of this writing, Phillip Tuwaletstiwa.
49. See Tony Anaya's obituary in *El Puente*, May 1997, and the article on Tobías in *El Puente*, Dec. 2001.
50. Hoback, personal communication, 1995.
51. Zeke Scher, "The Dons of Galisteo," *Sunday Empire/Denver Post*, Oct. 25, 1970.
52. "Nizhoni School: Not Closed, Just Stretched Out: An Interview with Chris Griscom," *El Puente*, Feb. 2004. This, too, is disputed by villagers who are insulted by the notion that they themselves don't respect their own histories. They often feel exploited by Anglo newcomers colonizing their stories, present company not excepted.
53. Romona Scholder, "Summers Past," *El Puente*, Sept. 2000 (reprinted from the *Santa Fe New Mexican*, Aug. 4, 1974).
54. "The (Difficult) Birth of the Galisteo Community Center," *El Puente*, April 2017.
55. Marie Ferneau, "The Old Railroad House," *El Puente*, Nov. 1998. Marie (1923–2008) was an artist and Doc had been a professor in the agriculture school in Tulsa.
56. Hart, Rhodes, and Morgan, *Unknown World of the Mobile Home*, 39.
57. Carlson, *The Spanish American Homeland*; J. B. Jackson's brilliant essay on the vernacular home, "The Mobile Home on the Range," 51–67.
58. Poet and architect Levi Romero, a professor at UNM, once tried to spearhead such an effort. The ever-more popular "tiny homes," some of which are produced by a former art critic in Santa Fe, appeal to the mobile young but not to traditional families. They are also far more expensive than

trailers and manufactured (or "modular") homes, which are considered permanent and a step up from double-wides.

59. Interview, "Alva Simpson's Nephew Robert Dobyn," in Eldorado Volunteers, *Windmills and Dreams*, 84.
60. Interview with Robert Dobyn, ca. 1996.
61. José Ortiz y Pino III, personal communication, 1999.
62. Metz, *Robert E. McKee: Master Builder*, 72.
63. Patrick McCaffrey, "McKee Ranch Converting to 'Rhodesia Plan,'" *Santa Fe Reporter*, March 24, 1982. Cook, when asked during court hearings how many ranches he owned and where, replied, "What do you mean by a ranch?"
64. For their obituaries, see *La Puente*, Jan. 1997, and *El Puente*, Dec. 2003.
65. In the western basin, near Bonanza Creek (the site of the original town of Los Cerrillos), the J. W. Eaves Movie Ranch, built in 1968–70 for *The Cheyenne Social Club*, starring Jimmy Stuart, Henry Fonda, and Shirley Jones, shared many of these honors. It's now rented for private parties, complete with "gunfights, Indian dancers," advertised as "Walk the same streets as John Wayne, Clint Eastwood, Kevin Costner, Kevin Kline, Johnny Cash and many more." But Bonanza Creek owner Glenn Hughes had no plans to open his set up to tourists: "Given the choice of supervising 200 tourists or 200 longhorns, I'd take the cows anytime" (Wall, "Movie Town Sets Stage," 30). This recalls a local bumper sticker from decades ago: "More Mining, Less Tourism."
66. Their obituaries are in *El Puente*: Andres, Oct. 2003, and Josefina, March 2004.
67. Galisteo residents unsuccessfully protested this addition.
68. See Princenthal, *Agnes Martin*. For Martin's time in Galisteo, see Woodman, *Agnes Martin and Me*.
69. Among them, artists Shaun Gilmore, Nick Merrick, Janice Wall, Steve Davis, Jim Sloan, Patrick McFarling, Peggy Diggs, and Ed Epping, and writer Margaret Wrinkle.
70. J. B. Jackson, quoted in La Farge, *Turn Left at the Sleeping Dog*, 277.
71. Its original name having proved elusive (maybe Cerro Matadero, or Cerro Lucero, or Cerro Ortiz), I knew it first as "Sacred Mountain." The tribes would prefer it remain anonymous and unvisited due to its sacred status.
72. See Basso, *Wisdom Sits in Places*.
73. The Ortiz Mountains, aka San Lázaro or Oso, then Oro Mountains, and possibly at some point the Perdenal (*sic*) Range (*pedernal* means "flint").
74. The name Galisteo may come from a Moorish fortress in Spain in the tenth and eleventh centuries called Medina Ghaliayah. The Moorish wall surrounding the village dates from the eleventh to fourteenth centuries, and Galisteo was also the site of a *juderia* (Jewish barrio). The Spanish town of Galisteo is first officially documented in 1217 and by 1451 there was a Count of Galisteo. Some say the name has a connection to Galicia. According to Roberto Valdez, "Galisteo is a Spanish name derived from *kálistos*, a Greek word meaning 'very beautiful.'" This seems unlikely (Valdez, "Living Down Country People," 10).
75. El Chical, a field in Galisteo, for instance, is Nahuatl for "underbrush," or "a thicket of Rabbit thorn brush (chicos)" (Cobos, *A Dictionary of New Mexico and Southern Colorado Spanish*, 5). Today there is widespread appropriation of Native names and sites, such as Paa-Ko, the site of an ancient Keres Pueblo village on NM 14, now the name of a neighboring subdivision.
76. Steele, "Naming of Places in Spanish New Mexico," 299, 300.
77. David Snow, personal communication, 2018.
78. For a more detailed exposition on roads, see King, *Speculations on the Economy*.
79. In the 1940s, what is now US 285 went over the hill to an earlier road behind Lamy. Lamy Canyon met old Ranch Road and came out by the Eldorado Community Center, where there was a ranch house, then through a pretty valley to Santa Fe (José Ortiz y Pino III, personal communication, 2001).

80. José Ortiz y Pino III told me that after passing through the break in the northern creston, NM 41 originally went west toward the railroad tracks (following an older road) where there was a dangerous curve along the river at what is now Nizhoni. It was straightened during the Depression (personal communication, ca. 2012).

Chapter 6

1. Simona García's mother, Mathilda Sena Baros, began each day with this prayer.
2. Patricia Marina Trujillo, quoting her "gramita" ("The Moon Rises over Hernandez Again and Again," *Green Fire Times*, Dec. 2016, 30).
3. Eduardo Galeano in interview with Gary Younge, "Eduardo Galeano: 'My great fear is that we are all suffering from amnesia,'" *The Guardian*, July 23, 2013.
4. At almost 53 percent, New Mexico ranks higher than California and Texas, according to numbers from the US Census Bureau compiled by the Metropolitan Policy Program at the Brookings Institution and summarized by Matthew Reichbach, *New Mexico Political Report*, July 11, 2016.
5. Rodríguez, "History, Memory, and Querencia," 197.
6. Ibid.
7. Steele, "Galisteo," 35. Steele lived in Galisteo for ten years in the 1970s and 1980s. His book on Galisteo was already typeset in the process of being published by Sunstone in Santa Fe when he died suddenly in 1986. It never appeared, though I have read the manuscript, and I have only photocopies of the photographs by Alisa Wells (who died in 1988). No footnotes survived, or perhaps ever existed.
8. At one point in the 1990s, an anonymous critic posted stickers announcing Galisteo as "Anayaville"—shades of an earlier attack on the Anaya family in which a photo of someone shoveling manure was captioned "Training for Politics: Anaya Ranch," an underhanded dig at the political power of one branch of the family. Joe M. (José Manuel) Anaya was chairman of the State Highway Commission, and the state transportation building in Santa Fe is named for him. Joe and his Anglo wife, Mary Ann, lived on the family ranch twenty miles south in Stanley (its road is named after his father, Basilio Anaya) and were joined there by some of their children. Their son Michael Anaya, who is a former president of the Galisteo Community Association, later became a two-term county commissioner (succeeded by his brother Robert for two terms), has worked for the State Land Commission, then came in second in his run for state senator in 2016. The departure of several Anayas from the village where the family had lived for generations signaled a waning of local power, and it is increasingly difficult to recruit members of the old families to participate in community activities.
9. In 2016, Galisteo had a population of 253: 121 males, 132 females, with a median age of 51.1.
10. José Ortiz y Pino III, personal communication, 1997.
11. Steve Gonzalez to artist Celia Muñoz (Lippard, *The Lure of the Local*, 4).
12. Price, *Dry Place*, xxii.
13. Wright, "On Modern Vernaculars and J. B. Jackson," 169.
14. Arjun Appadurai quoted in Rodríguez, "History, Memory, and Querencia," 199.
15. Rodríguez, ibid.
16. It hurts to work hard and sometimes be stabbed in the back. In the spring of 2004, an anonymous diatribe was left in community mailboxes attacking "community leaders" Tom Morin, Mike Anaya, and me. Outraged letters to *El Puente* (April 2004) ensued.
17. In 2014 I found myself in a Bicentennial committee that for the first time (after twenty-some years of meetings) was majority Hispano with only two Anglos. I was intrigued by the difference in the atmosphere. The conversation was relaxed, knowledgeable, reminiscent, and intimate.

18. Rodríguez, "Acequias," 7.
19. Christina Nealson, "A Wound Called the West," *Geronimo*, Jan. 1999, 8.
20. Michael D. Anaya, "Code of the West," *Bienvenidos* (annual), *Santa Fe New Mexican*, 2006.
21. Graciela Esperanza, speaking at the conference "Local Ingenuity," Portland, Maine, 1999.
22. Poster by Ricardo Levins Morales; the text originated in South Africa.
23. When I first moved to New Mexico, artist Nancy Holt and I attended, out of curiosity, a "Knowing" by Chris Griscom of the Light Institute. Speaking from a raised dais and dressed in flowing white robes, she declared that she was based in Galisteo because there are crystals underlying the entire basin. I was incredulous then (and more so later, when my well went bad) but amused by the connections to the work of Nancy's deceased husband, Robert Smithson, who was fascinated by crystals, the basis for his famous early Minimal sculptures.
24. In June the Board of County Commissioners accepted the development proposal with two modifications concerning water and drainage. Eventually the commercial project failed, but three new homes were built on the lot, which has a working well.
25. "La Puente" is recorded as a New Mexican idiosyncrasy in Cobos's *A Dictionary of New Mexico and Southern Colorado Spanish*. But according to one resident, it was merely "feminizing—cheap slang that came in with the pachucos" (personal communication, ca. 1997).
26. Saunders, *Bird Notes from the Galisteo Basin*. The highly respected botanist Bill Isaacs, who lived in Galisteo, had promised to be *El Puente*'s "nature columnist," but sadly succumbed to cancer in 1997.
27. In April 2004, at the demise of *El Puente*'s "El Arroyo" page, the anonymous editor (Isabella) came out: "As for my identity—it's as clear as a bell (AHH!)." Of its most popular contributions were the occasional "You know you live in Galisteo if. . ." "Your speech pattern changes during rodeo weekend," "You dress up to go to the Bobcat Bite" (a tiny hamburger joint formerly on Old Las Vegas Highway), or "You moved here because you LOVE the desert and promptly put in 10,000 feet of irrigation pipe to change the 'bland' color of the grass."
28. The first fire department—instigated by then resident Rosie Rosenwald, Roman Attenberger, Joe M. Anaya, and Charlie Holloway—the proud possessor of one vintage 1950s truck, lasted only a few months. In 1984 a Galisteo Basin Fire Brigade based at Girls Ranch near Lamy (with another ancient vehicle) also lasted only a few months.
29. I joined the GVFR Auxiliary in 1995. My contributions have been enthusiastic but minimal; I'm listed on the rolls as "Reporter" (and t-shirt deliverer).
30. The opening salvos for a Community Plan were published in *El Puente* in January, February, and Summer 1998.
31. These figures may be a bit skewed as some families did not reply. Those who did tended to be activist oriented.
32. See *El Puente*, February 2003 and Summer 2004.
33. *El Puente*, June 2006.
34. When our plan was accepted by the Board of County Commissioners, then county commissioner Kathy Holian was very complimentary about our work, writing on 2/28/12: "One of those issues was the new Galisteo Community Plan. . . . I would like to encourage communities that don't have plans to look at this one as a beautiful example of how planning should be done. This was the result of the hard work of many people in Galisteo over the course of several years. The Plan is an important step forward for the community, but the process of developing it was also important. It has the effect of bringing a community together to decide what is important and what they would like to preserve." The Galisteo Community Plan identified the historic Village Plaza area as a possible focus for potential small businesses and community activities that would "fit in" with existing historic patterns; a Plaza Nueva was suggested. In early 2018 the reconstituted Planning

Committee decided against a designated "commercial corridor" in "downtown Galisteo" and made all uses "conditional" anywhere in the village proper. Applicants would apply to the County and our Planning Committee to determine appropriate uses.

35. García, "Lucha Es Tu Herencia."
36. The City of Santa Fe recommends 8–12,000 gallons per month or 96–144,000 per year, per household. Santa Fe has one of the most successful conservation programs in the state at 54 gallons per capita per day (gpcd) for residential use and 90 gpcd in toto (all water used for all purposes in the city). Thanks to Roger Taylor for this information (personal communication, 2015).
37. In the early 2000s, desalinization of water from the Estancia Basin to the south of Galisteo was touted and almost initiated, but it proved too expensive, for now. The almost mythical San Juan–Chama diversion promised Santa Fe County a bright future, but in 2015 its infrastructure was failing.
38. Joe Cooper in *El Puente*, Oct. 1997. Previous proposals by "related landowners" included schemes to mine and flatten Buffalo Mountain west of the basin and create a new city of 70,000 people (*El Puente*, Nov. 2004). At the same time, the Cerrillos-based Rural Conservation Alliance was trying to raise $50,000 to oppose a water rights transfer from McKee Ranch to thousands of acres around I-25 for unspecified projects (Peppler et al. were the applicants). If the transfer had gone through, up to 80,000 gallons of water could have been diverted from the rest of the Galisteo Basin—Galisteo, Lamy, and Cerrillos—to Buffalo Mountain and La Bajada Mesa. That's so much "paper water," which may or may not exist underground, that would not have been available for domestic use (or development) in the eastern basin.
39. *El Puente*, Nov. 1998. Fortunately, in 2017, Moya was lured back onto the board, but not as president.
40. *El Puente*, Summer 2007.
41. The Barclays owned a ranch near Cerrillos that was EWI's project headquarters and home to the experimental "Flushing Meadows" gray-water project. Jansens is now an independent contractor with his own company, Ecotone, and continues to work with the village and public agencies.
42. Paige Grant and Neil Williams, Letter to the Editor, about the Santa Fe River, *Santa Fe New Mexican*, Nov. 23, 2005.
43. They remodeled the three big gullies between my house and the creek. Other parts of this reclamation project ranged from Jim Cummings's property in lower Cañoncito, to my then neighbors Barb and Wayne King, to Kathy Richardson's near Cerrillos.
44. See *El Puente*, Nov. 1998, May 1999, Oct. 1999.
45. Linda McKee, personal communication, 2002.
46. Some community leaders from old local families, who had gone to school in Moriarty with Governor King's family, were on Cook's side. The GCA opposed him, with the aid of attorney Booker Kelly.
47. From the author's notes on court proceedings.
48. In the early 2000s, that same strip was mentioned by new owner Tom Ford's ranch manager as a possible site for development. It is the obvious choice for divestment from Cerro Pelón Ranch because its location across the river makes it more logically part of the village than of the ranch itself, not to mention its historical significance.
49. The promise of thousands of acres of accessible open space, adjacent to county open space provided by bond issues, made the project popular with many neighbors. Others were adamantly opposed to the residential portion, which was eventually scaled back to 640 units on 450 acres with an 8 to 10-year buildout; this, too, eventually failed to get approval (*El Puente*, Jan. 2005).
50. *El Puente*, Oct. 2002, Summer 2003.
51. *El Puente*, May 2004, Jan. 2005.

52. *El Puente* scooped the *Santa Fe New Mexican* by interviewing the county fire marshal, who was outraged that the film company had upped the amount of dynamite used after the required fire inspection. "Editorial," *El Puente*, September/October 1998.
53. The village appointed a liaison with the film companies to minimize disturbance to locals, and the Community Association received generous subsidies, a custom that was dropped for a while in the early 2000s and then reinstated.
54. I was told that Ford had a vision of his horses swimming in the moat, until someone reminded him that they would be defecating in the water feature as well. An Ando-designed pet mausoleum was also mentioned, and other modernist structures were added to the ranch.
55. *El Puente,* Summer 2004.
56. *Leading Estates of the World*, June 2016; *El Puente,* Summer 2016. I was not permitted to reproduce the illustrations in this book.
57. The community water part was wishful thinking if it referred to Galisteo's system. See *El Puente*, March 2001.
58. In an unpopular move, the Archaeological Conservancy approved of the development and was involved in a plan to fence off a few Pueblo sites to "protect" them.
59. See "Nizhoni School: Not Closed, Just Stretched Out: An Interview with Chris Griscom," *El Puente*, Feb. 2004.
60. Despite our attempts to make NM 41 an official Scenic Byway, DOT is committed to its designation as a Commercial Thoroughfare, given that NM 14 is a Scenic Byway.
61. *El Puente*, Nov. 2001.
62. County records list this tract in the name of an Ortiz y Pino heir, although the local grapevine held that Concha had bequeathed the land to the cathedral in Santa Fe. In 2019, the GCA is pursuing a title search in yet another attempt to put all these questions to rest.
63. To add to the brew, grazing rights on the four acres had been permitted by Concha to a local Hispano family who also felt a sense of ownership through longtime use. Moreland also tried to pick off a nearby pasture that had been quitclaimed years before by Chris Griscom, former owner of the Durán compound.
64. The names Moreland and Purse were concocted by neighbors for a Rodeo Parade float protesting the land grabs.
65. Martínez, quoted in *El Puente*, Oct. 2004. See *El Puente*, Nov. 2004, Feb. 2005, Sept. 2005. In April 2006, *El Puente* interviewed the land grabbers.
66. *El Puente,* Feb. 2005. See chapter 4 for the backstory.
67. *El Puente*, Oct. 2006.
68. *El Puente*, Jan. 2007.
69. Around 1993, I found a very old, leaf-shaped, gray stone knife on a rise above my house. A visiting friend who was an aspiring archaeologist found more in the same place. Then more, washing out quite quickly: five stone knives and a series of glassy black obsidian chips, flakes, and cores, a beautiful red chert scraper, a broken San José arrowhead. I was given permission by a former state archaeologist to take them into my house as they were already "out of context." In 2016 more artifacts washed out, discovered by our local congressman, who was walking across my field to place a political campaign sign.
70. In 2006, the notion of a Galisteo Basin State Park was suddenly broached and greeted by communal horror. Even the most populist among us are ambivalent about an invasion of cultural tourists, and Pueblo peoples are steadfastly opposed. Nothing came of that idea, although Santa Fe County is now exploring plans for a "gateway" to the Galisteo Basin in its Lamy open space.

71. Mednick, *San Cristóbal*, 233.
72. I was first told that this area was Romeroville and then that the name was a hispanization of O'Meara or O'Mara, after an Irish settler or mine owner. Coal was being mined nearby when Nels Nelson was in the basin. Two mining claims were found in a survey, one with a post tagged "BENAVID LS #5824" southwest of the former Frank Anaya ranch.
73. See Lippard, *Down Country*.
74. There are neo-natives whose mantels or garden benches are literally paved with sherds found in the Galisteo area.
75. Water was one obstacle; its quality in this area is famously abysmal. King Cattle Company is owned by the family of former New Mexico governor Bruce King, who was once a truck driver for Don José in Galisteo and whose niece Rhonda King is a Realtor and former state legislator.
76. Cajete, *A People's Ecology*, 3, n. 77.
77. Ibid., 17–19.
78. Joel Glanzberg in Cajete, *A People's Ecology*, 227, 236.
79. Fiege, "Private Property and the Ecological Commons in the American West," 222–3.
80. See Flores, *Coyote America*.
81. When I first moved to Galisteo, I watched a porcupine high in an old cottonwood in the bosque next to the house. He stayed there for days. City girl that I was, I called Animal Control to say that he seemed to need help. "Lady," they said. "You should worry about the tree, not the porcupine."
82. A friend tells me that tourists have complained about "all the broken-down cars with their hoods up"—actually the most effective defense against rodents chewing engine wires in a cozy place.
83. All attempts at eradication of Russian olives and tamarisks had failed until the summer of 2016 when a large-scale, state–funded project cleared the central section of the bosque, opening up the cottonwood groves and planting hundreds of willows to replace the invaders. But within months, nascent Russian olives were back, and the 2018 drought endangered the new plantings. In 2017 another large grant tackled the rest of the bosque, north of the old bridge, with similar results. It remains to be seen if these massive efforts have successfully banished the culprits.
84. Paley, *The Collected Stories*, xi.

BIBLIOGRAPHY

1909–17 Proceedings of Case #6470, "Benjamin Pankey v. Juan Ortiz et al." in the District Court, Santa Fe County. Typescript.

Agnew, S. C. *Garrisons of the Regular US Army, New Mexico, 1846–1899.* Santa Fe: Press of the Territorian, 1971.

Arellano, Anselmo F. "The Never-Ending Land Grant Struggle." *La Herencia del Norte, Summer 1996.*

Bandelier, Adolph F. *The Southwestern Journals of Adolph F. Bandelier, 1880–1882.* Vol. 1. Edited by Charles Lange and Carroll L. Riley. Albuquerque: University of New Mexico Press, 1970.

———. *The Southwestern Journals of Adolph F. Bandelier, 1883–1884.* Vol. 2. Edited by Charles H. Lange and Carroll L. Riley. Albuquerque: University of New Mexico Press, 1966.

———. *The Southwestern Journals of Adolph F. Bandelier, 1885–1888.* Vol. 3. Edited by Charles H. Lange, Carroll L. Riley, and Elizabeth Lange. Albuquerque: University of New Mexico Press, 1975.

———. *The Southwestern Journals of Adolph F. Bandelier, 1889–1892.* Vol. 4. Edited by Charles H. Lange, Carroll L. Riley, and Elizabeth Lange. Albuquerque: University of New Mexico Press, 1984.

Basso, Keith. *Wisdom Sits in Places: Landscape and Language Among the Western Apache.* Albuquerque: University of New Mexico Press, 1996.

Batchen, Lou Sage, collector. "El Indio viejo (The old Indian)," 5-5-49 #7. WPA New Mexico Collection, 1936–40. Fray Angélico Chávez History Library, Santa Fe.

Baxter, William. "Cerrillos Area Names Database." May 1, 2009. http://www.cerrillosnewmexico.com.

———. *Gold and the Ortiz Mine Grant: A New Mexico History and Reference Guide.* Santa Fe: Lone Butte Press, 2014.

———. *The Gold of the Ortiz Mountains: A Story of New Mexico and The West's First Major Gold Rush.* Santa Fe: Lone Butte Press, 2004.

Benavides, David. "Lawyer-Induced Partitioning of New Mexico Land Grants: An Ethical Travesty." Research Paper No. 4., Center for Land Grant Studies. Unpublished manuscript, 1994.

Bloom, Lansing B. "Barreiro's Ojeada sobre Nuevo-México." *New Mexico Historical Review 3,* no. 1 (January 1928): 73–96; vol. 3, no. 2 (April 1928): 145–78.

Bowden, J. J. "Private Land Claims in the Southwest." 6 vols. Masters of Law thesis, Southern Methodist University, 1969.

Boyd, E. *Popular Arts of Spanish New Mexico.* Santa Fe: International Folk Art Foundation, 1974.

Briggs, Charles L. "A Conversation with Saint Isidore: The Teachings of the Elders." In *Hispanic Arts and Ethnohistory in the Southwest: Papers Inspired by the Work of E. Boyd,* edited by Marta Weigle, 103–15. Santa Fe: Ancient City Press, 1983.

Brooks, James F. *Captives and Cousins: Slavery, Kinship, and Community in the Southwest Borderlands.* Chapel Hill: University of North Carolina Press, 2002.

Brown, Lorin W., with Charles L. Briggs and Marta Weigle. *Hispano Folklife of New Mexico: The Lorin W. Brown Federal Writers' Project Manuscripts.* Albuquerque: University of New Mexico Press, 1978.

Brugge, David M. *Navajos in the Catholic Church Records of New Mexico, 1694–1875.* Tsaile, AZ: Navajo Community College Press, 1985.

Burchill, Mary D. *Lady of the Canyon: Evelyn Cecil Frey, a Tribute.* Los Alamos, NM: Otowi Crossing Press, 2001.

Caffey, David L. *Chasing the Santa Fe Ring: Power and Privilege in Territorial New Mexico.* Albuquerque: University of New Mexico Press, 2014.

Cajete, Gregory, ed. *A People's Ecology: Explorations in Sustainable Living.* Santa Fe: Clear Light Publishers, 1999.

Cannon, Hal. "The Perils of the Humanities or How I Became Human." *Grantmakers in the Arts Reader* 14, no. 2 (Summer 2003). https://www.giarts.org/index.php/article/perils-humanities-or-how-i-became-human.

Carlson, Alvar. *The Spanish American Homeland: Four Centuries of New Mexico's Rio Arriba.* Baltimore: Johns Hopkins University Press, 1990.

Chávez, Fray Angélico. *My Penitente Land: Reflections on Spanish New Mexico.* Albuquerque: University of New Mexico Press, 1974.

Coan, Mary W. "La Corrida del Gallo in Galisteo." *New Mexico Magazine* (December 1933).

Cobos, Rubén. *A Dictionary of New Mexico and Southern Colorado Spanish.* Santa Fe: Museum of New Mexico Press, 1983.

Concha Ortiz y Pino de Kleven Papers, Center for Southwest Research, University Libraries, University of New Mexico, Albuquerque.

Cooperrider, Charles K., and Barnard A. Hendricks. *Soil Erosion and Stream Flow on Range and Forest Lands of the Upper Rio Grande Watershed in Relation to Land Resources and Human Welfare.* Technical Bulletin no. 567, May 1937. Washington, DC: US Department of Agriculture.

Córdova, Kathryn M. *¡Concha! Concha Ortiz y Pino, Matriarch of a 300-Year-Old New Mexico Legacy.* A *La Herencia* publication. Santa Fe: Gran Via, 2004.

Correia, David. *Properties of Violence.* Athens: University of Georgia Press, 2013.

Dahl, Nancy. "Concha Oriz y Pino de Kleven Interview." Transcript of Living Treasures tape recording, September 27, 2000, Fray Angélico Chávez History Library, Santa Fe.

Davis, Sylvester. "Diary of Sylvester Davis." *New Mexico Historical Review* 6, no. 4 (October 1931): 383–416.

Davis, W. W. H. *El Gringo: or, New Mexico and Her People.* Chicago: Rio Grande Press, 1962. Reproduction of the 1938 edition published by Rydal Press, Santa Fe, NM. First published 1857 by Harper & Brothers.

deBuys, William. *Enchantment and Exploitation: The Life and Hard Times of a New Mexico Mountain Range.* Albuquerque: University of New Mexico Press, 1985. Revised and expanded edition, 2015.

Dike, Shelton H. *The Territorial Post Offices of New Mexico.* Albuquerque, NM: privately published by Dr. S. H. Dike, 1958.

Dunbar-Ortiz, Roxanne. *Roots of Resistance: Land Tenure in New Mexico.* Norman: University of Oklahoma Press, 2007.

Ebright, Malcolm. *Land Grants and Lawsuits in Northern New Mexico.* Albuquerque: University of New Mexico Press, 1994.

Ebright, Malcolm, ed. *Spanish and Mexican Land Grants and the Law.* Manhattan, KS: Sunflower University Press, 1989.

Ebright, Malcolm, Rick Hendricks, and Richard W. Hughes. *Four Square Leagues: Pueblo Indian Land in New Mexico.* Albuquerque: University of New Mexico Press, 2014.

Elder, Jane Lenz, and David J. Weber, eds. *Trading in Santa Fe: John M. Kingsbury's Correspondence with James Josiah Webb, 1853–1861.* Dallas: Southern Methodist University Press, 1996.

Eldorado Volunteers, eds. *Windmills and Dreams: A History of the Eldorado Community and Neighboring Areas.* Eldorado, NM: Eldorado Community Improvement Association, 1997.

Elkus, James. "Galisteo: 1500–1900." Senior honors thesis, Colorado College, 1974.

Elliott, Richard Smith. *Notes Taken in Sixty Years.* St. Louis: R. Studley and Co., 1883.

Federal Writers' Project. *New Mexico: A Guide to the Colorful State.* New York: Hastings House, 1940. Republished in 1989 as *The WPA Guide to 1930s* New Mexico.

Fiege, Mark. "Private Property and the Ecological Commons in the American West." In *Everyday America: Cultural Landscape Studies After J. B. Jackson,* edited by Chris Wilson and Paul Groth, 219–231. Berkeley: University of California Press, 2003.

Flores, Dan. *Coyote America: A Natural and Supernatural History.* New York: Basic Books, 2016.

Forrest, Suzanne. *The Preservation of the Village: New Mexico's Hispanics and the New Deal.* Albuquerque: University of New Mexico Press, 1989.

García, Paula. "La Lucha Es Tu Herencia (The Struggle Is Your Inheritance)." *Voices from the Earth* 5, no. 2 (Summer 2004). http://sric.org/voices/2004/v5n2/nmaa.php.

Graña, Mari. *Begoso Cabin: A Pecos County Retreat.* Albuquerque: University of New Mexico Press, 1999.

Graybill, Robert. "A Shot in the Dark: How a Famous Cowboy Detective Cracked a Baffling Case." *New Mexico Magazine* 84, no. 9 (September 2006): 62–65.

Gregg, Josiah. *Commerce of the Prairies.* Norman: University of Oklahoma Press, 1954. First published 1844.

Gutiérrez, Ramón A. *When Jesus Came, the Corn Mothers Went Away: Marriage, Sexuality, and Power in New Mexico.* Stanford, CA: Stanford University Press, 1991.

Hall, G. Emlen. *Four Leagues of Pecos: A Legal History of the Pecos Grant, 1800–1933.* Albuquerque: University of New Mexico Press, 1984.

Harrington, John Peabody. *The Ethnography of the Tewa Indians.* Washington, DC: US Government Printing Office, 1916.

Hart, John Fraser, Michelle J. Rhodes, and John T. Morgan. *Unknown World of the Mobile Home.* Baltimore: Johns Hopkins University Press, 2002.

Henderson, George L. "What (Else) We Talk About When We Talk About Landscape." In *Everyday America: Cultural Landscape Studies After J. B. Jackson,* edited by Chris Wilson and Paul Groth, 178–98. Berkeley: University of California Press, 2003.

Hoback, Priscilla. *Living Clay.* Santa Fe: Sherman Asher Publishing, 2000.

Holtby, David. *Lest We Forget: World War I and New Mexico.* Norman: University of Oklahoma Press, 2018.

Horgan, Paul. *Great River: The Rio Grande in North American History.* Hanover, NH: Wesleyan University Press, 1984. First printed 1951 by Rinehart.

Hughes, John Taylor. *Doniphan's Expedition: Containing an Account of the Conquest of New Mexico.* Cincinnati: U. P. James, 1847.

Jackson, John Brinckerhoff. *Discovering the Vernacular Landscape.* New Haven: Yale University Press, 1986.

———. *The Essential Landscape: The New Mexico Photographic Survey.* Albuquerque: University of New Mexico Press, 1985.

———. "The Mobile Home on the Range." In *A Sense of Place, A Sense of Time,* 52–67. New Haven: Yale University Press, 1994.

———. *A Sense of Place, A Sense of Time.* New Haven: Yale University Press, 1994.

Jensen, Joan M., and Darlis A. Miller. *New Mexico Women: Intercultural Perspectives.* Albuquerque: University of New Mexico Press, 1986.

Kammer, David. *Application for Registration: New Mexico State Register of Cultural Properties; Galisteo Historic District.* Typescript. Santa Fe: New Mexico Historic Preservation Division, 1999.

Kendall, George Wilkins. *Narrative of the Texan Santa Fe Expedition.* New York: Harper and Brothers, 1844.

Kenner, Charles L. *The Comanchero Frontier: A History of New Mexican-Plains Indian Relations.* Norman: University of Oklahoma Press, 1994.

King, Wayne C. *Speculations on the Economy and Roads at Galisteo.* Galisteo: El Puente Press, 2014.

Korte, Alvin O. "En el Renganche." *La Herencia* (Fall 2002).

Kutsche, Paul, and John R. Van Ness. *Cañones: Values, Crisis, and Survival in a Northern New Mexico Village.* Albuquerque: University of New Mexico Press, 1981.

La Farge, John Pen. *Turn Left at the Sleeping Dog: Scripting the Santa Fe Legend, 1920–1955.* Albuquerque: University of New Mexico Press, 2001.

Lamadrid, Enrique R. *La Geografía de Querencia: Land Grant Culture, Landscapes, and Communities.* A Treaty Day Address to the New Mexico Land Grant Consejo. Rotunda of the New Mexico State Capitol, February 2, 2015.

———. *Hermanitos Comanchitos: Indo-Hispano Rituals of Captivity and Redemption.* Albuquerque: University of New Mexico Press, 2003.

Lange, Richard W. *Archaeological Survey of Upper San Cristóbal Arroyo Drainage, Galisteo Basin, Santa Fe County, New Mexico.* Contract Archaeology Program Report no. 37. Santa Fe: School of American Research, 1977.

Larson, Robert. "The White Caps of New Mexico: A Study of Ethnic Militancy in the Southwest." *Pacific Historical Review* 44, no. 2 (May 1975): 171–85.

Lecompte, Janet. "The Independent Women of Hispanic New Mexico, 1821–1846." *Western Historical Quarterly* 12, no. 1 (1981): 17–35.

Lippard, Lucy R. *Down Country: The Tano of the Galisteo Basin, 1250–1782.* Santa Fe: Museum of New Mexico Press, 2010.

———. *The Lure of the Local: Senses of Place in a Multicentered Society.* New York: The New Press, 1997.

Lummis, Charles Fletcher. *Letters from the Southwest: September 20, 1884 to March 14, 1885.* Tucson: University of Arizona Press, 1989.

Madrid, Luis E. "Ciria's Tale and the Long Walk." *La Herencia* (Winter 2007).

Marcy, Randolph B. *The Prairie Traveler.* New York: Harper & Brothers, 1859.

Matthews, Kay. *Culture Clash: Environmental Politics in New Mexico Forest Communities, A Memoir, 1970–2000.* Santa Fe: Sunstone Press, 2015.

McGrath Morris, James. "A Mighty Balladeer: Actor and musician Burl Ives settles awhile in Galisteo." *Pasatiempo, Santa Fe New Mexican,* June 16, 2017.

McGraw, Patricia. *Tiffany Blue.* Santa Fe: Lone Butte Press, 2006.

McNitt, Frank. *Navajo Wars.* Albuquerque: University of New Mexico Press, 1972.

Mednick, Christina Singleton. *San Cristóbal: Voices and Visions of the Galisteo Basin.* Santa Fe: Office of Archaeological Studies, 1996.

Meketa, Jacqueline Dorgan, ed. *Legacy of Honor: The Life of Rafael Chacón, a Nineteenth-Century New Mexican.* Albuquerque: University of New Mexico Press, 1986.

Meinig, D. W. *Southwest: Three Peoples in Geographical Change, 1600–1970.* New York: Oxford University Press, 1971.

Merlan, Thomas. *Historic Homesteads and Ranches in New Mexico: A Historic Context.* Prepared for Homestead Workshop, September 25–26, 2010. Santa Fe: New Mexico Historic Preservation Division, March 2008.

Metz, Leon Claire. *Robert E. McKee: Master Builder.* El Paso: Robert and Evelyn McKee Foundation, 1997

Nelson, Ethelyn G. "Camp Life in New Mexico." *El Palacio* 4, no. 4 (November 1917): 19–34.

Nieto-Phillips, John M. *The Language of Blood: The Making of Spanish-American Identity in New Mexico, 1880s–1930s.* Albuquerque: University of New Mexico Press, 2004.

Olmsted, Virginia Langham. *The Ortiz Family of New Mexico: The First Six Generations.* Albuquerque: Olmsted, 1978.

Ortiz y Pino, José III. *Curandero: A Cuento.* Santa Fe: Sunstone Press, 1983.

———. *Don José: The Last Patrón.* Santa Fe: Sunstone Press, 1981.

Ortiz y Pino, Yolanda. *Original Native New Mexican Cooking.* Santa Fe: Sunstone Press, 1993.

Paley, Grace. *The Collected Stories.* New York: Farrar, Straus and Giroux, 2007.
Pancoast, Charles Edward. *A Quaker Forty-Niner: The Adventures of Charles Edward Pancoast on the American Frontier.* Edited by Anna Paschall Hannum. Philadelphia: University of Pennsylvania Press, 1930.
Peticolas, A. B. *Rebels on the Rio Grande: The Civil War Journals of A. B. Peticolas.* Edited by Don E. Alberts. Albuquerque: University of New Mexico Press, 1984.
Pino, Pedro Bautista. *The Exposition on the Province of New Mexico, 1812.* Edited and translated by Adrian Bustamante and Marc Simmons. Santa Fe: Rancho de los Golondrinas; Albuquerque: University of New Mexico Press, 1995.
Pratt, Boyd C., and David H. Snow. *The North Central Regional Overview: Strategies for the Comprehensive Survey of the Architectural and Historic Archaeological Resources in North Central New Mexico.* Vol. 1, *Historic Overview of North Central New Mexico.* Santa Fe: New Mexico Historic Preservation Division, 1988.
Price, Patricia L. *Dry Place: Landscapes of Belonging and Exclusion.* Minneapolis: University of Minnesota Press, 2004.
Price, V. B. *The Orphaned Land: New Mexico's Environment Since the Manhattan Project.* Albuquerque: University of New Mexico Press, 2011.
Princenthal, Nancy. *Agnes Martin: Her Life and Art.* London: Thames & Hudson, 2015.
El Puente de Galisteo. Monthly community newsletter, edited by Lucy R. Lippard, January 1997 to present, archived in the New Mexico State Library, Santa Fe.
Quintana, Frances Leon. *Pobladores II: Hispanic Americans of the Ute Frontier.* Aztec, NM: Frances Leon Quintana, 1991. Revised edition of Swadesh, republished by the author.
Rael-Gálvez, Estevan. *Identifying Captivity and Capturing Identity: Narratives of American Indian Slavery in New Mexico and Colorado, 1776–1934.* PhD diss., University of Michigan, 2002.
———. "Testifying to the Silence of Servitude: Two New Mexico WPA Writers' Project Interviews." In *Telling New Mexico: A New History,* edited by Marta Weigle, with Frances Levine and Louise Stiver, 285–92. Santa Fe: Museum of New Mexico Press, 2009.
Razac, Olivier. *Barbed Wire: A Political History.* New York: The New Press, 2002.
Reséndez, Andrés. *The Other Slavery: The Uncovered Story of Indian Enslavement in America.* Boston and New York: Houghton Mifflin Harcourt, 2016.
Rivera, José A. *Acequia Culture: Water, Land, and Community in the Southwest.* Albuquerque: University of New Mexico Press, 1998
Rodríguez, Sylvia. *Acequia: Water Sharing, Sanctity, and Place.* Santa Fe: School for Advanced Research, 2006.
———. "Acequias: Trust and Hydrosocial Territory." In *A Path to Sustainability: The Past and Future Role of Water Management,* edited by Jean T. Larmon, Lisa J. Lucero, and Fred Valdez Jr.
Louisville: University Press of Colorado, forthcoming.
———. "History, Memory, and Querencia." In *The Oxford Handbook of Southwest Archaeology,* edited by Barbara Mills and Severin Fowles, 193–205. New York: Oxford University Press, 2017.
Ruxton, George Frederick Augustus. *Adventures in Mexico and the Rocky Mountains.* Glorieta, NM: Rio Grande Press, 1973. First published 1847.
Sánchez, George I. *Forgotten People: A Study of New Mexicans.* Albuquerque: University of New Mexico Press, 1940.
Sánchez, Victoria D. de. *In the Footsteps of an Educator: The Memoirs of Victoria D. de Sánchez.* Privately printed, 1989.
Sauer, Carl Ortwin. *The Morphology of Landscape.* University of California Publications in Geography, vol. 2, no. 2. Berkeley: University of California Press, 1925.
Saunders, Jan. *Bird Notes from the Galisteo Basin.* Galisteo: El Puente Press, 2005.

Scholder, Romona. "Summers Past." *El Puente* (September 2000). Reprinted from the *Santa Fe New Mexican,* August 4, 1974.

Secord, Paul R., and Homer E. Milford. *Galisteo Basin and Cerrillos Hills.* Charleston, SC: Arcadia Publishing, 2018.

Shultz, Eric. "A Case for Revising the History of Chupadero and Rio en Medio." *La Jicarita,* May 16, 2013. https://lajicarita.wordpress.com/2013/05/16/a-case-for-revising-the-history-of-chupadero-and-rio-en-medio-2/.

Sides, Hampton. *Blood and Thunder.* New York: Doubleday, 2001.

Simmons, Marc. *Coronado's Land: Essays on Daily Life in Colonial New Mexico.* Albuquerque: University of New Mexico Press, 1991.

———. *Spanish Government in New Mexico.* Albuquerque: University of New Mexico Press, 1968.

———. *Spanish Pathways: Readings in the History of Hispanic New Mexico.* Albuquerque: University of New Mexico Press, 2001.

Sinclair, John L. "Galisteo of the Remedies." *Westways* 54, no. 1 (January 1962): 4–6.

Snow, David H. *Archaeological and Historical Investigations, Barclay Ranch–La Gotera Grant, Santa Fe County, New Mexico (April–May, 1993).* Arlington, VA: Conservation Fund, 1994.

Stanley, Father [Stanley Crocciola]. *The Galisteo, New Mexico Story.* Pep, TX: F. Stanley, 1965.

———. *The Lamy, New Mexico Story.* Pep, TX: F. Stanley, 1966.

Steele, Marion A. "Galisteo: A History and Guide to an Old New Mexico Village." Unpublished manuscript, 1986.

Steele, Thomas J. "Naming of Places in Spanish New Mexico." In *Hispanic Arts and Ethnohistory in the Southwest: Papers Inspired by the Work of E. Boyd,* edited by Marta Weigle, with Claudia Larcombe and Samuel Larcombe. 293–302. Santa Fe: Ancient City Press, 1983.

Swadesh, Frances Leon. *Los Primeros Pobladores: Hispanic Americans of the Ute Frontier.* Notre Dame: University of Notre Dame Press, 1974.

Tigges, Linda. "The Pastures of the Royal Horse Herd of the Santa Fe Presidio 1692–1740." In *All Trails Lead to Santa Fe: An Anthology Commemorating the 400th Anniversary of the Founding of Santa Fe, New Mexico in 1610,* 237–65. Santa Fe: Sunstone Press, 2010.

Toll, H. Wolcott, and Jessica A. Badner, eds. *Galisteo Basin Archaeological Sites Protection Act Sites Assessment Project.* Santa Fe: Office of Archaeological Studies, New Mexico Department of Cultural Affairs, 2008.

Tórrez, Robert J. *UFOs Over Galisteo and Other Stories of New Mexico's History.* Albuquerque: University of New Mexico Press, 2004.

Townley, John. "Mining in the Ortiz Mine Grant Area." MA thesis, University of Nevada, 1968.

Trujillo, Michael L. *Land of Disenchantment: Latina/o Identities and Transformations in Northern New Mexico.* Albuquerque: University of New Mexico Press, 2009.

Twitchell, Ralph Emerson. *The History of Military Occupation of the Territory of New Mexico from 1846 to 1851 by the Government of the United States.* Denver: The Smith-Brooks Company, 1909.

———. *The Leading Facts of New Mexican History.* Cedar Rapids, IA: Torch Press, 1911.

———. *The Spanish Archives of New Mexico.* Cedar Rapids, IA: Torch Press, 1914. Reprinted 2008 by Sunstone Press.

Turner, Henry Smith. *The Original Journals of Henry Smith Turner: With Stephen Watts Kearny to New Mexico and California 1846–1847.* Edited by L. Clarke. Norman: University of Oklahoma Press, 1966.

Valdez, Roberto H. "Living Down Country People: Names of the Galisteo Basin." *Land Water People Time Cultural Guide.* Supplement *Taos News* (2017–18): 10–14.

Van Ness, John R., and Christine M. Van Ness. *Spanish and Mexican Land Grants in New Mexico and Colorado.* Manhattan, KS: Sunflower University Press, 1980.

Vigil, Maurilio. "The Legacy of Our Land Grants." *La Herencia* (Spring 2003).
Walden, Moira. "Running Water for Galisteo." *La Puente de Galisteo* no. 1 (January 1997).
Wall, Dennis. "Movie Town Sets Stage for a Western Revival." *New Mexico Magazine* (June 1994): 26–32.
Walker, Hollis. "Diary Opens Another Page in the History of Santa Fe Trail." *New Mexico Magazine* 72 (May 1994): 44–51.
Waters, Frank. *People of the Valley.* Chicago: Swallow Press, 1941.
Weidemann, Paul. *New Mexico Real Estate Guide,* May 5, 2005.
Weigle, Marta. *New Mexicans in Cameo and Camera: New Deal Documentation of Twentieth-Century Lives.* Albuquerque: University of New Mexico Press, 1985.
Weigle, Marta, and Peter White. *The Lore of New Mexico.* Abridged edition. Albuquerque: University of New Mexico Press, 2003.
Weigle, Marta, ed., with Claudia Larcombe and Samuel Larcombe. *Hispanic Arts and Ethnohistory in the Southwest: Papers Inspired by the Work of E. Boyd.* Santa Fe: Ancient City Press, 1983.
Weigle, Marta, ed., with Frances Levine and Louise Stiver. *Telling New Mexico: A New History.* Santa Fe: Museum of New Mexico Press, 2009.
Westphall, Victor. *Mercedes Reales: Hispanic Land Grants of the Upper Rio Grande Region.* Albuquerque: University of New Mexico Press, 1983.
———. *The Public Domain in New Mexico,* 1854–1891. Albuquerque: University of New Mexico Press, 1965.
Wright, Gwendolyn. "On Modern Vernaculars and J. B. Jackson." In *Everyday America: Cultural Landscape Studies After J. B. Jackson,* edited by Chris Wilson and Paul Groth, 163–77. Berkeley: University of California Press, 2003.
Williams, Jerry, ed. *New Mexico in Maps.* Albuquerque: University of New Mexico Press, 1986.
Wilson, Chris, and Paul Groth, eds. *Everyday America: Cultural Landscape Studies After J. B. Jackson.* Berkeley: University of California Press, 2003.
Wilson, Chris, and Stefanos Polyzoides, eds. *The Plazas of New Mexico.* San Antonio: Trinity University Press, 2011.
Woodman, Donald. *Agnes Martin and Me.* Brooklyn: Lyon Artbooks, 2015.
Wroth, Will. "New Hope in Hard Times." *El Palacio* (Summer 1983).

INDEX OF NAMES AND PLACES

Page numbers in *italics* refer to illustrations.